Philosophy, Language and the Political

Poststructuralism in Perspective

Philosophy, Language and the Political

Poststructuralism in Perspective

Edited by
Franson Manjali
and
Marc Crépon

PHILOSOPHY, LANGUAGE AND THE POLITICAL
Poststructuralism in Perspective

Edited by Franson Manjali and Marc Crépon

First Published, 2018

ISBN 978-93-5002-484-3

Published by
AAKAR BOOKS
28 E Pocket IV, Mayur Vihar Phase I
Delhi 110 091, INDIA
Email: aakarbooks@gmail.com

Laser Typeset at
Arpit Printographers, Delhi 110 032

Printed at
Saurabh Printers Pvt. Ltd., Greater Noida

Contents

The Conference and the Book

All but three of the 20 papers being published here were presented at the international conference on *Philosophy, Language and the Political: Re-evaluating Poststructuralism* held at Jawaharlal Nehru University, on 10th, 11th and 12th December 2014. The papers by two French scholars who could not participate in the Conference owing to unforeseen difficulties, Gérard Bensussan and Jakob Rogozinski, both of the Philosophy department at University of Strasbourg, are included in the volume. Well-known philosopher, Jean-Luc Nancy, also of Strasbourg, presented his talk by way of a video-conference in the afternoon of the second day. Another late addition in this volume is a paper by Abhilash Nath that could offset the lack of a paper on Michel Foucault

Some of the participants, though they were actually present and read papers in the conference, have not been able to contribute their papers in the present volume. These are: Paul Patton, Professor of Philosophy at UNSW, Sydney, Aniruddha Chowdhury, ex-Fellow at Indian Institute of Advanced Study, Shimla, Soumyabrata Choudhury of JNU, Milind Wakankar of Indian Institute of Technology, New Delhi, Ranu Uniyal of Lucknow University and Anirban Das of Centre for the Study of Social Sciences, Calcutta. No gainsaying the fact this volume would have been considerably richer with their scholarly contributions.

We regretted enormously that in spite of our best efforts, we were not able to host and have the participation of the well-known philosopher and feminist writer Hélène Cixous, owing to her unexpected indisposition.

During the course of the conference, several colleagues and friends assisted us by presiding over different sessions and thus enhancing the intellectual value of the event. They are, besides Saugata Bhaduri and Saitya Brata Das, co-directors of the conference, Ayesha Kidwai, Asha Sarangi, Manidipa Sen, Brinda Bose, Sharad Baviskar and Lipi Biswas-Sen, colleagues of diverse Centres of the university, as well as Simi Malhotra of Jamia Milia Islamia, New Delhi, and Rina Ramdev of Sri Venkateshwara College, New Delhi. Assistance and untiring help rendered by Nimmi Nalika Menike and Sanjay Kaushal, then research students (now doctorates) of the Centre, also need to be mentioned.

The following is the description of the three-day Conference, organised under the direction of Franson Manjali, Saitya Brata Das and Saugata Bhaduri:

> While commemorating the death anniversaries (in 2014) of two major philosophers of our times, Michel Foucault (30th) and Jacques Derrida (10th), it is useful for scholars to attempt a reevaluation of the current of thought and academic practice that appeared and flourished in the last four decades of the 20th century, under the label of 'poststructuralism.' The trend may be said to have begun with the publication of Gilles Deleuze's monograph on Nietzsche in 1962. Since then, the decisive philosophical break with the hitherto dominant structuralist current owed itself to other philosophical antecedents in the works of Heidegger, Levinas and Blanchot. Indeed, a sense of the stultification of political thought in Europe both before and immediately after World War II contributed to the emergence of the new philosophical approach. Going beyond the Gramscian and the Althusserian concerns with hegemony and ideology respectively, philosophers resorted, following Nietzsche's philological and genealogical instincts, to a tracing of the discontinuous historical movements of dominant discourses, as well as to an effective critique of their modernising and totalising dimensions. Historically and discursively, fragmentation and multiplicity began to be seen as more real than the totality that many scholars had until then held on to as their major orientation. That totalities could and must open up to infinite multiplicities was one of the main tenets of the poststructuralists. Consequently, in addition to recasting the 'human sciences,' they sought to re-envision the aesthetic (especially the literary and the artistic) and the ethical domains, by inducing a much-needed political sensitivity into them. Contextually speaking, for many in India, not the least of the effects of post-structuralism was felt in the forging of postcolonial critiques and other movements initiated and pursued by Edward Said (Orientalism), Georgio Agamben (Bio-politics), Homi K. Bhabha, Gayatri Chakravarty Spivak and Paul Patton (post-colonialism, since the early 1980s). And more recently, it is evident that the field of religion, has also been impacted by poststructuralism, in bringing in thoughts on a discourse of God, that seek to undermine the pressure of a political theology with its adversely major role in the makeup of our modernity.
>
> In the three-day conference, several reputed scholars from different parts of the world, are expected to respond by highlighting the backgrounds and destinies, and the possible merits, achievements and difficulties of the poststructuralist philosophical movement, as well as address some of the diverse criticisms that have been leveled against it.

It pleases me to state here that the conference received financial or logistical support from several sources. Jawaharlal Nehru University, Indian Council of Social Science Research (ICSSR), and Indian Council of Philosophcial Research (ICPR) provided useful grants for the organisation of various aspects of the event, including the travel of Indian participants, while Institut Français de Delhi generously made available travel grants for the French scholars to attend the conference. Several individuals of these institutions wholeheartedly supported the event, especially S.K. Sopory, former Vice-Chancellor of JNU. Judith Oriol and Nicolas Idier of Institut Français who were both personally interested in the event, deserve our special and sincere thanks. One cannot avoid a word of acknowledgement of the facilitating roles of Mercy Helen at ICPR, Dhruv Raina at ICSSR Northern Region, and Balveer Arora, ex-Rector at JNU, who later served as the President of Alliance Française de Delhi.

This conference was the third in a sequel of major conferences that I have fortunately been able to organise at the Centre for Linguistics and English, School of Language, Literature and Culture Studies, JNU, in a span of 12 years. The first of these was held in 2002 under the title, *Beyond the Linguistic Turn – Poststructuralism and Cultural Theory*, and the second conference, *Nietzsche: Philologist, Philosopher and Cultural Critic*, was held in 2004. The papers of both these conferences were published by Allied Publishers, New Delhi in 2006.

These conferences, including the one of 2014, of which the present volume is a modest testament, can be seen to have a thematic continuity. They are concerned with questions of language, literature, culture, philosophy and indeed critique, a critique with a political content. It is worth mentioning that this intellectual trajectory was initiated in the erstwhile Centre for Linguistics and English of JNU by Professor Emeritus Harjeet Singh Gill, a pioneer of Structuralist and Existentialist currents of thought and academic activism in the whole of India. He has instilled his abiding interest in European philosophy in general and French thought in particular, and inspired many of his students, colleagues and followers with his infectious enthusiasm for nearly two generations. We are ever grateful to him.

A personal note of thanks is also due to Jean-Luc Nancy and Marc Crépon for their abiding friendship and co-presence from the distant Strasbourg and Paris respectively, ever since I met them in 2002. Udaya Kumar, friend and colleague has been a constant source of motivation and encouragement.

And there are still many friends and colleagues in the near and distant worlds, and near and dear persons, towards whom I should express my gratitude.

Last but not the least, my sincere thanks to Mr. K.K. Saxena, the publisher, for his ever-exuding enthusiasm for and interest in this book.

Franson Manjali

Preface

Against the Call for Blood, the Call for Critique

Marc Crépon

Whoever wishes to write the history of twentieth century will not escape these "magical" words that have acted upon our consciousness as ferments of violence: "Fatherland," "Civilization," "Race," "Identity," and even "Religion," whose capital letters are retained here as if they were idols of murder! If we are not afraid of being too schematic, we would willingly maintain that each of them carries within it a tension – within which we live – between two appeals whose opposition is irreconcilable and will have to remain so: the call for blood and the call for critique. On one side, these words are animated by an explosive force which drives, almost irrepressibly, to make the blood flow; on the other, the long history of their bloodthirsty usage should prompt every time they erupt in the public arena, whenever they are in the head or they appear at the tip of the tongue, a principled retreat, even more, the time for an introspection, a distancing and a suspension, which are the primary conditions for critique. But nothing is so simple, for where one would expect to find clear and precise distinctions, a sure line of demarcation between these two types of vocations, of very unequal potency, the risk of their confusion, contamination and mutual instrumentalisation can never be entirely eliminated. In the course of the twentieth century, and even today, on the one hand countless are the unjustifiable calls for blood (all of which have their roots in racism, xenophobia, anti-Semitism) that appear in the glorious garbs of a necessary critique of one or other form of imagined oppression, and on the other, the calls for the legitimate critique of real dominations which has "gone awry" or has returned as the murderous security for the most criminal regimes. Language itself, that of literature and of the human sciences, of history as well as of philosophy, will often borrow from each other hesitating between each other, and then falling one within the other. Many poets, novelists, essayists, but also philosophers have lost their way in the unusual experience of this reversal; and intellectual history of the last century cannot be separated from these multiple forms of "consent" to murder. To brandish these formula-words at random, like a "blood-stained banner" or a rallying symbol, will have too often constituted the refuge of a form of impotence, as if the radicality of the blood, asked or given, could offer *a contrario*, the illusion of a hypothetical power of thought and action.

Also we must know how to detect in every singular language, all idiomatic inventions, more or less radical, which have resulted from it, the traps they shelter. They are concealed, as we can discern, in the murderous power of these capitalized words, around which we have been hovering right now: terrible words which, assuming they have ever been credible (that is, the belief, with which they create the object, was not *always already* an illusion), should be able to lose some of their power of seduction and their illusory credit, in the course of the analysis. But nothing is so simple. What, indeed, *can* the critique be, faced with the seductions and the temptation of violence? And yet, we must resist a feeling of helplessness. Nothing would indeed be more serious than ceasing to believe in the necessity of opposing them. This is the call for critique, as we understand it, among others, of the whole post-structuralist tradition, to which this volume is dedicated. It seeks to deconstruct every discourse that produces violence, maintains or justifies it. It is a task that nothing can stop – and especially not those who continue to perceive it as a weapon that makes it possible to oppose the surrender of the thought that they might be tempted to organize. That's what makes this book a message of hope. It is in the force of the thought that it wants to restore confidence, like a bottle thrown into the sea.

Paris, December 2016.

(*Translated from French by Franson Manjali*)

Philosophical Critique and the Politico-Linguistic Aspects

Franson Manjali

The papers appearing in this volume refer to several areas of great importance to the poststructuralist thought. As Marc Crépon's prefatory words suggest it is most pertinent to identity poststructuralism today with the role of philosophical critiques that seek to question and overcome some of the prevailing discourses, especially the really or potentially violent discourses that in fact tend to define our epoch. They call for a critique, affirmatively against the call for violence... Directly or otherwise, as indicated in the conference note presented earlier, this openly critical approach has a long history going back to continental philosophy of nearly 150 years, beginning with Nietzsche. There can be no possible definiteness about the historical movement of the critiques, since sometimes, what began as a critically oriented discourse against certain oppressive regimes may itself unwittingly become or is allowed to become a source of violence and hatred. Sustained references to and thoughts on the other 'precursors' of poststructuralism, who implicitly or explicitly address these issues—Heidegger, Levinas and Blanchot—appear in several of the articles presented here.

Returning to the title of the book (and the conference, as well) it is useful to clarify some of the aspects of the *political* with reference to the *philosophical* and the *linguistic*. The linguistic in an earlier epoch (more precisely, what was prevalent then, the *philological*), was an arm of the European scholars in the 18th and 19 century colonial contexts. Following the acclaimed success of the Enlightenment (led by Voltaire, Diderot, Kant and others) against the Church and other resistant forces, many scholars brought languages to the fore to analyze their properties of being able to define and describe the mental and cultural 'character' of the people themselves. Here, what we see in the works of the German philosopher J.G. Herder (a reneged student of Immanuel Kant) or the British jurist-scholar William Jones, and later those of Wilhelm Humboldt or Max Müller, and many others, is the emergence of a *philological* movement that ran parallel to but outside of the mainstream mentalist approach that the early rationalist *philosophers* like Descartes and Kant had proposed and firmly established. If Rationalism helped philosophers to know what 'man' is, in terms of his primary mental make up, and to suggest what could be the 'universal' cognitive properties shared by the whole mankind, Romanticism (beginning with Rousseau) and then philology sought to see differences, and therefore the nature of the differences among the different peoples of the world, and even to suggest and sometimes define and predict the characteristics and the values of every people or nation that constituted the humankind. However, these differences between languages and between cultures were not to be reckoned as infinite or unbridgeable. They were readily and manifestly available for comparison to be able to determine the similarities and differences among them. Since, in any case, the Biblical (ancient theological) views insisted on a monogenesis of all the world's languages, the scholars who pursued *philology* (as distinct from *philosophy*), and claimed the unquestionable *scientificity* of this domain, sought to establish reliable connections and disparities among languages. The lexically and morphologically related languages were claimed to belong, again following a Biblical idea (referring to the narrative of humankind's assumed division and dispersal since Noah), to identifiably distinct 'families.'

Though pretending to be 'scientific' even while depending on beliefs from an antique Judeo-Christian theology, these 'families' were to be understood in terms of races of people and therefore carrying the marks of racial superiority or inferiority. Thus, the so-called Indo-European 'family' with its 'inflectional' morphological feature (found mainly in the 'classical' languages Sanskrit, Greek and Latin) was assumed to be at the highest level of the linguistic hierarchy while Chinese (with its 'isolating' morphological structure) was designated a position at the lowest level, while the Semitic family (with an 'agglutinating' morphology) consisting of Hebrew, Arabic, etc. was assigned an intermediate level. These racial prejudices maintained at the philological level were partially attenuated in Herder (for whom culturally, man was essentially made of a tissue of language), but paradoxically became severely pronounced in the philosophically enhanced approach proposed by Humboldt, who favoured the Kantian notion of universal functioning of the human mind, even if the diversity of languages resulted in disparate cultures and mentalities. Later in the works of Max Müller, who served as the Chair of Comparative philology at Oxford University (appointed in 1868), under the influence of the positivist philosopher Auguste Comte, and in tandem with the evolutionist Charles Darwin, and later the '*Junggrammatikers*,' philology sought the status of a rigorous science, indeed a 'science of language' as Müller called it. With this, what was intended to be a philosophical divergence from Kant, that his favourite, though renegade pupil Herder had insisted on, on the basis of philological and textual considerations, resulted in the formation of two distinct scholarly currents: *philosophy* and *philology*. The 'love of *logos* (language, discourse),' or philology, thus became separated from the 'love of wisdom or knowledge,' or philosophy with its emphasis on a direct cognitive understanding of the world, whether it is the world of empirical reality, of mind, and eventually of language itself. Later, Phenomenology (Brentano, Husserl) and Analytical Philosophy (Frege, Russell) would address these questions in their own quite different ways.

Following our primary concerns, it should be noted here that Nietzsche's role was to take philology back to philosophy in the second half of the 19th century. Nietzsche, as a young professor of philology and profoundly in love with the Dionysian (that is the artistic and the musical, as opposed to the intellectual or the Apollonian) strand of Greek thought, went on to interpret the words of the ancient Greek, and the later European languages, in terms of a historical differential of 'morality'. In doing so, Nietzsche was indeed redefining an originally philological term '*genealogy*' as a term for the shifting and contingent 'truths' of morality in philosophy. We can observe that this transformation of the language problematic from philology to philosophy played a major role in the transformation from structuralism to poststructuralism, as it had prefigured in Gilles Deleuze's seminal work, *Nietzsche and Philosophy* (1962).

Structuralism itself had emerged as a breakaway from the third and last phase of philology (the positivistic comparative and historical linguistics associated with the *Junggrammatikers*) in the conceptually delineated posthumous work of Ferdinand de Saussure (1916). Beyond its initial use in autonomously linguistic analysis, it had many later developments, in the form of its applications in related fields. Roman Jakobson, the polymath Russian émigré in the U.S. found it applicable in just about every field of humanities, especially in literature and aphasiology. At the same time, Claude Lévis-Strauss began to assiduously and almost euphorically apply Structuralism in the social sciences, that is, in what he founded as Structural Anthropology. Structuralism, in the social sciences, he claimed in his influential *Structural Anthropology*, is like atomic physics in the physical sciences. What followed was a profusion of somewhat politically neutral scholarly applications of Structuralist theory and practice. Prominent among them were Jacques Lacan who transformed Freudian psychoanalysis in unexpected ways with the aid of structuralism, Louis Althusser who sought to redefine Marxism as a scientific political theory following the basic structuralist principles, and Roland Barthes who reinvented the Saussurean proposal for a Semiology, that in fact flourished in the sixties and seventies as Semiotics, or a structuralist theory and practice of cultural and literary analysis.

Deleuze's recourse to the late 19th century philological philosopher Nietzsche must have surprised many, especially because of the extreme notoriety for his name being popularly associated with Hitler's Nazi (National Socialist) regime in Germany, for which the presentation of the former's writings in a prophetic and poetic mode as well as his sister Elizabeth's naïve enthusiasm were mainly responsible. Deleuze saw in Nietzsche's philologically-derived 'genealogy' a potential for radicalizing the field of human sciences—in a manner clearly distinct from that of both the Marxists and the structuralists —where for the sake of emancipation from hegemonic cultures and therefore politically constituted people, could be submitted to a 'clinical' and 'critical' treatment. If this was his philosophical move, in the climate of the sixties' France hitherto largely dominated by Structuralism, Deleuze sought to actively transform the sign-based approach of the semiotics, leading to his own proposal regarding 'sense,' a notion that is closely associated with Nietzsche's own aesthetics and linguistics based on the notion of 'sensation.' Meaning or signification, henceforth could not be seen as something merely intellectual, but material and embodied. It must be noted that Lacan himself distorted and transformed the Saussurean 'sign' which for the former was centered on the materiality of an ever shifting signifier, than on the signified.

Foucault was least concerned with the problematic of the sign. He in fact chose to abandon it totally, and with derision. Instead, and in spite of his own pronouncements, he employed a simple etic-emic structuralist model in his early work on the 'archaeology of the human sciences' (dealing with 'life,' 'language' and 'labour') and published as *Les mots etles choses* in 1966. He was in a way applying a 'scientific' structuralist model to unravel the history of the 'human' (life, labour, language) sciences, in terms of what he called 'epistemic' discontinuities. This model was clearly different from the merely descriptive approach proposed by Thomas Kuhn in his *The Structure of Scientific Revolutions* that appeared four years earlier. Historically speaking, and archaeologically, when a set of *etic* elements attains a saturation point, one can notice an *emic* shift or discontinuity. Foucault was attempting here a genuinely structural principle—through historicised—to reinterpret what Kuhn had earlier referred to as 'paradigm shifts' in randomly occurring scientific revolutions. The former was setting up what he called instead the 'history of systems of thought' in rather politically neutral terrains.

But this changed later with his adoption of Nietszchean principle of 'genealogy' presumably under the influence of Deleuze. Discursive formations and their discontinuities, he now saw, are not merely structurally ordered, but are performatively induced by human acts. And moreover in a rather Nietzschean and Heideggerian vein, he suggested a preordering of discourses into which subjects were inserted. This 'order', just as Deleuze understood it later, also meant a 'command,' and for Foucault, it constituted the realm of 'power.' Much of Foucault's genealogical effort was to show how such constituted power existed within discourses, and how performative acts of 'transgression' could displace and dislodge the structures of power ingrained in the prevailing and dominant discourses. If this idea has a resonance with Heidegger's understanding of truth as *aletheia* or 'unconcealment,' it certainly could not have been incidental.

Derrida, on the other hand, in two of his central works of the sixties, addressed the question of the 'sign' frontally: *De la Grammatologie* and *La voix et le phénomène* (both 1967). He was questioning an age-old Platonic bias (maintained by others down the line, till Saussure) in favour of a fixed 'meaning' (or what Derrida called 'transcendental signified') that is supposed to be always and already present in words, that is, in the use of language. Language does not have a pregiven or natural origin or source in the human thought, accompanied by a prelinguistic voice. Each time language is used, humans constitute it or reconstitute the elements of language that is already constituted in terms of differences (a principle that Derrida notes Saussure states, but by and large ignores). This constitutivity of language in terms of differences induced on the materiality of language can be nothing natural, but only the result of a 'cultural' process, itself effectively political, and thus to be understood just as writing has always been understood as cultural. Therefore, the whole of human language would be constituted culturally like writing, and that is what makes it possible to dislodge the belief in the 'secondariness' of writing. All language, be it speech or writing, is fundamentally 'arbitrary' or arbitrarily constituted, and this in-built arbitrariness can be ceaselessly questioned, critiqued, displaced and reconstituted, and this exactly is the infinite task of deconstruction, a deconstruction that can affect every domain of our linguistic, cultural or political existence.

Thus, critiquing and rejecting the assumed legitimacy of the discursive or linguistic blocks or totalised closures in any given, especially dominant society or culture, is what has been conceived as the central task of poststructuralism. In a manner of speaking, it questions language as a 'private property' where or whenever this idea is seen to be operative. Deleuze's notion of 'deterritorialisation,' Derrida's 'deconstruction' and Foucault's 'discontinuity' or transgression, or even 'fearless speech' (Gk. *parrhesia*) highlight this problematic. It can be seen that the 'precursors' had undertaken this task in their own ways. Broadly speaking, this can be identified as follows: Nietzsche questions the three foundational pillars of European society, namely a. Socratic philosophy rooted in a cerain essntialist ontology, b. the pietistic Christianity and c. modern science which ignores man's happy and aesthetic existence in favour of 'progress.' Nietzsche insists on the need for a constant renewal and *aesthetic* recreation of one's language alongside with and in response to the eternal transformation of the world around him in order to avoid and exit from such cultural entrapments. Heidegger in his highly regarded work, *Being and Time* (1927), introduces an ontology of subjective existence, where the self is seen moving along in time, and living is seen as struggling through daily conflicts and constraints up to the point of nonexistence in the inevitable event of his or her death. Faced with this possibility of the impossibility of one's own existence, the self is expected to resolutely create an authentic existence that links up communally with the existence of other related human beings, in a social process that enhances and enriches the state of one's own community or nation and resists being overtaken by other forces outside it. In his later works, Heidegger attributes the appearance of personal and communal indolence to the prevailing uncritical use of language, and emphasizes a recognition of and a return to the poetic freshness that defines language in its origins.

Levinas who was Heidegger's pupil and later became disappointed and extremely disillusioned with the latter's notorious association with the Nazi regime in the early thirties, sought to foreground *ethics* over existence. Philosophically situating himself outside the Greek-based ontology, he returns to the Talmudic Judaic sources to place the self's responsibility to the other as the starting point of philosophy. Death, for Levinas, can only suggest to us ultimately of our own self's impossibility or powerlessness in the world, and therefore the need for opening our being to that of the other, to our neighbor's appeal addressed to us —even if it would happen to be at our own peril. This would imply for him at another level, that our own language, cannot be solely about what is 'said' about the being of the world, in whatever mode, but is about what happens as our 'saying' or responding to the other. Our language can only be a response to the destitute 'other' signalling our infinite responsibility to the being other than us.

Blanchot, on the other hand chose yet another path, by introducing an exit from philosophy itself, by a 'refusal' of philosophy as such. Since man's relation to the world out there, whether aesthetic, existential or intersubjective happens in and through language, resulting in a stultification that is real or potential, this language itself must be understood in terms of how it connects with *non-existence*. This, in his view, is what literature does, connecting existence with non-existence, leading us from an account of what we deem as existence to that which does not exist, that which is yet to exist. Literature, that involves 'writing,' as another mode of language's existence keeps us in intimate touch with non-existence. In his extensive critical essays on literature, Blanchot endeavours to show that this is what great writers like Hölderlin, Mallarmé, Rilke and Kafka were doing. Their writing unfolds and flourishes when they were closest to their own non-existence, death or suicide, or to their unconsciousness in potential madness. Writing is where language is constantly transformed by the work of writers in their attempt to reveal what is outside known existence, in nonexistence. Language as literature is thus the continuous manifestation of the outside and the other that is yet to exist, or 'to come', if we say it in another register.

It is not difficult to see that writers in the so-called poststructuralist current take recourse to perspectives from one or other of the above philosophers (assuming Blanchot to be a philosopher, even if he 'refuses' philosophy). Understandably, they also have more contemporary reference points, such as (primarily) Structuralism, Psychoanalysis, Phenomenology and Linguistic Pragmatics. Being critical philosophers, we can notice their interactions and encounters with their precursors as well with their contemporaries. At the same time, we can find other contemporary philosophers engaged in either parallel currents of thought or critical rejections of their works. These include philosophers Alain Badiou, Jean-François Lyotard, Georgio Agamben and Jacques Rancière.

At the same time, their followers who are prepared to engage more or less favourably with their philosophical critiques with regard to the politico-linguistic, abound. These include those writers who are involved in feminist, postcolonial or other modes of critique. The names one is often reminded of are: Jean-Luc Nancy (a major philosopher in his own right), Philippe Lacoue-Labarthe, Edward Said, Héléne Cixous, Gayatri Chakravarty Spivak, Homi K. Bhabha, Judith Butler, Paul Patton, among many others.

Rather than seeing language as a mere tool for communication or for critique, these philosophers address and direct their criticism to the reality of the (structural) blocks and bounded totalities, often the source and depository of social and political repression and violence, within any and potentially every use of our own language. Thus, if Heidegger had affirmed that 'language is the house of being,' it should be noted that language is not just the source and shelter of our existence, it is also the depository of all our lived experience, our experience of living in a world of violent or quasi-violent, fearful, anxious daily conduct. Language, even when it aspires to be a mode of spiritual and worldy enhancement, is also at the same time, a warehouse of all the lies and hatred as well as unjust and violent discourses, both inherited or freshly proffered, the flotsam and jetsam that accumulates from our unpredictable and often angst-ridden daily life.

Evidently, Deleuze, Derrida and Foucault addressed these issues in similar or different ways, in a wide range of domains. They have dealt with issues ranging from reason to madness, from the treatment of madness to religion and God, from feminism and sexuality to literature and art. And each one of them did not ever insist on a single unchanging method for their critiques. What is already coagulated as unacceptable in the prevailing discourse must be critiqued with their own philosophical resources, and that was their motto. They did this, not all in one attempt, but in small and decisive steps, and their goal was of often clearer than the path to be taken.

Deleuze in his early work on Proust's literature, treated signs as some sort of pragmatic intermediaries, which were acting upon or negotiating between the characters, and collectively upon the readers of the novels. In his *Anti-Oedipus* (1971), along with Félix Guattari, he approached the Oedipus problematic, formulated by Freud in terms of the familial closure, as that which needed to be opened up to political and economic realities. In addition to the clinical identification of the principal psychoanalytical problematic, they also highlighted the critical opening and ('machinic') flow of the closed meanings in and through literature, as simplified in Balzac's novels. Their perspective on what is proposed as *schizoanalysis* in opposition to psychoanalysis proceeds from the above seminal ideas.

In his major methodological work *The Logic of Sense* (1968), with reference to Lewis Carroll's *Alice in Wonderland*, he introduces the problematic of a cleavage between what words in language which supposedly *signify* intellectually, and their *sense* that is never conclusive, and which therefore remains 'paradoxical.' Alice is both growing taller and shorter in Carroll, depending on which point of measure one approaches her fictional reality. Deleuze's emphasis here is on a constant lability of meaning as sense, which can never be bounded in an intellectual meaning. This sensible meaning in Deleuze and Gauttari's view ever remains open to new possibilities or variations, outside of what is assumed of language and its words at the intellectual level.

In *A Thousand Plateaus*, the second part of their *Capitalism and Schizophrenia*, Deleuze and Guattari launch the basis for a multi-pronged political critique. It's here they introduce seriously the concept of the *rhizome,* a non-hierarchical and horizontally connecting model of critical activity. In the politico-linguistic domain they resort to contemporary inputs from Pragmatics and Sociolinguistics. Using ideas from what they present as the meaning theory of the ancient Stoic philosophers, they demonstrate how language as 'command' affects the state of the human body. Language, they want us to understand, is not merely communication and statement, but that which seeks obedience from those people subordinated by authorities who acquire and command power over the former. As this language-power dynamics exists even at the level of quotidian use of language, they go on to show that 'pragmatics is a politics of language.' But at another level, particularly in the literary works of an author like Kafka, they identify a process of 'minorisation' of a major language, such as when a highly bureaucratic German language is internally transformed by the use of the same language by a Czech Jew, exposed to a familial Yiddish, that results in a 'minor' language. The minor language is more like a politically-charged 'foreign' language, within one's own more familiar major language. Clearly, Deleuze and Guattari are more concerned with the exterior surfaces of language use which has an affect on the body, both personal and political, rather than with any interiority. It is in this respect, one can understand Deleuze's interest in what he refers to as 'expression' in Spinoza's philosophy. This is in line with his rejection of all that is usually spoken of as interiority of meaning in language.

In a somewhat similar vein, Foucault speaks of the 'positivity' of discursive formations. He too is *not* interested in any intellectualized meaning in the politico-linguistic domain that would be the task of philosophy to criticize. On the other hand, he is also not interested in the problematic of sense and sensation à la Deleuze. Bodily problematic is treated differently by Foucault, in terms of *Biopolitics* that is further linked with what he calls the historical emergence of *governmentality* or relatedly in terms of sexuality. While, in his 'archaeology,' he shows the historical layering of knowledge discourses, later in 'genealogy,' the interfaces of the discourses, are to be seen as imbued with a power dimension. Even if individuals and societies are politically subjected in and by discourses of knowledge, they are nevertheless endowed with capabilities to overcome and transgress such discourses, irrespective of their actual content. But then such transgressive acts, essentially performative, are meant to result in the formation of alternative subjects that constitute a given society.

Derrida, on the other hand, relies on some of the strands of philosophical thinking opened up by Heidegger, Levinas and Blanchot. He is conscious of the role of 'deconstruction' as destruction of (linguistically constituted) metaphysical thought whether it is in the religious, political, psychological or artistic-literary spheres. In a Levinasian vein, he is, more than the other two discussed here, specially sensitive to the question of the 'other,' whatever be the domain considered, e.g. Colonialism/ Eurocentrism, Nationalism, and concomitantly one's own identity in language, culture, religion, etc. These are also areas that have often manifested themselves in violence of one degree or the other. This 'other,' for Derrida, does not have a 'phenomenological' reality as it was implied in Levinas' early work, *Totality and Infinity* (1962). The other does not have a manifest or real existence, which would make him or her a possible target of counter-violence. 'The secret of the other is that the other is a secret,' Derrida says. It is this vulnerability of the other, even in his status as a foreigner or an enemy, that makes him deserve one's hospitality and forgiveness.

But, the site of any philosophical critique that one can undertake is still, and always language. It is language that is culturally and politically constituted as texts. There is violence, hatred and hostility—real or potential—in our own texts, texts close to our selves or our sheltering homes. There is, as Marc Crépon seems to suggest in his preface, a 'call for blood' or even bloodiness, knowingly or unconsciously accrued in our texts that must be ceaselessly addressed and overcome by our relentless philosophical critiques. It involves, yielding every time, the uncertain, unpredictable and singular outside or the other of our own language/s as Derrida understood as our primary concern.

REFERENCES

Blanchot, M., 1955. *The Space of Literature,* (tr.) Ann Smock, University of Nebraska Press, Lincoln, 1982.

Deleuze, G., 1962. *Nietzsche and Philosophy*, (tr.) H. Tomlinson, Athlone Press, London, 1983.

——, 1968. *The Logic of Sense*, (tr.) M. Lester, Columbia University Press, New York.

Deleuze, G. and F. Guattari, 1971. *Anti-Oedipus*, (tr.) R. Hurley, M. Seem & Helen R. Lane. Penguin, New York, 1977.

——, 1981. *A Thousand Plateaus*, (tr.) B. Massumi. Minneapolis: University of Minnesota Press.

Derrida, J., 1967. *Of Grammatology,* (tr.) Gayatri C. Spivak, Baltimore: Johns Hopkins University Press, 1976.

——, 1967. (tr.) *Speech and Phenomena,* (tr.) D.B. Allison. Northwestern University Press, Evanston. 1973.

Foucault, M., 1966. (Eng. tr.) *Order of Things*. Tavistock, London, 1970.

Heidegger, H., 1927. *Being and Time*, (tr.) J. Macquarrie and E. Robinson, Oxford, Blackwell, 1962.

Kuhn, T., 1962. *The Structure of Scientific Revolutions.* University of Chicago Press, Chicago.

Lévi-Strauss, C., 1967. *Structural Anthropology,* (tr.) C. Jakobson and B.G. Schoepf, Anchor Books, New York.

Levinas, E., 1961. *Totality and Infinity*, (tr.) A. Lingis, Duquesne University Press, Pittsburgh, 1969.

Nietzsche, F., 1887. *On the Genealogy of Morals* (tr.) D. Smith, Oxford University Press, Oxford, 2008.

Saussure, F. de, 1916. *Course in General Linguistics.* (tr.) Wade Baskin. Philosophical Library Press, New York. 1959

1

The Invention of the Idiom: The Event of the Untranslatable

Marc Crépon

I

If we were to wonder as to what *made event* for us, *one* day, *once,* certainly amidst so many memories thar reveal themselves to us, we would have to grant some place to those books which we would recognise, repetitively and sometimes even unconsciously, that marked us, leaving an indelible trace in the language we speak and write, and in the way think and perhaps even how we perceive the world. And if now, we had to take the question from another end, by starting exactly from this singular language, it is at first a deluge of questions that would force upon everyone, not without concern—because, every moment of one's life, we should be able to stop and wonder: "What is the language I speak and write? What is the tone that I use? What is *my* voice? My delivery? My rhythm? How did I come to this"? And that is when a doubt would begin to appear: "As if all these books read, these languages passed through, this 'culture' appropriated, were not for nothing"! The share of these other languages (more than one really), those of philosophy and literature, which have their own codes, their impressive monuments, their obligatory passages, which impose their own demanding, distinctive, imperious system of values, which can turn out to be considerable, insidious, furrowing all kinds of divisions and estrangements, to begin with that between the nearest and the most loved ones, parents, children and friends. It reminds us that there is no "natural," homogeneous, self-identical culture, that any "particular culture," on the contrary, is made up of a complex play of appropriations and disappropriations—which, as such, comes from a process of differentiation which thus implies happy or unhappy events. Something (more than one thing) must indeed have happened to this language which we speak and write for it to be what it is. What we call "culture," is not a work internal to one's own self, as we might sometimes say hastily, it is a work of the other on oneself—a threatening hospitality, because it produces a separation, a difference, a loss, because it implies breaks and ruptures, extractions. To put it differently, every time I give *myself* a language—and we do not stop giving ourselves to it, incorporating ourselves in it, we do not stop making our own, the language of others (another language), —it possesses me, it constrains me, it seizes me. There is nothing more intimate and nothing more exposed. Who does not fear that the language that one speaks, as well as one's voice, does not betray him? Who has never suffered from the way it forced itself upon him, with the tone that he adopted in spite of him—as if he spoke or wrote, like a ventriloquist, a language which is not *his* ?

II

Behind these few introductory remarks, the reader would have doubtless perceived precisely an "other" language—a studied, meditated, incorporated, restored language, that is to say, translated, in more than one form, those of teaching, seminars or the essay: the language that Jacques Derrida writes in a book that speaks precisely of the relationship of each of us to *his* language and which he must invent *himself*, of what is translated or not translated in it—a book, *The Monolingualism of the Other,* the reading of which will have been for many, one of these events whose contours we try here to delineate. During a long anamnesis, Derrida speaks, in fact, of what he there calls an "intractable intolerance": the obsession with the purity of language, which must be understood in a very special sense. It is not merely a matter of purging the foreign words nor of any "contamination" by foreign languages; it does not refer to any origin, it does not articulate itself any exaggerated or fantasized identity. It has also no political or social dimension, in the sense that it would come to support any particular form of linguistic nationalism. What then is this "purity of language," in which undoubtedly we can recognize many other thinkers and writers, Kraus, Heidegger, Nietzsche, Kafka and so many others? And if it is true that one's "obsession" supposes a debt, what is it that the one who assumes it consider himself to be "in debt"? Conscious of all the ambiguities which the concept of purity conveys, Derrida specifies its exigency in the following terms: far from reducing it to a grammatical loyalty or even the search for a style, its role is to "bow to a more secret rule, to 'listen' to the imperious murmur of an order, with which someone in me, flatters himself in understanding, even in situations where he would be the only one to do so, in *a tête-à-tête with the idiom*, the final goal: a last will of language, even more, a law of language, which would confide itself only to me."[1] In other words, it is a matter of giving thanks, "to nothing that is given, but only to that which is to come."

This "face-to-face with the idiom," this "final goal," this "last will," that is what we would like to think today "as the event of language" and as the trial of the untranslatable. Because this "purity to come," this purity understood in a "hyperbolic" sense—consonant with the "hyperbolic" ethics that Derrida elaborates, during the same period, in the form of a thought of hospitality, forgiveness, secret or testimony—this desired purity is inseparable from the dream of *making happen* (here, is the event!) something in language. It is not to be thought otherwise than as the dream of a promised language, of a language to come, whose promise is the *event itself*. And if it is true that *The Monolingualism of the Other* does nothing other than explore what exactly is the "relation to language" in deconstruction—not what the so-called deconstruction would say of language, since the beginning of 1960s, but what it would have done, what it would have attempted to *make happen* in language in the movement of its writing, then it is necessary to recognize that this "hyperbolic" purity is situated at the core of what it has always sought. It does not amount to tics of writing, no more than it refers to a ruse of language; it is focused on the "madness" of its future.

III

It is, as everyone knows, not only about the books to which we keep referring, but also the sentences to which we return and which come back, while writing and teaching, by way of citation, as a *ritornello*. The trace which they have left in the memory of the one who remembers them is, doubtless, that of these events whose emergence we try to restore. The moment when in *The Monolingualism of the Other*, Derrida evokes the dreamt-of language, he uses a long sentence, marked by its breath and convolutions, often quoted, meditated and commented upon, which will have this strange resonance. In many respects, the reflections which follow do nothing but attempt to explain the echo. So we must listen to it:

> But the dream, which must have started to be dreamt, at that time, was perhaps to make something happen in this language. The desire to make it arrive here, by making something happen to it, to this language that has remained intact, always venerable and venerated, worshipped in the prayer of its words and in the obligations that are contracted in it, by making something happen to it, therefore something so intimate that it would no longer even be in a position to protest without having to protest, by the same token, against its own emanation, so intimate that it cannot oppose it otherwise than through hideous and unavowable symptoms, something so intimate that it comes to take pleasure in it as in itself, at the moment it loses itself, by coverting itself as the One who turns on itself, who returns (from itself) to itself, at the moment when an incomprehensible guest, a newcomer without assignable origin, would make the said language happen to him, forcing the language itself thus to speak itself, otherwise, in his language.[2]

Let us then try to decipher this sentence, of which the least we can say is that, in the actually endless and tortuous movement of its syntax, it makes something *happen* in language, saying what it does and doing what it says! What does it tell us by following its own dream, teach us of this *arrival*? Firstly, the *event* that concerns us, does not consist in doing violence to language, wounding it, torturing its grammar, syntax, disturbing its semantics. It is not, in other words, a break with what *is law* in language—with the law of language, in the name of a self-proclaimed originality and uniqueness. The movement is infinitely more subtle and more radical than all denial of this order. What Derrida has in view is something quite different: to accept until the end, the debt owed with regard to words. In other words, making something happen in language supposes that one is never able to rid of this debt, that one never acts with language, as if all has been said, everything was already sedimented, engraved in marble as immutable belongings. So it is with language as such, with what in it has remained unsuspected, unaccomplished, unexplored as coming from its future. And it is from this future (*à-venir*, to-come) that arrives, in its turn, what reassembles it. This undoubtedly is the first decisive point, as regards the thought of the event that is sketched in these reflections on language and writing. A language only leans itself towards future. It is held in the present only by its future (*à-venir*)—what is projected in it, beyond it, comes from this beyond. No way to exit from it: it is to the provenance of the future that it returns to make the present an event.

IV

Let us return to the question, from where we started initially: "What is this language that each one uniquely speaks and writes"?, "What *events*, traumatic (or not), does it keep in its memory"? Another way of posing the question would be: "Is there anything in this language, with all these encounters and readings which mark the trace of so many events which constituted it—is there anything there with which it can, still singularly, be identified for "discovering" or "retrieving" its own "identity"? An easy answer would be to invoke thus any belonging whatsoever, by supporting that such a written and spoken language, French for example, is to begin with, a common language, conceived as a definite "cultural" heritage, whose diverse institutions and varied circumstances would have permitted the appropriation. A "given," more or less strict milieu, a marked out schooling process would have determined its contours. But is this identification with a predetermined speech and cultural community sufficient and satisfactory? Is it not, on the contrary, really the best way of never acknowledging what *makes event* in the relation that we maintain with this legacy and all the debts which we owe. If, while speaking and writing, we imagine ourselves to have never done anything, and to do nothing, at the end of the day, than to restitute one or several languages we learnt, doesn't it amount to supposing, admitting or recognizing that ultimately, nothing ever happened, happens and will happen in that which constitutes the singularity of anyone? No event then, according to such a thought of the relationship with language and culture! All that we could say and write, we have been saying and writing, in such a perspective, would be since long and in advance a dead letter. But it is true that it is perhaps also the risk taken in every writing and speech, including the ones we address to those we love: that it is already dead.

So let us touch here upon the second decisive point, in this thought of the event, on which we have been dwelling for some time, namely what links us to the question of language and its survival (*survie*). How do we live on (survive) ourselves in language? What links language to life and death? Here it is appropriate to quote a second text of Derrida, another of these sentences which return as a *ritornello*, leaving traces in language of the one that welcomes them: an event. It is taken from the interview that Jacques Derrida gave to Jean Birnbaum, shortly before he was taken away by illness.

> The moment I leave (publish) "my" book (nobody obliges me here), I become, appearing-disappearing, as this uneducable spectre which will have never learnt to live. The trace that I leave signifies to me both my death to come, or already happened, as well as the hope that it survives me. It is not an ambition of immortality, it is structural. I leave a scrap of paper there, I die: impossible to get out of this structure, it is the constant form of my life. Every time I let go something, such a trace leaves me, "proceeds" from me in an unreappropriable manner, I see my death in writing. Extreme ordeal: we expropriate without knowing to whom properly the thing we let go is confided. Who is going to inherit and how? Will there be even any heirs?[3]

And everyone knows—for, the text is well known—that Derrida, very soon in the same interview, seems to ask himself if, two weeks after his death, there would still be something of what he could say, and even more, write, some traces that he would have left behind. How do we live on (survive) ourselves, in language, our language? What can we pose against the vanity of every speech and writing, indefinitely reproducible, so much repeatable that they eventually disappear in the flow of their inderminate repetition? And well, nothing less precisely than from where we left a moment ago, which is this "secret purity" enriched by a new determination—namely its "resistance to translation."

V

"Untranslatable," such indeed is the law of purity, that we must understand in a very precise sense. Thus, there is a "surviving (living on) oneself unto oneself" in one's language. Now, what this living on requires, primarily, is a singularity. Here is the paradox! In a sense, what is absolutely singular is absolutely mortal. Singularity as such, because it is absolutely singular, does not survive its disappearance. And nevertheless, it is indeed a matter of this survival. There remains, consequently, only a single possibility of living on oneself in language: the hyperbole of a radical purity, understood as resistance of what in language *makes event* to its dilution and disappearance in the indefinite repetition of its translations. Derrida says: "'Untranslatable' remains—should remain, my law tells me (it is Derrida who is speaking), the poetic economy of the idiom, the one that is important for me, for I will be dying even faster without it."[4] So why should we promise to ourselves, as well as to others, to be *untranslatable*? Why should we make our law about it? Because there is going to be a responsibility and it is aporetic. What is important to understand, indeed, is the link that connects, the responsibility of an impossible translation with that of a survival, in the event of "what *happens* in language." To speak (or to write), is to translate, it is to try to give rise in language, to a singularity: that of an experience, an encounter or an address—and it is, at the same time, the same moment, to experience the impossibility of such a translation. For, every time I try to translate a particular perception, an emotion, or any other experience, every time I also try to acknowledge, the singular one whom I address, in the unique and irreplaceable aspect of one's encounter, in the manner that I have to use language to go towards him, it is this common singularity that escapes me, it is that which *does not happen* in language. By not making a trial of it, we live in the illusion of a transparent translation, blindly trusting in what is said and written, convinced that language is nothing less and nothing more than a convenient means for communicating our thoughts. That's why what "makes event" is understood as the shared effort in translating the untranslatable, which is singularity itself. And this is also the reason why purity is always to come. For, we give in, most of the time, to the social and political exigencies, in order to go ahead in speech and writing. We do not necessarily speak for saying nothing, but what we say inescapably remains very far from or quite oblivious of the call (ethical, perhaps) of singularity. And most of the time, none of this, which remains very ordinary, banal or quotidian to the point of lethargy, boredom or nausea, makes event,

So it is understandable why the purity which should gives rise to the event by opening up its possibility, is doubly hyperbolic. It is so, firstly by what it urges to do the impossible, while placing itself at the same "height" (we dare not speak of transcendence) of what naturally escapes it. It lies so in the radicality of a gesture, that its aporetic responsibility is enough to qualify as "ethics"—a gesture which we shall call "vital," as soon as it involves the possibility of a survival, of living on with oneself in language. But it is so also in its extension from the text or the book addressed to every speech act. We doubtless think that we can dream of making writing a "perpetual revolution,"[5] as Derrida reiterates, in a quasi-testamentary way in the interview already cited above. But the radicality of the promise that this dream expresses (this is what is at stake in *The Monolingualism of the Other*) is that it extends the aporetic character of this responsibility in every word addressed.

VI

We mentioned a while ago that this book with its event-sentences presents itself as an impossible anamnesis. It is characterised, among all the thoughts that seek the concept of idiom, like that of Jean-François Lyotard in *The Differend*, by the enigmatic connection that he proposes between "a universal structure and its idiomatic witness." Also the thinking of the event that is presented therein does not escape the intimate story—as if, ultimately, the tradition to which it had to adhere was less of attempts at language than of confessions, wherein, precisely due to language, their very possibility becomes infinitely complicated. What the book confesses about our relation to language (this unique language that we speak and which is not ours, that we never really possess), reflects not particularly the nature of this confession, but of all confessions in general and, still more broadly, of all writing. This relation, as one can understand it, is dominated by the impossibility of identification with anything stable, reassuring, simple, and comfortable whatsoever. Neither does it let itself fold back on the belongingness to a given community nor on the legacy of a determined culture and even less on the "roots." Because most of the time the language we speak and write does not belong to us, and that we are thus uprooted in this language, exiled—as Kafka had felt in the family, in office and everywhere, or nearly so, in society—, we are forever in quest of the invention of an idiom, in the very language, which allows us to find ourselves again. The desire for an untranslatable idiom, this is the truth of the event, as if there was a link between this foreignness to oneself that we recalled a moment ago (and who has not experienced it) and the drive which pushes us, for example, to write—as if, to put it yet differently, everything was woven between this genealogical drive which comes to us from an impossible anamnesis, from the opacity of every singular history, and this vital need that we have to exist in language in a singular manner.

There would therefore be always something lost, and at the same time distraught, in our relationship with language, the nostalgia for an untraceable origin. Let us try to recapitulate: if I have but one language which is not mine, there is no transparent relation to oneself which can guarantee the ego of its identity. The ego, in this sense, is untraceable. Here is, undoubtedly the great lesson of *The Monolingualism of the Other*: nothing proves to me, nothing guarantees me that I would find myself in what I say, in what I think, and in what I believe to be convinced of thinking by myself. Nothing assures me that I will not be always lost, really lost in language, (in my) language, forever.

VII

We now begin to understand better why, already in *Writing and Difference*, but even more in this event-book which is the object of our reflections, the question of language, translation and the untranslatable, is related to that of madness. That's when indeed, all the threads are connected, making the very promise of the idiom and with it, of the untranslatable, this promise of an event to come, a threat. But what madness are we speaking of? We are touching here the very heart of what *The Monolingualism of the Other* confronts. Three forms of madness haunt, in a spectral way, our relation with language. No way to escape it. The universal structure revealed by the idiomatic testimony of the impossible identification of the self with one's language, first and foremost, is that of these three possibilities. The first form of madness is the complete "disintegration" of identity: a relation to oneself and to the so-much-fragmented and de-structured language that the very possibility of an idiomatic invention is foreclosed: a quasi-aphasia. We then think of Hölderlin, in his abandoned tower in the care of a carpenter Zimmer, and of Nietzsche, looked after by his sister, of all those years that both of them spent in mad silence. We also think of Paul Celan, whose work is situated undoubtedly at the threshold of this madness, and of the poem titled *Tübingen Janner* ("Tübingen, January") which evokes precisely the silence of Hölderlin in his tower:

TÜBINGEN, JANUARY

Eyes talked into
blindness.
Their— "an enigma is
the purely
originated"–, their
memory of
Hölderlin towers afloat, circled
by whirring gulls.

Visits of drowned joiners to
these
submerging words:

Should,
should a man, should a man come into the world, today, with
the shining beard of the
patriarchs: he could,
if he spoke of this
time, he could
only babble and babble
over, over
againagain.
("Pallaksch. Pallaksch.")

The second form of madness is never admitted as such. Far from being perceived as madness, it is convinced, on the contrary, of its "normality"—and nothing can be as mad and threatening as this conviction. This madness, is that which characterizes all normative identification with a language learnt, including what it can have exclusively, distinctively, if not as potentially murderous. It represses the work of *différance*, in the illusion of an identity with itself which is, at the same time and wholly with a collectivity with which it identifies itself. To this collectivity, it even happens to give a universal dimension —and such is the madness of "globish," to which nothing is more foreign than the trial of an untranslatable, either interlingual or intra-lingual, since it believes that everything is translated in the common language with a perfect transparency.

But this madness of the normativity of a translation without remainder, it is also, indubitably, the one which we are most inclined to accept as its law, since childhood, to the extent that it can often appear as a necessity of existence. Family, school, religious community are so many forces which are predisposed to it. There again, we are not counting the borrowings from literature and cinema in order to exhibit, in all its facets, the mad part of this integration. One of those which imposes itself in the first place, is the multiple figure of the submission to law (and to the mimicry of the language of parlours and courtrooms, and more generally of bureaucracy) in the stories and novels of Kafka: *The Trial* and *The Castle*, which speak perhaps of nothing else—to say nothing of *The Metamorphosis* that we can always read as the story of a social, familial and professional totality that bursts in a terrible short-circuit of the body and language: madness. The ideal of a perfect transparency therein is pushed to the point of everything becoming obscure and everything disjointed.

And then there is this third form of madness in which Derrida hardly conceals the fact that he recognises his own story: that of a hypermnesia which constitutes ultimately the truth of his obsession with a "purity to come" and of the messianic waiting for what should or could in the end happen in language. Let us listen for a last time: here are the precise terms in which this third form is described:

> The madness of hypermnesia, a supplement of loyalty, a surfeit, of even excrescence of memory, to commit oneself, at the limit of the two other possibilities, to traces—traces of writing, language, experience—which carry anamnesis beyond the mere reconstruction of a given heritage, beyond an available past. Beyond any cartography, and beyond any knowledge that can be taught. At stake there is a wholly other anamnesis and even anamnesis of the wholly other...[5]

"An anamnesis of the wholly other"! If we could understand what it is about, then we would not be far from having understood what the situation is regarding this thought of the event which produces it, at the same time as it is elucidated. Let us go back, to begin from the point which we have just reached: the impossibility of a "stable identification of the self" by and in language, by and in the mastery, the possession, the disposition of a language that everyone could consider his own in his heart of hearts, and with which it would be possible for him to find and re-find himself—a language whose intra-lingual and interlingual translation would not pose any problem.

Here is the point: we cannot cling on to our supposed mastery and possession of a given language (and of all the cultural markers, identifiers that it carries) in order to answer the question "who am I"? And nevertheless, there is for everyone a language: the language he speaks. There should be, in reality, more than one language. Every singular event, every perception, every emotion, every sensation which seizes hold of us, we try to translate them in a language which is appropriate to them—that is to say which gives rise to what makes their arrival a singular event. In other words, every time we must invent in language, the language itself, the expression of a singularity, not to give rise to ours, but to be at the level of (we dare not say at the height) what happens and what makes event. That is why Derrida can write, paradoxically, that our monolingualism is constituted only by the languages of arrival. And that is the reason for plurality. If such were not the case, had we postulated in advance that there must not be anything of that sort, had we submitted ourselves to the codes of a programmed, formatted language for normative uses in every circumstance and were we to think that it is an illusion to imagine that there would be plurality, well, then we would be situating ourselves, in spite of us, near this other madness, that of the integration that we evoked a while ago: the madness of the mastery and possession of a source language.

But however little we admit and recognise that such a language does not exist, there exists in reality only languages of arrival, but whose arrival remains precisely indefinite and never succeeds in arriving at its end point—as Derrida writes, "an arrival which does not succeed in arriving." Why? There lies the most decisive or the nodal point. That's because (which resonates with so many readings, and events as can be discovered in the stories of Kafka and Borges), the termination, the end, and the completion are impossible. If such were not the case, there would not be any madness of language (and therefore, no event)—only programmes which would run and which would return each time to the same thing: the reduction to the same. What the madness of language does, on the contrary, is the irreducible transcendence of what happens to it, what befalls on it—that is to say what makes us open our mouth. Every time I speak (or write), I experience the trial of this transcendence, I feel the irreducible otherness of what happens. And there is no self-sameness, no relation with oneself, outside this trial. There is no self-sameness which is constituted outside the desire for recognising this otherness, where, in fact, it is however never possible to succeed in arriving. Everything passes, therefore (here is the madness) as if the constitution of the self-sameness, incomplete, was always in suspension—suspended in the desire of inventing a language, in the promise of a language to come.

That is why, if we follow *The Monolingualism of the Other*, there is no "first language," but only what Derrida calls a "prior-to-the-first language." Indeed, there is "first language" only for the systems—which can claim to have completely understood their object in a conceptual language that is appropriate to it: the first language. And we know how much the history of philosophy is replete with such "first languages." They constitute, undoubtedly, the secret ambition of all the great philosophers and metaphysicians: speaking-writing a new "first language." What do Plato, Descartes, or Spinoza, Kant, Fichte, Hegel, Nietzsche or Heidegger do, if not decree (because they imagine that they are using a language of departure) that their language is the first one, that it is "the first language" of "the first philosophy." But we also know how every time we translate them from one language to another, we experience the untranslatable, their ambition turning out to be an illusion.

We thus need to understand finally why this prior-to-the-first language is impossible and necessary—and why there is no other responsibility (the one that we accept every time we open our mouth) than that of promising (of promising oneself and of promising the other) to render it possible. Let us return! Every time we speak, we see ourselves thrown into an absolute translation. Because there is no original language to which we can hold on, the language we target does not exist differently but in the eschatological or messianic horizon of its promise. Only that's why! This horizon, we are inclined to forget it every moment at least in two ways. The first, as we have seen it, is the illusion of a language of the ordinary and general communication in which everything is perfectly translatable. It assumes—this is its credo—that every intra-lingual or interlingual translation is without remainder. The second is that of the mastery and possession of a mother tongue or national language, understood as an absolute language of departure (legacy, heritage), in which there is nothing that we can perfectly express and therefore perfectly translate. Of these two illusions, we can easily weigh the political implications which connect globalisation of communication and the nationalisms of linguistic belonging.

Consequently, how to dissipate the illusion? It is here that the experience and the ordeal of the untranslatable, even more so when they are from philosophical languages, turn out to be inevitable. To recognise or give rise to the untranslatable, is indeed to underline first of all in a performative manner that every thought written in a given language is the result of an impossible intra-lingual translation and that in this respect, it always supposes an idiomatic invention of the singularity—to put it differently, it is a language of arrival and not a point of departure. But this would also mean that this arrival is at the same time confirmed and repeated, intensified by every inter-lingual translation, as if this impossible and necessary language of arrival should never cease replaying its arrival, every time it passes from one language to the other.

(*Translated from the French by Sharad Baviskar and Franson Manjali*)

NOTES

1. Derrida, J., *The Monolingualism of the Other or, The Prosthesis of Origin* (tr.) P. Mensah, Stanford, Stanford University Press, 1998, p. 47.
2. Ibid., p. 51.
3. Derrida, J., *Learning to Live, finally – Interview with Jean Birabaum*, (tr.) Pascale-Anne Brault and M. Naas, New York: Palgrave, 2007, pp. 32-33.
4. Derrida, J., 1998, op. cit., p. 56.
5. Derrida, J., 2007, op. cit., p. 19.

2

Jouis Anniversaire!
("scenes of inner life" for the tenth anniversary of the death of Jacques Derrida)

Jean-Luc Nancy

I

From afar he saw us coming, of course, as always; and from afar he forewarned us. He was always one step ahead of us and our initiatives. Not only for ten, but for four-times-ten years he has waited for us at this turning point. What turning point? It's obvious: the point where it has to turn, absolutely; where it has to go round and round to come back to itself – be this re-turn infinite and, hence, without return.

Four-times-ten years ago, in 1974, he wrote: "How is the event of an anniversary possible now? What gives itself in an anniversary"? (*Glas*[1])

As Hegel says (more or less), this "now," this *maintenant*, loses nothing from being reread outside of its present: outside it, "now" gains the possibility of a meaning distinct from sense certainty. It gains the iterative now-ness, the *maintenance*, of signification. Now is always now. "It is *there*, but out there, *beyond*, within repetition, but eluding us there [...] the third party between the hands holding the book, the deferral within the now of writing, the distance between the book and the book, that other hand."(*Writing and Difference*[2])

What other hand? This text doesn't say. But another, later text, gives us at least some indication. Dealing with "Heidegger's Hand," this other text notes that, for Heidegger, clutching with both hands betrays "the eagerness of utilitarian violence," and that both hands should rather join together and unite "in prayer or in oath."[3] Thus, Derrida remarks, "nothing is ever said of the caress or of desire" (*Psyché* II).[4] He adds that Heidegger could counter by saying that the caress comes only after the "coming of the hand from speech" and as a result of this coming– "the hand that gives, gives itself, promises, lets go, gives up, hands over, and engages in the alliance or oath."[5] Yes, he could; but he doesn't.

"But why not say it then?," asks Derrida. He poses this question to his reader, he poses it to himself, he poses it to Heidegger. Likewise, he asked just before: "Does one make love [...] with the hand or with hands"? and in the prosopopoeia expressing Heidegger's potential retort, the latter recalls this question by evoking, "what you vulgarly call making love, caressing, or even desiring."[6] The adverb "vulgarly" conceals at least part of the answer to "why not say it?" or "why not have said it?" There is a romantic, erotic, desiring vulgarity to which will not condescend the thought of the single hand originating in speech and that, as such, offers and receives, offers itself and receives itself in such a way that "All the work of the hand is rooted in thinking" (cited by Derrida[7]).

We're not disputing this claim. We're simply asking what authorizes reserving the thinking and speaking work (loquacious or silent) for the single or unified hand; what authorizes subordinating, even abandoning, the vulgarity of two hands making love, the two hands of the one on or inside the body of the other, as well as the hands of the one interlaced with the hands of the other, given forth, abandoned to the caress, to manipulation and sexual jubilation (which, in turn, is a citation; we'll come to it elsewhere).

... We will hence have to return to this suspicion of sexual and manual vulgarity. But first, now, where has the anniversary gone? It isn't far off; it waits for us always in its reiterated now, *maintenant*, another hand that distances the book from the book at the same time that it distances, brings closer together, and handles two hands in love.

What other hand and what distance?

II

Precisely where, in the left column, at its summit, the question appears in *Glas*, "What gives itself in an anniversary?," the symmetrical summit of the rather dissymmetrical yet parallel right column contains the phrase: "The absence of the hand was as real and effective as a royal attribute, as the hand of justice."[8] The hand in question is the severed hand of Stilitano, the hand whose absence and supplement were brandished by the division or dissemination of the word *moignon*, or "stump," into two pieces—the severed *moi* followed four pages later by *gnon* (meaning a "stroke" in slang, especially a punch). Between the *moi* and its stroke, long sexual, biblical, and tattooed variations have followed this imperative instruction: "What is necessary here: hands induced to bandage the column. The column is wounded, otherwise it would not be a column."[9]

Colloquially, the column is also the erect penis (for example in the expression "se taper la colonne," meaning: to masturbate). That the column is here, at the same time, the column in the book, the book itself reminded us when it spoke of "two supplementary columns that seem detached from one another"[10] just before the severing of the *moi*—a castration, however, that does not deprive of the column without also erecting it. Indeed, he writes: "Nothing ever bands erect, it seems, except a stump, a *moignon*."[11]

The wounded column, circumcised, "covered with scars and legends"[12]—this is the circumcision of the beyond-Jewish, the circumcision of the heart, of that Saint Jude who, on the next page, he will search for in Jean-Paul's *Fibel*, that is, the *Bible* in dialect, in the vulgar tongue, this Jude—Christian name for Judas—who "seeks to create a common asset of the Old and New Testament"[13] and "never tires of converting."[14]

—to which he, Derrida, adds "Perhaps what I am doing with you."[15] (yes, he adds, he throws that out, *casually*, just across from the "gift of the *es gibt*" that "gives itself to be thought before the *Sein*," and which thus "displaces all that is determined under the name *Eriegnis*, a word often translated as *event*,"[16] upon which, turning the page, at the top of the column, ensues: "How is the event of an anniversary...?" —but let's be patient just a bit longer.) Let's be patient even though he annoys us tremendously with his being on the lookout for us in this way, and his converting himself at each turning point while nonetheless remaining the same; yes, the eternally dissimilar same, he himself provoking his own distension. He is introducing us *to how to remain oneself without oneself, how to appropriate improperly, to erect by cutting, and to be gendered without being differentiated.*

To dress the column is thus to care for—in particular, to bandage, *bander*, with "meters of white gauze"[17] —the wounded member. But it's not to heal, it's not to return to the same, and it's not to identify via separation, either. To band erect, *bander*, the wound: this not only thwarts the logic of subtractive castration—the logic, in general, of a loss or a lack—, it also, by the same stroke/*gnon*, blurs the distinction between the sexes, since the erecting wound, the *blessure bandante*, must also, at the same time, henceforth, be related to what we are here told of the Torah wearing "a robe and a crown" and whose "two rollers are then parted like two legs"[18] after its bands are unwrapped (after it has been unbandaged, *débandée*).

(It should not be forgotten that the column of God guiding the people is also double: a column of fire by night and of clouds by day, a fact that makes it necessary to reckon with the "indeterminate play"[19] of these two types of unformed matter: flame and cloud, light, darkness.)

And, finally, let's not forget that "the column *has* no Being, nor any being-there, whether here or elsewhere." (*Dissemination*[20])

III

But the anniversary was there, already there, in the left column across from the Torah. There, it's a question of the erectionof the pyramid that "guards life—the dead—in order to give rise to the for-(it)self of adoration."[21] The for-itself is not given with adoration: with adoration nothing is given. Adoration gives, gives itself, devotes itself. It addresses the other without getting back its address. But all the Hegelian logic here brought to light consists in sacrificing to the for-itself the initial "panicked and pyromaniac dissemination"[22] (the fire that consumes all, the holocaust). Without this sacrifice—which sacrifices the integral sacrifice that preceded it (if it took place, if the originary ever takes place)—the adoration itself wouldn't take place, for it is adoration of the initial fire and its dazzling invisibility).

The pyramid allows adoration to find itself and to preserve itself for itself. In preserving itself adoration sacrifices itself; it is exiled from its "consuming instant"[23]and from "the eruptive event of the gift."[24] There's the anniversary: the gift annuls itself in returning to itself. It converts itself into a "gift for (it)self," according to the incisive expression that will soon appear. The gift for itself is "the annulus, the ring or collar or necklace, the chain."[25]

Anniversary, annulus, annulment of the eruptive gift, chaining to Being or of Being, return to self and reappropriation. But propriation in general—or the *Ereignis*, since this is another and necessary translation—, is it not, might we say, just as much *Ereignis* and *Zeugnis*, even *Übereignis*?

The *archi*-initial event—older, buried deeper than all archaeology and all "logoarchy"[26]—is so archaic that it does not even precede: it does not take place or "*is not*". (To be sure, at one point he speaks of "Being's all-powerful precession"[27] from which is torn the "*es gibt*." But we must understand that [along] with Being the gift also exceeds precession or precedence.)

"The gift *is not*."[28] It bursts, it burns, it burns all and burns itself. Like the "archangel" mentioned long before, the "virgin born of a virgin, who announces himself,"[29] it shines, it sparkles. "To come, glisten, shine, appear, be present...*phuein*: to band erect. [...] In the beginning, *en arché*, that will have banded erect."[30]

Archangel, *arche*-messenger, less herald of the *arche* than *arche* of the announcement, news of the news: everything begins with some news, an announcement, a message, and it's the gift itself, nothing that is, nothing that subsists but the fire, the appearing, *phuein*.

(We should also understand: each time that it burns, each time that man "is ablaze in the light,"[31] since he does not receive light but is rather its property, its own, each time as well that "the secret of the gluing, milky substance that is pressed out of the object and shines like gold, astonishes,"[32] each time *es gibt*, it gives, it gives itself to be adored, it appears and disappears in its appearing.)

It shines, this fire, it burns, burns itself and reflects itself— "reflected and cooled by the glass, the ice, of the mirror"[33] that is, the mirror of the "*speculum,*"[34] of philosophical speculation. The latter is thus both the effect of the "blazing" and its reflection. A reflection, thus: an exact image and reflection of the itself-burning-itself. That which annuls itself reflects simultaneity in its annulus, the "*simul* of erection and castration."[35] Yet simultaneity beckons to, attracts, the homophony of simulation, just as the exactness of the mirror image and the reflection cunningly attracts the dissimulation of what, in a reflection, is lost. Perhaps the at-the-same-time of the banding erect and the contra-banding dissimulates a semblance, something like the "endless simulacrum" of writing[36] or like transvestism ("Would you like me to dress up as a woman?" I murmured"[37]—written at the top of the right column,[38] on the erected wound, or again as a simulation of enjoyment: "Perhaps you were playing at coming."[39])

And yet: "at the climax, you were lit up with a quiet ecstasy, which enveloped your blessed body in a supernatural halo."[40] The play at coming makes one come all the same. On the other side of the page, according to the *simul* of the columns, we are reminded that: "Natural things do not exist for themselves."[41] The spirit that rends itself from nature, appears to itself, frees itself and becomes for-itself. The supernatural halo of the pimp, of you whom "I, all attention, felt [...] flow into me, warm and white, in little continuous jerks,"[42] this halo of sainthood bears the play's reflection, the self-feeling ("the felt sensation (*Empfindung*),"[43] the left column clarifies). *To play at* is to simulate and simultaneously feel, to represent what is played.

Self-feeling is precisely to feel, the play makes up precisely the truth of that which annuls itself. The present of being-present cannot not be exceeded—presented, perhaps, even re-presented —by the gift and the *archi*-archaic putting-into-play. That's what's at stake: as much as the eruption of the beyond-*arche*— the gift, the enjoyment that gives, the ecstatic abandon– must lose itself to make itself

("the end of enjoyment is the end of enjoyment: the final point, period. The bone or snag of enjoyment, its chance and its loss, is that enjoyment must sacrifice itself in order to be there, in order to give itself its *there*, in order to touch, and tamper with, its *Da-sein*."[44]).

— as much as its loss reflects, mirrors, re-presents, and re-appropriates for itself that which wasn't even itself, neither self, nor law, nor faith,

— but as much as, too, begins to shine and burn a *moi* cut into *gnon*, a stroke –

a dirty trick or stroke of force a that does not reappropriate reappropriation, that reopens the night in the back of the eye and, from there, casts a glance not only "on Hegel's system,"[45] as he says with Feuerbach, but also into the inmost depths what this system dissimulates, simulates, and reveals all at once, namely "a sort of signifier without signified, the wasting of an adornment without the body proper, the total absence of property, propriety, truth, sense, a barely manifest unfolding of forms that straightaway destroy themselves."[46]

The glance hence strikes in this "fire artist without being,"[47] a blazing, sizzling expression that seems to designate the impossible "other without self, that means (to say) nothing, whose language is absolutely empty, void, like an event that never comes about itself" just as little as, at the same time, simultaneously, the writing here and now of this book "will never return, by some proper or circular course, to its own place."[48]

IV

The annulus, the ring, is not simply annulment. It returns to itself, but it divides itself as well. Broken into the two pieces of the symbol, it "does not form itself again."[49] The symbol, the symbiosis that it signals, is not visible from the outside. "It is a question of 'mystical action';"[50] that is, as the text itself repeats elsewhere, it is a question not of a dissimulated secret but of that which reveals itself in proper clarity (in the improper clarity of the proper). A precise analysis of the oft-evoked "Mystic Rose" would demonstrate this. We can bet that it applies equally to the annulment of the *arche*-an-archic gift, the anniversary, and the return to self: clarity and obscure light of self-abandonment.

"Today, here, now, abandoned, me"—and just across from this, on the left: "the result, in the enjoyment, is itself robbed of its being-there."[51]

Let's return to the page with the annulus, the ring, that does not close itself, does not form itself again. In the right column one reads the following: "Writing remains modest because it is caught in a fleece. [...] Freud proposes a model natural to the feminine technique of the text: the hairs that dissimulate the genitals."[52] A bit further down: "The gulf hides its borders there. In the weaving of this dissimulation, the erection is produced only *en abyme*."[53]This means all at once: the erection is engulfed in the collapse by which the column's elevation annuls itself, it places itself *en abyme*, taken up into itself, within its own insignia, infinitely, all the way to invisibility."A phallic upsurging *and* a vaginal concavity (small *glas* grown, summarized in between, at the back of the glottis), intact virginity *and* bleeding castration."[54]

Mystical action indeed: no symbol, synthesis, or sympathy, no copula or coupling without the link of the relation involved being dissimulated from view, from being grasped, from the concept, and revealed, exposed to another gaze, one that is not fixed on any form.[55]

"[S]mall *glas* grown, summarized in between": here, the book itself, the book with two columns, the law with legs open, and the God of fire and smoke crosses it self while shrinking to miniature scale, resonating and summarized—that is, taken up again, repeated and tightened, even sucked again, as we can read earlier on.

The book, not even properly his—to whatever self or for-itself one may wish to relate this possessive, this book cites or re-cites the following: "This book aims to be only a small fragment of my inner life."[56]—citing, appropriating, therefore, without returning to any self whatsoever except the self of this "this [book]," written, reread, rewritten here and now. But on the other side, to the left of the gap in-between, the other column tells of the slaying of the Sphinx and the solution to its enigma, which is "*man, free, self-knowing spirit*."[57]

What self-knowledge responds—from one column to the other, across the rift, the slit and the empty white space—to this book that never stops engulfing itself and putting itself *en abyme*? Without a doubt: the self-knowledge of an essential waiting. Between without-self and for-itself, there is awaiting oneself, there is straining oneself in waiting.

"I await myself, and nothing else; I myself await myself in myself; and this is the most identifiable and identifying self-relation, i.e. the ego's memory or promise of itself." (*Aporias*[58])

But we know that awaiting oneself and expecting can only come down to waiting for the other and expecting her arrival or departure. If I await myself, it's the other. If it's the other, the wait is not attainment—save for that attainment "reaching the far-off without harming it." (*Parages*[59]) The other remains at a distance, in the proximity of her remoteness that lends her the appeal, the attraction into which I am drawn.

This is what happens with: "a book from which poisoned, feathered phrases swoop down on me. The hand that launches them sketches, as it nails them somewhere, the dim outline of a Jean who recognizes himself, dares not move, awaiting the one that, aimed at his heart in earnest, will leave him panting."[60]

That's what he expects, he who writes the book, writes it by copying out so many, many phrases—"each phrase, each word, each stump of writing"[61]—he who is not Jean but Jacques, [something] which cannot but remind us of Jean-Jacques ("*In all this, love of myself does all the work; self-love has nothing to do with it*."[62] (*Reveries*, 8th Promenade)—that's what he expects from love come from the other, from Jean to Jacques and also from Wilhelm, or even from Jesus, whose favorite disciple, as Wilhelm tells us again and again, is John.

He waits to be loved, to love himself being loved by the other, without self-love, receiving his arrows, he awaits, he strains towards them, tensed in the desire to hear the strokes stick into his gasping flesh—his flesh, the flesh of the reader, of the lover, of the beloved, of he who dresses his own wound.

He writes: "If I write two texts at once, you will not be able to castrate me. If I delinearize, I erect. But at the same time I divide my act and my desire. I—mark(s) the division, and always escaping you, I simulate unceasingly and take my pleasure nowhere. I castrate myself—I remain(s) myself thus—and I 'play at coming'.

Finally almost."[63]

What is "almost"? Here: "Almost: the ideal place for transvestism is, of course, *presqu'île*, almost an island, peninsula. *Péninsule.*

He becomes almost a woman on a tongue of lone land penetrating in mid-Ocean."[64]

V

He divides himself, simulates himself at the same time and cross-dresses or trans-genders himself by means of a tongue that penetrates the Ocean. Just across, in the other column or other peninsula (lone penis?), it is a question of "the *inner* process of the plant's *relation to itself* [...] uprooted from itself, toward the outside, by the light"[65] but that, in the flower, reveals itself in the light emanating from inside the plant. And "[t]his passage is analogous to the one that sublates the outer resonance of the noise in(to) the voice."[66] Voiced sound, song, speech, sonorous tongue in the Ocean – meaning, in the *archi*-originary element; where the eruptive event takes place and engulfs itself, annuls itself and propriates itself, just as when "the galley slave exhausts himself over his oar [...] In cadence he attacks the surface of the sea that glistens, herself; he makes a mark there, finds support there, but the movement is endless, the element is equal to itself, re-forms itself, impassible, engulfs the wake or the foam."[67]

But this galley slave is the author; and in case you hadn't noticed, you're told a bit further on. He is "driven to write by orders received at the back"[68] while just across, on the left, it is a question of the reading that sublates written words into the truth of their meaning just like the mystic enjoyment of bread and wine annuls these as objects and sublates them into Christ. Reading takes pleasure in writing's slavish toil. The author reads himself as well—"he shows you this or that with a finger, and yet [...] fucks you, his eyes elsewhere. He fully comes then."[69]

Fully? Fully engulfed, yes.

He takes pleasure in his anguish like the one who remains there, gasping under the impact of phrases shot like arrows. And we return to the hand: the one that erupts from the book, that bends the bow and shoots its arrows. This is "the other hand" which calls out for, invites to the game, the work of the two hands. Like those of this woman, "this whore," who tends Jesus' feet: "she adored him, pressed him gently with her hands, soothed him with a holy pomade, wrapped him with strips the moment he begins to stiffen."[70] Across from these strips, on the right, a necklace, a Golden Fleece (which will become pubic [hair] further on) around the neck of "Harcamone the Christ."[71]

Sexual attributes are exchanged, intermixed, transformed, cross-dressed, transubstantiated. During Christ's Last Supper the "mystical action" is played out: "This is my body" proceeds to a "copulation without any proper object of its own" and "[m]ore precisely [...] a penetration."[72] There where, on the left, begins the analysis of transubstantiation, on the right we read: "The golden fleece surrounds the neck, the cunt, the verge, the apparition or the appearance of a hole in erection, of a hole and an erection at once, of an erection in the hole or a hole in the erection: the fleece surrounds a volcano."[73]

The volcano and the "erected hole,"[74] which appeared earlier in the text, designate or rather produce, exhibit, engrave and throw out arrows of that which, when it is a question of naming the communion with the body and blood of Christ, is also called "such incalculable enjoyment."[75] The hole is thus no more a secret abyss than the bandaged rod is a glorious plenitude: the one passes into the other, passes to the other; they are not determinable, just like *différance*, which "is never offered in the present,"[76] but does not "dissimulate itself" either, "as a mysterious being, in the occult of a nonknowledge or in a hole with indeterminable borders (for example, in a topology of castration)."[77] It is in this way that *différance* "exceeds the order of truth."[78]

"That is because in truth [read: the truth that is exceeded] a sexual difference is still necessary,"[79] states the left column, there where, in the right one, the "de-generated gl"[80] is indicated, that is, the emblem, the glairy gurgling and the speculative looking glass where the blaze of everything before everything is "reflected and cooled."[81]

A sexual difference is necessary. It still is, and it's necessary that it be different from sexual difference as opposition, distinction, distribution or attribution; different from a difference between the sexes.

A differing difference is necessary, playing itself out from column to column, from edge to edge and without edges or limits. Necessary, an annulus not returning to itself, a difference or rather a plurality, a dissemination of "unheard of and incalculable sexual differences." (*Points*[82])

VI

The sexual organ, if one can name it in the singular in this way (if one can name it at all in a sense other than anatomical), the sexual organ is by no means brought in here to serve as an example or analogy for the exorbitant problem of the "for-(it)self of adoration,"[83] that is, the problem of how a surge, a surrender, an ejection towards absolute exteriority can be related to the self in such a way as to appear in disappearing, as to annul the annulment of everything while losing itself again in the annulus, in the anniversary, and in their symbolic breaking apart. "Sexual organ"creates this constraint: "the necessity for the singular to look for the 'self-feeling' in the other."[84] This is the exact opposite of adoration: adoration disappears in the "jerk," the "jump" or the "breaking in"[85] it adores, whereas the sexual organ seeks itself for itself outside, seeks out the jerk, the jump, and the breaking-in. As we've already seen, "the natural tendency of sperm is opposed to the law of *logos*." (*Dissemination*[86])

But this self-feeling does not appropriate, does not reappropriate an identity that might have been already given. The self of adoration—of enjoyment—seeks itself in the other and hence doesn't find itself there. One doesn't find oneself there, speculative sublation or not—or rather, speculative reflection is no more to be found there than, on the other side of the page, "the stroke of the *'je m'éc,' exchange, disgust, flow, write, listen to* [*myself*]"[87]can be reflected in "Rembrandt's looking glass."[88] This stroke is only one of the endless redoublings of strokes that hammer, punctuate, cut and re-cut his texts and his cries: thus-strokes, gong-strokes, tail-strokes, glottis-strokes, gl-strokes.

He does all that—exchanges himself, flows himself, etc.—stroke by stroke and simultaneously, he trades his sexual organ, he disgusts himself with phlegm, he flows from himself in sperm or drool, he writes himself and cries out loud, he listens to himself—not speaking, however, but flowering. It's a book about flowers, about the flower that "equals castration, phallus, and so on"[89] and which, signifying opposites while deposing them, "overlaps," that is, passes through, cuts, crosses and uncrosses"virginity in general, the vagina, the clitoris, 'feminine sexuality,' matrilinear genealogy, the mother's *seing*, the integral *seing*, that is, the Immaculate Conception."[90] Elsewhere the "virginal flower" will be called "varginal: between verge and vagina of the virgin, little stone or clitoral bell"[91]

Flowers take up a considerable part of this book: both their religion according to Hegel and, on the other side of the page, the "general tendency to unisexuality among floral systems,"[92] which is a mode of mixture, combination, and dispersion of sexual products. This is why the flower or flowers can be distributed across all sexual organs, that of the virgin and of the "handsome soldiers," whose removed trousers reveal "those heavy flowers whose odor strikes me like thunder."[93] It's in this way that "The religion of flowers follows the religion of the sun."[94] It covers and doubles the pyramid, as it were, doubles the for-itself of the adoration and the opening of the anniversary annulus.

The color of one flower in particular, the color of the *genêt* or broom, this "corn mush yellow," gives rise to a "brushstroke," which, he says, he doesn't know "where to place in my adoration."[95] This brushstroke, whose place he indicates ("here") as erratic and arbitrary, is nonetheless the brushstroke intended to be the most deeply touching: "I will have done nothing if I have not succeeded in affecting you with *genêt*, in coloring, smearing, gluing you, making you sensitive [...] out of the most proper affect of this text."[96]

Immediately, he adds: "But is there any? And of what text? of his? of mine?"[97] But it's just after this that he makes sure to "place this brushstroke here," this yellow flower color he says he doesn't know where to place. Another yellow flower, the reseda, provided the color for the trousers from which stem "those heavy flowers." "Yellow and waxy" is, too, the stain—and the feel—of the "unctuous" balm with which Mary Magdalene "made the body of Christ glisten."[98] (We should bear in mind that in French slang, to make someone glisten, *faire reluire*, means to make someone come, *faire jouir*.) Also, pollen in its "disseminance"[99] is said to be yellow. Yellow is "like gold or betrayal,"[100] like the sun or like transvestism.

Elsewhere, he evokes Celan who spoke of "my yellow spot, my blind spot, my Jewish spot,"[101] something he annotates as follows: "*Macula*, the word for the spot (yellow, at the back of the eye) clearly retains this connotation of a mark soiling the immaculate; this mark stains or inculpates the immaculate, like an original sin of sight" ("Rams"[102]).

The most proper affect of this text by one-knows-not-whom is the affect with which he wants, with which he must soil us, smear us, glue us; it's the balm, the semen, the milk, the divine sap of unity or the sibylline whiteness of the woman,[103] as well as the "the clitoral glue, the cloaca of the abortion, the gasp of the sperm."[104] We would then need to follow up here with all the jolts and jerks, the secretions, the suctions, the glottis strokes and "the streaming, gleaming, gliding emergence" that makes Jean come as he lifts the baptized bodies from the water—"desire to immerse oneself in the water's fullness."[105]

Across, in the right column, flows the interminable dictionary article on the word *classum* with all its references to *glas*, to sounds of bells and trumpets. It flows and it clacks, it gets muddled up and drowns there, in this mush of plenitude where the unity of a new life copulates with every dispersion and scattering, every *débandade.*The most proper affect is that which affects the proper in general: the "contradiction that inhabits the proper itself,"[106] its original sin, its sin as origin, and which demands the proper be taken from itself to be properly what it is, a proper related to a non-proper or to another proper (which, in turn...). All turns round—though there's no turn nor all—that which he calls in another text "this collusion without identity of the near and the far" (*Parages*[107]), which agitates the most proper proper, and of which the sexual organ is the exhibition, the annulment, the annulus, that is, simultaneously both the neutralization and the division, the excess and the excrescence, the "verginity;"[108] which is, finally, that which "in sexual difference carries beyond the one and the two, dual or oppositional difference." (*Points*[109]) Meaning, again, beyond the proper and the improper. Thus, also: beyond the *propre*, or clean, and the dirty.

Beyond: that is, always further on in the braid of the two, the braid that cannot be disentangled.

VII

This affect of the proper—impropriety of the flower's name,[110] or, across from that, of the family that collapses by its own doing, "logic of the antherection: prosperity/misery, shame/glory, wild/tame, proper/improper"[111] (on the lice) etc., etc.,—this affect is of course not unrelated to the "organizing affect" of writing, nor, that is, to its "compulsional matrix" characterized as a "coagulation of sense, form, rhythm."[112] Across from the marriage contract and from the necessity of getting beyond its formalism in order to accede to that modesty that restrains instinct only to make it surge forth even stronger,[113] this coagulation is presented as a sort of twisting round oneself, as a spasm of the one who writes (himself) and feels the jolts of a meaning that is made in rhythm, a meaning that spurts forth with the pounding of the words and phrases. He had already quoted Freud: "the sexual-symbolic meaning of the penholder merges into the act of writing that the latter discharges" (*Grammatology*[114]), making note, of course, of the odd regime of this symbolic meaning that here, quite literally, discharges itself.

The same quotation from Freud contains the following remark: "at the root of the sexual-symbolic meaning of the penholder lay probably originally that of the weapon and the hand,"[115] an aggressive hand, then, one that is sadistic or exhibitionist, as the citation specifies. Perhaps the hand that jerks off the man who's jealous of himself, who misses himself, and who cannot even reappropriate his jealousy as his own and "touch himself, deliver himself, give birth to himself [...], then band himself erect to death, masturbate himself or fuck himself in flowing out of himself: *je m'ec, je m'enc.*"[116]

From the very first page, "*je m'ec*" appeared as a "stump of writing" whose first extension, "I write myself," was followed by "I exchange myself, disgust, listen to, flow" and, elsewhere, "I move myself away" or "I crush myself."[117] But "*je m'en*" remains without extension, a stump wielded at us, the readers, uneasy even though forewarned.

Because it's vulgar, isn't it? It's very vulgar, more vulgar than obscene (which would be modest, he says[118]). The vulgarity of "making love" and "with two hands"was part of the prosopopoeia of Heidegger's objection. But Heidegger was elsewhere subject to a lengthy examination regarding another vulgarity he rejected: the "vulgar concept of time." Against Heidegger, *Ousia and Grammé* teaches the impossibility of distinguishing between two concepts of time without borrowing from the most metaphysical lexicon of the "authentic and the inauthentic, the primordial and the fallen." (*Margins*[119]) Yet here the death knell sounds, indefinitely, only for a remnant, by and for a remnant that does not subsist—especially not in the condition of "a scrap that falls or remains"—but that "suspends itself."[120]

The impossibility of separating the vulgar from the noble— from the *sublated*—, the fall from the rise, the slit from the protrusion (the column from its wound, the penis from the vagina), is what this whole text has been scheming, along with the impossibility of distinguishing the authentic from the inauthentic (or the fake), the proper or clean from the improper or dirty. In the heart "in the heart of the heart" of which it is a question—one column from the other—with the Hegelian dialectic of hermaphroditism inherent in the process of sexual differentiation, in this heart of the heart, face to face with a "red rose of monstrous size and beauty,"[121] there is no longer opposition or distinction (in every sense of this word). There, to be sure, is played out that "setting free of the gift of Being's all-powerful precession"[122] initiated by the very same Heidegger (but, we can bet, not with only one hand).

If nothing *is* vulgar or distinguished but always begins in the "neither-nor of the ghouls (between man and woman, between man and nonman, language and nonlanguage, and so on"[123](across the page from Hegel caught in the "intertwining"[124] of a university position with a wedding reception), then the "for-itself of adoration" is straight away affected by a self-exiting or self-starting, corn mush is regurgitated on the pyramid and the incendiary eruption of the gift endlessly haunts and sings across all reappropriations.

Which is also why this book, double and more than double, stages multiple scenes at once: grandiose familial, genetic, evangelical, or tragic scenes, scenes that are obscene or infested by lice, scenes of robbery and crime, and then, as the swapping and confluence of all the other sorts, scenes of inner life: "I am a prisoner who plays (plays for himself) scenes of inner life, you will require nothing other than a game"[125] (this is an incision, a groove, a notch made in the edge of the column). The inner is the for-itself, but also a break from it, the inside of the trousers,[126] the irony inside the community (the woman[127]) or the "inner hammer" of the bell,[128] and many others still. The scenes the prisoner plays for himself, scenes he can do no more than play—(the text everywhere assures the proliferation of the game, all the way up to the game of God "playing with himself as the infinite becoming finite"[129])—all these scenes are played out because the inner is play through and through, it plays itself while exiting itself, breaking opening its own annulus, the anniversary annulus of the proper producing a scene.

It's a game above all when he says "I," there where I play(s) at saying "I". Elsewhere, in a film (another type of game), he says he would like for philosophers to talk about their sexual lives. He was just playing. Yes and no; he was playing at playing. But he does it here; he tells, that is, not of his own, but of Hegel's sexual life—Hegel carved into a medal as "philosopher seated before a column";[130] and of Kant's who, for Hegel, was guilty of "remaining still no further than the fetish,"[131] and of some others, like Socrates, who tried to slide his tongue across the "*liparon* (the sleek), *kollodes* (glutionous), the *gliskhron* (gultionous) [...] and *gloiodes* (gluey)" until "the coming floods" forth,[132] or like Rousseau, who "loved balls,"[133]but in whom we above all recognized the pen-holder.

Even the flower is here stripped bare: "naked, veiled, fuzzy, eriopetal flowers (all this is very burdened, isn't it: too rich and in bad taste, the gendarme or the upper bourgeois would say)"[134] —vulgar, then, "a sort of popular novel,"[135] he says across from "the secular complicity of philosophy and religion."

But is it really a matter of life when the sexual is the matter?

All these inner lives, shaken, wobbling, flowing, and glued together... put outside, thrown, no longer able to return, ejected, ejaculated indiscriminately and amalgamated, coagulated, agglutinated in the glue of *différance* ("The detached remains glued thereby, by the glue of différance, by the a"[136]). *Différance* no longer differentiates; it brews and mixes in spasm, in embrace, in "everything that can happen to the porridge, to the mush of gluttinous."[137] The sexual organ unintelligibly mixes its natural vulgarity into its adoration. It smears the one with the other, since "[n]atural desire, as such, is destined to lose itself, to be incapable of reflecting itself in its naturalness,"[138] and adoration gets bogged down in its yellow stain. The sexual organ doesn't ever come down to the same thing. It doesn't come back to itself at all. It is not for-itself; it *is* not.[139] It glues. It pastes together while with both hands spreading apart the Being-less columns and the distended annulus of its anniversary.

(Translated from the French by C. Còrdova)

NOTES

1. *Glas* (Lincoln: University of Nebraska Press, 1986), p. 242; Fr., p. 270.
2. *Writing and Difference*, trans. Alan Bass (U Chicago, 1978), p. 300; *L'Ecriture et la différence*, p. 436.
3. "Heidegger's Hand (Geschlecht II)," translated by John P. Leavey Jr. and Elizabeth Rottenberg, in *Psyché: Inventions of the Other,* Vol. II (Stanford, Stanford U Press, 2008), n.12, p. 302.
4. Ibid., p. 50.
5. Ibid.
6. Ibid. "commonly" removed, "vulgarly" put in its place.
7. Ibid., p. 43; in the French, p. 50.
8. Glas, p. 242b.
9. 239 b.
10. *Glas*, p. 238b.
11. 238 b.
12. 239 b.
13. 242 b. made present tense
14. 242 b; translation mine, since "ne se lasse jamais de se convertir" is mistranslated in English as "Nor did he ever let himself be converted"; Eng. made present tense; Fr. 269b.
15. 242 b.
16. 242 a.
17. Citation not yet located; i.e. my translation.
18. *Glas*, p. 240b.
19. Eng not located; Fr. 58 [?]; "jeu infini" pg. 59 a...
20. *Dissemination*, Barbara Johnson trans (U Chicago/Athlone, 1981), p. 352; Fr. 427
21. Ibid., p. 240 a.
22. Ibid., p. 241 a; English trans. has "panic".
23. 240 a.
24. 242 a.
25. 243 a.
26. 76 a; Fr. 88.
27. 167 a; Fr. 188.
28. 242 a; Fr. 270 a.
29. 82 b; Fr. 95 b.
30. 148; Fr. 168: "Reluire, briller, paraître, être présent, *phuein* : bander. [...] Au commencement, *en arché*, ça aura bandé."
31. 86a; Eng reads: "he is ablaze in it"; Fr. 100 a, "il flambe en elle".
32. 144b, ", the substance," cut out of "shines, the substance, like gold, astonishes"; Fr. 163.
33. 242 a.
34. 242 a; Fr. 270.
35. 22 b; Fr. 30.

36. 237 b; Fr. 265.
37. 223 b; fr. 271.
38. In fr. p. 271.
39. 25 b; fr. p.32.
40. Ibid., 'halo' replaces 'nimbus'.
41. 24 a.
42. 24-25 b.
43. 25 a.
44. 260 a; fr. 289.
45. couldn't find it in Eng; Fr. supposedly 225.
46. 239 a; fr.266.
47. 238 a.
48. 56 b; Fr. 66.
49. 67 a; fr. 79.
50. 67 a.
51. 260; fr. 289.
52. 67 b.
53. 68 b. "in" taken out, "en" replaced.
54. 69 a.; fr. 81.
55. Cf. 49 a; Fr. 59.
56. Glas, 256 b; citing Genet, *Our Lady of the Flowers.*
57. 256 a.
58. Aporias (Stanford/Meridian, 1993), p. 64; *Apories*, p. 116.
59. *Parages* (Stanford, 2011), Leavey (tr.), p. 18; Fr. p. 29.
60. 201-202 b; fr 226; D citing Genet's *Our Lady of the Flowers.*
61. Glas 1b (trans. altered); fr. 7.
62. *The Reveries of a Solitary Walker*, Butterworth trans. (Hackett, 1992), p. 117.
63. Glas, 65 b; fr. 77.
64. 245-6 b "mid-Atlantic" changed to "mid-Ocean"; Fr. 273.
65. 245-6 a.
66. 246 a; 'relieves' taken out; 'sublates' put in'
67. 63-64 b, "scours" changed with "the foam"; Fr. 75.
68. 70 b.
69. 108 b last sentence changed from "He thus fully comes" to "He fully comes then."; Fr. 124.
70. 62 a all "it"s [referring to Jesus' corpse] changed with he/him as fits Nancy's use of the citation; Fr. 73-4.
71. 62 b.
72. 68 a. 'operation' put for 'action', though I'm insure as to whether action is on the page here cited.
73. 66 b; fr. 78.
74. 37 b.
75. 68 a.
76. *Margins*, Alan Bass (tr.) (Chicago, 1982) p. 6; Fr. p. 5.
77. Ibid. – note that in Bass's text he writes "without dissimulating itself".

78. Ibid.
79. 149 a. Fr. 169.
80. Ibid., word order swapped.
81. 242 a.
82. *Points*, Peggy Kamuf et. al. (tr.) (Stanford/Meridian, 1995); p. 93; Fr. 99.
83. *Glas*, 240 a.
84. 111a; Fr. 128.
85. cf. 105-7a; Fr. 123.
86. *Dissemination*, Barbara Johnson (tr.) (Continuum, 2004), p. 153; Fr. 193.
87. '[myself]' added, CC.
88. *Glas*, 111 b; note that I translated what the translators left in the French. Fr. 128.
89. 47 b; fr. 57.
90. 47 b.
91. 85 b.
92. 251 b
93. 17 b.; Fr. 24.
94. 240 a; Fr. 268.
95. 105 b word order changed; Fr. 121.
96. 104-5 b.
97. 105 b
98. 63 a; I replaced "unctuous" for "oily-like"; Fr. 74.
99. 255 b.; Fr. 283.
100. 42 b, "as" taken out, "like" put in; Fr. 52.
101. "Rams" in *Sovereignties in Question*, Thomas Dutoit & Philippe Romanski tr. (Fordham, 2005), p. 154.
102. "Rams," p. 209, "sullying" changed to "soiling" n.33; *Béliers*, 60.
103. 159 b 180 b.
104. 121 b Fr. 138.
105. 89 a; Fr. 103.
106. 138 a; Fr. 157.
107. *Parages*, p. 25; Fr. p. 36.
108. 15 b; Fr. 22.
109. Weber's introduction in *Points* (Stanford: Meridian, 1995), p. 3; Fr p. 9.
110. 188b; Fr. 211.
111. *Glas*,164 b; Fr. 185.
112. *Glas*, 195 b; Fr. 219
113. Cf. 196 a.
114. *Grammatology*, Spivak trans. (JHUP, 1997), p. 334, n. 37 (the citation is in fact from M. Klein, "The Role of the School in the Libidinal Development of the Child," which the Eng. edition of *Grammatology* appears to reproduce in the Eng. original, as I do here); Fr. 133.
115. Ibid.
116. *Glas*, 180 b, I changed 'oneself' to 'himself' and took out the 'to's; Fr. 202.
117. Cf. *Glas*, 64 b; the translators opted for "I'm removed" and "I'm crushed".

118. 129 b; Fr. 147.
119. *Margins*, Bass (tr.), p. 63 trans altered to fit Nancy's altering of the Fr original; Fr. 73 (original reads: "Et toutes les oppositions conceptuelles qui servent la destruction de l'ontologie s'ordonnent autour d'un axe fondamental: celui qui sépare l'authentique de l'inauthentique et, en toute dernière instance, la temporalité originaire de la temporalité déchue.")
120. *Glas*, 226 a; Fr. 253.
121. 112 b; Fr. 129.
122. 167 a trans altered to fit Nancy's French citation, from "Heidegger sets free the *es gibt*, in *es gibt Sein*, of Being's all-powerful precession"; Fr. 188.
123. 157 b; Fr. 178.
124. 157 a Hegel writes "'everything is so intertwined that...'"
125. 126 b, "for" added, and "the" in "the inner life" taken out; Fr. 145.
126. 201 b; Fr. 236b.
127. 187 a; Fr. 210
128. 228 b; Fr. 254.
129. 30 a; "play" changed to "playing"; Fr. 38.
130. 184 a; Fr. 206.
131. 197 a; Fr. 232.
132. 236 b, word order changed from "floods the coming"; Eng. trans has two instances of "glutinous"; Fr. 263.
133. 151 a; Fr. 171a.
134. 129 b; "naked" put instead of "downy" for *à poil*; Fr. 147.
135. 201 b; Fr. 226.
136. 167 b; Eng translation altered; it reads: "The detached remain(s) collared thereby, by the glue of difference, by the a."; Fr. 188b.
137. 121 b, "gluttinous" changed for "nurslings who are gluttinous"; Fr. 139.
138. 148 a; Fr. 167.
139. No italics in original.

3

Can a Toolbox Go to War? The Political Legacy of Poststructuralism

François Cusset

I would like to start by taking three things seriously, be it for strategic reasons.

First, the poststructuralist label itself: it might be a form of academic packaging, the artificial gathering of very divergent lines of thinking, a shallow designation hiding yet revealing a certain fear before History (like any *post* word does), but one can not deny, in sheer terms of intellectual history, that there is a relatively homogenous and inter-referential corpus formed around the names of Foucault, Deleuze, Derrida, and to a lesser extent, Lyotard, Barthes, Baudrillard, but also their American offsprings and critical discussants, such as Judith Butler or Gayatri Chakravorty Spivak, their British or German respondents such as Manfred Frank or Terry Eagleton, and the great historiographic or conceptual revisions it has inspired in many countries, India included. Second thing I want to take seriously is the old performative notion that concepts can indeed change one's life, or that building a critical argument *is* doing certain things with words. And third, against the binarism of theory *vs.* practice, we need to endorse, even tactically, the idea of a specific political potential of *theory*, theory understood here as an academic byproduct, as the leading institutionalized paraphilosophical discourse of today, but able to debunk or deconstruct hegemonic views and phallogocentric or Western signifiers in ways which can be indeed put to use in real social and political life.

Then we need a starting point, which will be dramatically simple: we are at war, a form of open civil war at the global level which has very little to do with the military, nation-based, ideologically polarized conception of war of 20th-century politics—a war induced by our current form of disenchanted and disinhibited neoliberal violence imposed without alternatives and all the more openly that the supposed necessary knot formed together by capitalism and democracy has now been untied for good, or more exactly for worse. And a war complemented by religious and ethnocultural conflicts rising everywhere to rechannel a more general social unrest and dissatisfaction, as well as by actual local conflicts which are now beyond control in many places, from the Middle-East to old Soviet Republics and even Mexico's cartels.

A multifaceted war, complete with a faceless enemy, a disorganized popular mass, lonely and alienated life forms, and its many cultural diversions, against the background of a rising yet unexpressed north-south tension, and with no more safeguards such as the nuclear threat or an international peacekeeping force as was the case a few decades ago. A war, in other words, waged on local battlefields and more broadly at the intersubjective level, with free-floating subjectivities devastated by social anomie, economic precariousness, cultural scepticism, and our terminal inability to collectively imagine ANY viable future.

In such a context can theory, especially poststructuralist theory, be of any help?

Theory is itself at a turning point. Our present theoretical moment, after the poststructuralist moment *per se* (which dates back to the last quarter of the 20th century), has to do with three converging evolutions characterizing this turn of the millenium:

1. the final demise of meta-narratives and all-encompassing theories, whether they take the form of orthodox historical materialism at odds since the end of Soviet communism and revolutionary promises, or of civilizational totalisations *à la* Huntington or Fukuyama proved wrong by recent social reawakenings (from the ill-named Arab "springs" to the failed yet decisive Occupy Wall Street movement)

2. a first wave of intellectual decolonization and active questioning of the West's cultural and espistemological hegemony, palpable in the emerging world's recent set of political and critical experiments (from South America's indigenous socialism to the groundbreaking rethinking of domination currently at work in countries such as Brazil and India)

3. the overall decline of lateral solidarities and traditional sociopolitical institutions, which makes non-governmental (or protest) politics both unlikely, in the absence of institutional support, and yet all the more promising, once disanchored from the collective structures inherited from two centuries of so-called "modernization": for better or worse we have been deprived of an explanatory worldview, of a pregiven sociopolitical (collective) subject, of an epicenter or point of reference to which a transversal struggle or collective project could be actually connected.

All in all, this is both good and bad news: the disconnexion between academic overtheorizing and grassroots social life is more blatant than ever, while there is also a certain reopening of stakes, and of the social imaginary, a vivid need to (re)invent ourselves both intellectually and socially, and therefore an unprecedented potential for real conceptual audacities to anticipate/inspire/transform/perform our global social world —in other words, there are high expectations, especially from today's youth, and the necessity to largely renew our conceptual arsenal.

This is where these bodies of conceptual work altogether forming the poststructuralist canon (French but not only, between German sources and American or Indian continuations...) can indeed be put to use again, and anew. Such works, which are must-reads on most campuses now, had been marginalized or despised or even boycotted in cold war times, to the extent that they fell in the cracks: being neither Marxist nor liberal, neither micro nor macro, neither metaphysical nor analytical, they were then seen less as an *Aufhebung* of such polarized conflicts than as a freestyle, somehow dandy, or "literary," third term. But in our changing context these texts and concepts which literally found no place (or were out of place) back then, can now turn out to be providential, or at least directly helpful when Karl Marx and Adam Smith, Hegel and Tocqueville, or even Lenin and Lennon (as one might say), have been partly disactivated, conceptually devalued, when they are a bit off duty, at least in their orthodox versions.

For one should at least recall the power of anticipation these texts all had vis-à-vis the major changes of the last fifty years, and with regard to the amazing plasticity and ideological opportunism of our dominant neoliberal regime: Foucault with his much-debated microphysics of power (the understanding of biopolitics as the new nature of power, and of governmentality and control as more decisive than constraint and classical domination); Deleuze and Guattari with the deterritorializing/reterritorializing (or micro/macro-political) oscillation of modern capitalism, and its central element of Desire; Lyotard by promoting intensity (and the libidinal impulse) as the new frontier of a dematerialized freemarket nightmare; and even the less explicitly subversive approach of Derrida, through his exploration of writing but also of power as both ghostly and permeating our historical time, both absent and present, inscribed yet endlessly self-erasing. It is as if they all had in mind, to cover these famous examples respectively, the new dissemination of power among invisible and countless shareholders (Foucault), the unexpected tensions but also alliances between the freemarket and religious power, or between consumer society and moral repression (Deleuze and Lyotard), as well as the larger distancing of life and the world once they went virtual and started taking place *online* (Derrida) —if you allow me to translate these famous poststructuralist conceptual lines into later, contemporary global realities.

In that sense maybe they are precisely what we need, or at least can be put to use again. When the old totalizing regime of political thought is dreaded by both specific radical activists and by passive users or consumers, and when it turns out to be utterly inappropriate in a world of which the West (or the "north") is no longer the hegemonic center, then the strategic humbleness of the poststructuralist toolbox (as Foucault and Deleuze famously qualified the role of intellectuals in the 1970s, against the sacred figure of the Intellectual, and its nostalgic traces of idealism), then such a deliberate humbleness can indeed make a brillant return, or at least come back and help us.

But wars are real, they are brick and mortar (or missile and torture), and both these new shapeless social mobilizations and these scattered conceptual inventions of poststructuralism are a bit of a blur, they remain hard to grasp, locate, identify: so, in the same way that we may ask, 'how many batallions does a small group of sexual activists or a band of cultural anarchists actually have to oppose real power?,' we are entitled to ask in turn whether a toolbox, a modest yet very subtle theoretical supplement, can *de facto* go to war.

I will answer this seemingly silly question with the example of three of these tools, by juxtaposing three key notions taken from the poststructuralist canon, where they served to displace older regulatory signifiers: the notion of friendship, or bonds of affect, against the older desincarnated "social interaction" derived from political philosophy and social sciences; the notions of becoming and subjectification, against the old rigid notions of History and the homogenous individual Subject; and the notion of life itself, mostly against... itself, or life trying to disentangle itself from a value system of which it is the teleological horizon. All in all, three fuzzy notions, less specific or problematized than actual philosophical concepts can be, but in various ways three notions which are haunting the works of these different authors with enough persistence to be a kind of philosophical signature (among other possible ones), and again, three notions which I believe can actually, if not wage war, at least serve and enlighten in the specific agonistic situation we are dealing with, the situation of these radical activists and these disillusioned social forces, or of this larger people "without-a-subject" (or this larger collective subject without a politically constituted "people").

These notions also offer a form of overlap, as I will try to associate each of them with more than one author, hence forcing to bridge the many gaps that still separate them...

It will all be just very allusive and superficial, given the extent of this approach and the lack of time.

Friendship

An offensive, subversive, demanding notion of friendship, close enough to the one present in the famous Derridean concept of a "Politics of Friendship":

a strange way of bonding, still undefined and unnecessary, a dis-anchored, always-already deconstructed, expropriated and reappropriated, sentimental and anti-institutional, contingent and radically democratic bond which, for these very reasons, could fit today's struggles and social reinventions better than organized and compulsory collective bonds, and at the theoretical level provide the missing link between structures and feelings, between objective forces and unstable subjectivities, oppositional logics and romantic rebelliousness, spontaneous refusal and organized resistance – or between "the two Marxes," as Lyotard would have it in his *Libidinal Economy*: between the old bearded totalizing master and the intensive, sensitive, impulsive German waitress which in Lyotard's provocative view he also is.

Friendship in that sense has to do with what Foucault said (in a famous 1981 interview with French magazine *Gai-Pied*) of "invented relationships," the need to invent new forms of interaction irreducible to blood ties, to social dependency, and even to the old, culturally specific romantic paradigm of love (his two exemples then were gay communities and the bonds born in world war one trenches). It is not far either from the concept of friendship elaborated in a famous correspondance between Gilles Deleuze and the French writer Dionys Mascolo as a "communism of thinking," a certain sharing or putting together of our individual aphasias, amnesias, political impossibilities. And indeed it is closely related to the late politicization of deconstruction attempted by Derrida in his 1994 *Politics of Friendship*, in which he replaced the arrogant certitude of a planned future by the fragile promise of a *maybe*, a modality, said Derrida, which does characterize friendship.

What is at stake here is to get out of the old aporia typical of the left-wing tradition between the organized people and the romantic people, between the institutional strategy and a more sentimental, spontaneous anarchy. The stake here is to better be in tune with today's youth, born from online social networks and wary of prefabricated frames, a youth whose fights and mobilizations retain an affective, sentimental, subjective and enraged dimension unknown in the days of strong unions and rigid political parties—a new generation of social tricksters and well-informed dreamers, whose conceptions of counterpower can be best seen in such recent examples as the Occupy Wall Street and Indignados movements in the West, but also in South America's indigenous brand of socialism, India's urgent feminist struggles, the vanguard of the Arab Springs of three years ago, and even young pacifists struggling to live in Israel.

With the poststructuralist focus on structures of feeling at the expense of social objectivism, on the contingency of interpersonal meetings at the expense of holistic, generalizing views, and on invented/fabricated relations at the expense of pregiven/inherited relations, we are coping with an operational bias, a working notion of what can bond us to each other without tying us nor reducing our inner power.

And we shouldn't forget either the role played by friendship in these thinkers' biographical itineraries, friendship with each other, in the aftermath of 1968 and decolonization, which saw them march together against racism or consumerism, sign petitions together, join causes beyond their many philosophical disagreements.

Becoming

The concept of becoming in Deleuze, Guattari, or even Lyotard, refers to unpredictable forms of infrasubjectification, to the intricate multiplicity of (individual or collective) subjective lines, and to a radically transformational ontology. It connects in their works with various signifiers, such as nomadic science, molecular inputs, lines of flight, nondialectical difference, a local or on the contrary extended subject but distinct from the liberal tradition of a homogenous, strictly individual Subject. Here what we inherit from poststructuralism is a materialistic, non-separatist, post-Spinozist notion of the subject, or the replacement of the old Subject altogether by an endless process of subject*ification*, as clearly opposed to the abstract individual subject of Cartesian metaphysics and liberal legal systems, as happening below and/or beyond that (mostly administrative) compulsory individual scale. The morphing and hectic transformations of this poststructuralist plastic and dividual subject, which can be a group, a desiring machine, a situational combination, or a virtual part of me that I just send on-line, all open onto various becomings which help us break with traditions, origins, and the burden of the past, becomings as pure deployments of nondialectical difference and ontological change, but not from scratch, not bubbling up where nothing was, more like the momentum, or the continued logic of being, already present in Spinoza's concept of *conatus*, and the power of agency stemming from it. And if Derrida's work is less immediately associated with such notions, his endless critique of the dictatorship of presence (in phenomenology) and origins (the ever-paralysing *arché*) also connects in its own way with the concept of becoming.

This fragmented yet unlimited ever-becoming subject, advert to liberal individualism and to the metaphysics of presence, is recurrent in Deleuze and Guattari's inquiry into contemporary modes of subjectification, throughout the two volumes of their *Capitalism and Schizophrenia* project (*Anti-Oedipus* and *A Thousand Plateaus*), but also in Foucault's notion of "discursive formations" (discourse is not located in subjects of enunciation but is blooming everywhere, in fragments and wholes, layers and bonds, in bits and pieces), and somehow also in Derrida's notions of "dissemination," "event," "aporias," always raised by him against logocentrism and the supposed homogeneity of presence and the present cohesive Subject of here and now.

Becoming and subjectification are also key notions to better understand, and even make the best of, the emancipatory potential of schizophrenia and identity swaps in our transformist, plastic, web 3.0 "schizo-culture". Which might be why such odd, almost science-fictional concepts as these end up more at home in the horizontal vertigo of American capitalism, or even in the vertical metamorphoses of contemporary Indian society, than they are on the more substantialist grounds of old Europe, where they were fashioned a few decades ago by a handful of free thinkers at odds with their own dominant *episteme*, and who turned out to be strangers on their own land.

Life

Our third notion opens onto the old ambivalence of vitalism: life at a still-undefined stage, life in all its conceptual blur, is precisely the conceptual supplement by which we initially slipped, or drifted, from structuralism to poststructuralism— as was the case with Derrida's famous paper at the inaugural (or primal) scene of poststructuralism, the October 1966 Johns Hopkins symposium on "The languages of criticism and the sciences of man," when he inserted life within the inner workings of the Structure under the changing names of 'play,' 'desire,' 'laughter': the decentering and destabilizing of organized structures which this very gesture triggered made structuralism problematic and the flesh of life the ultimate stake of its philosophical critique. Life here is the Nietzschean imperative of emancipation and willpower, radically emancipatory to the extent that it exceeds the rhetorical structures of commandment, but it is also the new frontier of capitalism, the heart of neoliberal governmentality, life as precisely what is ceaselessly favored and controlled and incented and confiscated for our good (or benevolently taken care of) in what Foucault coined as biopolitics. Life as an emancipatory burst and life as the always-already available site of neoliberal control, both and at the same time.

In Deleuze's energetics, in Foucault's genealogies, or even in Derrida's slippages, life thus is a double-edged concept, located at the border between emancipation and control, free unfolding and strict valuation: Marxists and liberals alike still have trouble with a certain vitalism characteristic of poststructuralist theory, or its vitalist immanentism, more suspicious than the orderly description of historical materialism and the ontological coherence of liberal metaphysics – but still, it remains the best conceptual guide to understand the new texture of contemporary hegemony, to understand the consented domination on our lives of the media spectacle, of the pharmaceutical industry, of the insurance (and risk) paradigm, of all the plastic and cosmetic transformations of the self, of the obligation made to all of us to develop and unleash all our productive resources, of a certain compulsory sexual drive also, and even of the dis/identificatory potential of our online adventures. Life here is the only thread.

The very ambivalence typical of such fuzzy concepts, derived from our uneasy and indeed diverse readings and reenactings of these few crucial late-20th-century philosophical works, might be simply the ambivalence of politics and resistance in our strange present times—ambivalence of friendship as the most commodified affective bond AND the last one freeing us from our many professional and biological alienations; ambivalence of becoming when it not only shifts and moves and deterritorializes subjectivities but also makes it difficult to anchor any struggle or solidarity in the long term and an instituted force; ambivalence of life when it is the Trojan horse of governmentality and the ultimate horizon of (environmentally conscious and socially reinvented) emancipation... A conscious and critical form of intellectual ambivalence, with which we are or maybe better off today than with cold, dead, disconnected certitudes: we are doomed to ambiguity, and our struggles too.

I shall end on this unending, or open-ended, note.

4

Jürgen Habermas and Jacques Derrida as "Good Europeans"

Samir Gandesha

The less stable necessary ideologies are, the more cruel the methods by which they are protected. The degree of zeal and terror with which tottering idols are defended shows how far dusk has already advanced.

– Max Horkheimer

Introduction

According to E.M. Butler, in the aftermath of the Napoleonic conquest, the German-speaking world was profoundly captivated by the image of the Athenian polis.[1] So great was Greece's hold that she famously described it as the "tyranny of Greece over Germany." Today, the situation appears to be inverted. Germany now, undeniably, exercises a tyranny over Greece. And, within Butler's schema, this makes perfect sense insofar as such an overwhelming tyranny as Greece exercised over Germany gives rise to an equal and opposite impetus to rebellion. So, if the contemporary German tyranny over Greece is an inverted repetition, it is a repetition with a difference. This is a tyranny of a very different kind than the one exercised by Greece over Germany two centuries ago. Unlike the admittedly phantasmal relationship Butler famously describes, it is far from the cultural-intellectual or spiritual tyranny once wielded by Greece, centering on what Joseph Chytry calls the quest for a re-founding of the "aesthetic state,"understood as "a social and political community that accords primacy, although not exclusiveness, to the aesthetic dimension in human consciousness and activity."[2] This was a state in which Eudaimonia or a full flourishing of the total human personality might once again be possible in a Germany that had passed through the aftermath of the French Revolution, the Napoleonic conquest, and the ensuing crisis of diremption (*Entzweiung*) Hegel describes in the so-called "*Differenzschrift*" or the *Difference Between Fichtean and Schellingean Systems of Philosophy*. In this text, Hegel argues that the need (*Bedürfnis*) for philosophy arises from painful historical divisions and conflicts. In his mature work, like virtually all those of his generation, Hegel took the Kantian Critical System, with its opposition between the noumenal and the phenomenal realms, the rational duty of will and embodied, sensuous inclination, ought and is, to be uniquely expressive of the diremptions of modernity that were in need of supersession. The means by which this would be accomplished, in Hegel's view, was through a conception of Experience or *Erfahrung* as the basis of Spirit's journey "home" to itself through the painful labour of externalization and alienation.

Today, the tyranny of the reunified German state is, arguably, the tyranny of the creditor over the debtor.[3] The post-1789 German preoccupation with what Novalis had famously called "*transcendentale Obdachtlosigkeit*," "transcendental" or ontological homelessness, has given way to a preoccupation with recuperating financial debts whose material effect, in Greece, is leaving in its wake an all-too *ontic homelessness* as middle-aged public servants and old-aged pensioners alike lose the roofs above their and are thrown out into the streets of Athens and Thessaloniki. And such debt becomes *infinite* and therefore almost theological in provenance,[4] insofar it can never be repaid because its harsh terms of "austerity"simply inhibit the kind of economic growth to generate sufficient revenue to redirect to the Troika. What does seem to be in the offing, however, is a brutal appropriation of Greece's now greatly devalued public assets such as the Port of Piraeus and its airport, in lieu. If, as Walter Benjamin argued in a brilliant unpublished fragment from 1921, just as the infamous German inflation had begun to spiral, if capitalism were to be understood as a "religion," "it is a religion which offers not the reform of existence but its extreme destruction." (*Selected Writings* Vol. I, 289)

The contemporary tyranny of Germany over Greece raises several questions, one of the critical ones being: "What is it to be a good European today?" Since re-unification, Germany had sought to remake itself in the post-war period as a "Good European" state but, now, it would appear that there is something rather different afoot. This question concerning the "Good European," of course, was famously first posed by Nietzsche who was witness to the very formation of the German State in 1870-71. In a letter to his mother on August 17th, 1886, from Sils Maria, Nietzsche writes: "For, even if I should be a bad German. I am at all events *a very good European.*" This statement, then, helps us to refine our question thus: What is a bad German (*schlechter Deutscher*) and what is a good European (*guter Europäer*)? Could it be the case that just as Butler's thesis is turned on its head, as suggested above, to its Nietzsche's formulation that, today, to be a *good German* is to be a *bad European*?

Any answer to the first must include at least some response to Nietzsche's critique of Bismarckian Prussia: its nationalism, militarism and xenophobia. And, as I ust suggested, Nietzsche saw the effects of this first-hand as an orderly in the very crucible out of which the German state was forged under Prussian leadership, namely the Franco-Prussian War. As many commenters have previously already noted, echoing, of course, the singular voice of Walter Kaufmann, it is, therefore, doubly ironic that Nietzsche's work could have been so easily appropriated by his sister, Elizabeth, and her husband in support of German imperialism and fascism.

But at a deeper level, Nietzsche's grappling with his German identity had, in part, to do with his own formation as the son of a Lutheran minister. Nietzsche's injunction in *Beyond Good and Evil* to practice a "hardness against oneself" was, in this sense, articulated against his own early "hard," which is to say, ascetic, Protestant formation. It was kind of negation of a negation, though, of course, his deep suspicion of Hegel and Strauss would not permit him to describe it that way.That is, much of his own anti-Christian polemics was articulated in the form of such a practice. It was, as it were, an act of alienation, a leaving home, a form of spiritual wandering throughout Europe (see *The Good European: Nietzsche's Work Sites*). This constituted no less than an escape from his father's home, which Nietzsche describes as a "sick house." As Julian Young explains:

> Though the recollections of his father in *Ecce Homo* are a eulogy, they contain, nonetheless, an emphasis on sickness.: 'My father died at the age of thirty-six: he was delicate, loveable and morbid, like a being destined only temporarily for this world—a gracious reminder of life rather than life itself.' And...that he owes his father every 'privilege' of his nature *save for* 'life, the great Yes to life [which is] *not* included' in his debt.[5]

Nietzsche can be considered a "good European" insofar as his work, in a very substantive way, is infused by the atmosphere absorbed via his many walking tours through Switzerland, the South of France, Italy. What was Nietzsche leaving behind? He was leaving behind, I would suggest, the land in which, what he called in the *Genealogy of Morals* the "ascetic ideals" reasserted themselves with tremendous force through Luther's Reformation. It was at this decisive moment, as Marx had already remarked, that each "man becomes his own priest." Nietzsche shows elaborates on this insight with tremendous precision in *On the Genealogy of Morals*. The key problem of which is the problem of relation between memory, debt and guilt (*Schulden* and *Schuld*). The faculty of memory, itself, arises in Nietzsche view, to remember debts and plays a key role in the constitution of guilt that lies at the heart of "slave morality." Earlier, in his *Second Untimely Meditation*, Nietzsche argues for the kind of "active forgetting" entailed by a critical writing of history—against both antiquarian and monumental modes—that would be placed in the service of life. So, Nietzsche's remarks here, may also be taken to stand for his *Abscheid* not only of the "sick house" of his Lutheran *father* but also for that of his Lutheran *fatherland.*

But this does not mean that Nietzsche seeks to absolve himself from all debts per se, from an economy of debt. Rather, for him the question of the "Good European" is bound up with the assumption of debts of a rather different order than what confronts Greece today. Nietzsche evinced debts to the Roman Stoics and, especially after his break with Wagner, the French enlightenment and Italian renaissance, Machiavelli in particular. However, it was really his debt to Greek thinking that was most pronounced in Nietzsche, not to mention several previous generations of German thinkers Of course, as if well known, rather than trotting out the usual platitudes as per Winkelmann, Nietzsche drew attention to the explosive character of the Dionysian music of the 5th century. But this was already a curious kind of debt—one that was also, for a time, owed to Schopenhauer and Wagner—but also to a Dionysus that, as he indicates, hailed from beyond Greece and Europe, itself, in Asia Minor. It was in Greece that it was met with and subdued by the Apollonian forces of order, plasticity and visibility that constituted classical tragedy.

Nietzsche's practice of a "hardness against himself" as a way of being a "*schleter Deutscher*" and therefore a "*guter Europäer,*" a "Good European" can been seen also in Habermas's and Derrida's respective approaches to the intellectual traditions which they inherit. In their open letter on the emergence of a "European public sphere" and their subsequent conversations with the Italian journalist Giovanna Borradori, we find a rejection of Europe as simply just a fiscal entity organized along neo-liberal lines— "vampiric commercialism"—from Maastricht onwards that solidifies an up-dated version of the ascetic ideals, now with no apparent alternative. These ascetic ideals could be said to lie at the inverted kind of tyranny I alluded to above: the tyranny of a fiscally conservative, frugal and hardworking Germany over a prodigal, spend-thrift and lazy Greece. In place of this burden of *Schulden* and *Schuld*, debts and guilt, we find the attempt at establishing the conditions of the acknowledgement of a certain kind of inheritance and therefore a debt of another kind entirely. One condition of such an inheritance is a critical leave-taking of one's own intellectual tradition, a certain kind of leaving home and "pathos of distance."

On February 16, 2003, the *New York Times* startlingly announced that there were now *two* superpowers: the United States and global public opinion. The *Times*'s declaration was in recognition of the widespread protests, which had taken place throughout the world on the previous day, against the mobilization of U.S. military might against Iraq. In a surprising letter to the *Frankfurter Allgemeine Zeitung*, dated May 31, 2003, one which we can only read with a certain amount of wistfulness today, Habermas and Derrida argued that these events constituted no less than the "harbingers of a European public sphere" that could serve as a counterweight to an ascendant United States. Just as it had served as a model for social welfare, Habermas and Derrida suggest, Europe possessed the capability to advance "a cosmopolitan order based on international law." Europe was uniquely placed to meet this challenge not so much because of its positive achievements but because of its common historical experience of catastrophe (this therefore also echoes Nietzsche's revulsion at German militarism): from the bloody religious wars of the sixteenth and seventeenth centuries, through the brutalities of empire and two world wars fought mainly upon its soil, to the Shoah itself. By reflecting on these experiences, Europeans were able to distance themselves from their own particular traditions and, in the process, forge a "post-national constellation." Conflicts were henceforth institutionally sublimated, leading to the realization that differences—"the mutual recognition of the other in his alterity—can also be the mark of a common identity." What seems to have made this joint intervention possible were earlier discussions that took place in the aftermath of the attacks of 9/11 among Habermas and Derrida and Giovanna Borradori.

Habermas and Derrida's letter was surprising given the nature of prior philosophical antagonism that had existed between the two thinkers. In his philippic against postmodernism delivered as a series of twelve lectures in the mid-1980s, Habermas argues that, like Heidegger, Derrida "degrades politics and contemporary history to the status of the ontic and the foreground, so as to romp all the more freely and with a greater wealth of associations, in the sphere of the ontological and the archewriting" (*The Philosophical Discourse of Modernity*, p. 181). Six years later, Derrida counters: "Claiming to speak in the name of intelligibility, good sense, common sense, or the democratic ethic, this discourse tends, by means of these very things, and as if naturally, to discredit anything that complicates this model. It tends to suspect or repress anything that bends, over-determines, or even questions, in theory or in practice, this idea of language" (*The Other Heading*, p. 55).

Despite the significant philosophical issues that separate them, these interviews reveal many commonalities. One may view such commonalities as attributable to a shared sense of European identity that has become sharpened by the events of the past half-decade. Indeed, these interviews raise the intriguing yet largely overlooked question of the specifically *geo-political* dimension of philosophy. Both Habermas and Derrida are committed to the idea that philosophy might have something to say about contemporary history—a view that is, by and large, anathema in the Anglo-American world, as was richly demonstrated by the disgraceful spate of obloquy masquerading as "obituaries" that followed upon Derrida's death. Moreover, the two philosophers can be considered *Good Europeans* inasmuch as each takes up a critical stance towards his own national philosophical tradition. In seeking to develop a rational critique of reason, Habermas trenchantly engages the anti-Enlightenment currents that had come to dominate German thinking in the wake of post-Kantian Idealism, from the Romantics down through Nietzsche to Heidegger. Derrida, in marked contrast and drawing upon a certain Heideggerianism, deconstructs the metaphysical rationalism, most clearly associated with the name of Rousseau—that reaches its practical apotheosis in the French Enlightenment and its practical culmination in the Revolution of 1789.

In these interviews, both Habermas and Derrida are skeptical of the view that the attacks of 9/11 inaugurate a new epoch in human history. While arguing that it is still too early to judge, Habermas suggests that two things distinguish this event from previous comparable events such as Pearl Harbor. The first is that the event unfolded before a "universal eyewitness of a global public" (p. 28) and the second is that, unlike past conflicts, the nature of the enemy and the risk he poses is radically indeterminate (p. 29). Unlike the Palestinian suicide bombers and national liberation movements, al-Qaeda possesses no realistic political objectives, only a vaguely articulated *jihad* against the West (p. 29). Similarly, Derrida emphasizes the ineffability (p. 86) of the event: it lies beyond our ability to give a coherent account of it, and is for that reason traumatic (p. 89). As with all forms of trauma, it engenders its own specific repetition-compulsion—both in the repeated screening of the horrific images of the attacks and in the naming of the event itself (pp. 87-88). The trauma that calls forth such a work of mourning is not so much the fact of the event itself but, rather, what it portends, that is, the possibility of far more sinister forms of violence "to come"; violence not on the order of the spectacularly large and visible, but rather on the order of the minute and invisible, as in nanotechnology (p. 102).

Both Habermas and Derrida see the event as resulting from the uneven nature of globalization, which has explosively combined a widening of social and economic inequities between North and South with the destruction of the symbolic resources of various lifeworlds, particularly in Islamic and Arabic regions. Such a convergence has led to a distinct backlash not simply against the United States but against modernity per se and the "unfinished project of Enlightenment" to which both Habermas and Derrida subscribe, albeit in different ways. This backlash, according to Habermas, takes the form of fundamentalism, the distinctly *modern* phenomenon whereby "the guardians and representatives of the true faith ignore the epistemic situation of a pluralistic society and insist—even to the point of violence—on the universally binding character and political acceptance of their doctrine"(p. 31). In contrast, in the experience of Western Europe, the claim of certain world religions to universality could only be sustained on the basis of empires whose farthest edges were blurred. In the course of modernization, understood in distinctively systems-theoretic terms, as the "accelerated growth in complexity," such claims could no longer be sustained. For, central to modernization was what Habermas calls a "double relativization"—the relativization of religious traditions in relation to one another and in relation to an emergent scientific discourse. It was the "cognitive thrust" of such a double relativization that forms the bedrock of the liberal discourse of "tolerance" and, ultimately, the separation of church and state (p. 31).

While in the West, modernization was understood as a process of creative destruction and the losses were, in the long run, more than compensated for by the increase in individual freedom and material prosperity, in the developing world modernization is *perceived* almost exclusively in negative terms. This state of affairs is only exacerbated by the dialectic of globalization in which material inequalities become intensified via communications technologies. The sheer ubiquity of global capitalism subjects the normative resources stored up in local traditions to an almost unbearable pressure. Terrorism, then, is the response to the increasing colonization of lifeworlds by strategic forms of rationality.

Derrida also roots the emergence of global terror in the context of globalization. He deconstructs the idea that the attacks of September 11, 2001 inaugurate a qualitatively new epoch and rightly points out, as many others have done, that the forces that attacked the United States on 9/11 and other occasions were initially created, trained, and funded by the United States itself during what would prove to be the endgame of the Cold War. Derrida thus goes one step beyond Habermas's analysis of terrorism as a revolt against modernity and asserts that it is an "autoimmuniary process... that strange behavior where a living being, in a quasi-*suicidal* fashion, 'itself' works to destroy its own protection, to immunize itself against its own immunity" (p. 94). This autoimmuniary disorder has three dimensions: (1) the suicide of the individuals responsible is a double suicide inasmuch as they use Western technology and training against the United States itself; (2) the change that 9/ 11 has effected simply intensifies the conditions from which terrorism springs; and (3) the "War on terror" leads to reprisals on the other side, reprisals which in turn produce a redoubling of the war effort (pp. 94-102).

The crux of the difference between Habermas and Derrida has to do with the normative positions in which they ground their accounts of political violence. Habermas attributes terrorism to *distorted* communication. Thus, it follows that the answer to political violence lies in the mutual understanding that underlies communicative as opposed to instrumental and strategic forms of action. Habermas's liberalism could be viewed as a species of the discourse of toleration that arose in the aftermath of the Protestant Reformation. Political inclusion is here understood as the propensity to recognize and engage with the other under clearly delimited, formal conditions.

Yet there is a deep ambivalence in Habermas's account of the normativity of communication, an ambivalence which has to do with the tension between the social-historical and the philosophical-transcendental vectors of his project. A full discussion of this conflict is neither possible nor appropriate here. Suffice it to say that if the normative ideal of mutual understanding emerges only through a "rationalization of the lifeworld" specific to the historical experience of Western Europe, then the understanding of violence as the culmination of distorted communication has purchase only within societies that have relatively robust and open public spheres. However, if mutual understanding is a transcendental structure inherent in language per se, then it follows that not just modern violence but violence per se results from distorted communication. But is it really plausible to understand the Peloponnesian War, the sacking of Rome, or the Crusades as so many effects of distorted communication? Has consensus always been the implicit normative horizon shared by all human beings in all times and places by virtue of the simple fact that they are language users? Ultimately, Habermas's analysis of terrorism fails to convince because, like the evolutionism that underlies its basic account of modernization, it is unable to account for the *differential logics* of modernization in the West, on one hand, and in its former colonies, on the other. This difference has to do with the history of the *subordinate inclusion* of colonized societies into the structures of global capitalism.

While not completely opposed to the idea of toleration, Derrida is suspicious of it for two reasons. The first is that it lays down a set of conditions that the other must meet if she is to be included; toleration is a limited form of hospitality. Secondly, those conditions imply that there is a certain threshold above and beyond which the other cannot be tolerated in much the same way that a body is said to be unable to tolerate an infection or disease. Derrida suggests instead, without offering any compelling arguments, that limited—or what we might term *thin*—forms of hospitality are ultimately parasitic on a strong notion of unconditional hospitality. This understanding of ethics stems from Derrida's reading of Emmanuel Levinas and is premised on the idea that, understood phenomenologically, ethics involves a relation between self and other in which my responsibility to the other takes precedence over that which I owe myself. Such a form of hospitality, rather than setting conditions for the other's participation, would let the other be in her "otherness" without condition or qualification.

Derrida's conception of ethics as unconditional hospitality raises different, yet equally troubling, questions. While Derrida acknowledges the practical limitations of the idea of unconditional hospitality, one must nonetheless question its pertinence to "actually existing" politics. Consider, for example, Turkey's bid to become a member state of the European Union within the next decade—the prospect of which would effectively deconstruct the equation of Europe with "Christendom" broadly construed. Were it to come to pass, Turkey's ascension would make Europe live up to its own promise, which, as Derrida articulated in *The Other Heading*, is to be *non-identical* with itself. Yet, it would seem that it is precisely a *conditional* hospitality that is required here, in order to pressure the Turkish state to uphold human rights, particularly those of its minority Kurdish population, not to mention not bombing Kurdish territories in Iraq and Syria and assassinating members of the PKK. Indeed, it is difficult to see how the thought of unconditional hospitality could avoid the very traps of the liberal discourse of tolerance that it seeks to deconstruct. Why? Because the other, understood in nontheological terms, is inherently plural and constituted via relations of recognition with other "others." In the case discussed above, for example, unconditional hospitality for members of one group (Turks) translates into a *very* conditional hospitality for another (Kurds), if not its negation. This is precisely the problem that a normative liberal theory such as Habermas's seeks to address: how can the claims of particular groups be reconciled within the overall framework of basic human dignity? Such claims can only be reconciled at the level of agreement on the process by which possible disagreements can be settled. At the same time, however, it would seem that the complementary role of deconstruction would be to draw unrelenting attention to forms of exclusion and repression that result from such proceduralism. In this sense, genuine democracy is, in Derrida's terms, always already oriented towards an as-yet undetermined future. Genuine democracy, therefore, is truly a democracy *to come*.

What neither philosopher properly grasps, however, is the way in which the commodifying or reifying logic of globalization unleashes profound and troubling anxieties within societies in which centuries-old traditions that are already under siege are challenged not just from the outside but from within as well.[6] The best account of the transformation of the conditions of cultural life by an ever-globalizing capitalism remains, of course, Marx and Engels' Shakespearean paean to the transformative, liberating dynamics of capitalism in the *Communist Manifesto* in whose English translation one can hear clear echoes of the *Tempest*:

> Constant revolutionizing of production, uninterrupted disturbance of all social conditions, everlasting uncertainty and agitation distinguish the bourgeois epoch from all earlier ones. All fixed, fast-frozen relations, with the train of ancient and venerable prejudices and opinions are swept away, all new ones become antiquated before they can ossify. All that is solid melts into air, all that is holy is profaned and man is at last compelled to face with sober senses (*mit nüchternen Augen*) his real conditions of life, and his relations with his kind. (Marx and Engels, 2008, pp. 38-39)

The uprooting of traditional social relations and community based forms of life produces a political vacuum, very often filled with the spectacular imagery of concreteness, idolatries and violence. This is made especially clear in the media strategy of the newly arisen geo-political player in the Middle East: the Wahabi organization Daesh. Since its emergence in the chaos that unfolded in post-invasion Iraq, post-civil war Syria and in the aftermath of the Gaddafi regime in Libya, this formation has orchestrated a particularly deft media-strategy by releasing high-definition video clips of its atrocities[7] via the internet to prospective recruits but also to a Western media which, in a state of crisis and intensive competition, compulsively and pathologically relies upon ever-more sensationalistic content to package, gloss and market. Most recently, of course, Daesh has targeted the spectacles of a heavy metal rock show at Bataclan and an international football match between France and Germany at Stade de France. In its quest for ever more sensationalistic events to package and sell to an international viewership, however, the Western media aids and abets Daesh in accomplishing its stragetic aims: inducing nothing less than a condition of latent if not manifest panic in ever-larger swaths of the population.[8]

In the absence of an organized Left in the Arab and Persian worlds, either via co-option or elimination, to enable popular forces to truly face the 'real conditions of life', namely, *social relations* as such, what has come to occupy the space of resistance are conservative revolutionary movements. The latter, for example, took power in Iran in 1979 and momentarily Egypt in the aftermath of Tahrir Square. The 'fundamentalist spectacle' (Lütticken, 2009), however, structurally repeats the nihilist vision of capitalist modernity in more than one respect: Where representation rules (both in the realm of the visual and in the realm of politics), alternatives will be rare if not merely apparent.

The critique of reification and spectacle therefore also suggests an epistemic shift (a change of standpoint) from the atomized reality of reified social relations and the glossy surface of hyper-capitalist idolatry on the one hand to the self-organization of those social forces who constitute and produce social reality in the other. In other words, in the absence of an organized, self-confident, radically democratic movement prepared aggressively to take up Nietzsche's dictum that 'Whatever is falling deserves a push,' what we see is a quintessentially modern mobilization of the very tradition organized around the idea of the 'holy,' under attack by an all-too 'profane' logic: what Marx elsewhere in the *Manifesto* deems the 'callous cash payment.'

However distorted the spectacle of terror might be, it may still contain an obscured image of social totality. The object of the attack on 9/11 was the multinational workforce housed at the World Trade Centre as well as the military and security apparatus whose role it was to maintain the stability of the economic and geo-political order established via Bretton Woods. On the other side of spectacle (see Lütticken, 2009), an equally distorted but equally symptomatic image was given: While typically understanding very little if anything and, indeed, visibly shaken and seemingly paralyzed upon learning the news about the attacks on the morning of September 11th, George W. Bush did, however, possess unique insight into the real objective of the attack—the nihilism of capital accumulation without end. He unwittingly made this clear the day after the attacks when he enjoined US citizens to do their duty and go shopping or, indeed, to visit Disney World in Florida. This makes perfect sense: In the minds of those in power the world is truly a Manichaean one, not so much divided by 'good' *versus* 'evil,' as such, but rather by opposing versions of spectacle (Disney World *versus* 9/11).

But the problem of the spectacle which emerges anew on September 11, 2001, has a more complex valence: the long gestating Arab Revolutions.[9] Ten years later, sparked off by the tragic self-immolation of Mohamed Bouazizi, the road-side fruiterer constantly harassed by the Tunis police, massive regional political convulsions were rapidly set in motion leading to, among other things, in the region's most important state, Egypt, the rise and fall of the Muslim Brotherhood in elections that followed the toppling of the Mubarak junta which, itself, in a farcical repetition that echoed that of Napoleon III so acerbically described by Marx whereby Mubarak was replaced by Mubarakhism in the form of General Sisi.

So, however much both Habermas and Derrida embody a certain spirit of the "Good European" in Nietzsche's sense, they don't properly pose the question of nihilism that terrorism represents in Europe today. It could also be argued that what we see in the suicide bomber, in particular, is a crisis of modernity that is highlighted by those who have been displaced and dislocated by the processes of capitalist globalization themselves—processes that Habermas and Derrida are quite well aware of. It is in these figures that, I would suggest, we see what I call a paradox between liberal freedom, on the one hand, and the idea of a "meaningful life" on the other. This was a problem that Nietzsche had called "nihilism" by which he meant that the highest values cannot sustain themselves—that the old religious values cannot maintain themselves in light of their own contradictions, for example, the injunction to tell the truth undermines the "evidence of things not seen" of Abrahamic faith—and *political* will existed that had the capacity to create genuinely new values to fill the void left by the mechanistic worldview of modern science that destroyed the meaningfulness or purposefulness of life at an existential level.

If the philosophical use of the term nihilism can be traced to Jacobi's critique of Fichte's subjective idealism,[10] Nietzsche drew the term "nihilism" from the Russian writer Turgenev who, himself, was responding to anarchist bombings directed against the oppressive regime of the Tsar in the context of Russia's modernization in the last third of the 19th century. In Turgenev's novel *Fathers and Sons*, nihilism, personified by the physician and moralist Bazarov, signified the reduction of nature, human emotion and, indeed, artistic expression to abstract, mechanistic processes that came increasingly to be understood through the lens of naturalistic materialism. In so doing, Nietzsche anticipates what many consider to be the meaning-destructive role of cognitive science today in reducing the human mind, human consciousness, and ultimately human freedom, to deterministic organic bio-chemical processes. And such processes are, of course, mirrored in the instrumental reason of the market. Terrorism represented in Russia an equally reductive response to the inequality and irrationality of the *ancien regime*. So the idea of "terrorism" in perhaps its earliest modern manifestation was tied to a discussion of nihilism.

One way of understanding the problem of "nihilism" as Nietzsche took it up is in terms of a seemingly unresolvable tension or a trade-off between liberal or negative "freedom," on the one hand, and "meaning," on the other. In the West, the formal freedom of the individual—which we should be very careful not to dismiss so glibly—arises on the basis of a profound crisis of the established orders of meaning that take their bearings from the "revealed truths" of the Abrahamic religions (the same could, by the same token, be said to apply to Hinduism and its strict caste system and relation of culinary and sexual practices not to mention the interaction of members of the different castes and the Sudras, themselves). This was the idea that the world was inherently meaningful insofar as it was divinely ordained and revealed. An individual situated within these traditions had limited freedom, by which I mean the capacity to author her own fate, to write her own script, for a variety of sociological and metaphysical reasons, yet her life was, in fact, full, perhaps over-full, of meaning. Life from its inception to its end, and indeed beyond, had a purpose which was often tied inexorably to conditions of labour. For the modern, middle class, Western "emancipated" individual, the situation is the obverse. As a result of age of revolutions from 1789-1848,[11] the individual is progressively liberated from any kind of tradition that could be said to limit her capacity for self-determination. Those with a certain level of affluence can choose from a seemingly limitless set of different ways of living one's life (difficult to properly distinguish, though, from passive consumerism), and indeed one can now, all other things being equal, even choose one's own gender and/or sexual identity with the aid of bio-technology as a consequence of which meaning enters into a profound crisis. As Jean-Paul Sartre famously stated in his lecture "Existentialism is a Humanism," existence precedes essence, we are left, now, with the difficult burden of fashioning ourselves rather than situating ourselves in larger meaningful contexts that transcend us—that precede us and will survive us upon our death.

This throws some important light on the claim made by Westerners that "they" hate "our" "freedom." It's not that they hate our freedom in particular rather it is that the articulation of freedom in liberal terms, as it is a narrow conception of freedom that seems aimless, empty decadent and licentious. We are condemned to freedom, but we do not live under conditions in which that freedom could be meaningfully exercised. This is the liberal conception of negative freedom: ability to choose in the absence of impediments, as opposed to the genuine capacity—what Nietzsche called "Will to Power"—to participate in making meaningful decisions about our lives, indeed, in authoring "new values." If our contemporary relativism makes all forms of life equally valuable, then none of them is valuable at all. Perhaps this is what explains the attraction of the "escape from freedom," promised by the certainties of fundamentalist religion and right-wing populist movements in the West are proving themselves to be to growing numbers of people.

It is precisely this seemingly unresolvable crisis that suicide bombers seek to resolve. Combine this crisis of meaning with exclusion from the conditions of the formal liberal freedom described above, from the very possibility of redeeming some of the promise of material happiness and fulfilment that capitalism offers everyone but actually delivers to very few, with racism and neo-colonial realities in which young Muslim men experience humiliation on a global scale and you have a recipe for massive disaffection and, ultimately, radicalization. As Max Horkheimer once suggested during a previous time of crisis: "The less stable necessary ideologies are, the more cruel the methods by which they are protected. The degree of zeal and terror with which tottering idols are defended shows how far dusk has already advanced."[12] Suicide bombing reassembles the broken unity of meaning and freedom in a single act of extreme violence. And it is an act that is sure to beget more violence in Iraq, Syria, Pakistan, Afghanistan, etc. as well more reprisals on the streets of major Western cities on innocent Muslims which, itself, will no doubt of course further fuel the fire of extremism. Today we clearly stand at a threshold. There seem to be only two alternatives in Europe and beyond. The first is a continuation of this vicious circle under increasing militarization, authoritarian undermining of civil liberties and, ultimately fascism. The second, is a strengthening of genuinely democratic forms of self-governance and self-organization in which new life-affirming rather than life-denying values could be constituted.

Conclusion

Derrida and Habermas could be said to embody the idea of the "Good European" along lines laid down by Nietzsche. They do so, therefore, by taking up a critical, sceptical stance towards their own intellectual traditions. If Nietzsche presciently identifies the struggle for the control of the earth as the birth of Grand Politics, then Derrida and Habermas are witnesses of precisely these Grand Politics in the 20th century and engage in what Habermas calls "learning by catastrophe."

While it is beyond question that Derrida partakes of the larger reception of Nietzsche in post-war France as model of *affirmative* thinking intended as the counter-point to the negativity of Hegel and Marx, Habermas cannot, of course, be so easily understood as "Nietzschean" in any straight-forward way. While Habermas and Derrida both participate in what Richard Rorty has called the "linguistic turn," they do so in radically different ways. For Habermas, the unforced force of better arguments presented in the space of reasons represents the normative horizon against which power or distortions in communication can be exposed. For Derrida, communication, beset by an infinite play of deferral and difference, is thus as tropological as it is conceptual, and, as a consequence, is invested with a logic of undecidability. Power is the capacity to fix or arrest the play of signification in such a way that it temporarily yields a stable meaning. We might say, then, that if for Habermas power is external to the inherent normativity of discourse, for Derrida the hegemonic working of power is internal to it. While Habermas emphasizes the universality of moral norms as the outcome of a concrete discourse in which the other is included, Derrida's deconstructive interventions are articulated in solidarity with an other always already excluded as a condition of her *inclusion*.

In fact, on the face of it, Nietzsche could be said to be, perhaps even more than Heidegger, to be Habermas' principal intellectual foe. For example, already in his 1968 *Knowledge and Human Interests*, Habermas mounts a powerful criticism contra Nietzsche of what he will call in the *Philosophical Discourse of Modernity,* some seventeen years later, the intertwining of validity claims, on the one side, and forms of power on the other. Indeed, one could claim that communicative reason, and therefore the normative bedrock of Habermas' entire position, is grounded in the idea of an institutionalized *differentiation* between force and manipulation, on the one hand, and a form of mutual understanding grounded in the "unforced force of better arguments," on the other. In contrast, Derrida, with Nietzsche insists upon the undecidability of concept and metaphor, denotative and connotative uses of language. So, for the latter, power, or what Nancy and Lacoue-Labarthe call the "political" (*la politique*) is, in a sense, prior to this opposition.[13]

Yet at the same time, there is an undeniable aesthetic and deeply Nietzschean dimension in Habermas's very conceptualization of modernity, itself, as embodying a kind of "will to power," as no longer relying on the "traditional authority" embedded in past forms and practices, but, rather, heroically, to quote Habermas, "generating its normativity out of itself." Like Derrida, Habermas draws upon his own de-familiarizing distance indeed one could say *alienation* from the Third Reich in which he spent his youth as well as the mentorship of returned exiles—Horkheimer and Adorno—caused both philosophers to look at the world from what Edward Said calls a "stereoscopic" perspective. Ultimately, if what I have said is true, that is, if Derrida and Habermas can be considered as Good Europeans, who evince an intellectual and philosophical debt, even when in Habermas's case it is disavowed, to Nietzsche, and if Nietzsche identifies with a Dionysus who hails from beyond Europe's border, in Asia Minor, then we must conclude that to be a "Good European" is to positively affirm or re-affirm Europe's own non-identity with itself.

NOTES

1. E.M. Butler, *The Tyranny of Greece Over Germany.*
2. Joseph Chytry, *The Aesthetic State*, xii.
3. See Maurizio Lazzarato's *The making of Indebted Man* and *Governing by Debt.*
4. See Deleuze and Guatarri's analysis of the "infinitization" of debt in capitalism in *A Thousand Platueas* and also the work that it has inspired such as Maurizio Lazzarto's *Making of Indebted Man* and *Governing by Debt.*
5. Julian Young, *A Philosophical Biography of Nietzsche,* Cambridge: Cambridge University Press, 2010: 11.
6. The following few paragraphs draw form the Introduction to *Reification and Spectacle: On the Timeliness of Western Marxism*, Samir Gandesha and Johan Hartle (eds.), Amsterdam: University of Amsterdam Press, 2017.
7. One of the worst being beheading of some twenty-one Coptic Christians on a Libyan beach.

8. So much so that in Europe, many prepare themselves for an imminent invasion of ISIS fighters.
9. One must not forget that the ground of the Arab Spring was, to some extent, prepared in Persia, i.e. the 2009 Green Revolution in which the 'micro-spectacle' is turned in the direction not of rendering the population more passive but for creating conditions under which the Ahmadinejad regime could be challenged (unsuccessfully as it turned out).
10. Michael Allen Gillespie, *Nihilism Before Nietzsche,* Chicago: University of Chicago Press, 1994.
11. Eric Hobsbawm, *The Age of Revolution.*
12. Max Horkheimer, *Dawn Aphorisms (1926-1931).*
13. This is also why Kompridis in *Disclosure and Critique* makes the strong claim that Critical Theory requires a phenomenological supplement that centers around the notion of "disclosure."

5

Cryptonymy: Deconstruction, Psychoanalysis, Politics

Anup Dhar

What is it to reevaluate post-structuralism? How does one reevaluate? Can there be a general evaluation? Or do we reevaluate 'at the seams'? Evaluate where post-structuralism is most edgy, most attacked and yet most creative: the question of the (geo)political? Which thinker do we take recourse to, to reevaluate? Do I take to Lacan? Or do I do it through Derrida? Perhaps, find instead a Lacan in Derrida. Or a Derrida in Lacan. The paper takes off from Derrida's "Geopsychoanalysis: and the rest of the world" ... and arrives at Derrida's Foreword— titled "Fors"— to Nicholas Abraham and Marie Torok's *The Wolf Man's Magic Word: Cryptonymy*. It remains a trifle undecided: does it arrive at Derrida's Foreword to *Cryptonymy*? Or does it arrive at Derrida's *cryptonymy*, at what is *cryptonymic* in Derrida's work, itself? The Moebius of this indecision forms the context of the paper's 'reevaluation of post-structuralism' from first *without* (titled 'politics of psychoanalysis') and then from *within* (titled 'psychoanalysis of politics').

Derrida's "Geopsychoanalysis: '... and the *rest of the world*' "[1] works at the troubled interface of the deconstructive, the psychoanalytic or more precisely, the *crypto-analytic* and the political; it raises at least three questions and offers us a way of reevaluating post-structuralism from first, *without* and then, *within*:

(i) the question of the geo-graph, the geo-political graph of psychoanalysis
(ii) the question of the politics of psychoanalysis; the politics of space-place in psychoanalysis; and
(iii) the question of the psychoanalysis or crypto-analysis of politics.

It is the question of the geo-politics of psychoanalysis that takes the paper to the psychoanalysis of the *world of the rest* or more precisely "a new theory of mental life" that emanates from the world of the rest. It is the question of the psychoanalysis of politics ('psychoanalysis of torture' to be more precise) that takes us to crypto-analysis, and to cryptonymy; we ask:

where in Derrida's work is there a footprint of the psychoanalysis of politics? Is cryptonymy a way of approaching the question of the political in general and of *Hegemony and Socialist Strategy* by Ernesto Laclau and Chantal Mouffe, in particular? The paper hence asks: what if one writes hegemony and socialist strategy once again *after* cryptonymy? Or more precisely what if one reevaluates the question of hegemony after cryptonymy? The other question the paper asks: does late Foucault's re-reading of psychoanalysis (just like Derrida re-reads psychoanalysis in *Cryptonymy*) in *Hermeneutics of the Subject* (as against his reading of psychoanalysis in *History of Sexuality*) as *askesis* give another turn to politics—politics *as* askesis; socialist strategy *as* askesis? Thus if the cryptonymic in Derrida takes us to the *secret* of the hegemonic, or the hegemonic as secret, the psychoanalytic in Foucault takes us to the *subject* of socialist strategy. Both contribute to the rewriting of not just post-structuralism but of the political in general and hegemony and socialist strategy in particular.

Reevaluating Post-structuralism from *Without*: Politics of Psychoanalysis

I take off from Derrida's somewhat uncharacteristic assertion in *Geopsychoanalysis: '... and the rest of the world'*: 'there is practically no psychoanalysis in Asia, or in the South Seas'. One would like to ask: why would he say this? Is it because he is unaware of the presence of psychoanalysis in Asia? Or is it because he actually thinks 'psychoanalysis has never set foot' on Asian soil (this being the question of *location-space*)? Or is it because *here* psychoanalysis 'has never taken off its European shoes' (this being the question of *character-disposition*)? Is it because as Derrida says 'De facto and de jure. African [or Asian] psychoanalysis was European, structurally defined in the profoundest way by the colonial state apparatus'? Is it because much of Asian or African psychoanalysis were 'merely emanations of what we used (how accurately!) to call 'metropolitan' organizations.'" (1998: 69)

Derrida begins the piece with the International Psychoanalytic Association's proposed Constitution of 1977, which contains a 'parenthetical sentence' which attempts to 'map the divisions of the psychoanalytic world.' The map is as follows: 'The Association's main geographical areas are defined at this time as America north of the United States-Mexican border; all America south of that border; and the *rest of the world*' (italics mine). It is the 'rest of the world' that animates Derrida; it is the 'world of the rest' that animates me. He asks: why does the rest of the world remain unnamed in the Constitution? Or more particularly, why does 'Latin America' remain unnamed? This according to Derrida is as if the 'psychoanalytic colonization of a non-American rest-of-the-world, the conquest of a virginity parenthetically married to Europe.' This leads to first what Derrida calls a *homogenization* of the rest of the world. To me however the crisis is in the *hegemonization* of the world of the rest. Because, even in his naming of 'Latin America' Derrida falters; it appears there is no psychoanalysis in the rest of the world; the world of the rest remain barren in terms of the production of 'theories of mental life.' It appears all of psychoanalysis even if present, is European, or a *derivative* of the European. The work and world of the rest looks like a slightly modified or a displaced version of the European/American Original. One needs to ask: how have the 'rest' received psychoanalysis in the rest of the world? What has it done to the world of the rest? What has the world of the rest done to psychoanalysis? How do I make sense of the above discussion—a discussion premised on the (absence and presence of) psychoanalysis in Asia (and Africa)? How do I map the difficult work of psychoanalysis in Asia? Has it produced something different from what Derrida calls 'metropolitan organizations'?[2] What does the layered life-history[3] of the first 'savage' psychoanalyst, Girindrasekhar Bose, who also practiced psychiatry in a mental hospital, taught psychology and psychoanalysis in the University and wrote (psychoanalytically signed) commentaries on the Bhagvad Gita (1948 [1931]), the Yoga Sutras (1966), the Puranas (2001 [1934]) and proposed in lieu of psychoanalysis, *A New Theory of Mental Life* tell us? Does it give us a sense of something different from what Derrida calls "metropolitan organizations"? Is it the history of a new theory of mental life and of *sexuation*, different from the one offered by Freudian psychoanalysis? It is possible that taking off from an extant logic of the Indian psyche (exemplified by epic manuscripts like the *Mahabharata* as against Greek Tragedy[4]) it offers to the west the *Indian logic of the psyche* (and not just the logic of the *Indian psyche*).

It is also possible that Bose was giving birth to an aboriginal form of psychology where aboriginal psychology was not about an isolated insight or data but about questioning the basic paradigm, architectonics and culture of western psychology; this could possibly grant alternative/aboriginal psychologies the right to integrate within, what they see as the best of modern psychology and to reject the bad; and inaugurate in the process a new theory of mental life and of sexuation marked, in this case, by the interminable see-saw of what Bose called the eroticized *double wish*. It is possible that Bose was actually giving back to the west an *aboriginal* insight—an insight that would need to be adopted by the West as well; and this insight was not about *who we were*; it was not just about the Indian psyche; it was not about the possibility that Indian males don't have the castration complex; it was about questioning the very deployment of the castration complex and by default of the phallus as a constitutive node/anchor of sexed psychic life. It was not about saying that we are or were different. It was to build on this difference and give to the West *and* to ourselves a *different* psychology.

Bose was neither accepting or repeating the judgments passed on us by Western culture, nor impotently resenting them. Either way, there are no estimates of our own, wrung from 'an inward perception of the realities of our position' (Bhattacharya, 1954 [1931]: 104). Bose was resisting both an 'unthinking conservatism' and 'an imaginary progressiveness merely imitative of the West' (Bhattacharya, 1954 [1931]: 104). In other words, Bose was resisting *hegemonization.*

Reevaluating Post-structuralism from *Within*: Psychoanalysis of Politics

Derrida invokes psychoanalysis' a-politicism as also a-psychoanalyticism in politics in the context of 'torture' and human rights. He asks: what is that form of violence that we call torture? Where does it begin and end? What is the status of the suffering inflicted or undergone in torture? What is the substance of torture? What is the phantasy structure of torture? What is the symbolic logic of torture? Derrida asks: "why is the International Psycho-Analytic Association, unable to take up a position on certain kinds of violence in any other terms than those of a *pre-psychoanalytic* and *a-psychoanalytic* juridical discourse, even then adopting only the vaguest and the most impoverished forms of that traditional legal idiom, forms deemed inadequate by modern human rights jurists and lobbyists themselves?" (1998: 76)

Derrida suggests: "at present there exists no approach to political problems, no code of political discourse, that has in any rigorous way incorporated the axiomatics of a possible psychoanalysis." What then, is it to put (not just *someone* [which is our usual understanding of psychoanalysis], but) *something* 'in analysis'; in this case, the question of torture? What is it to put the 'political' in analysis? The first "concerns the neutralization of ethics and of the political realm, an utter dissociation of the psychoanalytic sphere from the sphere of the citizen or moral subject in his or her public or private life; and a consequent circumscribing of psychoanalysis within the realm of the 'clinical'. The other "involves the retreat toward ethical-political positions whose neutrality is rivaled only by their seeming irreproachability; they lean, moreover, away from the political and toward the ethical ... It is in this context that a doctrine of human rights is evoked—a doctrine, what is more, itself ill-defined—the shelter is taken behind a language with no psychoanalytic content or pertinence, a language that takes no risks of a psychoanalytic nature and that should certainly satisfy no one present here today. What is an "individual"? What is a "legitimate freedom"... what is the "political" from a psychoanalytic point of view? (1998: 77) This also relates to so many "vast and pressing issues [like philosophy of law, its history, the problem of its relationships to ethics, politics, ontology, and the value of the person or even of the humanity of the human individual—the possibility (or impossibility) of forming the notion of dignity, in the Kantian sense, which would transcend all values, all exchange, all equivalence, and perhaps even go beyond the idea of law itself, beyond judicial weighing-up] which the psychoanalytic problematic should no longer be able to evade and about which it ought to open a debate with Plato, Kant, Hegel, Marx, Heidegger, and several others, as well as with jurists and philosophers of law. A debate of this kind has never been more apropos, and when I say that psychoanalysis should no longer be able to evade it, this also implies, in my view, that psychoanalysis cannot itself in this respect be evaded." (1998: 78)

Derrida shows how the Association "dispenses with any properly *psychoanalytic reflection* upon human rights, upon what the meaning of "right" might be in a world where psychoanalysis is a contemporary reality." One hence needs to look for the "theoretical constructs best able to bring out the conceptual inadequacy of the axiomatics of human rights and of Western political discourse, and to show the way in which these are rooted in deconstructible philosophemes ... they indicate the necessity for a new ethics—not just for an 'ethics of psychoanalysis' (see Lacan, *Seminar VII*), but for another ethical discourse on ethics in general, another political discourse on politics in general, a discourse that would take into account deconstructive and psychoanalytic factors."

Derrida thus argues for a (deconstructive and) psychoanalytic rethinking of the political; however this is possible only when, and if, there is a political rethinking, and why not, a political re-evaluation of the psychoanalytic corpus. What is known as 'psycho-social studies' could be the ground for such a psychoanalytic rethinking of the political and a political rethinking of the psychoanalytic; the letters exchanged between Louis Althusser and Jacques Lacan, between 1963 and 1969 (see Dhar and Chakrabarti, 2014: 220-233) could also form the backbone of such a dialogue between the psychoanalytic and the political. In this paper, however, I try to develop a rethinking of the cusp of the deconstructive and the political through a turn to cryptonymy; and hegemony and socialist strategy serve as the placeholder of the cusp of the deconstructive and the political.

Hegemony and Socialist Strategy after Cryptonymy?

This section of the paper asks: what would it be to rethink the question of hegemony after cryptonymy in particular and Derrida in general? Would a dialogue between the Lacanian Real and the Derridean understanding of the 'crypt' enrich our understanding of hegemony? It also asks: what would it be to rethink socialist strategy after cryptonymy/Derrida? The section thus builds on Derrida's question: what would be a "socialist" approach to the 'social'?

Marx engendered a socialist approach to the early nineteenth century Comte-ian social. What would it be in the contemporary? Would it be a "*socius* no longer defined solely in terms of classic, i.e., socioeconomic, concepts—where a psychoanalytic contribution might be considered essential?" (1998: 79) What would then be a socialist strategy? Would it be a kind of decipherment of what Abraham and Torok calls the crypt? Or would it be what Foucault in *Hermeneutics of the Subject* calls *askesis* (in fact, Foucault sees Lacanian psychoanalysis itself as an *asketic* tradition; *askesis* was also central to the Gandhian project of non-violent reorganization of desire in the *socius*)? Derrida however talks of an *occlusion*, "which effectively bars the emergence of an ethics or politics truly *contemporary* with psychoanalysis." How to rethink the political beyond this occlusion; as also, how to rethink psychoanalysis beyond the usual and customary occlusion of the political in psychoanalysis?

Hegemony: Neurotic or Psychotic Phenomenon?

Lacan in *Seminar III* (1953) is taking us beyond the 'manifest clinical symptomatology' of neurosis and psychosis to a structural difference between the two, one that is not based on a psychosexual aetiology. Lacan opens *Seminar III* by saying that he wants to address not the treatment, but the *question* of the treatment of the psychoses, a fact that is reflected in the title given to the paper that emerges from this Seminar and is included in the *Écrits*—"On A Question *Prior* To Any Possible Treatment of Psychosis". That is, Lacan is not simply aiming to propose a better technique for working within the established theoretical framework, but rather attempting to re-examine the theory of psychosis and propose something Freud never fully achieved – a structural distinction between the neuroses and the psychoses. It is with respect to psychosis—i.e. the Wolf Man Case and the case of Judge Shreber that Lacan inaugurates thinking around 'foreclosure' or primitive *verwerfung* (as distinguished from classical psychoanalysis' insistence on *repression*); thinking around foreclosure (and not repression) could in turn help one rethink the political, rethink theories of hegemony and theories of the outside. (see Chakrabarti, Dhar and Cullenberg, 2012)

> The progress of the analysis of the [Wolf Man], the contradictions which are revealed by the traces through which we follow the specification of his position in the human world, point to a *Verwerfung*, a rejection (and not *Verneinung*: 'repression')—literally, it has always been for him as if the genital plane did not exist. ...There is no trace of this plane in the symbolic register ... Castration, which is precisely what didn't exist for him, manifests itself in the form of something he imagines—to have cut his little finger, so deeply that it hangs solely by a little piece of skin... There is a sort of immediate external world, of manifestations perceived in what I will call a primitive *real*, a non-symbolized *real*,

> despite the symbolic form, in the usual sense of the term, that this phenomenon takes... it really is a *psychotic phenomenon* that we are dealing with. (Lacan, 1997: 58-59)

While Lacan inaugurates thinking around foreclosure (i.e. *Verwerfung*), as against 'The Repressive Hypothesis', in psychoanalysis, Derrida focuses on the *number* of wolves. For Derrida what is important is that there are *six* wolves; and six in Russian is *siestorka*; siestorka *is* sister or stands for sister. This keyword, *siestorka*, for Derrida, "no doubt unutterable" and "unknown for the moment," would have to be polysemic, expressing multiple meanings through a single phonetic structure. One of these would remain shrouded, but the other, or several other meanings now equivalent, would be stated through distinct phonetic structures, that is through synonyms." Derrida would call them *cryptonyms*[5] ("words that hide") because of their allusion to a foreign or archaic meaning, apparently not having any phonetic or semantic relationship to the *prohibited* [or the *taboo*] *word* (Abraham and Torok, 1986: 18–19). One hence needs what Derrida calls "the science of cryptological interpretation" (1986: xv) or *cryptoanalysis* (see Chakrabarti, Dhar and Dasgupta, 2015 for a rethinking of the political in terms of the crypt, cryptonymy and cryptoanalysis).

Taking off from Lacan, one can now think of two ways of conceptualizing the hegemonic: the hegemonic thought and conceptualized in terms of what Lacan calls the *neurotic phenomenon* (i.e. through the contingent *suture* of an incomplete and open-ended totality replete with antagonisms) and the hegemonic thought and conceptualized in terms of what Lacan calls the *psychotic phenomenon* (i.e. through the production of a *spectral/delusional appearance of things* premised on the lurking feeling that something is amiss and a lid or a cloud cover is what can hide the rent in reality produced by *fore*-closure; hence there are two closures: one, foreclosure, which is not a closure but a *rent*; i.e. an opening, a kind of primal/primitive opening, an opening caused before the actual/delusional closure; and, two, the closure of the rent of foreclosure through the production of a delusional cosmology). We have seen how it is with respect to the Wolf Man Case that Lacan speaks of foreclosure or primitive *Verwerfung*:

> The progress of the analysis of the subject in question [i.e. the Wolfman] ... point to a *Verwerfung*, a rejection ... We have been led to locate this rejection on the level, I would say, of the *non-Bejahung*[6], because we cannot, in any way, place it on the same level as negation... In a general way, in fact, the condition such that something exists for the subject is that there be *Bejahung*; this *Bejahung* which isn't a negation of a negation. What happens when this *Bejahung* doesn't happen, in such a way that nothing appears in the symbolic register? Just let's look at the Wolf Man. There was no *Bejahung* for him, no realization of the genital plane.

> *There is no trace of this plane in the symbolic register* ... it really is a *psychotic phenomenon* that we are dealing with. (Lacan, 1997: 58-59)

What then is the 'psychotic phenomenon'? "It is the emergence *in reality* (emphasis ours) of an enormous meaning that has the appearance of being nothing at all—in so far as it cannot be tied to anything, since it has never entered into the system of symbolization—but under certain conditions it can threaten the entire edifice." (Lacan, 1997: 85) It is *perceived* as absent in the received consensus, in institutions and disciplinary bodies, in the Law; it does not exist as such for the subject; something else emerges in their place to cover up for their absence as also to silence, mute their subject-effects; it is a process of putting a cloak over their very existence; the delusional cosmology is such a cloak. The question that haunts this paper: can hegemony be re-thought in terms of what Lacan calls the psychotic phenomenon, i.e. in terms of (i) foreclosure and (ii) delusional closure, in their mutual constitutivity? The question of hegemony, where hegemony is itself the delusional cosmology or the cloud-cover, is thus not to be predicated in the image of the Lacanian 'model of neurosis' or more precisely in the image of the 'neurotic phenomenon' (*Verdrangung* or repression is the founding concept of neurosis), but in the image of the Lacanian 'model of psychosis' or more precisely in the image of the 'psychotic phenomenon' (primitive *Verwerfung* or foreclosure marks the entry point concept in psychosis). (Lacan, 1997: 85; Chaudhury, 2012: xv–xxvi)

Our understanding of the hegemonic, thus, has two components: One, it is neither merely real nor unreal; it is *irreal*; it is spectral; however, that of course does not mean that it has no subject-effects. Two, it is delusional; it is productive of a delusion; the delusion of the American Dream, for example, however, once again, that does not mean that it has no subject-effects. In fact, delusions or the world of phantasy can have subject-effects far stronger than what could be called real perceptual-conceptual apprehensions or comprehensions of the world. In that sense, the delusional sets up a certain relationship with the world; it gives a certain shape to the being-in-the-world; it also engenders a certain kind of subjectivity; a subjectivity circulating obsessively and repetitively around a delusional vortex/cloud; Marx called it the 'delusive appearance of things'; the task of the political is to *work through* this delusional appearance of things in the everyday and in every pore of life (we would, however, desist the reduction of this formulation to the appearance/reality, false/true consciousness model so rampant in conventional or classical Marxism).

In this paper, we thus understand hegemony as that phantasy, that phantasmatic whole, that delusional lid that fills, or covers up the hole created by what we designate as foreclosure (i.e., primitive *Verwerfung*). The hole in the Symbolic engendered by foreclosure is closed, is sutured with the help of a delusional cloud cover of phantasies, dreams, even out and out suicidal attractions. We, thus, move away from a realist rendition of the hegemonic to an irreal understanding of the hegemonic, an irreal (combining real-unreal) that has deep-seated subject effects. This is an understanding of the hegemonic that is 'phantomatic' (see Marx, *The German Ideology*). It is, as if, premised on the 'mystical character of the becoming-fetish'. It is the 'ghost [that] gives its form, that is to say, its body, to the ideologem'; it is as if one will have to reckon with the 'invincible force and the original power of the "ghost" effect'. (Derrida, 1994: 186)

This is, however, not to suggest that the delusion cosmology is not real or is an absolute outside to what could be called materiality. Rather such delusions are a constitutive component of a deeper and expanded understanding of materiality, produced through practices in as much as it produces practices. The dream-like nature of hegemony does not make it unreal. It puts it at the cusp of the real–unreal.

We also argue for a deeper and expanded realism by invoking foreclosure and the Lacanian 'real', a notion that is placed once again at the cusp of the real-unreal-irreal. The foreclosed is neither present (in a simple sense in the Lacanian Symbolic) nor is it absent (in a simple sense in the subject-world). It is both absence and presence; presence in the sense that it has real subject-effects; absence in the sense that the discursive structure resists it. What one had conceived of as reality is a fiction, a world of phantasy (as in Lacan), a delusive appearance of things (as in Marx). It is in fact a 'cover' for that which has been foreclosed. *What is foreclosed is real.* On the one hand, what is foreclosed is a necessary fragment of reality. Thus, its absence creates a 'hole' in reality, which the world of phantasy concomitantly fills.

On the other hand, it also has real subject-effects (as we have suggested above); more importantly, it continues to haunt, torment, threaten the hegemonic; the crux of the hegemonic is, thus, constitutive of or is premised on the interminable 'keeping at bay', 'putting to burial', 'rendering dead', 'tabooing', 'silencing', 'keeping in a secret *crypt'* the *real*; in a word, *the hegemonic must resist the return of the real*; it must mutate, transit, change form in order to keep the crypt a secret, keep secret the crypt, or keep the secret of the crypt a secret; and this is where Derrida (or the perspective of the Derridean psychoanalytic: cryptonymy) comes to supplement Lacan. Spectrality (*à la* Derrida) and delusion (*à la* Marx-Lacan) on the one hand, and foreclosure (*à la* Lacan) and secrecy (*à la* Derrida) on the other, are two concept couples through which we access the question of hegemony.

The thinking of the political post-psychoanalysis thus takes us beyond the simple distinction realism/unreal. Dreams, hauntologies, spectrality, delusional, hallucinatory, the Lacanian real, fetishism, phantasy, are all attempts at making sense of or representing the cusp of the real–unreal, or occupying the hyphen between the two through the invocation of the irreality of the hegemonic.

The Scrypt[7] of the Hegemonic

The *keyword*, no doubt unutterable... and unknown for the moment, would have to be polysemic, expressing multiple meanings through a single phonetic structure. One of these would remain shrouded, but the other, or several other meanings now equivalent, would be stated through distinct phonetic structures, that is through synonyms... We would call them *cryptonyms* (words that hide) because of their allusion to a foreign or archaic meaning... Certain words suffered an extraordinary exclusion and that this same exclusion seemed to confer on them a genuinely magic power... because a given word was unutterable that the obligation arose to introduce synonyms even for its lateral meanings, and that the synonyms acquired the status of substitutes. Thus they became *cryptonyms*, apparently not having any phonetic or semantic relationship to the *prohibited* [or the *taboo*] *word*. (Abraham and Torok, 1986: 18–19)

We shall also ask in this context: Is the hegemonic a *cryptonym*, a cryptonym to render 'unutterable' and 'unknown', to 'shroud', 'hide', 'exclude', or 'prohibit' some key word(s)? The re-reading/re-working of Freud's Wolf Man 'case history material' (and associated material including Wolf Man's auto-psycho-bio-graph)—"dream by dream, and symptom by symptom"—by Abraham and Torok through

i) the "progressive elaboration" of Wolf Man's "personal dictionary" (Abraham and Torok calls it The Wolf Man's *Verbarium*)
ii) cataloguing of "deciphered hieroglyphics" and
iii) *anasemic* research (anasemia "creates an angle. Within the word itself"; anasemic research approaches symbols as an archaeologist struggles to decipher documents in an unknown language; however, to fully complete the work of deciphering, "one must restore the entire functional circuit, which implies and implicates a multiplicity of teleological subjects, and within which the symbol-thing acts as a mere relay")

show how behind the many facets and phases of Wolf Man's expressed sufferings—one could call it Wolf Man's *symptomatology*—there *was/is* "a precocious traumatic scene, removed, sent to the crypt, encrypted." (Abraham and Torok, 1986: lxxi) Within the expressed and changing phases of transition, the crypt is, as if, a "tombstone of the illicit" but which paradoxically "marks the spot of an extreme pleasure [*jouissance*] [for the hegemonic], a pleasure entirely *real* ['real' also in a Lacanian sense] though walled up, buried alive" (Derrida in Abraham and Torok, 1986: xxxiv). One may ask what a crypt is. Derrida inaugurates three understandings of crypt:

(i) crypt as "a certain organization of places [*lieux*] designed to *lead astray*" (xxxvi); "the crypt hides as it holds"; the grounds [*lieux*] are so disposed as to "disguise and to hide ... but also to disguise the act of hiding and to hide the disguise ... what is at stake here is what takes place secretly, or takes a secret place, in order to keep itself *safe* somewhere." (Derrida in Abraham and Torok, 1986: xiv)
(ii) crypt as "a topographical arrangement made to keep (conserve-hidden) the *living dead* (xxxvi). The cryptic place is also a "sepulcher," the "place of a non-place". The inhabitant(s) of a crypt are always a living dead, a dead entity, semantically dead; as if neither can be inserted in the syntactic chain; or even the chain of signifiers; as if both are "words buried alive" [1986: xxxv]; both are "defunct words" [1986: xxxv], words "relieved of their communicative function."
(iii) crypt as "a cipher, a code"; this is a movement as if from crypt as noun to crypt as verb. "To crypt is to cipher, a symbolic or semiotic operation that consist of manipulating a secret code."

Hegemony is then about a secret script; the script of a crypt; or the crypt of a script; a *scrypt*. "Secrecy is essential," whence the crypt becomes, "a hidden place, a disguise hiding the traces of the act of disguising, a place of silence" (xvii); the crypt is however also and at the same time "the outcast safe," "a commemorative monument," "the vault of a desire". One hence needs what Derrida calls "the science of cryptological interpretation" (1986: xv) to make sense of the subject. This is also because the scrypt of hegemony follows the division of a "fantasmatic double(ness)"; the subject is a neither-nor; where a "world of phantasy" or a "delusional appearance of things" is covering, clouding the crypt.

Socialist Strategy: The Old

"Our relations are old, Althusser"—this is how Lacan begins his letter to Althusser on Nov 21, 1963. One can ask: what is *old* about the relation? Where is *that* connection that comes to be designated as old? What is the nature of the old? How old? Where is it emanating from? Can one insert Foucault's *Hermeneutics of the Subject* between Lacan and Althusser to make sense of the old: "It seems to me that Lacan has been the only one since Freud who has sought to refocus the question of psychoanalysis on precisely this question of the relations between the subject and truth. This is to say, in terms which are of course absolutely foreign to the historical tradition of this spirituality, whether of Socrates or Gregory of Nyssa and everyone in between, in terms of psychoanalytic knowledge itself, Lacan tried to pose what historically is the specifically spiritual question: that of the price the subject must pay for saying the truth, and of the effect on the subject of the fact that [s]he has said, that [s]he can say and has said the truth about [her/]himself. By restoring this question, I think Lacan actually reintroduced into psychoanalysis the oldest tradition, the oldest questioning, and the oldest disquiet of the *epimeleia heautou*, which was the most general form of spirituality" (Foucault, 1982 [2005]: 30). Foucault is of the opinion that 'in both Marxism and psychoanalysis, for completely different reasons but with relatively homologous effects, the problem of what is at stake in the subject's being (of what the subject's being must be for the subject to have access to truth) and, in return, the question of what aspects of the subject may be transformed by virtue of [her] access to the truth, well, these two questions, which are once again absolutely typical of *spirituality*, are found again at the very heart of, or anyway, at the source and outcome of both these knowledges' (Foucault, 2005: 29). Taking a somewhat wide-angle historical view over two millennia, Foucault finds again in Marxism and psychoanalysis 'the questions, interrogations, and requirements which ... are the very old and fundamental questions of the *epimeleia heautou*, and so of spirituality as a condition of access to the truth' (Foucault, 2005: 29).

However, Foucault laments, neither of these two forms of knowledge/praxis has openly considered this point of view clearly and willingly. There has been an attempt to conceal the conditions of spirituality specific to these forms of knowledge. This perhaps explains why it becomes difficult to make the political and the psychoanalytic come face to face. While at the core they share an *old* relation, they have increasingly got separated and have come to be distant and foreign to each other.

Here one needs to understand what Foucault means by *spirituality*. This is important because the Foucauldian turn to spirituality (as distinct from what Parker has rightly called 'pop spirituality') is emerging, somewhat retrospectively, in this paper as one of the cusps between the political and the psychoanalytic. Foucault begins by first making a distinction between philosophy and spirituality. He calls 'philosophy' the form of thought that 'determines that there is and can be truth and falsehood and whether or not we can separate the true and false' (Foucault, 2005: 13). He calls 'philosophy' the form of thought that asks what it is that enables the subject to have access to the truth and which attempts to determine the conditions and limits of the subject's access to truth. He calls 'spirituality the search, practice, and experience through which the subject carries out the necessary transformations on [her]self in order to have access to the truth' (Foucault, 2005: 13). For Foucault, 'spirituality, as it appears in the West ... postulates that the truth is never given to the subject by right. ... truth is not given to the subject by the simple act of knowledge (*connaissance*), ... *for the subject to have right of access to the truth he [or she] must be changed, transformed, shifted, and become, to some extent and up to a certain point other than himself [or herself]*. The truth is only given to the subject at a price that brings the subject's *being* into play. ... *there can be no truth without a conversion or a transformation of the subject*, without a long labor of *ascesis* (*askesis*)' (Foucault, 2005: 15-16). Such labor of askesis give to psychoanalysis and the political, especially 'socialist strategy', a character that also and in turn makes them apposite.

While Foucault reached the psychoanalytic understanding of the political through the invocation of concepts like askesis, Derrida reaches the psychoanalytic understanding of the political (in turn related to a political understanding of psychoanalysis) through questions of what Marx called the 'secret thereof' and what Derrida calls the 'break-in technique.'[8] For Derrida:

> What is at stake [in politics] is *what takes places secretly* [i.e., that which deludes], or *takes a secret place* [i.e., that which is crypted], in order to keep itself [i.e., the hegemonic] safe... . (Derrida, 1986: xv)

In *a-psychoanalytic* understandings of the political, there are no 'secrets thereof'; there is no need for a 'break-in-technique' or a 'cryptological interpretation'; as if there is no need to take note of *what takes place secretly*, what takes place behind the veil or how one is deluded; as if there is no need to develop an appreciation of *what takes a secret place*, or what is crypted.

Derrida, on the other hand, taking off from a psychoanalytic understanding of the political (one could call it 'post-cryptonymic renditions of the political') imagines a politics of *working through* the 'delusional appearance of things' and foregrounding the paradoxical truth; a politics of *breaking into* the crypt, the encrypted; breaking into the crypt by working through the substitute signifiers; a politics of an encounter with the crypted, with the 'tombstone of the illicit', but which paradoxically 'marks the spot of an extreme pleasure [*jouissance*] [for the hegemonic], a pleasure entirely *real* ['real' also in a Lacanian sense] though walled up, buried alive'. One could call it the politics of the *living dead.* The politics of an encounter with tabooed key words, through a working through the hegemonic's *Verbarium. It is a* politics of the 'progressive elaboration' of the hegemonic's 'personal dictionary', the politics of the cataloguing of 'deciphered hieroglyphics'. One could call it the politics of *decipherment.* One could also call it the politics of the *secret,* about the secret, around the secret, on the secret. Because what is at stake [in politics] is *what takes places secretly* [i.e., that which deludes], or *takes a secret place* [i.e., that which is crypted], in order to keep itself [i.e., the hegemonic] safe.

NOTES

1. This essay was the opening address to a French-Latin American meeting convened in Paris in February 1981 at the initiative of René Major. The proceedings of this event, which was devoted mainly to the institutions and politics of present-day psychoanalysis, were published under the same title as the meeting itself: *Confrontation* (Paris, Vert et noir, 1981), and subtitled *Les souterrains de l'institution* (The Underground Corridors of the Institution). Translation first published in *American Imago* 48.2 (1991). Translation by Donald Nicholson-Smith (1996).
2. Post-structuralizing is a kind of possible culturalizing; and culturalizing could be a kind of post-structuralizing. However, there is no guarantee that one would lead to the other. One hence needs to keep the work of culturalizing alive in poststructuralism and the work of post-structuralizing alive in the 'cultural turn'.
3. When graduate training in psychology was introduced at the University of Calcutta, Girindrasekhar Bose, already a medical professional, obtained a Master's degree in psychology (1917). He was awarded the first doctorate in psychology at an Indian university in 1921. His dissertation was titled 'The Concept of Repression'. Bose was thus developing an elaboration of/on the *concept* of repression; in other words, he was not taking repression or what Foucault in *History of Sexuality* calls 'The Repressive Hypothesis' as given; he was, on the contrary, and in contradiction to most analyses of his time, reflecting on the *concept* of repression.
4. When one takes Oedipus Rex as the 'text of the psychic' one ends up with a narrative of 'acts committed in the context of non-knowledge/ignorance' (Oedipus did not know who his parents were), remorse/guilt at what one has done, self-chastisement or sacrifice to atone for one's deeds (Oedipus blinds himself). This guilt-ridden traumata sets off the 'psychic teleology'. Freud tries to make a case for such a psychic teleology in *Moses and Monotheism*. However, if one takes the Bhagvad Gita as the text of the psychic, as Bose does, one gets a different psychic teleology, a teleology sparked off by an affront to a menstruating woman in the blind king's court of justice now being avenged by the collective of husbands she has; however there is a deferral; one of the five husbands is haunted by a near-primal doubt that could be so characteristic of the conception of *dharma* (what should I do?) and why not the human (who am I?) as well; the doubt is premised on the question: can I kill?
5. *Crypt* for Derrida is "a certain organization of places [*lieux*] designed to *lead astray*" (Derrida in Abraham and Torok, 1986: xxxvi). Crypt is also "a topographical arrangement made to keep (conserve-hidden) the *living dead* (xxxvi). The cryptic place is also a "sepulcher." Crypt is "a cipher, a code;" this is a movement as if from crypt as noun to crypt as verb. "To crypt is to

cipher, a symbolic or semiotic operation that consist of manipulating a secret code."

6. In his 'Reply to Jean Hyppolite's commentary on Freud's "Negation"' (1954), Lacan describes a primordial act of affirmation which is logically prior to any act of negation. Lacan uses Freud's German term, *Bejahung* to denote this primordial affirmation. He posits a basic alternative between *Bejahung* and the psychotic mechanism he later calls 'foreclosure'. *Bejahung* designates a primordial inclusion of something in the symbolic, whereas foreclosure is a primordial refusal to include something... in the symbolic' (*Encyclopedia of Lacanian Psychoanalysis* http://nosubject.com/index.php?title=Bejahung).
7. *Scrypt* is both the 'script' of the hegemonic and the 'crypt' *within* the script of the hegemonic, that is *hermetically* sealed.
8. 'Before turning our minds to the break-in technique that will allow us to penetrate into a crypt (it consists of locating the crack or the lock, choosing the angle of a partition, and forced entry), we have to know that the crypt itself is built by violence' (Derrida, 1986: xv).

REFERENCES

Abraham, N. and M. Torok. 1986. *The Wolf Man's Magic Word: A Cryptonymy.* (Tr.) Nicholas Rand. Minneapolis: University of Minnesota Press.

Althusser, Louis. 1999. *Writings on Psychoanalysis: Freud and Lacan.* ed. Corpet, Olivier and Matheron, François. *European Perspectives.* New York: Columbia University Press.

Bose, Girindrasekhar. 1948. 'A New Theory of Mental Life.' *Samiksha*, 2(2): 108–205.

Chakrabarti, A., A. Dhar and B. Dasgupta, 2015. *The Indian Economy in Transition: Globalization, Capitalism and Development.* New Delhi: Cambridge University Press.

Chaudhury, A. 2012. 'Foreword,' in *World of the Third and Global Capitalism,* by A. Chakrabarti, A. Dhar A and S. Cullenberg. New Delhi: World View Press.

Derrida, J. 1998. 'Geopsychoanalysis: and "...the rest of the world"', in C. Lane (ed.) *The Psychoanalysis of Race.* New York: Columbia University Press.

Foucault, M. 2005. *The Hermeneutics of the Subject: Lectures at the College de France 1981-1982.* (Tr.) Burchell, G., London: Palgrave Macmillan.

Lacan, J. 2006. *Écrits* (Tr.) Bruce Fink – New York, W.W. Norton.

Lacan, J. 1977/1998. *The Four Fundamental Concepts of Psychoanalysis.* New York: W.W. Norton.

Lacan, J. 1998. *The Seminar of Jacques Lacan.* Ed. Jacques-Alain Miller. *Book XX. On Feminine Sexuality: The Limits of Love and Knowledge ... Encore (1972-1973).* (Tr.) Bruce Fink. New York: W.W. Norton.

Laclau, E. and C. Mouffe, 1985. *Hegemony and Socialist Strategy: Towards a Radical Democratic Politics.* London: Verso.

Parker, I. 2011. *Lacanian Psychoanalysis: Revolutions in Subjectivity.* London: Routledge.

6

(De)constitutive Theories of Language and the Politics of Change

Siby K. George

Changes beckoned by political communication are a significant site for the manifestation of the power of words. But the classical understanding of words as representations of independent realities cannot account for the power of words and the changes it beckons. At the same time, the deconstitutive understanding of the power of words as in Heidegger, though seminal and compelling, does not call into question the dark side of that power. Levinas's understanding of the self as exposure to otherness, the moral abground which is aboriginal articulation as such or saying, can be seen as setting the moral limits on all that is deliberately asserted and thereby made in words. The essay will begin with Charles Taylor's distinction between enframing and (de)constitutive theories of language. It will then explore Heidegger's deconstitutive view of the power of words, and move to show how this view helps clarify the issue of the arising of new realities. The final part proposes that Levinas's deonstitutive understanding of the aboriginal saying can be seen as the moral limit set on the power of words.

1. Two Types of Language Theories

Charles Taylor makes a grand bipartite division of theories of language. Enframing or designative conceptions of language in modern philosophy (which Taylor attributes to Hobbes, Locke and Condillac) have Cartesian representational epistemology as their basis. Ideas in the mind are representations, which are to be squared with correlative reality, whether internal or external, according to a 'responsible procedure' of synthesis. Meaning is generated through associating signs or words (signifiers) with their referents that are conceptual representations (signifieds) of things. Language makes for a cohesive and responsible picture of reality as a connected whole. Language in such theories is imagined as arising out of the prelinguistic association of ideas with signs. Signs and ideas exist before and after language, but language makes us realize that we can associate signs and ideas imaginatively and direct these associations to explain phenomena in powerful ways. The enframing view of language fits very well within the modern scientific culture, propelled by instrumental rationality and the technological worldview. In this view of language, the preoccupation is with eliding ambiguity and with picturing or representing reality rationally. The great progress made by modern science by the use of the formal language of mathematics and logic is an example of the limits and scope of the enframing conception of language. While it can go on extending the representational logic of the same paradigm, it cannot trigger alternatives outside it.

The constitutive or expressivist theories of language, on the other hand, find their early expression in the works of Herder and Humboldt, and their animated twentieth century revival in Heidegger, hermeneutics, poststructuralism, Wittgenstein and others of that ilk. According to Taylor, the crucial point is, constitutive theorists think that the semantic dimension is impossible without language, just as language is impossible without that dimension. We cannot show meaningfully that things have significations without language. Inasmuch as language and meaning in this broad sense are constitutive of being human, we are language animals. There is no prelinguistic realm of signs, which is always already linguistic. Taylor's emphasis, however, is that a constitutive theory of language makes room for huge, unprecedented historical transformations. In such theories, the obsession of corresponding expressions with accurate representations is replaced with describing things in powerful and newly meaningful ways. Our being in the linguistic-semantic dimension makes it possible for us to 'treat the things which surround us in new ways.' We move in this dimension whether we are making sense of things for our very simple purposes or we are conferring on things 'meanings of a new kind.' Since things cannot have meaning for us without language, it follows that our powerful use of language can invest things with new and forceful meanings.[1]

However, the transformative theories of language of Heidegger and others in the twentieth century can be better described as "(de)constitutive" than 'constitutive'. They are deconstitutive inasmuch as what is constituted by language and meaning is constantly deconstituting and reconstituting itself. That is to say, what is constituted in language is never a permanent presence, refusing to withdraw and recede to the background in order to let what it is not to come into presence and thus into being. When Heidegger speaks of language as "the house of Being,"[2] Levinas of "a saying prior to language,"[3] and Derrida of there being "no outside-text,"[4] they are arguing that there is no prelinguistic sphere of ideas. However, by this they do not mean that reality can be framed up as a permanent presence or, in Levinas's idiom, reduced to an absolute 'said'. Rather, they mean that since the constitutive realm of meaning is language, an important human task is radical critique or destructing/deconstructing/deessentializing/questioning already constituted meanings through creative and powerful use of language. Language is also deconstitutive of human experience as such because identities created through language in experience are constantly undermined, deconstructed and reconstituted through language itself. The constitutive force of language is constantly destabilized and undercut by its own deconstitutive and reconstitutive forces.

The deconstitutive conception of language, then, is much broader in scope than the enframing view of language. Language, in this view, is expressive, dynamic and engaging rather than the mere capacity of the mind to relate signs to ideas. It is dialogical and thus presupposes interlocutors and the community of speakers. The power of language is immediately evident in such a view. The power of words means the power to move and sway human beings, the power to bring about a new world.

2. Heidegger's Deconstitutive Theory of Language

The classic case of the deconstitutive theory of language is Heidegger, whose destructive hermeneutics of over two millennia old philosophical 'words' of the western tradition attempted to recover from that same tradition certain 'unprecedented words,' which according to Taylor, are "words of power... words of retrieval."[5] These words of retrieval of "[t]hose who think and those who create with words"—thinkers and poets—accomplish "the manifestation of Being insofar as they bring this manifestation to language and preserve it in language through their saying."[6] Being for Heidegger is both the background intelligibility that makes possible the manifestation of beings as well as the historical-cultural manner of manifesting or presencing of beings. Humans belong to the earth through their intimacy with beings as a whole, which unfolds as history or the making or unmaking of the 'world' of their involvements. A historical world can arise only because humans have the gift of language. By means of language they become historically intimate with beings "through the creation of a world and through its rise, as well as through its destruction and decline."[7] The ontological fact of world-formation by means of language gives rise ontically to cultural-historical worlds, which manifest unique ways of being intimate with beings as a whole. Human language "gives expression to what is most pure and most concealed, as well as to what is confused and common," to "*beings* which press upon him and inflame him in his existence, or *nonbeings* which deceive and disappoint him."[8] Powerful sayings or words that bring to expression the most hidden aspects of beings that can inflame us and press upon us have the power to transform our world.

There is no idea or representation separate from the word. "If the word did not have this bearing," remarks Heidegger, "the whole of things, the 'world', would sink into obscurity."[9] 'Logos,' according to him, is the oldest word for 'the rule of the word'; it was the word both for saying and Being/ 'presencing of beings'. Logos means "saying which, in showing, lets beings appear in their 'it is'."[10] That is: word "makes the thing be a thing... first brings what presences to its presence."[11] The cosmos is before there are words, but there is no world of human involvements, wherein realities are invested with meaning and force. Without the meanings words give to things, without meaningful relations between things and without the powerful significations we attach to them when we speak of them, things are meaningless, inert stuff. Without words, things are outside the ambit of human meaning and mediation.

Hence, Taylor notes that for Heidegger 'humans are language animals.' "They are beings who somehow possess, or are the locus of, this constitutive power of expression. In order to know the essence of human beings, you have to understand this power, i.e. language in the broad sense constitutivists use the term."[12] Notice that Taylor is repeatedly using the word 'power' to refer to language. Heidegger does, too, as in this startling statement: "Even if we had a thousand eyes and a thousand ears, a thousand hands and many other senses and organs, if our essence did not stand within *the power of language*, then all beings would remain closed off to us—the beings that we ourselves are, no less than the beings that we are not."[13] In an attempt to retrieve 'the authentic philosophical naming force of the Greek word,' which is said to be destroyed by the translation of philosophy from Greek to Latin, Heidegger claims "to win back intact *the naming force of language and words*; for words and language are not just shells into which things are packed for spoken and written intercourse. In the word, in language, things first come to be and are."[14] The human capacity to say is not a mere ability but a powerful ability.

Heidegger performed several such acts of retrieval in his writings, the best known of which was the retrieval of the word 'Being' in *Being and Time*. While at another well-known attempt to retrieve the sense of the word 'building' (*Bauen*) as 'involved caring dwelling' in the 1951 lecture "Building Dwelling Thinking," he remarks that language retracts the original meanings of its essential words, although "its primal call does not thereby become incapable of speech; it merely falls silent."[15] We can retrieve forgotten meanings of words and re-power them because (i) "[t]he word itself is the giver... the word gives Being...," and (ii) the word can also deny or 'hold back' Being. When we ponder over such withdrawals of meaning, emphasizes Heidegger, "it comes to light how astounding a power the word possesses."[16] It is the power of the word to reveal and conceal that gives things their rich meaning and gives rise to a world that matters to us rather than a universe that is indifferent to us.

The power of words, however, has its limits. While powerful deployment of words can transform our world, words themselves are not subjective creations arising from an imagined inner depth of individuals. We begin to exist by entering and inhabiting linguistic worlds rather than by constructing or making them. The cultural-linguistic community is a space of truth and reality, which the speaker cannot override if he/she wants to remain in the truth. At the same time, truth is neither permanent nor historically absolute.[17] As Joseph Kockelmans argues, each linguistic world at a particular historical moment is characterized by a certain 'naught' inasmuch as it is delimited by "what a language does not show" on account of "its mistakes, one-sided views, and errors."[18] Truth itself, therefore, arises from a domain of error and concealment. That is why Heidegger writes that "errancy belongs to the inner constitution of the Da-sein into which historical human beings are admitted."[19] All possibilities of questioning the true and recasting meaning arise in terms of the historically contingent linguistic world. The contingent expressive space provided by language (de)constitutes the very finite essence of human existence. In this sense, Heidegger's conception of language would appear banally (de)constitutive.

However, the powerful deployment of words does not mean that everything is possible with words. Words are always circumscribed by a linguistic world, 'one of the houses of Being'. Humans, nonetheless, are not fully conditioned or totally determined by their world inasmuch as they can project their existence upon several meaningful possibilities yet to appear concretely within that world but still are hidden within its expansive horizon of possibilities. Like a wave that occasionally ventures farther into the shore of the sea, human existence sometimes uncannily strives to go beyond the boundaries set by the world of praxis and language. Anxiety about the total absorption of existence into the inauthentic world that socializes and levels down authentic existence triggers original expressions, although, as Heidegger repeatedly insists, these still are hermeneutically relatable to the concealed horizons of one's linguistic world. Words of power in such instances can be genuinely original. This is why Kockelmans remarks that "[t]he new meaning that man can always force to 'light up'... originates, as it were, in a 'realm of emptiness'."[20] The most original realm of meaning is empty because it is difficult to show in what way the new meanings forced into emergence from the cultural-linguistic world are related to that world, which is the horizon of meaning as such, except probably as words that totally negate and undermine that world. In this sense, such creations of language are genuinely poetical because they bring the genuinely new, an alternative world, into presence.

The poets of original thought 'first reach into the abyss' beyond the traditionally interpreted and taken for granted cultural-linguistic world, risk more than ordinary mortals, 'risk it with language' and "since only those who risk more are capable of it, the saying that says more is only occasional. For it remains difficult."[21]

Philosophy takes what is revealed originally by poetic thought even further, and so it is "the terrifying, though rare, questioning of the truth of being."[22] It cannot be so except through words that relate to the cultural-linguistic world and yet go beyond it, beyond the given understanding of beings as a whole. Hence, the contingent expressive space provided by language also deconstitutes and reconstitutes the finite historical essence of human existence. It is in this sense that Heidegger's conception of language is deconstitutive. World-transformation is not a unilinear, necessary or history-denying development but is a response to historical Being in terms of its yet not realized possibilities. Imaginative retrieval, therefore, repeats as well as transforms the world.

If words have power, they can also lose power as the meanings that resound in them fall silent. "In the word, in language, things first come to be and are. For this reason, too, the misuse of language in mere idle talk, in slogans and phrases, destroys our genuine relation to things."[23] Heidegger sees in the modern technological culture—idly talking, information-driven, willful and subjectivistic—a peculiar loss of the power of words and assertion of the power to make. It is difficult for moderns to experience the power of words because "modern thinking is ever more resolutely and exclusively turning into calculation... calculating how man may soon establish himself in worldless cosmic space... This type of thinking is itself already the *explosion of a power* that could blast everything to nothingness."[24]

What Heidegger means by calculative thinking is objectivistic expression arising out of the modern subject-centric representational thinking and instrumental understanding of language. This type of thinking turns technological when all things manifest themselves to the modern subject as objects standing ready for endless manipulation and gratification, made possible through scientific-technical reductionism. Technology and language are both powerful, but the power of modern technology is to reduce all the manifold meanings of phenomena into the single formula of efficiency and resourcefulness; whereas, the power of words means protecting this very manifoldness in its variety. The monological power of technology colonizes and levels the manifoldness of meaning inherent to language.[25] The power of words that makes things 'near' to the human respondent, both as dear and dangerous, is lost in calculative abstraction and objectification. For Heidegger, a representational and instrumental understanding of language is a consequence of the trajectories of modern thinking. And so the antidote to technologism and objectivism is the power of expression in all its force and danger; it is poesy, art, meditative thinking and the rule of words. Heidegger coins a whole array of new and mainly verbalized nouns to convey the sense of the non-substance ontology he was inaugurating. The strategy of retrieval brings to the fore what language withdraws and makes silent. We cannot anymore say there is nothing in a name; in fact, there is nothing outside names/words. Such a conception of language has made it difficult to rehabilitate pejorative words and usages enmeshed in questionable histories. Sexist, racist, casteist words are banished and made to disappear from our sensibilities. The power to change is couched in words; it is not a reticent, wordless capacity to act. What is the force of this conception of language for the politics of change? How does the power of words come to effect in far-reaching political changes and transform our world?

3. Deconstitutive View of Political Change

Enframing theories of language also try to grapple with the power of words. Powerful words are more accurate representations of prelinguistic realities. Powerful descriptions help their authors wield greater control over what they describe. In deconstitutive theories on the other hand, radical revolutions and deep, smoldering political transformations create new meanings and conceal past meanings. Political transformations can help withdraw erstwhile realities and give rise to new ones. Of course, the later Heidegger is wary of all politics of the will, machination and techno-modern, techno-capitalist calculation. Yet, there is no reason why poetic political activism and creating new forms of our shared realities in response to questions arising from the ontological site of our existence should be an anathema.[26] What Heidegger is in fact wary of is the techno-capitalist politics of liberalism, which institutes "a process of ontological mono-politics enframing the real as such in terms of available, usable, orderable, and makeable reserve."[27]

Otherwise, Heidegger considered politics as an originary, reality-defining possibility. Truth for him is possible not first as correspondence or as givenness-beforehand. Truth emerges rather in 'the opposition of clearing and concealing'. Clearing of an open field of beings or a world, and concealing or withdrawing an erstwhile field of beings, at least partially, is necessary for the establishment of truth. While speaking of the different language-mediated ways of the establishment of truth in "The Origin of the Work of Art" (1935), Heidegger notes that an essential way in which truth establishes itself is "the act that founds a political state."[28] Heidegger considers founding of a political state as a "specific domain of creativity, decisions, and peaks and valleys within history" like sculpture or poetry, which ought to be the historical thinker's matter for thought and presentation.[29] The power of the word is central to both the work of art and of politics. Referring to Aristotle's statement that the human being is a political animal, Heidegger adds that it can be so only because it is an animal that has the word or logos or "that being that can address beings as such with respect to their Being."[30] Now, truth or unconcealment is poetic as it brings reality to the fore. Julian Young calls events such as political beginnings 'charismatic events' and for Heidegger such events, just as the works of art, bring forth truth. Young exemplifies charismatic events by referring to Hitler's founding of the Nazi state in 1933, Pericles's founding of Athenian democracy, Yahweh's covenant with the Jews in the desert and the central Christian event of the crucifixion.[31]

The Buddha's first sermon delivered to five companions in Sarnath and Gandhi's first nationwide noncooperation movement against the British Raj in 1920 are no less charismatic events. Gandhi's symbolisms and the discursive imagination of the nation he set in motion became in some ways central to the historical essence of the young Indian nation. His articulations involved overcoming and withdrawing from view alternatively imagined nations. Ashis Nandy observes that Gandhi "knew well that he would have to fight hard in India to establish his version of nonviolence as 'true' Hinduism or as the central core of Hinduism" because nonviolent Hinduism was not a sealed fact. Swami Vivekananda for example, adds Nandy, made the sarcastic comment at the end of the nineteenth century that the British excelled in the authentic teachings of the *Shastras* to be manly and this-wordly, whereas Indians foolishly took up the authentic teachings of the New Testament to be "passive, life-denying, feminine subjects."[32] Gandhi was not putting into words what was unchangeably essential in Hinduism or Hindustan but what he saw as an interpretive appropriation of the tradition; he was opening up or unconcealing an authentic possibility of the tradition, and in so doing, was concealing other constellations of meaning with regard to that tradition. This is what Heidegger means by the assertion that the essence of the word is to 'let beings appear in their Being' and that "Being manifests itself primordially in the word."[33] In this sense, if Heidegger dared "to take up the great and lengthy task of tearing down a world that has grown old and of building it truly anew"[34] in a philosophical way, Gandhi was attempting an improbable political reconstitution of the tradition. The nation born out of Gandhi-Nehru legacy, however, began to be caught up in new webs of words after about fifty years of its life. A narrative that Gandhi successfully concealed and never allowed to come to the foreground of national consciousness is suddenly finding wings, words and a world. The Babri Masjid demolition of 1992 and the nuclear tests of 1998 were also charismatic events that unconcealed other realities and stoked up old, suppressed narratives of "rage-

and-shame" in the words of Pankaj Mishra. According to him, this is "just the kind of retrograde 1920s-style nationalist dogma that is making a big comeback in India."[35] A new world of words, celebrated and believed to be an ultramodern repetition of the ancient, is thus being born, just as the Gandhian world is facing deconstitution and dissolution.

Taylor notes that the (de)constitutive understanding of language has both positive and terrifyingly dangerous uses and that Heidegger is aware only of the former. The ecological insights Heidegger draws from his (de)constitutive view of words, Taylor says, is a 'benign' use that Heidegger's thinking can be put into.[36] However, this is certainly a misstatement. For Heidegger, language is the most dangerous good because "it first creates the possibility of a danger,"[37] and it alone can expose humans to something manifest, whether it be good or evil as we read in "Letter on 'Humanism'". Heidegger goes on to argue that language alone can first create the threat or danger to Being, the possibility of the loss of Being, just as the possibility of the emergence of Being. Language always hides within it the danger of the loss of Being. Language must suffer this danger in order to be language. Hence, the custodians of language, poets and thinkers, are in that much more danger. Not that the thinker and the poet is in a more perilous condition than the child in tears for food or the inhumanly treated outcast. But the danger Heidegger speaks of is real because the creative pursuit of the thinker and the poet can banish the suffering of the outcast into oblivion or call it forth into being. Heidegger's later turn away from the decisionism and subjectivism of *Being and Time* can be seen as an acknowledgement of the negative uses of the deconstitutive power of words of the willful subject, as apparent during the Nazi period of his intellectual career.[38]

4. Moral Circumscriptions of Deconstitutive Theory of Language in Levinas

Heidegger has a genuinely deconstitutive and critical conception of the power of words, and yet, the response of the Heidegerian deconstitutive view of language to the dark and sinister words of power would simply be that they are contingently dependent on the demands of the world. Interlocutors may be thought of as broadly delimiting the power of words since words are always responses. But Heidegger is least interested in dwelling on these limits and the consequent possibility of ethics. The deconstitutive power of words is extremely important to Heidegger's project, but what violence this power can do in its sheer upsurge in the face of the Other was never a focus of his attention. This cannot go unnoticed when we think about words and politics, especially in the light of Heidegger's Nazi sympathies.

Undoubtedly, then, the politics of words, which is capable of beckoning new realities to presence, necessarily involves the question of ethics/justice. While there are resources in Heidegger for a political ethics centered on *Being and Time*'s notion of Being-with[39] and for an ecopolitical ethics of the thing and the earth in his later writings,[40] I want to invoke Levinas's notion of otherness because there is a clear sense of ethical delimitation of the deconstitutive power of words in his writings. However, I want to take this turn here without doing any disservice to the interpretation of Heidegger offered above, and so, I approach Levinas with two Heideggerian caveats.

Firstly, Levinas is inescapably humanistic. Speaking of his Kantian predicament, Edward Casey writes that for Levinas "ethics is human or does not exist at all."[41] In his response, Diane Perpich recognizes that Casey's environmental ethics is invoking Levinas, despite his humanism, because Levinas's notion of responsibility for the Other arises from the irreducible alterity and singularity of the Other and not because the Other serves our interests, and is sufficiently like us to deserve equal treatment or because we have natural sympathy for the Other. For Perpich, the attempt to see Levinasian 'face' in otherness as such, human and non-human, is doomed because the Levinasian oeuvre does not permit it. [42] However, such a reading has been an important line of Levinas scholarship and for good reasons.[43] Tom Sparrow, for example, argues that being human is not a condition for being a Levinasian 'face'. The face is that which is capable of experiencing and expressing a need in a non-representational way.[44] For Levinas, this non-representational expression is aboriginary language or what he calls 'saying,' which, like discourse in *Being and Time*, goes before the 'said' or the language of deliberate assertions. So, I take it that the face that makes demands on me is otherness as such that I encounter, and not particularly human otherness.

Secondly, to this reading of the notion of otherness, which definitely is an undercutting of and going ahead from the humanism of the Other that Levinas champions,[45] we must attach the post-Heideggerian mood of the later Levinas (Of *Otherwise than Being, Or Beyond Essence*, 1974) that Michael Fagenblat recently took note of. He writes: "Unlike Levinas 1, Levinas 2 thinks it impossible to 'escape' from Being to get a clear moral point of view that transcends the plane of history and the evil of mere Being. Ethics is refigured as the 'exposure' to the other in the very inwardness and passivity of the self."[46] The deconstructive, post-Heideggerian turn in Levinas, thus, means the passive exposure of the self from out of itself to otherness. Levinas sees the exposure itself as language in a deconstitutive sense and I shall argue that this view of language as ethical exposure may be thought of as the limit and measure of the dark side of the power of words. Thus, for both Heidegger and Levinas, words are responses to otherness as such and both acknowledge their deconstitutive power, but Levinas undercuts the 'power' of the deconstitutive word in invoking the aboriginal ethical upsurge.

For Levinas, before verbs and nouns (the said or *dit*), before Being or intelligibility, language is *saying* (*dire*), which involves "a positive and antecedent event of communication which would be an *approach* to and a *contact* with the neighbor, and in which the secret of the birth of thought itself and of the verbal statement that bears it would lie."[47] Levinas's emphasis on human-to-human contact may be considered as the predilection involved in our dialogical relationships, but should in no way deter us from thinking of the moral demands made upon us by what is not human, especially when our sensibilities are so conditioned through our aboriginal exposure to otherness as such.[48] He writes that "saying is communication, to be sure, but as a condition for all communication, as exposure."[49] The saying that underlies constitutions and laws, words of power and sobs of powerlessness, is "the trace—the unpronounceable writing— of what... does not enter into any present, to which names designating beings or verbs in which their *essence* resounds are no longer suited... but which marks with its seal everything that can be named."[50] It is deconstitutive of the said because the said cannot exhaust it. Thus, saying comes to mean the antecedent exposure of the self to the Other, the non-indifference to the Other.

For Levinas, the ethical sense of exposure to otherness is presupposed by language in the Heideggerian sense of interdependence of Being and word. Words involve 'the subordination of the saying to the said.' Language in this sense permits us to utter by a necessary betrayal what is otherwise than Being, the ethical exposure to otherness, which is saying. The language of saying is prior to and is the condition for the linguistic system of the said. The word-Being interdependence cannot 'exhaust what there is in saying.' Since temporalization of the understanding is essence and Being, synchronic temporalization is allergic to the saying, which is diachronic and deconstitutive. John Llewelyn writes that the priority of the saying is "prior both to the priority of formally logical system and to that of historical events. So the priority of neither, a priority that is constitutive and at the same time deconstitutive of the continuum of time and of the order of logical implication and presupposition."[51] For Levinas, Heidegger's verbal words still vibrate with 'essence,' although they are temporal and historical. The meaning of words, even powerful words, says Levinas, cannot be irresponsible caprice. A kerygma or fiat hinged on the saying gives to 'historical languages spoken by people a locus.' Words speak "the saying that bore the said, but goes further, was absorbed and died in the said, was inscribed."[52] Hence, while the intelligibility of words, the realm of the said, is a play without responsibility, "where everything possible is permitted," says Levinas, saying bears "an intrigue of responsibility."[53] That is, Levinas agrees with Heidegger that words are not representations of pre-existing ideas. But they signify a saying that goes before them.[54] Our exposure to otherness and its exigencies are at the origin of the meaning of words. When we utter words, they do not exhaust the full force and power of their original meanings, but they still are (and we are called to be vigilant about this) traces of those meanings. Magical, powerful but dangerous words betray the responsibility to the Other that are at the origin of words themselves.

What do we make of the Levinasian interjection that prior to word and Being there is exposure to otherness or saying? Only this: "there is question of the said and Being only because saying or responsibility require justice."[55] Without it, there is no limit or measure to the said. It is exposure to otherness as such that makes us what we are and gives meaning to our things. In this sense, the self is already a tending towards otherness, which Levinas calls responsibility, but more accurately it is the requirement to respond to otherness (response-ability). The excess of this tending towards otherness or response-ability is reduced to worded forms of law and justice, state and its systems, politics and public life, to bearable forms distributed across our encounters with otherness. We need to be continuously vigilant about the ways in which politics constantly strives to discredit and deceive the saying that gave rise to the state and the constitution. The danger of the betrayal of the saying by the said of politics prompts Levinas to call competitive politics "the art of foreseeing war and of winning it by every means."[56] The politics of equality, Levinas writes, is born out of the inequality and the surplus of my duties over my rights.

The aboriginal upsurge of the ethical, the saying, is to be necessarily betrayed and reduced to the said, for there is not only the Other but the Other's other or the third or society and, we must add, otherness as such, for there is nothing stranger to the self than the alterity of nature and animals. Reason, state and justice, born out of the betrayal of the original ethical upsurge, Levinas says, should be mediated by the traces of that very ethics. Self-interested individuals looking out for security and freedom, for which they are willing to enter into a social contract and produce the liberal society, are not Levinas's political beings. Prior to the needs and interests of the self, justice or society is always already conditioned by ethics, which makes justice never blind to the cries of the Other, the most genuinely Other in a polity. At the most aboriginal level of ethics, the saying, my responsibility for the Other always exceeds her/his responsibility for me. Hence, what moves justice is the forgetting of self.[57]

There is a restless, anarchic hither side to order and foundation/ *arche*, which is saying or responsibility for others. The power of words and the realities they make cannot be a case of freewheeling volition or even response.

The power of words is measured by the demands of the Other and the 'height' of her/his needs. For Levinas, this measurement constitutes language as such, which Heidegger's deconstitutive theory of language does not see. When the power of words calls forth new realities, justice which somehow undercuts the self, the we, listens to the Other and answers to her cries for justice. It is not the *presence* of otherness that "puts into question the naive spontaneity of the ego,"[58] but it is the *passive obsession* with otherness, already forming the folds of the self. Unlike the uncanny angst-filled Dasein of *Being and Time*, Levinas's human being is not intoxicated with the concern for own existence but its disquietude and insomnia 'comes from the destitution of the others.'

Saying is an asymmetrical obsession with otherness as such. From this unreasonable obsession, there arise words of power which shape reality one way or another. The saying already "cries out for justice, demands measure and knowing."[59] The demand for justice is met in fixing and reducing the saying to the said in the forms of consciousness, reason, comparison, law, technology, science, state, society, coexistence and the like. The abuse of what is fixed in a said is thus taken to be not giving ear to the saying that conditions the said. Levinas looks at technology, for example, as that which lets society meet the needs of the Other (of course, without considering its ecological consequences), but criticizes the consumerist society as the "accumulation of useless wealth" without circulation and distribution, concretion of a magnificent science into suffocating technology or "matter metamorphosed into walls."[60] Similarly, Levinas attaches democratic liberalism to 'the ceaseless deep remorse of justice.' The demands of the saying on the said of democracy constantly deconstitutes what is fixed and written down with regard to it.[61] Politics is about ensuring happiness to citizens who are equally recognized but ethics is "the surplus possible in a society of equals, that of glorious humility, responsibility, and sacrifice, which are the condition for equality itself."[62] The limits placed by the ethical surplus alone can guide the power of words that beckon new political realities. New political realities are new responses to the responsibility to the other that underlies sociality, not new strategies to undermine otherness.

Without the rupture introduced to the power of words by the authentically Other interlocutor, the politics of change is nothing but the tyranny of the self, of the same over the other, the stranger; without giving ear to the question posed to the speaker of magical words beckoning new realities by the genuine Other to the political self of the polis, the change thus beckoned turns out to be nothing but oppressive, vulgar display of the victorious self, the 'we', over the 'they', the totally other, whether it be the stranger, the animal or nature. Political reason, represented in the enframing words of power, explains the concerns of the other in terms of the common good. The same danger does not go away even when we recognize the deconstitutive power of words, unless we recognize the deconstitutive ethical sensibility that interrogates and examines the narratives spun by words and the power they wield. That which prompts to deconstitute the spell of magical words is a saying that goes before the words are uttered.

NOTES

1. See: Charles Taylor, "An Issue about Language." In *Language, Culture, and Society: Key Topics in Linguistic Anthropology*, ed. Christine Jourdan and Kevin Tuite (pp. 16-46). Cambridge, Cambridge University Press, 2006.
2. Martin Heidegger, "Letter on 'Humanism'" (1946), tr. Frank A. Capuzzi. In *Pathmarks*, ed. William McNeill (pp. 239-276). Cambridge, Cambridge University Press, 1998, p. 239.
3. Emmanuel Levinas, *Otherwise than Being, Or Beyond Essence* (1974), tr. Alphonso Lingis. Dordrecht, Kluwer Academic, 1991, p. 16.
4. Jacques Derrida, *Of Grammatology* (1967), tr. Gayatri Chakravorty Spivak, 40th Anniversary Edition. Baltimore, The Johns Hopkins University Press, 1997, p. 158.
5. Charles Taylor, "Heidegger on Language." In *A Companion to Heidegger*, eds. Hubert L. Dreyfus and Mark A. Wrathall (pp. 433-455). Malden, MA, Blackwell, 2007, p. 452.
6. Heidegger, "Letter on 'Humanism'," p. 239.
7. Martin Heidegger, "Hölderlin and the Essence of Poetry" (1936). In *Elucidations of Hölderlin's Poetry*, tr. Keith Hoeller (pp. 51-65). Amherst, NY, Humanity Books, 2000, p. 55.
8. Ibid., p. 54.
9. Martin Heidegger, "The Nature of Language," (1957-58). In *On the Way to Language*, tr. Peter D. Hertz (pp. 57-108). New York, Harper & Row, 1982, p. 73.
10. Martin Heidegger, "Words" (1958). In *On the Way to Language* (pp. 139-156), p. 155.
11. Ibid.
12. Taylor, "Heidegger on Language," p. 443.
13. Martin Heidegger, *Introduction to Metaphysics* (1935), tr. Gregory Fried and Richard Polt. New Haven, Yale University Press, 2000, p. 86; my emphasis.
14. Ibid., p. 15; my emphasis.
15. Martin Heidegger, "Building Dwelling Thinking" (1951). In *Poetry, Language, Thought*, tr. Albert Hofstadter (pp. 143-159). New York, Harper & Row, 1971, p. 146.
16. Heidegger, "The Nature of Language," p. 88.
17. Taylor argues that what gives meaning to reality for Heidegger is neither Plato's human-independent world of ideas nor Hegel's human-dependent *Geist.* Rather, Heidegger postulates the clearing out of which meaningful reality emanates, which is human-related and yet human-independent. Taylor remarks that Heidegger "doesn't place the clearing simply inside us as a representation...

[but] puts it instead in a new space constituted by expression" ("Heidegger on Language," p. 444). The expressive space is the essence of sociality or being-with.

18. Joseph J. Kockelmans, "Language, Meaning, and Ek-sistence." In *Heidegger on Language*, ed. Joseph J. Kockelmans (pp. 3-32). Evanston, Northwestern University Press, 1972, p. 30.
19. Martin Heidegger, "On the Essence of Truth," tr. John Sallis. In *Pathmarks* (pp. 136-154), p. 150.
20. Kockelmans, "Language, Meaning, and Ek-sistence," p. 31.
21. Martin Heidegger, "Why Poets?" (1946). In *Off the Beaten Track*, ed. & tr. Julian Young and Kenneth Haynes (pp. 200-241). Cambridge, Cambridge University Press, 2002, p. 237.
22. Martin Heidegger, *Contributions to Philosophy: Of the Event* (1936-38), tr. Richard Rojcewicz and Daniela Villega-Neu. Bloomington, Indiana University Press, 2012, p. 30.
23. Heidegger, *Introduction to Metaphysics*, p. 15.
24. Heidegger, "The Nature of Language," p. 84; my emphasis.
25. About the domination of natural language by technological objectification, Heidegger writes: "Framing—the nature of modern technology holding sway in all directions— commandeers for its purposes a formalized language, the kind of communication which 'informs' man uniformly, that is, gives him the form in which he is fitted into the technological-calculative universe, and gradually abandons 'natural language'" (Martin Heidegger, "The Way to Language," [1959]. In *On the Way to Language* [pp. 111-136], p. 132).
26. See: Mikko Joronen, "Dwelling in the Sites of Finitude: Resisting the Violence of the Metaphysical Globe." *Antipode* 43:4 (2011: pp. 1127–1154), p. 1144; and, Jeff Malpas, *Heidegger's Topology: Being, Place, World*. Cambridge, MA, MIT Press, 2006, p. 300.
27. Mikko Joronen, "Conceptualising New Modes of State Governmentality: Power, Violence and the Ontological Mono-politics of Neoliberalism." *Geopolitics* 18:2 (2013: pp. 356-370), p. 367.
28. Martin Heidegger, "The Origin of the Work of Art." In *Poetry, Language, Thought* (pp. 17-86), p. 60.
29. Heidegger, *Contributions to Philosophy*, p. 120.
30. Martin Heidegger, *Holderlin's Hymn 'The Ister'* (1942), tr. William McNeill and Julia Davis. Bloomington, Indiana University Press, 1996, p. 83.
31. Julian Young, *Heidegger's Philosophy of Art*. Cambridge, Cambridge University Press, 2001.
32. Ashis Nandy, *The Intimate Enemy: Loss and Recovery of Self under Colonialism*. Delhi, Oxford University Press, 1983, p. 51.
33. Martin Heidegger, *Parmenides*, tr. André Schuwer and Richard Rojcewicz. Bloomington, Indiana University Press, 1992, p. 76.
34. Heidegger, *Introduction to Metaphysics*, p. 133.
35. Pankaj Mishra, "Modi's Idea of India." *The New York Times*, 24 October 2014, accessed 3 March 2015 http://www.nytimes.com/2014/10/25/opinion/

pankaj-mishra-narendra-modis-idea-of-india.html

36. Taylor, "Heidegger on Language," p. 453.
37. Heidegger, "Hölderlin and the Essence of Poetry," p. 55.
38. See: Siby K. George, *Heidegger and Development in the Global South*. New Delhi, Springer, 2015, pp. 20-26.
39. See: Michael Lewis, *Heidegger and the Place of Ethics: Being-with in the Crossing of Heidegger's Thought*. London, Continuum, 2005; Jean-Luc Nancy, *Being Singular Plural* (1996), tr. Robert D. Richardson and Anne E. O'Byrne. Stanford, Stanford University Press, 2000; and Siby K. George, *Heidegger and Development in the Global South*, Chapter 5.
40. See: Mikko Joronen, "Dwelling in the Sites of Finitude: Resisting the Violence of the Metaphysical Globe."
41. Edward S. Casey, "Taking a Glance at the Environment: Prolegomena to an Ethics of the Environment." *Research in Phenomenology* 31: 1 (2001: pp. 1-21), p. 6.
42. Diane Perpich, *The Ethics of Emmanuel Levinas*. Stanford, Stanford University Press, 2008, p. 159.
43. See: William Edelglass, James Hatley and Christian Diehm, ed., *Facing Nature: Levinas and Environmental Thought*. Pittsburg, Duquesne University Press, 2012; and, Peter Atterton and Matthew Calarco, ed., *Radicalizing Levinas*, Part III: Animals and the Environment. Albany, State University of New York Press, 2010.
44. Tom Sparrow, *Levinas Unhinged*. Alresford, John Hunt Publishing, 2013, p. 76.
45. See: Emmanuel Levinas, *Humanism of the Other*, tr. Nidra Poller. Urbana, University of Illinois Press, 2003.
46. Michael Fagenblat, *A Covenant of Creatures: Levinas's Philosophy of Judaism*. Stanford, Stanford University Press, 2013, p. 101.
47. Emmanuel Levinas, "Language and Proximity." In *Emmanuel Levinas: Collected Philosophical Papers*, tr. Alphonso Lingis (pp. 109-126). Dordrecht, Martinus Nijhoff, 1987, p. 125.
48. Levinas's seminal thesis in *Otherwise than Being* is that it is the aboriginal impingement of otherness upon the self before time, care, interest, Being and freedom that forms the self's identity or selfhood. In this sense, the self is always already given over to otherness or, in Levinas's words, substituted for the Other. Hence, Levinas's formulation of selfhood is 'the Other in the same.' My aboriginal responsibility for the Other undercuts the demand for demonstration of their right. Reason and words of power are themselves based on that which is 'without reason par excellence'. The rational-semantic space itself hangs on meaningless, sublinguistic, subliterary, subpoetic murmuring, which in many ways is comparable to the inarticulate and deconstitutive-reconstitutive space of meaning of Heidegger (Llewelyn, "Levinas and Language," In *The Cambridge Companion to Levinas*, ed. Simon Critchley and Robert Bernasconi [pp. 119-138]. Cambridge, Cambridge University Press, 2002, p. 132).
49. Levinas, *Otherwise than Being*, p. 48.

50. Ibid., p. 185.
51. John Llewelyn, *Emmanuel Levinas: The Genealogy of Ethics*. London, Routledge, 1995, p. 140.
52. Levinas, *Otherwise than Being*, p. 36.
53. Ibid., p. 6.
54. Ibid., pp. 37-38.
55. Ibid., p. 45.
56. Emmanuel Levinas, *Totality and Infinity: An Essay on Exteriority*, tr. Alphonso Lingis. Dordrecht, Kluwer Academic, 1991, p. 21.
57. Levinas, *Otherwise than Being*, pp. 159-60.
58. Ibid., p. 91; compare, Levinas, *Totality and Infinity*, p. 43.
59. Ibid., p. 158.
60. Emmanuel Levinas, *In the Time of the Nations*, tr. Michael B. Smith. London, Continuum, 2007, p. 84.
61. Emmanuel Levinas, "The Other, Utopia, and Justice." In *Entre Nous: Thinking of the Other*, tr. Michael B. Smith and Barbara Harshav (pp. 223-233). New York, Columbia University Press, 1998, pp. 230-31.
62. Levinas, *Totality and Infinity*, p. 64.

7

Resisting the Work of Mourning: Survival and Resurrection of Jacques Derrida

Jacob Rogozinski

"Fire-Death" (*Feu la mort*) is, to begin with, an indirect quote, alluding to the title of one of Derrida's books, "Cinders" (*Feu la cendre*), an admirable reflection on the remainder (*le reste*), mourning, sacrifice, the holocaust, on "dispersion without return". Cremation is there the mark of what resists the work of mourning, of an "affirmation of fire without place or mourning." But ashes are not death and every death does not necessarily leave ashes: there are several ways of dying, several ways of thinking death. "[Fire –] Cinders" or "Fire – Death": these titles draw on a homonymy, on the two meanings of the French word "Feu," whose semantic ambiguity (*equivocité*) perhaps covers two different relations to death. "Feu," in French, designates most often "fire," the flame that heats or destroys—and, by derivation, the mortal order *to make fire/light with fire [faire feu]*. Understood this way, the expression "Fire–Death" would ring out as a declaration of war: "death to the fire!," "fire over death!" But we also know that the term "feu" is equally employed in French in a somewhat old-fashioned locution to qualify a deceased person: "*feu* so and so". In this case, the title would no longer let itself be understood as a belligerent rallying cry, but rather as this strange and paradoxical statement: death is dead, death is over and done. This is because we are not talking about the same fire—fire as flame derives from the Latin word *focus*, hearth, whereas fire as designating a deceased person comes from the Latin word *fatum*, destiny. "[Feu] so and so" is thus said of someone who has fulfilled her destiny, the inexorable destiny of every human, of every living being, which is dying. This puts into play a certain conception of human destiny, of existence as finitude, and assigns a task to thought: to teach us how to die, how to train ourselves for it or to anticipate it, according to the venerable tradition that goes from Plato and the Stoics up to Heidegger. It differs from another conception that calls for an ultimate victory over death, to the point of announcing *the death of death*. An ardent vision where a flame is in play, where in the end of times death is precipitated into a "lake of fire" and consumed forever. In these words you have probably recognized the final proclamation from the *Apocalypse of St. John* (20, 14-15), the eschatological News that radically opposes the other thought of death I have just mentioned, which teaches us to welcome it and thus to accept our finitude.

In this conflict, this disagreement between two ways of thinking death, where would Derrida situate himself? On the side of finitude, of accepting destiny and of anticipating this being-able-to-die [*pouvoir-mourir*]? Nothing is less certain. He had already measured himself up to the apocalypse, to the News and to apocalyptic tone. In taking as point of departure a writing where Kant denounces the "tone of grand master" used by "mystagogues," Derrida had come to question this "powerful program" which, throughout Western history, does not cease to "announce the end." He had asked himself whether "it is a tone, the eschatological, or whether it is voice itself"; that is, whether every voice is not in fact that of the "last man" (literature is thus briefly summoned, with Blanchot's name, which we will soon find again). He had asked himself lastly whether that which is called apocalyptic would not be a "transcendental condition of all discourse, of all experience even, of every mark and every trace (...), that is to say, of the divisible sending for which there is no auto-presentation or assured destination."

This affirmation is pivotal between his earlier works on sending or "destinerrance," and certain themes that he would subsequently deploy, such as the promise or messianism, "messianity without a Messiah." But without ever taking up that which is nonetheless at the heart of the messianic and/or apocalyptic News (supposing that these two notions are coextensive, which is not certain): the promise that, "in the days of the Messiah, the dead will resurrect." What's the relation between this promise, and the "logic of mourning" he never stopped working on? Without forgetting this enigmatic aim of a "mourning of mourning," that of a "beyond the mourning principle" which is, as he said, "the only thing that finally interests me," that which "makes me write and speak," which "gives me and takes away idiom." To experience mourning always boils down to—according to the psychoanalyst Daniel Lagache's expression—"killing the dead" in us: to draw a limit between the living ego and the dead, in order that we may succeed in separating ourselves from the lost object, while introjecting it, while directing it so as to better expel it—it is important to distinguish this *introjection* process from the "cryptic" *incorporation* of the dead object in the ego, which so much interested Derrida. To kill *the* dead by mourning, could this be the matrix of this messianic promise of killing death? Isn't mourning also each time a mourning of death itself, to proclaim here and now the death of death?

If it is not the case that, in affirming the mourning of mourning or the death of death, one paradoxically preserves the instance that one expected to revoke; one reinforces it even in doubling it, since it is about, still again and always, the work of mourning or of putting to death... *Fire – Death* only announces the paradox in which death wins every time. Without a doubt we will have to confront such statements with the different occurrences of the Derridian gesture which consists in redoubling a concept.

— "the truth of truth," "the sublation of sublation," "the gift of gift," etc.—as if this redoubling permitted to bring out his quasi-transcendentals. *Fire – Cinders, Fire – Death*: in what atopic place, in what pre-originary or post-terminal time is one situated to be able to proclaim this? Is it a time always to come, that of prophecy, of the messianic and apocalyptic News, or on the contrary is it a time already past, since ashes and mourning are here traces of an event from bygone times, of an extinguished flame? And above all, *who* will dare to pronounce it? Who can be sufficiently alive or sufficiently dead to declare not that "I am dead," as Derrida never stopped writing throughout his life, but that death itself is dead, that we are over and done with mourning? A declaration even more incredible than the "I am dead" of Poe's *Valdemar*, since it supposes a step beyond death. That is to say, a survival (*survivance*). But what kind of survival is here at issue? What relationship is there between the Derridian theme of *survival (survivance)* and that old word – which he almost never uses—of resurrection? It is impossible to approach this question without confronting survival's (*survivance*) ambivalence; for "to survive" and its derivatives are in French as ambiguous as the verb "to relive/to revive" [*revivre*]. A survivor is someone who has gone through an ordeal where death was at stake and who has nevertheless come out of it alive. Every survivor is in this sense an apparition (*revenant*), even if this reappearing (*revenance*) is not necessarily that of a ghost: it can also name the survival of a living being that has triumphantly faced death. This is why a feeling of triumph—a manic elation—often characterizes the survivor's experience and can make it so frightening for herself and others. Numerous examples attest to it: surviving can drive someone crazy, or it can make people kill themselves or others. Now would be the moment, if we had the time, to go over those striking pages of *Crowds and Power* where Elias Canetti, a Jew who survived Nazism, questions the "passion for survival" and the unsettling enjoyment (*jouissance*) it can procure: he there sees a sort of "curse" and the matrix of all tyrannies... Let us not forget by the way that the verb "to survive" equally names in French the fact of remaining alive after having lost that which gave meaning to our lives, such as those close to us (*proches*), our loves, our honor, or even our vital faculties: thus one sometimes speaks of people who have lost everything as though they had "survived themselves." Understood in this way, survival would rather designate a sub-life, the quasi-spectral existence of a living being that has almost already died, a living-dead. Does this ambiguity hold when one crosses over to another language? Does it get resolved, at least partially, in the duality of verbal expressions that translate "to survive" in German (*überleben/fortleben*) or in English, where three possibilities obtain: to survive, to live on, to outlive?

In going back over this term to make of it a major theme of his thought, Derrida inherits its ambiguous meaning without ever questioning it. He sometimes presents "survival" as a hyperbolical life, an extra, an increase of life, and the pre-fix "over" (*sur*) henceforth echoes a quasi-Nietzschean accent. This is especially the case in the interview where he declares—a couple of weeks before his passing—that "deconstruction is on the side of the yes, of the affirmation of life," that "surviving death [...] is the most intense kind of life possible." But in spite of its quasi-testamentary character, this declaration does not necessarily give us his *last word*, the ultimate truth or the finally revealed secret of his work (if there could be one...). We who so loved him would have loved that his *Yes come* be a yes to life, that his thought be an "athanatology," a meditation on life and not on death, the affirmation of "a life previous to the opposition between life and death." And yet, this is not always the case: in his previous texts, survival is almost never determined as an "extra-of-life" (*sur-vie*), as resurgence of life in its most extreme intensity. Instead of artificially bringing Derrida a bit closer to Nietzsche, to Bergson, to Rosenzweig or to Henry, it is appropriate to take note of his ambiguities, of his hesitations, and even of his contradictions, in order that we can avoid passing over in silence the *melancholy of deconstruction*, the thanatological temptation that so often made his thought of survival (*survivance*) give out to the hold of death. Perhaps because he characterized—a bit too quickly—logocentrism as zoologocentrism, as a metaphysics of Life; and that he was always wary of a univocal affirmation of life, of a life that would purport to radically demarcate itself from death and to put an end to it, for in the end it would only be pure presence without *différance*, that is to say another name for death. For "pure life," as he used to say, is synonymous with "pure death"—"and all I say goes as much against a philosophy of pure life as against its simple opposite." This explains why, as is often the case, he identifies the survivor, the ghost [*revenant*] and the specter; why he understands survival as the spectral existence of someone who's neither-alive-nor-dead, and who survives herself without having ever been her-self. Because "the survivor is always a ghost," always already engaged in a mourning of self, in mourning this unique singularity, irreplaceable, that she never was, for this mourning is born "from the standpoint of the death of one who has never been a living being."

It is impossible to understand anything out of the Derridian theme of survival if one does not take account of the combat he waged for so long on two fronts, to loosen the noose of a *double-bind* that, up until now, has trapped every thought of death. A double obligation that takes the form of a double aporia: to say it quickly, let us name these two poles *the aporia of sublation* and *the aporia of finitude*. He gave an explanation of the first one in *Writing and Difference*, then in *Glas*, but it is impossible for me, within the limits of this paper, to follow the thread of this long and patient explanation. He confronted the second one precisely in the book that bears this title: *Aporias*. He there questions the Heideggerian conception of an anticipatory grasp of death by Dasein, which would give access to "her most proper possibility," thus ensuring her most radical individuation. This presupposes that Dasein can attest to her death "as such," that she can become the witness of her "own" (*propre*) death, while she must remain alive to do this: for it is only "as a living being or dying being—dying *while remaining* (*demeurant*) alive—that she can attest to a being-for-death." The analytic of Dasein thus stumbles upon the enigma of a neither-living-nor-dead being, still alive in the "already there" of her death, which is precisely survival (*survivance*) as a mourning of self. But Heidegger "wants to have nothing to do (*connaître*) with mourning or the revenant." In wanting to ground Dasein's selfhood (*ipséité*) in the anticipation of her future (*à venir*) death, *Being and Time*'s author was thus unaware of another possibility: that this self (*ipséité*) be constituted "from an originary mourning," which would be at the same time a mourning of *self* (*de soi*) and the mourning of an *other* (*d'un autre*); to the extent that "the relation to self (*rapport à soi*) carries or presupposes the other as different from self within this being-self (*être-soi-même*)." Selfhood (*ipséité*) is thus discovered as irreparably cracked, as undercut by this pre-originary relationship to the other, by the structure of an irreducible auto-*hetero*-affection. It is this pre-originary alteration of self (*soi-même*) that Heiddeger—different from Levinas, and perhaps already Hegel—cannot come to think. Nor can he come to grasp the temporal torsion implied by this originary mourning of self, this dying that Blanchot sometimes designates as the "unremitting imminence (...) of what has always already happened."

Neither Hegel, nor Heidegger: how to escape the double aporia towards which these two names point? How to thwart the aporia of finitude without falling into the sublation one? By avoiding the reverse gesture, where thought would surely let itself be trapped; for it is about overcoming these two aporias: even if it is sometimes presented as an aporetic-trial, we would do no good to deconstruction were we to maintain that it must simply dwell in the aporia instead of searching to cross over it. When Derrida attempts to escape from philosophy's aporias, he often resorts to literature; for example when he plays Mallarmé "against" Plato, or rather *in lieu* of Plato, Bataille and Genet *in lieu* of Hegel ("in lieu" [*au lieu de*]: which does not mean that literature comes to occupy the place of philosophy, but rather that it destabilizes it without substituting it). It is to Blanchot that Derrida refers in order to loosen the *double-bind* of the finite and the infinite, of the being-of-death and of absolute life; he refers to Blanchot's affirmation of a "survival without survival"—in which we hear: without an extra of life—where the undecidable contamination of life and death is revealed. In reading Blanchot, he notes that "if one wanted here to speak at all costs of resurrection (...), there would neither be a Christology nor a speculative Holy Friday, nor a truth of religion in absolute knowledge. But all that, the Passion, Resurrection, Absolute Knowledge, is mimed, repeated and shifted in the life without life of this survival (*survivance*)."[15] Blanchot in lieu of Hegel: the dying without death of a survival without life instead of death's sublation in the self-affirmation of absolute Life. But also Blanchot in lieu of Heidegger, for the trial of death of which he bore witness dissolves the self's identity and singularity in the experience of an anonymous death where "*I* do not die, I am deprived of the power of dying, (where) "one" [*Man*] dies, one never ceases nor does one ever finish dying."

What we are dealing with here, explains Derrida, is "a death that, to be irreplaceable, and because it is unique, is not even individual, (...) a proposition that would trouble even this *Jemenigkeit*, this 'each time mine'" of Heideggerian Dasein. It is to this neutralization of life/death that Derrida points to in one of Blanchot's texts, *The Instant of My Death*, which stages what we could call a *death without death of death*. This account of autobiographical—or rather autothanatographical—style narrates an episode that happened not long before Liberation. Whether it be an authentic or fictional testimony is here of little importance. "I remember a young man, (...) prevented from dying by death itself." Suspected of participating in the Resistance, the account's anonymous narrator had been apprehended by the Germans and placed before an execution squad. At the moment where the "Nazi lieutenant" was about to cry "fire!," "another 'fire' comes, a 'backfire'," gunfire unleashed by the Resistance. It is then that the soldiers let the narrator go, who thus finds himself living beyond his death, forever haunted by the impossible experience of this death that did not take place, that took place without taking place, that only happened by not happening. Long from freeing him or bringing him back to life, this "interruption of dying" will forever leave him with pending death, a death that is not *his own* death, that stripped him of all identity by rendering him to the survival (*survivance*) of a living (*vivre*) without life. That which Derrida proposes to call *demeurance*, in which we should understand not only "that which dwells and remains over time in an abode [demeure]," but also the "unexperienced experience of who dies, there where two die, do not die or un-die (*dé-meurent*) in the moment where they die." To die without dying —and hence to survive—at the *same instant* [*à l'instant même*] one dies, within this instant that will never cease ending [*n'en finira plus de finir*], the time of a lifetime stretches monstruously to the point of lasting (*durer*). Such is the trial of *demeurance*, of this un-dying (*dé-mourir*) to which Blanchot makes us part.

At this point, two series of questions force themselves here:

(1) We find here what Derrida had noticed earlier on in Blanchot, namely the insistence of an *X without X* ("name without name," "misfortune/affliction (*malheur*) without misfortune/affliction," "being without being," ...) that culminates in a series of statements about life/death: "death without death," "surviving without surviving," "living without a living being like dying without death," etc. Without a doubt, we should confront this logic of the X without X to the Derridian gesture of quasi-transcendental redoubling (in the mode of the X of X). It does happen, by the way, that he comes to conjugate both gestures, like when he speaks for example of "the truth without truth of truth." What happens thus when the X of X gets interlaced with the X without X and lets itself be contaminated by it? To be sure, the Blanchotian theme of the Neutral does not let itself in any case be reduced to a simple cancellation of opposites. It nevertheless implies their neutralization in the mode of a neither/nor, and Derrida ratifies this gesture in several decisive passages of his work. Surviving, in this sense, is neither living nor dying, as much as the *pharmakon* is neither simple remedy, nor uniquely poison. What this neutralization of opposites forecloses is their asymetrical position within their opposition, the primacy of one term over the other, the preference that one might decide to grant to life over death (or to death over life). When Derrida made the effort of describing the "general strategy of deconstruction," its double gesture or double scene, he underscored however the fact that it must avoid restricting itself to the "simple form of a neither/nor," to "simply neutralizing the binary metaphysical oppositions," thus remaining ignorant of their asymmetry and the necessary reversal of their hierarchy. Did he sufficiently take this exigency into account? In letting himself be captivated by Blanchot's X without X, did he not only too often yield to what I would gladly call (please forgive this bad Witz!) a *ni-nihilisme* of the undecidable? And what would the consequences be for the question with which we are here concerned? To refuse, within the intertwining of life/death, to affirm the primacy of life over death, does it not necessarily equate to maintaining the reverse primacy, to *preferring death* and to thinking survival—even life itself—as a mode of death?

(2) In the singular experience of *demeurance* that Blanchot's account stages, a certain relationship to Nazism is at stake, with all that this implies: absolute disaster, "death without a name," that which Derrida calls, in reading Celan, the "menace of an absolute crypt"; but his patient and rigorous reading of Blanchot's text never evokes this. And yet, this spectral surviving (*survivance*) that is implicit in all of Blanchot's writings, is it that different from the unbearable trial Adorno spoke

> about, this "death worse than death" the possibility of which the 20th century taught us? Although Blanchot tackled it repeatedly in his texts, most notably in *The Writing of Disaster*, it is a theme that Derrida did not commit to pursue. We know that, contrary to Lyotard, and Lacoue-Labarthe (to name only close ones), Derrida will have left this crypt sealed. If we could take full account of this in thought and writing – but is this even possible? – all the questions that here arise, all the aporias of life/death, of mourning, of the specter, of surviving (*survivance*), shouldn't they all be deeply redrawn? How does one survive the trial of a death worse than death? How does one survive in order to bear witness? Wouldn't this testimony always remain the fact of a "subject," of what Artaud calls an *ego survivor* (*moi survivant*)? In accentuating the anonymity of dying and the spectrality of surviving, following Blanchot, doesn't the Derridian conception of surviving (*survivance*) risk being ignorant of it, of evading it?

Who is the survivor? If someone could survive the instant of her death, could she still bear witness to it in the first person? Blanchot chose to let the narrator of his account remain anonymous, surely because he had already accounted for this mourning of oneself, this neutralization of the *I* in the anonymous instance of the *One dies* a long time ago. In *The Instant of My Death*, this destitution of the I takes the form of a dialogue, or rather an appeal to the I by another "subject," another voice, just as anonymous: "I am alive. No, you are dead." This is the same as saying, notes Derrida, that "she who was an ego is no longer an ego, the *ego cogito*" and that "that which separates the two egological identities is nothing less than death itself." The unbearable trial of a death without death irrevocably divides the I itself, it splits it into an *I* affirming that he is alive and a *you* that appeals to him as already dead; which forbids him to gather together in the self-consciousness of the Hegelian subject or the finite selfhood (*ipséité*) of the Heideggerian *Dasein*. This is a lesson that is awfully close to the one drawn by Derrida from Poe's *Valdemar*: the impossible utterance *I am dead* also means the *death of the I*, its bereaved and spectral return. All this according to an ego demoting gesture that he shares with his contemporaries—Sartre, Bataille, Lacan, Deleuze...— and that I have proposed to call *egocide*. A gesture that is always tied one way or another, to a thanatology, that is to say a preference given to death over life. It is not the issue here to deploy all the implications of such a gesture, to expose its presuppositions and limitations. But simply to recall that this (non) experience of death that was, the one of Blanchot, is not the only one attested to by the literature and art of our times; that another relationship to life/death and another survival are possible. It is impossible for me to analyze here, among so many other significant examples, the role this going through death played in the path of two contemporary visual artists, two war pilots, the one American and the other German—Sam Francis and

Joseph Beuys—both of them victims of an airplane crash, and who drew from the dying-without-death of a traumatic coma all the material for their work. I will make do by alluding, much too briefly, to a testimony we get from a poet. "I died a long time ago" wrote Antonin Artaud in the Twenties, "I have already committed suicide, ONE has made me commit suicide [*ON m'a suicidé*]"—and, a few years later, "I always knew I was Artaud the deceased." He considers himself indeed as a "fresh flesh mummy," a "still-born," dedicated to the spectral survival of that which is "neither dead nor alive". So many thanatographical utterances where the strange knowledge of a previous mourning of oneself is affirmed, of a becoming-neutral of "his" [*sa*] death, which would situate him close to Blanchot's "one dies" [*on meurt*]. Except that, starting from a certain point – which coincides with his going through madness, his "healing" (if this term is suitable here), his return from the Rodez asylum—such utterances will make room for the affirmation of a life more powerful than death: "I have overcome (*franchi*) death, dreadful death through life, and to remain death [*la mort*] is to betray life." Like Blanchot and so many others, Artaud saw himself as a survivor, among a "dust of surviving egoes [*moi*]"; but he now identifies his survival as a resurgence of life: namely, the clearing of a limit, of that point he names the "point of death" and that designates the no-(step-of)-death [*pas-de-mort*] as well as the inanity or imposture of death. If he continues to affirm a preference, or rather a precedence, it is no longer that of death over life in the temporal twist of a previous mourning, but rather that of life, seen as continuous re-creation, perpetual renaissance: it is about "being born to life *in* life. For at each lived instant we precede our own birth." How can we understand [*entendre*] these incredible utterances? Like those of Blanchot, they are rooted in a personal experience: his collapse in Ireland, his being institutionalized in several asylums, the ordeal of electric shocks to which he was subjected at the Rodez asylum, his return to writing, this "healing" that he lives as resurrection. And yet, as much as Blanchot, Artaud's thought and writing cannot be "explained" by auto-bio-thanatographical circumstances. Must we identify in Artaud's work, as Derrida sometimes suggested it, the ghost of an absolute parousia, the imprint of a metaphysics of life, of *a life without death* that would imagine it has done away with specters and mourning and that would thus remain a prisoner to the Christian conception of resurrection and salvation? Nothing prevents us from thinking that. Except, perhaps, for a number of Artaud's own statements where he affirms the irreducible linkage of life/death in existence and the poem, their interlacing or chiasm, *but under the primacy of life*: for "the secret of my existence is that I am a dead piece of wood that is still alive," "all the more alive because he's dead." Wasn't this his singular way of affirming survival, of *preferring life always*?

REFERENCES

Blanchot, M., *The Space of Literature,* (tr.) Ann Smock, Lincoln: University of Nebraska Press, 1982.

Blanchot, M., *The Instant of My Death,* with J. Derrida, *Demeure, Fiction and Testimony,* (tr.) E. Rottenberg, Stanford: Stanford Universtiy Press, 2002.

Canetti, E., *Crowds and Power,* (tr.) Carol Stewart, New York: Continuum Press, 1962.

Derrida, J., *Learning to Live Finally. The Last Interview,* With Jean Birnbaum, (tr.) P.-A. Brault and M. Naas, New York: Palgrave, 2005.

Derrida, J., *Cinders,* (tr.) N. Lukacher, Lincoln: University of Nebraska Press, 1991.

Derrida, J., *Death Penalty,* Vol. 1, (tr.) P. Kamuf, Chicago: University of Chicago Press, 2014.

Derrida, J., *Points… Interviews, 1974-1994,* (tr.) P. Kamuf et al., Stanford, Stanford University Press.

Derrida, J., *Resistances of Psychoanalysis,* Stanford: Stanford University Press, 1998.

Derrida, J., *Aporias: dying—awaiting (one another at) the "limits of truth",* (tr.) T. Dutoit, Stanford: Stanford University Press, 1993.

Derrida, J., *Positions,* (tr.) Alan Bass, London: Athlone, 1981.

Derrida, J., *Schibboleth – pour Paul Celan*, Paris: Galilée, 1986.

Derrida, J., *Parages*, (tr.) T. Conley, J. Hulbert, J.P. Leavey, and A. Ronell, Stanford: Stanford University Press, 2010.

Derrida, J., *Glas.* (tr.) J.P. Leavey and R. Rand, Lincoln: University of Nebraska Press, 1986.

Derrida, J., "The Ends of Man," *Philosophy and Phenomenological Research* 30.1 (1969): 31-57.

8

Fear of Spinoza: Derrida as Reader of *Theological-Political Treatise*

Gérard Bensussan

I would like to start by situating my paper almost topologically: first, with respect to the precise occurrence (in Spinoza as well as in Derrida) of the *fear* which my title evokes; then, I will turn to the typescript, with which I was able to become familiar through the care of Willi Goetschel,[1] and, finally, I will address the spectrality that inhabits and permeates this text, the remarkable "ghost of Spinoza" of which Derrida speaks on page 17 of the third lecture on the "Théologico-Politique" that was at my disposal. In particular, I would like to suggest that this specter or ghost is even more present in Derrida's commentary by virtue of remaining nameless and it is precisely towards the naming of this spectrality that I myself will proceed. This preliminary remark will allow me to engage with the material of my "investigation" and to accurately circumscribe it as follows:

1. I will limit myself to the reading, commentary and interpretation of Derrida's notes, which are essentially contained in the lecture on 'Nationality and Philosophical Nationalism' (referred to as Théologico-Politique 1) and the two lectures on the Theological Political (referred to as Théologio-Politique 2-3) which were sent to me – and more specifically pages 1 to 3, page 17, and nearly the whole of the fascicle containing these lectures on the *Theologico-Political.*
2. If I allow myself such a selective reading, it is because even together these notes do not form in any way a coherent or organized reading of Spinoza. It is remarkable that the only texts with which Derrida engages—and again, we will see in what manner—are the *Treatise on the Emendation of the Intellect* and the *Theological-Political Treatise,* and that *Ethics* is scarcely mentioned even in an almost anecdotal mode.

We have all three of us, Willi Goetschel, Warren Montag and me, more or less entitled our papers: "Derrida, Reader of Spinoza." However, in my estimation, there is nothing of the sort between the two, no actual or rigorous deconstructive reading of Spinoza, like there is, and with what force, of Hegel (one would only have to open *Glas* to make the observation). We could explain at length and with much ease that between these two philosophers, Spinoza and Derrida, there is little common ground, affinity or dialogue, in the same way that the history of philosophy, to a great extent, is itself constituted, inventing itself, in a way, from these dialogues of thought, which can attest to profound discord or even relative agreement. Nothing of the sort, in my view, between Spinoza and Derrida—a point which merits more discussion, but which shall not be developed here.

3. In addition, the method of my reading is to elaborate on the one Derrida himself undertakes of Spinoza, the fragmentary character of which I have just outlined. In his own words: "my intention is not to engage in a systematic and internal reading of the *Treatise*" (*Théologico-Politique* 2, 1); "[my] very oblique and selective reading of the *Theological-Political Treatise*" (ibid., 17); "I could have called on other texts of the tradition, Kant" (*Théologico-Politique* 3, 17), he also says; "the reading [of Spinoza's text] will have had the significance of an inscription, an inscription within an inscription, resembling even something like opening credits, while titles, names and references appear, we already see the first scene in the background" (3, 1). This "first scene" is described by Derrida as "Judeo-German," where the hyphen is as "paradoxical" and as "difficult" as the one in "theological-political." This is of particular interest for my argument. In fact, the ghost of Spinoza's ghost that I clearly discern throughout Derrida's commentary is precisely, and may it be said right away, "Judeo-German." Derrida explains (1, 6) that he will not depart from "a modern Judeo-German text, but from one of the great texts of the philosophical tradition itself wholly devoted to the theological-political dimension in which the example of the Jewish people as a chosen people is of crucial importance," namely the *Theological-Political Treatise*. Not a starting point then, since he evokes Spinoza as a digression and as a simple but exemplary passage; in fact, Derrida goes to him or returns to him incessantly, and I myself will have to revisit this revisitation. In any case, the reading of Spinoza by Derrida is truly, in his own words, selective, oblique, contingent, whose function is simply that of a prelude, or even a pretext, or conversely, that of a postscript. Furthermore, he is often the sort to argue the incompletion of *Treatise on the Emendation of the Intellect*, and of his *ci falt,* that is to say of his last "word," *reliqua desiderantur* (La langue et le discours de la méthode 13, 3-4).

These preliminary considerations indicate already the methodological limit and paradox of any position which implies that the "Derrida, Reader of Spinoza" is perfectly evident, or is a sort of pseudo-evidence which needed to be isolated from the scope of a discussion on the reading of Derrida's reading.

In all of these course notes where we find this proposed "reading" of Spinoza, not deconstructive but spectral and outlying, where is the pivot-point, or more exactly, the diagonal of this change in perspective, so to speak?[2] This is found, according to me, around Spinoza's precise exclamation, undoubtedly recurrent in Derrida's commentary: *Nec satis mirari possum.*[3] Derrida reflects on multiple occasions on Misrahi-Francès' translation with his characteristic care in dealing with these matters: *"je suis frappé d'une véritable stupeur"* ("I am seized by a veritable stupor"). He adjusts and inflects the form of this statement through many significant variations: "stupefied, horrified" (Nationalité et nationalisme philosophiques 1, 24); "inextinguishable surprise, almost infinite" (*Théologico-Politique* 2, 2); "fascination" (ibid., 3); "all of Spinoza's discourse connotes a horrified admiration" (ibid., 10). Stupor, dread, admiration and fear all contribute to the meaning of *nec satis mirari possum.* Derrida puts these words into Spinoza's mouth: "I cannot be astounded enough, be fascinated enough, I cannot tire of looking; but I look while turning away, full of fear." (ibid.) In fact, a preliminary question or clarification is necessary: what is it that causes, in Spinoza's own text, in chapter 17 of the *Theological-Political Treatise*, this remarkable dread, this fascinated interruption which so captivates Derrida? It is the wrath of God, his violence, his ruse, his destructive fury, his vengeance:

> The more I ponder, the more I must exclaim, in Tacitus' words, that at that time "God did not wish to save them but to punish them."[4] Nor can I sufficiently express my amazement[5] that there was so much anger in the divine mind, that He should actually make laws (which are normally designed to protect the honor, safety and security of all the people) to avenge himself and punish them, and thus the laws seemed to be not laws (i.e., a protection for the people) but penalties and punishments.[6]

I can recall the context of this passage as it is relates to the *nec satis mirari possum.* It concerns the explanation of the degeneration or the "corruption," terms that Derrida extracts from the vocabulary of the *Treatise,*[7] of the State of the Hebrews. How and why has the State of the Hebrews veered from its egalitarian form of strict theocracy towards the "monarchical Mosaic Law"? Their State was originally founded on the equality of all through the abandonment and the transfer of their power of agency to a sole being, God, immaterial and, in a way, apolitical. It is therefore presented, in its "initial pact," as a quasi-democracy.[8] But, as it happens, this initial pact gives way to a personal allegiance under the authority of Moses. The reason for this substitution, the replacement of a pact of equality for all in God by a pact of submission to one man, is, of course, the *fear* of the Hebrews, "struck with fear" because they were having to "address God, to receive and interpret his laws," plunged "in such a state of anguish that they believed their final hour had come" and that they preferred, "trembling, to turn to Moses" so that he might take care of the political and hermeneutical task in their place[9]. If fear is truly the cause and source of the transition from a theocratic pact to another, from quasi-democracy to monarchy, where does the fear itself come from? We would have to retrace the whole story starting from the Exodus from Egypt, such as it is recounted by Spinoza in his *Treatise*, and not without a certain amount of empathy, even though he is particularly severe with the Jews in his analysis as a whole. In their relationship to God, from the Exodus to the granting of the Law and the episode of the golden calf, the Hebrews, having accepted the pact of the transfer of power and law, were in a way tricked by God, who acted as a father to them; a father who was not only very strict, but also unjust, and profoundly so. But what does this ruse entail, this infamy of God, in Spinoza's reading of the State of the Hebrews after their historic leaving of Egypt? Spinoza insists on the liberty with which the Hebrews' consented to the Law:

> Once liberated from the intolerable oppression of the Egyptians, they were not bound by a pact to anyone; rather they regained the natural right to all that they could get, and everyone was once again free to decide whether they wanted to retain this right or give it up [...] they resolved [...] to transfer their right to no mortal man but rather to God alone. Without hesitation, all equally with one shout promised to obey God absolutely in all his commands, and to recognize no other law but that which He himself conferred as law by prophetic revelation.[...] [C]rying with one voice [the Hebrews said]: "We will do whatever God shall say" (making no mention of an intermediary).[10]

What is at issue here is the very famous *naase v'nishma,* from Exodus 24: 7 *All that the Lord has spoken we will do, and obey,*[11] a declaration that preoccupies so many rabbinic commentaries which, in general, stress that only the Hebrews had accepted obedience without any conditions from their side, while the other peoples had responded with demanding reasonable conditions for their eventual obedience. But what happens at the end of the story? The Hebrews, Spinoza explains, are the victims of what they accepted without reluctance. Only they accepted the unacceptable, to obey without even knowing why, as this was the order from God and no one else. This was their political demise. They were cruelly tricked by God and destined to be destroyed. Derrida comments at length the quote from Ezekiel 20: 25 inserted by Spinoza in his text (it is the same quote by L. Segon that the edition La Pléiade uses, to which Derrida adds the exceedingly cruel quote of Chouraqui): "So I gave them rules of government which were not good and laws under which they could not live—while also letting them ruin themselves through their offerings ... I had to destroy them, so that they would know I am Jehovah."[12]

God gave the Hebrews impractical rules of government and treacherously left them to fend for themselves with these commandments. He pushed them therefore to "corrupt themselves" in their efforts to practice his word; he corrupted them himself "with their offerings," in Chouraqui's translation. Even without having to explain the particular circumstance of this corruption, or the delegating of power to the Levites, we can see that God, according to the Spinozian retelling that Derrida examines, made the Hebrews unworthy to his own eyes, "to the eyes of his name," as we should say, the name being an important question in the seminar, and more precisely the divine name, *shem*, which is related to its homophone *"schème"* (schema): "this word *'schème'* amuses me," Derrida writes because "if Spinoza refuses or contests the existence of a schema in the Greco-Kantian sense, it's perhaps because he conserves the Hebrew sense of the word" (*Théologico-Politique* 2, 1). God decides then, in the name of his name, so as to make it known and to impose it, to "destroy" the Hebrews as a political community according to his avowed "plan"[13]: *"Je vais leur apprendre comment je m'appelle"* ("I will make them learn my name"), as Derrida puts it, playing with the French expression (2, 13).

The construction of the narrative is terribly violent. The Hebrews accept unconditionally the Law. Even their pseudo indocility (a "childish" argument according to Spinoza[14]), or their recriminations under the yoke of a cast, the Levites, is yet another side of their unconditional obedience to God. They accept therefore to "be obedient even before hearing his word." And so they are struck by the terrible vengeance, this "vengeful, demanding violence, or revenge" (ibid.) of God in order to impose his name. It is here, at this point, where Spinoza admits his fear. But why this fear, which, in his words, seems especially mysterious? It is surely not the effect of some sort of empathy that he feels towards the Hebrews. On the contrary, the circumstance will eventually be considered their own fault. He describes rather a sort of horrified stupor towards this vengeful and cunning God, this wicked God. If the circumstance is deemed the fault of the Hebrews, it is not God who should be held in contempt, but the Hebrews. This God, in order to impose his name on those who have forgotten it (we are still dealing with Spinoza's reading), deceives his sons and punishes them. It is unnecessary to explain how and why this vengeful God is on all counts incompatible with the *Deus sive Natura*. The question that we must ask is something else: does this God avenge himself or does he avenge *injustice?* Let us first remember some preliminary elements. Everything that man does for the conservation of his being depends strictly on the laws of nature, that is to say the government of God in its universal decrees and its "internal assistance," according to the proposed distinction in the third chapter of the *Treatise* between this "internal assistance" and the "external assistance," or in other words "whatever proves useful to man from the power of external causes,"[15] the "fortune" as Spinoza says also, the government of God as it acts on human affairs by means of external and unexpected causes. Thus, "whether therefore we say that all things happen according to the laws of nature, or are ordained by the edict and direction of God, we are saying the same thing."[16] Without difficulty, we understand that the vengeful, violent, and even spiteful God, —and, again, I will leave aside the question if this very literal reading, *sola scriptura*, is compatible or not with particular rabbinic commentaries – that this furiously anthropomorphic God is absolutely heterogeneous to the *Deus sive Natura.* With this being said, the actual question can now be specified and duplicated according to the perspective of Derrida's reading. 1. Why is it the fear of Spinoza rather than his mockery?[17] 2. What is the nature of Derrida's reworking of this fear?

To the first question (why the fear?), Derrida's response is very simple: that which is afraid and steps back in horror in this passage, is Reason, "Spinoza's rationalist and universalist system" (*Théologico-Politique* 2, 16) with "all his oppositions," his binary structural apparatus (internal/ external, spiritual/literal, rational/temporal, universal/corporal), with his "system of dissociations" (temporal and sensory election/natural law) and especially with his universalizing and Christianizing method (2, 11). Even Derrida explains that it is "rationalism as a whole," and not only Spinoza's, that would turn away, fascinated, from this violent vengeance of God. This fascinated Reason is haunted by the terrible fear of petrification as if faced with the Gorgon. Spinoza, Derrida explains, turns away but he still wants to look. *Nec satis mirari possum*: literally, "I cannot look enough." What fascinates Spinozian Reason, what it would want to look at in the face, is *"inextricability,"* or "the contamination, the contact between different meanings which Spinoza tries to keep separate" (2, 3). When it comes to Gorgon and Medusa, we say that they were inseparably of a splendid beauty and/or of a repugnant ugliness, as if the peril for whoever yielded to the desire of looking at them was found in this fearful indeterminacy. This leads to the second question. What exactly is the meaning of Derrida's reading of these pages, which I said was symptomal and not properly deconstructive? It is fairly clear: rationalism in its whole constitutes "a system of protection" against the threat of petrification which terrifies Reason. And what gives merit to this protection, what threatens to petrify in compact inseparability all of its dissociative and analytical operations? "The name" of God, Derrida insists: "is it not the case that all of Spinozian discourse acts as a protection against the name of God, of this God that becomes a nameless God in the *Ethics*?" (2, 17). *Reason against the Name*—but if Reason is a rampart against the Name, it is only secondary, a sort of product derived from the Name, invented to oppose its threat, archaic and fearfully cold. Derrida's fundamental contribution in the lectures on the Theologico-Political is to displace the anthropological representation of divine violence—which, for Spinoza or even Maimonides and the rationalist philosophers of the Middle-Ages, would have come across as an ignorant gesture—towards an absolutely and irreducibly originary status. It is precisely this radically non-anthropological originarity that could not see, or rather, as we know now, would not want, or could not see the system of rationality.

This situation [...] would be that of every institution, of every foundation of law which, by definition, is anterior to law, and would therefore be an act of originary violence, an act of war, but an act of originary war which can only be justified before the law by attacking another pre-originary violence, to which it responds, originarily, by taking the form of vengeance [...] But this vengeance can no longer be confined peacefully inside the limits of an anthropology or a psychology of the passions. But perhaps it founds the possibility of a human society (2, 5).

A "logic of vengeance" (ibid.) would therefore command and radically precede Law, Society and Reason. In truth, it is not a logic that we are dealing with, unless this term is simply used out of convenience, but a real *destructive force*. But Derrida, when he talks here of "logic," affirms very strongly that "vengeance" is not a pre-logical, anthropomorphic, anthropopathic, or anthropological figure. It is in fact the rational presupposition (which is a particularly apt oxymoron) that guides, for example, Maimonides' allegorical reading of the text of the Torah. It is also this presupposition whereby hermeneutic reason imposes itself on the biblical text in order to allow for a "rational" reading. To strengthen and to reinforce his position, Derrida calls upon two figures, two paradigms: the idea of a vengeance of history in Heidegger and the idea of a vengeance of language in Scholem. This double invocation has a precise function in Derrida's process: to show that in all cases (vengeance of God, of history and of language), the power or the insistence of vengeance is too large for the human subject, for the individual, the conscience, or even the unconscious of the individual subject: language and history, then, are laws to which the individual is subjected, for which he is perhaps responsible, but which surpass him and which he cannot master. These are not finite or empirical instances, even if they are not infinite in the positive sense of major rational theologies or traditional metaphysics. How are we to conceive of a vengeance which is not an extension of an anthropological subjectivity? (ibid., 2-3).

The two passages from the seminar that I have just cited delve into the "Judeo-German" indicated by Derrida as the actual horizon and genealogical framework of his reading of Spinoza. The Judeo-German figure, however, that would lend itself most manifestly to a real, explicit invocation by the needs of this reading, such as it is undertaken by Derrida, is not named. According to me, it is Walter Benjamin and, more precisely, some pertinent elements found in *Zur Kritik der Gewalt (Critique of Violence)*, which literally haunt Derrida's approach to the *Theological-Political Treatise*. Benjamin is the monumental ghost who walks through the entirety of the lectures on the Theologico-Political, and the ghost of Spinoza who attributes to him the place of an "inscription."

The whole thought process of the *Critique of Violence* is animated by the category of "divine violence," opaque in many regards but transparent in the essay from 1920-1921. It is very much this violence, which is at issue for Spinoza and Derrida. Benjamin opposes this "divine violence" to "mythic violence." If mythic violence is inspired by a directing and orienting principle, *power*, divine violence is entirely driven by another principle, absolutely "contrary," says Benjamin, that of *justice*.[18] Therefore, "God" replaces destiny, and the justice of ends replaces the violence of means. The first salient feature of this divine violence, for Benjamin, is that it gives definitive leave to law and that it commands a "politics" which is divorced from any relation to the judicial and is subject to the sole justice of ends. On the one hand, mythic violence combats violence by violence, a classic situation brought on by any form of power relations, its conflicts and political transformations. On the other hand, divine violence combats violence by justice. But it may only do so by radically destructive means: "limitlessly destructive," Benjamin writes. Through destruction, divine violence opposes the foundation and conservation of law held by mythic violence (something to which Derrida seems at times to reduce divine violence even though he does not refer here to Benjamin). In order to express and illustrate the destructive justice brought on by divine violence, Benjamin refers in particular to the biblical episode of the rebellion of Korah which he opposes to the myth of Niobe, punished for having considered herself superior to the goddess Leto. Korah and his two hundred and fifty companions who accompany him in his revolt are exterminated one by one, "the earth closed upon them, and they perished from among the assembly" (*Numbers*, 16, 33). Even Spinoza uses the example of Korah: "So they instigated a commotion and went to see [Moses], claiming they were all equally sacred and that it was not right that he should be elevated above all the rest. Nor was there anyway that he could pacify them; however, via a miracle which he invoked as a token of his high standing with God, they were all annihilated."[19] Both Spinoza and Benjamin refer to the same biblical passage, but they infuse it with symmetrically opposite significations. For Benjamin, God smites "the privileged ones" of Korah's group, the priests and the notables (and this is exactly what is said in the biblical text of the *Numbers* 16, 2: "princes of the congregation, the elect men of the assembly, men of renown"). For him, Korah's group unites all who incarnate, represent and assure institutionally "the domination of law on the living" and on justice. For Spinoza, however, the group is the representative of the people's protests against Moses' arbitrariness, fantasy and ambitions of a perpetual law, a pontificate, or in a word, his ruse. The violent destruction of Korah and his companions is in the name of "justice," albeit against law, according to Benjamin. According to Spinoza, it is, on the contrary, an abominable "denial of justice." Both are in agreement that a terrible act of violence is committed (Benjamin goes as far as to consider it an act of divine hyperviolence, whose complex status will not be discussed here), but it is *justice* which separates them.

The vengeful God who inspires Reason's fear is unjust. Stupefaction is borne out of God's injustice—which, not being able to stand this performative contradiction, calls on allegory for its anthropological contents in the figure of a God who is always equal to himself, or in other words, Nature, an equivalence which Reason perpetually creates. This God, whose injustice has been erased, is, Derrida insists, a *nameless God.* The question of the name is strategic in Derrida's reading. The *Treatise on the Emendation of the Intellect* analyzes very precisely what follows the confusion between name and thing. According to Spinoza, this confusion is at the origin of our belief in fictions as well as most of philosophy's errors. And yet the nameless God of *Ethics* represents a reversed reflection of a veritable fiction denounced by the *Theological-Political Treatise,* which is the Name without God as pure *flatus vocis*, destined for rumination and empty and superstitious invocation. This fiction indicates and attests to a powerlessness or a lesser intellectual power. Philosophy must then constitute a critique of language, since it is in language, in the words governed by the body, such as memory and imagination, that fictions are formed. In regards to this coherent and rigorous relationship between philosophical reason as a critique of language and, inextricably, as an operation of perpetuating an equivalence between God and Nature, I will refer back to Derrida and the very start of the lecture on 'Language and the Discourse on Method'.

Divine violence as it is distinguished by Benjamin from mythic violence, its foundation and conservation of law (an evidently decisive distinction), can only be expressed through Justice. It is Justice that smites Korah and his friends, the representatives of institutionalized law. It is Justice which destroys all in its path, that is to say all foundational or conserving violence, or all mythic law. For Benjamin, Justice is very much *the name of God*, to such an extent that we could even say that the God in the *Critique of Violence* is a *Deus sive Justitia.* He delivers "law" by smiting those who play with law and enforce it against Justice. It is without question that Benjamin leaves many aspects of the destructive or even exterminative violence of God in the dark, or in the darkness of God, as Nietzsche would have us say. But, in any case, what we are able to retain from this is that the violence of the vengeful God, or the God of Justice, is looked at by Benjamin straight in the eyes, without any avowed sense of fear, which does not help to comfort the reader, but does so with a rectitude that is authorized by the equivalence of divine violence with Justice and its extra-subjective power, something much more vast than any notion of subjectivity, consciousness or of individuality— a power which is neither finite nor empirical (*Théologico-Politique* 2, 3).

The symptomal reading of Spinoza's fear refers Reason back to its non-deductive genealogy, to an originarity that precedes it. God's vengeance is the operator of this genealogical operation undertaken by Derrida. It is true, however, that the seminar does not turn to this ghostly and very "Judeo-German" *Deus sive Justitia.* But it seems possible to me to decipher in Derrida's symptomalization of the *Theological-Political Treatise* a sort of secretive, marranic defense, "marranic of marranic," of the biblical-Hebraic literality, with regard to the vengeful God. This is shown in a series of inversions and displacements of fear. The text of these lectures on the Theologico-Political attests to an extraordinary mimetic force of the fear of Reason, towards and away from Spinoza. On page 10 of *Théologico-Politique* 2, Derrida puts forth the following hypothesis: "If I use the word fear or fright, it is in order to suggest now what I will get to in a moment and to risk a *rapprochement*, a troubling analogy between the stepping back/attitude of Spinoza before the vengeful God and the fear of the first Hebrews [...] at the immediate provocation and the fire of the divine speech." This remark pertains to the passage of the *Treatise* that I already cited in which Spinoza tries to determine the cause of the substitution of the pact of relinquishment for the pact of equality: "[O]n the first occasion, they all equally approached God to hear what he wished to decree. But in this first encounter they were so exceedingly terrified and astonished when they heard God speaking that they thought their final day had come. Gripped by terror, they approached Moses."[20] Being very reasonable, we could say, or even, to a certain extent, "rationalist," the Hebrews know very well that direct contact with God would be fatal for them. They are thus seized by a movement of stepping back that anticipates the stepping back of Spinoza, who, in a way, simply repeats the same gesture. But in turning to Moses and delegating all power to him, this movement would turn out to be fatal to the rigorous equality that united them, forever lost, replaced by a stately organization, structured by mediations, mediators and rules. The Hebrews sacrificed their liberty and their equality *because of their fear*, their panicked fright towards the violence of God, unbearable and fatal to men (this is the meaning of *Exodus* 33: 23, where Moses himself cannot see God, by virtue of an ontological impossibility, and not because of some hierarchical restriction). Filled with dread, the Hebrews prefer to enter into a rational transaction of the delegation of power as a system of protection against the terrible power of the Name. But they remain nevertheless assured, rightly or wrongly, of the Justice of the Name. It is truly the question of Justice which is at stake. The undeniable merit of Benjamin is his understanding of this very point, something which Spinoza's reading glosses over. What we are dealing with is a sort of chiasm in which, one against the other, Justice and Reason are playing—and for Benjamin, this speaks precisely to the conflict between justice and law. Rationalism's exaggerated premise entails a belief in which reason is always and necessarily on the same side as justice, or justice on the side of reason. And what if this wasn't the case? This is the dreadful suspicion that Benjamin's text on violence secretly and remarkably carries; it is undoubtedly here where his obscure enigma resides. It is as if we were to be confronted with, in twisting Spinoza's doctrine,[21] a *fiction of reason!* Spinoza's fear would therefore emanate from a certain recognition, evanescent, fugitive, unavowed, of this terrible and immediate incompatibility between reason and justice, just as the fear of the Hebrews (1, 25ff.) is at the core of the transition from a direct quasi-democracy to the delegation of power and to representation. Representation then, either in the philosophical and metaphysical sense or in the political sense of a transfer of power, sutures the impossibility of a full presence of God, within God. There would be therefore a manifest relationship between the "rationalist and universalist system of Spinoza" and "the transition whereby the Hebrews organize their State" (2, 16). If the God of the Jews is a God "who carries death [...] in the name of his name" (ibid.), there are ultimately two choices. On the one hand, with Spinoza, as well as with the rationalist stream of medieval and Jewish philosophy before him, we change paths, by going towards this *nameless God* who is the *Deus sive Natura*—and it's all of modern philosophy which participates in this movement. On the other, we will have understood that this Name means Justice, *Deus sive Justitia*, and we do not let go of the enigma, as it is scarcely possible—this is Benjamin's stance, despite many considerable difficulties that the *Critique of Violence* does not alleviate. This position is not Derrida's within the sixty odd pages of the lectures on the *Theological-Political*, which do not engage with any alternative but take the blade of undecidability right to the heart of Spinoza's argument. However, Derrida's position cannot be understood, in my estimation, without this Benjaminian foundation (messianic) of justice and its aporias, of which reason is terrified.

There is another side to the mimetic power of fear—a sort of secondary power, albeit very instructive. Derrida writes (2, 2) that, considering "the continuation of vengeance," the vengeance of history (Heidegger), the vengeance of language (Scholem) and of course the vengeance of God (Spinoza), he feels himself constant stupefaction, fear, astonishment and fascination; he could himself cry out *nec satis mirari possum.* What does this mimesis of fear signify, its repetition, by Spinoza, who gives fear its motive, by the Hebrews, who are subject to the fatal consequence, and by Derrida, whose revisiting, more or less feigned, is an operative gesture? What all this means, I said it from the very beginning, is an opening or a philosophical emotion, or affect, that can be likened to a procedure or a method whereby "objects" are assigned to thought outside any sovereign understanding, without any grounding, if it were, which would exclude fear in order to attain mastery, by of course a necessary and inevitable inversion of it. Fear is a virtue of Reason which Reason holds as a vice—the moment when Reason considers itself and, at the same time, questions itself in front of the abyss of its possible *deposition*, of its "ecstasy" and of its "stupor," to use Schelling's famous words. Derrida's text offers us a subtle, layered exposition that can take the form of a stratified cross-section of this spectrality.

Firstly, *the fear of the Hebrews,* as understood and explained by Spinoza. This constitutes the moment in which fear shows its two sides. In consenting, out of fear of death, to the relinquishment, the Hebrews fall into a new type of slavery, while at the same time constituting a multitude that "would surely be more fit to rule than to be ruled" according to the words of § 27 of the *Political Treatise.*[22] What would be needed here is a sort of simulation, an auto-commentary on behalf of Spinoza which would be, in fact, a counter-commentary of the passage in question from the *Theological-Political Treatise* by § 27 of the *Political Treatise.* I will of course not attempt this here but I would like to suggest the possibility that, in the very least, Spinoza's fear is spectrally linked to his own reflections on the multitude. Certainly, Spinoza's anti-Judaic passion in the *Theological-Political Treatise* hinders the possibility of such a dialogue. Spinoza is torn between a fear of the plebes, always ready to support the worst tyrants and to massacre the wise, and the radical affirmation that there is no sovereignty outside the *multitudo.* This significant inconsistency between a multitude which is ideally free and reasonable and an ignorant crowd, "terrible when it is without fear" effectively clarifies the situation of the Hebrews, the relationship to Moses and the theological-political question itself. It is through this problematic that we can understand that the transition from quasi-democracy to monarchy, from liberty in the equality of all to the relinquishment of all to the command of one person, is an expression of Spinoza's aporia of the multitude.

As for *Spinoza's Fear*, it is the fear of Reason and, at the same time, the reverse realization that this fear constitutes a "system of protection" (2, 16). In this fascinating expression of Reason, the symptomal reading reveals and circumscribes a greater frame for Spinoza's rationalism, a rationalism within a rationalism—une *mise en abîme*—of which Martial Guéroult has identified certain traits: an absolute, ontological and univocal rationalism, where being holds an absolute unity in terms of modes, causes and attributes. This ontological structure is determinant and automatically hinders the possibility of any separation between Reason and Justice. The metaphysical reappropriation or naturalization of God leads, therefore, to the nameless God of *The Ethics:* a God who has been emptied of any possibility of injustice, but who is, conversely, a God without Justice. Moreover, if God is to be but a naturalized (or naturalizing) God, and his kingdom equivalent to the law of nature, what happens to his Justice? This is the dilemma.

Our fear, finally, the one which Derrida takes on as his own, sharing it with us, can perhaps be seen as a reappraisal of philosophy itself. The stepping back of the Hebrews from God, of Spinoza and Derrida from God's violence, reminds us of an increasing significance for whoever encounters a text of the tradition. This movement is doubtless the same as what animates philosophy. The *thaumazein,* or 'wonder', is a contemplative stepping back of the same type; indignation, as well, or all of the other names that have tried to determine "the beginning of philosophy." Fear designates a pre-philosophical emotion, or affect, which can legitimately appear in the list. This question is fully undertaken from the very start of the lectures on Language and Descartes' Discourse on Method according to what Derrida describes as a "fatal topic [. . .] which constrains all philosophical discourse" (Language and the Discourse on Method, 13, 2), in taking the example of the *Treatise on the Emendation of the Intellect* as well as *Sein und Zeit,* of the *Phenomenology of the Spirit* and the *Manuscripts of 1844*. The stepping back, in so far as it is repeated, engages thought in the fateful topic of the beginning. There where fear fears, thought steps back to think: this is precisely what should be looked in the eyes.

(*Translated from the French by Richard Spavin*)

NOTES

1. Thanks to the kindness of Warren Montag and Willi Goetschel, I was able to work on the lecture notes of J. Derrida—also, I have to thank here the *Department of Special Collections, UCI Libraries, University of California, Irvine* where they come from. The typescript comes from two courses, lectures 10-13 of

'Language and the Discourse of Method' (*La langue et le discours de la méthode*) and lectures 1-3 comprising the lecture on nationality and philosophical nationalism (*Nationalité et nationalisme philosophiques*) and two lectures on the Theological-Political (*Théologico-Politique*). The latter are referred to throughout as *Théologico-Politique*, 1-3. It is on the basis of this distribution, uncertain and temporary, that I will cite here Derrida's notes.

2. One can say that Derrida and Spinoza are like two opposed angles of the philosophic field, as far away from each other in the space of a square as possible. And nevertheless, a diagonal can be drawn between them the way Derrida's lectures trace it. This diagonal is the diagonal of "fear." With this line of fear the field is traversed, without that, the opposition between the two "angles" occupied by the two philosophers could be abolished or tempered without reducing the space that opposes them.
3. Benedict de Spinoza, *Theological-Political Treatise*, ed. Jonathan Israel, trans. Michael Silverthorne and Jonathan Israel (Cambridge: Cambridge University Press, 2007), 226: "Nor can I sufficiently express my amazement [...]"; *Traité des Autorités théologique et politique*, trans. Misrahi-Francès in Spinoza, *Œuvres complètes*, ed. and trans. Roland Caillois, Madeleine Francès et Robert Misrahi, Bibliothèque de la Pléiade (Paris: Gallimard, 1954, reprinted 1988), 867.
4. Tacitus, *Histories*, 1.3.
5. The Pléiade has: "une véritable stupeur."
6. Spinoza, *Theological-Political Treatise*, 226.
7. All of the lectures on the *Theologico-Political* originate from the trinomial proposed by Derrida at the beginning of his analysis (*Nationalité et nationalisme philosophiques* 1, 8): corruption/vengeance/spectrality.
8. Spinoza, *Theological-Political Treatise*, 214: "The Hebrews did not transfer their right to another person but rather they all gave up their right, equally, as in a democracy [. . .]."
9. Ibid.
10. Spinoza, *Theological-Political Treatise*, 213 f.; Ibid., p. 848 et p. 849. The mediator is Moses, particularly in this story since he is the one who recommends that the Hebrews "relinquish" their State of equality before finding themselves within a monarchy. Moses is the only beneficiary of this transfer of the natural rights of the people.
11. Translations from *Exodus* and *Numbers* are from *The Jewish Bible* of the Jewish Publication Society, Philadelphia 1917.
12. Spinoza quotes Ezekiel 20: 25, Spinoza, *Theological-Political Treatise*, 226.
13. Ibid., 227.
14. Ibid., 225.
15. Ibid., 45.
16. Ibid., 45.
17. This is what the editors of the *Pléiade* believe—incapable of taking Derrida's interpretation of Spinoza's fear seriously. Derrida harshly criticized them for this.
18. Walter Benjamin, *Critique of Violence* in Benjamin, *Reflections: Essays, Aphorisms,*

Autobiographical Writings, ed. Peter Demetz, tr. Edmund Jephcott (New York: Schocken, 1986), 277-300, 296f. I will refer back to this same passage on page 296 f. in continuation of my argument.

19. Spinoza, *Theological-Political Treatise*, 227.
20. Ibid., 214.
21. This is what Derrida does at the beginning of the lecture on 'Language and Descartes' *Discourse on Method'*, when he deconstructs the founding proposition of Spinoza's principle of reason in the *Treatise on the Emendation of the Intellect,* according to which we cannot, once we have understood through intellect the nature of the body, form a fiction about an infinite fly. "Is it more difficult to form a fiction of a philosopher in a finite and mortal mode [...] What difference is there between Spinoza and an infinite spider" ('Language and the Discourse on Method', 11, 6)?
22. Spinoza, *Political -Theological Treatise* in Spinoza, *Complete Works*, tr. Samuel Shirley, ed. Michael Morgan (Indianapolis and Hackett, 2002) cap. 7, § 27, 720.

9

Not This, Not That...[1]: Maurice Blanchot and Poststructuralism*

Rustam Singh

The concept paper of the conference mentions Maurice Blanchot as one of the precursors of the so-called poststructuralism. However, it seems to me that if there was indeed such a thing as poststructuralism, Blanchot belonged to the very heart of this movement, he was located at its very centre. It also appears that some of the changes that took place both in the content and the form of the discourse in the West, with the result that the changed discourse came to be called poststructuralism, began much earlier, even a bit earlier than what is called structuralism, and the person who began them was Maurice Blanchot. Finally—and I say this with a lot of caution—I cannot help feeling that in some respects Blanchot went further than poststructuralism.

Let us look, first, at Blanchot's essay "The Myth of Mallarmé" which first appeared in French, under a different title, in 1946. This is the essay in which Blanchot expands upon Stéphane Mallarmé's (1842–1898) thoughts on language and in the process develops his own thoughts on language and literature. In my view, this is a crucial essay in Blanchot's trajectory as a philosopher and critic and probably even as a writer. The English translation of the essay can be found in Blanchot's collection *The Work of Fire* (*La Part du Feu,*1949), published by Stanford University Press in 1995, on pages 27 to 42. We can see in this essay how a particular view of language that became a dominant view in the Western discourse in the late 1960s and in the 1970s had its germination, in a certain way, nearly a hundred years earlier. We will see later that in practice this view not only reached its apogee via Maurice Blanchot but, apart from Jacques Derrida to some extent, also *in* Maurice

* Earlier published in *Comparative and Continental Philosophy*, Vol. 8, No. 1 (2016), pp. 72-82. The editors are grateful to Taylor & Francis Ltd. for granting the permission to republish the paper.

Blanchot. In fact, in my opinion, in the twentieth century Western discourse Blanchot was the most subtle practitioner of this view of language.

This language is what Mallarmé had called the "essential" language, which is different from the language that is "crude and immediate." What are the characteristics of this language? Firstly, this language is "impersonal"; it has an existence which is "independent and absolute." Blanchot also uses for it the word "autonomous." This language "does not imply anyone who expresses it, or anyone who hears it: it speaks *itself* and writes *itself*."[2] It is "never the act of someone who is speaking in the presence of someone who hears him..." "It is a kind of awareness, without subject..." Thus, this language—and this is an important point—is subjectless. "That is the condition of its authority." We can see that in this early essay the displacement or, what I would like to call, the defamation of the subject or the author has already begun.[3]

The second characteristic of this language is that it destroys the object that it names. "It causes to vanish, it renders the object absent, it annihilates it." Citing Mallarmé, Blanchot says: "'I say: a flower!' and I have in front of my eyes neither a flower, nor an image of a flower, nor a memory of a flower, but an absence of flower." This absence, nevertheless, is not an absence of reality. Rather, "we are once again in contact with reality, but a more evasive reality, one that presents itself and evaporates, that is understood and vanishes ... so that if in one respect it is done away with, in another respect it reappears ... like a series of fugitive and unstable nuances... ." This being so, we can see here the beginnings of the instability of meaning. We can also see here the beginnings of neuter or the neutral, a notion that is central to Blanchot's work and also, in my view, to poststructuralist thought. As such, it is pertinent to ask here: what is neuter or the neutral? A preliminary answer to this question is: it is *that* in language which, among other things, makes it difficult for us to grasp and retain sense or meaning, or the 'reality' of things.

We will come back to neuter, in order to comprehend it in a fuller sense, but here we should continue to attend to those disturbing characteristics of language that Mallarmé and Blanchot have brought to the fore—characteristics that seem to be opening a crack between language and understanding or even, one may say, between language and thought. We will see later that this crack will become, over a period, a wide gap, an almost unbridgeable distance that will set up language and thought in opposition to each other.

Style will play an important role in this process and things that come with style, things such as sounds, rhythm, the sheer physicality of words—physicality through which they become visible and erect a barrier between "what is and what they express." Speaking of words especially Blanchot says: "Their duty is to draw the gaze to themselves and turn it away from the thing of which they speak." This is not what everyday language can do. Such language only names the object; it does not make it disappear. Rather, it leaves a picture of it. It "gives way to the pressure of the thing it designates...[I]t hands us over to the presence from which it was supposed to defend us." And it was from this kind of language that Mallarmé "desperately fled." Therefore, "If language's distinctive feature is to nullify the presence it signifies, then transparency, clarity, commonplaces are contrary to it...they thwart its progress toward a signification free of any concrete reference."[4]

We can see here how language is beginning to take "precedence... over thought," if thought is defined by things such as transparency, clarity and concreteness. Another thing we can see is the deprecation of what is called 'presence'—in this case the presence of the being of things, of the facts of the world. But there is one more thing that is taking place here: It was claimed earlier that language is impersonal, that it is independent of the one who writes, speaks or hears it. However, if it is the "duty" of the words "to turn [the gaze] away from the thing of which they speak," if Mallarmé "desperately fled" from the language that does not do this, and if transparency and clarity are "contrary to" the language that is desirable— then the impersonality attributed to language is being taken away; then we are talking of a language that has to be created; then this language is expected to perform a certain function; then language is no longer a domain which is independent; rather this domain is under the shadow of a 'presence.'[5]

Oblivious of this transformation that is taking place in his *own language*, oblivious that thought is taking over language in his own engagement with language, Blanchot goes on to tell us what he means by the absence that is created by language in order to "free us from what is," from the entire "domain of the objective world." This absence is an emptiness, a silence, a lack "that is the purpose and true creation of language." He says: "Literature's law is this movement toward *something else*, toward a *beyond* that yet escapes us *because it cannot be*,[6] and of it we grasp only 'the knowing lack' that 'we have.'" Thus this movement, which is "the work of erosion," ends up creating a meaning that only "indicates itself, a still suspended meaning, of which we hold only the empty outline."

What has Blanchot done here? Firstly, he has equated meaning with what he calls 'something else,' 'a beyond.' Secondly, he has told us that this beyond cannot be reached, for it cannot exist. Therefore, thirdly, what *can* be reached—and is actually reached, actually realized—is its lack.

Now, the implications of this argument of Blanchot are far-reaching, but they are also problematic. We will sum them up as follows. What is called meaning cannot be reached. It cannot be reached because it cannot exist. Therefore what can be reached is only the lack of meaning, what Blanchot calls 'a still suspended meaning,' which is only an 'indication' of meaning, its 'empty outline.' This is what 'essential' language can attain.

We can see that Blanchot has moved here beyond the instability of meaning that we talked about earlier. But where exactly has he reached? Has he reached what will later be called the deferral or the slippage of meaning or some such thing? Yes. Certainly. However, if we look closely we find that he has reached beyond deferral either; he has crossed that point. And by doing that he has reached what can only be called the end of meaning. He has reached the place where the word no longer creates meaning; it does not perform that function. What the word does now is this: it erodes the reality of things, of the world as we know it. But does it fill the space that results from this erosion? No. Rather, it leaves us suspended between the world it is eroding and a world it does not create, between a lack that is growing and another lack that this growing lack generates at the edge of the 'beyond,' the edge of 'something else' which itself does not exist.

It seems to me that this is not the place where one would like to be.

And this brings us back to *neuter* or the neutral, for what we have just talked about is precisely the task of this 'entity' that 'exists' in the 'essential' language and which Blanchot has imbued with some more 'properties' in what we have seen above. Now neuter is not only *that* in language which makes it difficult for us to pin down or grasp sense or meaning; it is also what creates the illusion of a thing that cannot exist. At the same time, it creates the illusion that this thing, which is illusory, can be captured.

We will see some further additions to this notion called neuter. It will then become *that* which will turn a thing into something about which we cannot say: it *is* or it is *not*; it is *here* or it is *there*. The only way we would then be able to 'describe' this thing is this: *it neither is nor is not; it is neither here nor there.*[7]

Meanwhile, we should note that by introducing the notion of lack, Blanchot has opened up space for some stylistic innovations that will transform the form of his work. For, lack means a break too, that is, a crack or a gap. It is something that divides a thing into fragments, for example, a thing like discourse; or something that breaks a narrative, even breaks it down. However, as we will see, Blanchot will deploy it more radically, that is, as a void, and to achieve that aim he will once again use neuter.

Blanchot wrote about the fragment in his major later books *The Infinite Conversaton* and *The Writing of the Disaster*, published in French in 1969 and 1980 respectively. (In the former, he also wrote about its use by Friedrich Nietzsche.) But he had started using it in his own texts much earlier. For example, he had used it in his stunning essay on "Waiting," which appeared in French in 1959. Then he used it in what maybe called his last full-length fictional work or récit, *Awaiting Oblvion*, published in 1962. Later, he used it in his essays as well as in books, including the book called *The Step Not Beyond* published in French in 1973. From the stylistic point of view, *The Step Not Beyond* was a pivotal book, in Blanchot's own work and also in the so-called poststructuralist discourse. Why do I call it pivotal? Not because it was written in the fragmentary way, but because in this book, for the first time in Blanchot's work, there was a mixing of genres. *The Step Not Beyond* is primarily a philosophical book, but in between the philosophical fragments, at a number of places in the book, Blanchot has inserted pieces of fiction that read like a récit or a narrative. And these fictional pieces have been italicized. Thus the book has added three new elements to the fragmentary: mixing of genres, multiple typefaces and multiple voices. Earlier, in some of the essays in *The Infinite Conversation* too, he had used the device of multiple voices (what he called the "plural speech") talking to each other in such a way that we can't determine or fix their identity from what they say. Their identity seems to be shifting with every piece of speech that they utter. They seem to be giving up one identity and assuming another, and in the process losing identity altogether. The mixing of genres and the use of multiple typefaces continued, to some extent, in *The Writing of the Disaster*.

Needless to say, Blanchot used this fascinating array of devices in order to erode even further the being of the thing and the world, but also the subject and identity in general—what is called the presence—an erosion that is supposed to inhere in the 'essential' language itself but is unleashed with a particular force by the fragmentary style whose effect is intensified by these devices. At the same time, Blanchot was using these devices in an effort to erode the difference between philosophical and literary writing, an effort that he had begun much earlier, with *Awaiting Oblivion* in 1962, a book which is primarily fiction but is beginning to show elements of philosophical meditation.

But there is another device that Blanchot used time and again throughout his work, which enabled him to go even further in this erosion. This device, in a way, erodes language itself or rather erases it even as it unfolds itself. This device is the following: Blanchot makes a proposition and then withdraws it, partly or fully, either in the same sentence or in the sentences that come immediately later. Here is a quotation from what I would call a rather early text that demonstrates the use of this device. It is a part of Blanchot's short prefatory note to his monumental work *The Space of Literature,* published in French in 1955:

> A book, even a fragmentary one, has a centre which attracts it. This centre is not fixed, but is displaced by the pressure of the book and circumstances of its composition. Yet it is also a fixed centre which, if it is genuine, displaces itself, while remaining the same and becoming always more central, more hidden, more uncertain and more imperious.

Now, the fragmentary perhaps is supposed to do away with the centre of a book. But here is a book, which, let us say, is fragmentary, but has a centre and this centre attracts it; probably it gathers it together. However, this centre is not fixed because it is displaced by the book itself, by its pressure. So we may presume that it has moved from the centre of the book and has gone elsewhere. But no. This doesn't seem possible, because it is still a fixed centre. However, although it is still fixed, perhaps it is not a genuine centre. In other words, perhaps it is not a centre at all. But if it is genuine, then it displaces itself, something that earlier seemed to have been done by the book. And while it displaces itself, it remains the same, that is, probably a centre, at that place in the book where it has displaced itself and therefore perhaps is no longer central. Nevertheless, in this process of displacing itself, it has become even more central. At the same time, it has also become even more hidden and more uncertain, which means that it was already hidden and uncertain but not to this extent. Finally, while it has become even more hidden and uncertain—probably because it is not certain of being a centre and central, and thus is hiding—it has become even more imperious, that is, certain.

As we can see, Blanchot begins by saying that a book has a centre, but the entire quotation seems to say that perhaps the book has a centre but, at the same time, perhaps it doesn't have it. Or, if it has it, then the centre itself is not certain that it is. This is an example of how Blanchot in his language proposes something but then withdraws and erases it. And in the process, what he is able to achieve is the void.

Before we proceed any further, I will quote some more passages that have the same nature as the prefatory note I quoted above. The first passage is from the essay "Waiting," published in 1959. We will see here that 'play' of language that Derrida talked about in his essay "Structure, Sign and Play in the Discourse of the Human Sciences," as if for the first time, in 1966:

> Waiting gives time, takes time, but it is not the same that is given and taken. Waiting does not leave him time for waiting.
>
> ....
>
> In waiting reigns the absence of time where waiting is the impossibility of waiting. Time renders seemingly possible impossible waiting, which is governed by absence of time.
>
> In time waiting comes to an end without an end being put to waiting. Waiting which takes place in time opens up time to the absence of time where there is no place for waiting.
>
> In waiting, if time always gives us something to wait for, be it only our own end or the end of time, we are doomed to the absence of time which has always already detached waiting from this end and from every end.[8]

The second passage is from *The Step Not Beyond* (1973) that I spoke about earlier:

> "You will come again."—"I will come again."—"You won't come again."—"When you speak like that, I understand what it means: I'm here by way of the return, I'm thus not here: and I understand that this would be in the past, in a time so ancient that there has never been a present to correspond to it, that you have been here."—"But I am here, you see that."—"Yes, he said seriously, I'm here on condition that I forget that I'm here, remembering it one time, forgetting it another time, and just the same letting memory, forgetfulness, unfold themselves, close themselves back up, without anyone who remembers, who forgets."[9]

The next passage is from Blanchot's récit *Thomas the Obscure*, whose first version appeared in French in 1941:

> There was, then, henceforth, in all the sepulchers where he might have been able to take his place, in all the feelings which are also tombs for the dead, in this annihilation through which he was dying without permitting himself to be thought dead, there was another dead person who was there first, and who...[was] identical with himself.[10]

Now, if Blanchot in his language is able to *achieve* the void, then, can we say that this language is impersonal, a question I had raised even earlier? Can we say that what is going on here is language and not thought, in this case the thought of Maurice Blanchot? Thought which is arrived at by making use of a certain device, a certain way of deploying language? Isn't it thought here which is primary and not language, and behind that thought, more primary than it, a certain presence, which is personified by the person of Maurice Blanchot? Surely it is this same presence, or even the person too, who, in all of Blanchot's work, deploys all those techniques and devices that we have mentioned above, in order to use language in a certain way. The result is a thought, a theory, a way of looking at the world, including language. But here is a paradox. A thought that presents language as independent and impersonal is precisely the thought that twists and turns it, even manipulates it, probably more than any other thought, in order to achieve an effect, in this case the effect of a void, an erasure.[11]

And here I would like to come back to the prefatory note of 1955 from which I had quoted earlier. As we saw, Blanchot seems to be saying in this text that perhaps a book has a centre but, at the same time, perhaps it doesn't have it. But in the book itself, that is, in *The Space of Literature*, Blanchot suggests that there is actually no centre, and, in fact, no structure either. Speculating on what would happen if there is no totality or a whole, he writes:

> If the whole, though, is no whole at all, the movement that goes from me toward others never comes back toward me. It remains the circle's broken call. Moreover, the movement does not even go from me toward others; no one answers me, because I do not call, because from 'me' nothing originates.[12]

However, it is in a later text, called "The Narrative Voice: (the 'he,' the neuter)," first published in French in 1964, that Blanchot says, in so many words, that there is no centre. This is one of those texts where Blanchot tells us in his own voice what neuter is and what it does. Blanchot is writing here of the impression one often gets while reading a story that "someone is speaking in the background..." According to Blanchot, this impression "is really part of the singularity of narrative" and what he calls "the truth of the circle..." "as though the center of the circle lay outside the circle, in back and infinitely far back, as though the *outside* were precisely this center, *which could only be the absence of all center*."[13]

Now, if we treat 'the book' as well as 'the circle' above as a structure, then, Blanchot goes on to argue that the book, what he also calls the work, *itself does not exist*. For example, further on in the same essay, talking of the narrative voice Blanchot says,

> [I]t always tends to absent itself in its bearer and also to efface him as center, thus being neuter in the decisive sense that it cannot be central, does not create a center, does not speak from a center, but on the contrary, at the limit would prevent the work from having a center...*and also not allowing it to exist as a completed whole, once and forever accomplished*.[14]

Elaborating this view in the essay, "The Absence of the Book," published in 1969, Blanchot adds: "The Work, the absolute of the voice and of writing, is *unworked* even before it has been accomplished..."[15] This happens because of the very act of writing. Thus, "To write is to produce absence of the work...Or: writing is the absence of the work as it *produces itself* through the work and throughout the work." Writing, as such, is indeed an "insane game," as Mallarmé had termed it. But "What happens to the book during this 'game,' in which worklessness is set loose during the operation of writing?" What happens is that "Writing passes through the book, but the book is not that to which it is destined..." The book is only "a ruse by which writing goes towards the absence of the book."[16]

It is clear that what destroys the book in order to produce writing is worklessness, which inheres in the act of writing and which is another name for neuter. But what is important is that even as writing makes an appearance, the book gets destroyed; it disappears even before it could appear. And with this disappearance also disappears, *that is, does not come into existence*, what is called the structure—which is what the book essentially is.

Overall, for Blanchot, in the 'essential' language—that is, language which is impersonal—many things disappear: first it is the subject, then it is the being of the object and of the objective world, then the book along with its centre which again is the subject, and, finally, as we will see below, the being itself as well as the non-being. Insofar as the subject is concerned, what disappears is also the author as well as the listener or reader. And since literature or writing is supposed to move towards 'the beyond,' 'the something else,' which cannot exist, I have argued above that what disappears is also meaning. And Blanchot confirms this in his essay "René Char and the Thought of the Neutral," of 1963. Criticizing what he calls "ontological argument" in which God remains God "whether he is or is not," he tells us how the neutral speech is "always in excess" "in relation to Being" where it is "empty of meaning and through this emptiness absolutely separate from all meaning and non-meaning."[17]

Continuing in the same vein in the essay "The Narrative Voice," Blanchot writes: "[T]he neutral speech neither reveals nor conceals. This is not to say that it signifies nothing...it means it does not signify in the same way the visible-invisible signifies, but that it opens another power in the language, one alien to the power of illumination (or of darkening), of comprehension (or of misapprehension)." But what is this another power that the neuter opens up in language? "[I]t could be that telling (writing) is drawing language into a possibility of saying that would say without saying being and still without denying it either..." So that "speaking is not a matter of affirming being nor of needing negation in order to suspend the work of being, the work that ordinarily occurs in every form of expression."[18]

We need not mention that Blanchot has here imbued the neuter with another property. While earlier it eroded the being of things or made them disappear, or, even, made us believe that a thing was there when it was not, or that the thing did not exist, now it has moved out of the very structure of being and non-being, the structure of the 'is' and 'is not.' As I had hinted above, once this form of the neuter has become operative in language, we can no longer be sure whether a thing is there or is not—which is different from saying that the thing is there but cannot be captured.

So that it is as if the 'thing' here is like the Brahman of the Upanishads. It reminds me especially of the description of the Brahman in the Brhadâraòyaka Upanishad, and Blanchot was surely familiar with it. In the Brhadâraòyaka Upanishad Yâjñavalkya tells Gargi: "That, O Gargi ... is neither gross nor fine, neither short nor long...(It is) neither shadow nor darkness, neither air nor space, unattached, without taste, without smell, without eyes, without ears, without voice, without mind, without radiance, without breath, without a mouth, without measure, having no within and no without..."[19]

At the end, it would be interesting to compare, very briefly, Blanchot's notion of neuter with Derrida's différance, which perhaps is regarded as a central notion in poststructuralism.

We have seen that the neutral speech evades both meaning and non-meaning. And it is able to do this by sidestepping the very structure of being and non-being or that of presence and non-presence. Now, it seems to me that *différance* fails to do that; it continues to operate within that structure

This is how it happens.

Derrida tries to locate *différance*—what he also calls "the play of differences"—*prior to* the structure of presence and absence and he does this because he wants to conceive presence and absence, to conceive being, on the basis of *différance*. However, it is not clear where differance comes from if it is prior to the structure of presence and absence, the structure of being. It is as if différance—the "systematic play of differences," the play of the "traces of differences," and so on—exists on its own, prior to being, and as if it springs out of nowhere.[20] And if this is so, then, *différance* turns itself into a presence—a presence that looks like an originary presence, a presence that cannot be accounted for.

When we turn to the narrower field of language, it seems that here too *différance* precedes it, and the differences in the field of language, in the system of signs, are the product of *différance*. Further, it appears that the signs themselves—or elements—are the products, in fact, the effects of *différance*. To quote Derrida: "Nothing, either in the elements or in the system, is anywhere simply present or absent. There are only, everywhere, differences and traces of traces."[21] We can see that signs or elements turn here into ghostly presences which cannot exist unless there is present between them, and, in fact, within them, another presence, a presence that moves around and moves them around, even changes and shapes them, and is always present—the Presence of what can only be called, with a capitalized D, *Différance*. These instances show how *différance* gets caught into the very trap it wants to break.

Overall, difference has the structure of: *this, but also that*. It is located in presence but always points to the other in presence and also outside it. Neuter, on the other hand, believes in bypassing, making a detour, a tangential movement. It has the structure of: *neither this nor that nor any other thing*.

Thus it goes further than and beyond *différance*, although it emerged on the scene much earlier.

NOTES

1. The first part of the title is a play upon what, in Brhadâraòyaka Upanishad, the philosopher Yâjñavalkya says about the Brahman. Addressing Úâkalya, he said: "That self is not this, not this." See, *The Principal Upanishads*, edited with introduction, text, translation and notes by S. Radhakrishnan, Indus, New Delhi, 1994, p. 243.
2. Emphases, unless otherwise stated, are in the original.

3. We may recall here Roland Barthes' essay "The Death of the Author," published more than twenty years later.
4. Thus, to quote Mallarmé: "the silent thunder scattered in the foliage; not the intrinsic, dense wood of the trees."
5. But this problem is not peculiar to Blanchot. The discourse of some poststructuralist thinkers who came later suffers from the same defect, and probably even more so. Let me cite only one example, this one from Jacques Derrida. Long after Blanchot had carved a language that did not seem to have a centre and more than ten years after Blanchot had suggested, in his own voice, that perhaps there is no centre, Derrida, in his essay "Structure, Sign and Play in the Discourse of the Human Sciences," (first delivered in 1966), makes the same point in different words and tries to elaborate the concept of play in language. He says: "This field [that is, the field of language]...is that of play...Play is the disruption of presence...Play is always play of absence and presence, but if it is *to be thought radically*, play *must be conceived of* before the alternative of presence and absence. Being *must be conceived* as presence or absence on the basis of the possibility of play and not the other way around." (See *Writing and Difference*, Routledge and Kegan Paul, London, 1981, pp. 289 and 292. Emphasis added.)

   We can see the contradiction in Derrida's argument here. Even as he is speaking of the inherent play in language, which disrupts the presence, there is little play in his own language and, as such, we can read only one meaning in his sentences, quite possibly the meaning that is intended by him. In other words, his own language fails to disrupt his own presence. In fact, this is true of the entire essay that I have cited here and of the book from which I have cited it. In this particular quotation, note the use of phrases such as "if it is to be conceived radically," "play must be conceived of," and "Being must be conceived," etc. Derrida is trying his best to convince us that there is only one way. Quite a heavy presence, that!

   We will see below that Blanchot, in comparison, fared much better. Much before Derrida wrote this essay, Blanchot had actually invented a language that shows us how play in language can be made to occur, if it does not take place on its own.
6. The words "because it cannot be" are emphasized by me.
7. For a brief critique of Blanchot's notion of neuter, see my essay "Gift, Passivity, Neuter," in my book *'Weeping' and Other Essays on Being and Writing*, Pratilipi Books, Jaipur, 2011.
8. See *The Blanchot Reader*, edited by Michael Holland, Blackwell, Oxford and Cambridge, 1995, pp. 273-74.
9. See *The Step Not Beyond*, SUNY Press, Albany, 1992, pp. 16-17. The text is italicized in the original.
10. See *Thomas the Obscure*, in *The Station Hill Blanchot Reader: Fiction and Literary Essays*, Station Hill Press, New York, 1999, p. 73.
11. And this reminds me once again of Jacques Derrida. There are some texts by

Derrida where he introduces play in his language, for example *The Post Card.* These are also the texts where, I presume, he tries to bring the language of philosophy closer to the language of literature. He, too, uses some techniques and devices in order to realize this project. It is difficult to say whether he succeeds, unlike Blanchot who does, in at least some of such attempts. But the point remains that, like in the case of Blanchot, these are deliberate attempts to deploy language in such a way that certain effects are attained. This is different from there being an inherent play in language which problematizes meaning.

However, in some other texts by Derrida the language is conceptual. And these texts show that he is an impossibly logocentric writer. In these texts meaning is asserted with a terrible force, through a tightly controlled language. Reason rules his sentences, in a way it does in few other philosophers. Prominent examples of such texts are *Of Grammatology* and *Writing and Difference.*

So far as *Of Grammatology* is concerned, Derrida even talked about the "guiding intention" of this work. Even if the intention here is attributed to the book, we may note that an intention is a thing of the mind; reason is involved in a thing like that. The intention, which was not necessarily confined to *Of Grammatology*, is also revealed in what he said about his words when he wrote about animals. These words, he said, were "words from the heart." In other words, what he wrote in books like *Of Grammatology* was not necessarily from the heart but rather from the mind. This is a significant admission from someone who questioned things like the subject and presence in his work. But it is equally significant to note that we cannot question reason and then deploy precisely *that* in our work. (See Derrida's preface to *Of Grammatology*, tr. Gayatri Spivak Chakravorty, The John Hopkins University Press, Baltimore, 1997, and Simon Glendinning, *Derrida: A Very Short Introduction*, Oxford University Press, New York, 2011, p. 109.)

12. *The Space of Literature*, translated, with an introduction by Ann Smock, University of Nebraska Press, Lincoln, 1982, footnote 2, p. 164.
13. See "The Narrative Voice," *The Station Hill Blanchot Reader*, op. cit., p. 460. The word 'outside' has been emphasized in the original. The rest of the emphasis is mine.
14. Ibid., pp. 467-68. Emphasis added.
15. "The Absence of the Book," *The Station Hill Blanchot Reader*, ibid., p. 478. Emphasis added.
16. Ibid., p. 473.
17. See *The Infinite Conversation*, translated, with a foreword by Susan Hanson, University of Minnesota Press, Minneapolis, 1993, pp. 303-04.
18. "The Narrative Voice," op. cit., p. 468.
19. See, *The Principal Upanishads*, op. cit., p. 571.
20. Actually, it springs out of Derrida's head.
21. Quoted by Jonathan Culler, in *On Deconstruction: Theory and Criticism after Structuralism*, Routledge, London, 1998, p. 99.

10

'Being-outside and Yet Belonging': Political Philosophy of Giorgio Agamben

Manas Ray

The events of 9/11 and the 'war on terror', bear all the hallmarks of what Carl Schmitt—the anti-liberal German philosopher of the first half of twentieth century —described as a 'state of exception'. In the present political context, a state of exception refers to the ways by which the major liberal democracies are driven by the growing accretion of discriminatory executive power, thus bypassing existing legislative and juridical institutions. This indicates the ever fluid threshold of indeterminacy between democracy and absolutism. The crucial issue is whether the state of exception is becoming a permanent feature of governance across nation-states. And it is here that the political treatise of the Italian philosopher Giorgio Agamben becomes relevant.

Agamben refuses to accord modernity any epistemic break in political rule. Instead, he argues that the very same lineage of Western metaphysics of political power runs abated from the classical Greek time onwards. Modern political rule, if different, is only so in its manner of ceaseless intensification of sovereign power. He identifies the Camp (meaning, Auschwitz) as the abiding metonym of modern power. Human rights are at best a ruse and at worst grist to an all-powerful sovereign that reduces humans to mere amorphous mass of living bodies bereft of all political claims—bare life or '*nude vita*' (i.e., nude life), if one goes by the words of Agamben.

Agamben began his career and worked for a long time in classical rhetoric and aesthetics. His turn to political philosophy was only in the 1990s, with the publication of *Homo Sacer* (1995) —the first of his trilogy (or, 'tetralogy' as he prefers to call)— the other two being, *Remnants of Auschwitz* (1998) and a collection of essays, *State of Exception: Homo Sacer II* (2003). Since his claim as a political thinker rests primarily on these three books, the present essay will be concerned mostly with these.[1]

Prior to Agamben, the French philosopher Michel Foucault had argued that the regime of power that emerged in Europe between late seventeenth and early eighteenth centuries and came into its own towards the middle of nineteenth century occasioned a crucial shift in the existing principles of power. He claimed that whereas pre-modern sovereign power operated on the principle of the right to 'commit its subjects to death' (i.e., deductive power) in order to enhance the strength of the sovereign, modern power turns around this axis and works through the administration of life. The entry of life itself into the operations of power and the arrangement of political calculations around the survival of the species constituted for Foucault the 'threshold of modernity': "What might be called a society's 'threshold of modernity' has been reached when the life of the species is wagered on its own political strategies."[2] Since the late eighteenth century, the traditional role of the sovereign expressed as 'the right to kill and let live' has been on the decline. Instead, what we have is the emergence of the modern 'governmentalized state' that rules through a new combination of discipline and biopolitics, replacing to a large extent the earlier sovereign power. Foucault epitomized the modern thrust of political power as 'to make live and to let die'.

The historical claim that biopolitics emerged during the eighteenth century provides the point of purchase of Agamben's own critical thesis on biopolitics, which he describes as an attempt to 'correct'—or at least 'complete'—Foucault's analysis of the relation between biopolitics and sovereign power.[3] Agamben's major departure lies in this: whereas Foucault sees in 'biopower' the primary orientation of modern politics working through a broad spectrum of areas like hygiene, demography, social welfare and insurance systems, Agamben postulates his concept of biopolitics as the bare essence of the sovereign right to kill and let live. Thus, according to Agamben, the concept of biopower means at the political level what is at stake is the very life itself of the subject, not the intervention into the processes of living. Hence if for Foucault, biopolitics is a life-administering power working towards creating homogenous social body, for Agamben biopolitics (or, biopower) is the other name of same subtraction mechanism of earlier times, now more holistic, comprehensive and devastating in its range and scope. Agamben claims that rather than being characteristic of the modern era, sovereignty articulates with biopolitics in a much more fundamental way, such that the "production of a biopolitical body is the original activity of sovereign power" and "biopolitics is at least as old as the sovereign exception."[4] The political status and function of the legal exception is central to Agamben's analysis of biopolitics, and it is this that allows him to identify the contemporary condition of politics which he characterizes as one of abandonment and nihilism.

Homo sacer

To explain his position, Agamben redefines the sovereign/subject relation completely. Foucault had already questioned the idea of sovereign and subject as each other's mirror.[5] Agamben puts this relationship as two sides of a paradox. On the one hand, there are the operations of democratic politics which necessarily have to assume the whole subject, the subject of rights based on liberal consensus. On the other hand, we have the ceaseless production of bare lives through biopolitical-sovereign nexus that reduces life to its minimum essentials, a 'spectral lump' bereft of all rights, but who at the same time has to be located in the interstices of the juridical.

Excavating ancient Roman law, Agamben finds the right trope for this state: the figure of *homo sacer* ('sacer' here means both sacred and accursed: Latin *sacrificium/sacr/sacer*). Borrowing from the Roman writer Pompeius Festus, Agamben frames the *homo sacer* as the quintessence of extreme marginality, one who cannot be sacrificed to the gods (for his death is of no value to the gods) but who can be killed with impunity (because he enjoys no legal protection). For Agamben, the figure is neither merely historical nor a residuum, but a generalized trope for included exclusion of modern life, "an epitomic site of the social markings and symbolization of the workings of the sovereign."[6] In other words, it is a limit concept, the source of sovereign power. *Homo sacer* is at once sacred and accursed since it is located exterior with respect to the human order that it helps to establish. In the eyes of the *homo sacer* everyone is a potential sovereign; conversely, to the sovereign, everyone is a potential *homo sacer*. Destruction of such life does not mean homicide; killing here does not involve law and yet it does not indicate lawlessness.

As is evident here, it is through the exception of law (legally performed) that sovereignty and life are brought into conjunction; in other words, even though the sovereign defines and ratifies the exception, it is exception that founds sovereign power and allows the law to take hold of life. Law is fully operative in exception. Sovereignty's power resides in the state of exception produced by the legal order, which in turn draws its life from sovereign decision. The sovereign, much like the *homo sacer*, is a point of exteriority to the legal order. The difference is, while the sovereign constitutes the law by its decision of exception, the *homo sacer* brings out the specificity of law by being reduced to the site of the law's interminable gaze and violence. As the sacred, *homo sacer* occupies a space in-between the profane and transcendent. Peter Fitzpatrick observes: "These two dimensions can only be combined in *homo sacer* because of the confident reference beyond, because of a sacrifice which has brought the beyond into the measure and contingency of a profane world."[7] This beyond one can argue is as much the sovereign as the law—or better, the sovereign as law. In what follows, I shall focus on two aspects of Agamben's more explicitly political thought around biopolitics: his conception of sovereignty and the exception, and his understanding of the interrelation of life and law in the notion of 'bare life'.

First, however, let us ask: did the *homo sacer* ever exist? Or, at least, in the way Agamben frames him to be? Agamben is evasive: "It appears that we are confronted with a limit concept of the Roman social order."[8] James Leigh Stratton-Davidson in his authoritative book, *Problems of Roman Criminal Law* (1912), argues that the *homo sacer* did actually exist. But the meaning he gives is significantly different. He has the following to say: when a devotee of early Roman religion committed a serious crime, he was called a *homo sacer*. He was taken out of the jurisdiction of the religious authorities and left to the local magistrate and wasn't allowed the benefit of the so-called 'right' to appeal. Very often the religious authorities disputed the justice meted out to the *homo sacer* by the magistrate. Stratton-Davidson sees in the *homo sacer* the point at which the pre-legal passed into the properly constituted legal in imperial Rome. If the decision to take the plaintiff out of the jurisdiction of the religious authorities to the purview of the local magistrate is the moment of the reduction of life to *homo sacer*, then the figure belongs to a moment of transition from the pre-legal to the legal. Read in this light, *homo sacer* is indeed, even historically, a 'threshold' figure that Agamben considers it to be who indicates to a skewed fact that Agamben upholds—that is, by being located inside the law fully we run the risk of losing all rights at a particular point of emergency. This for him is the constitutive lacuna of the modern law.

Agamben makes a crucial reversal of Aristotle's distinction between bare life (*zoé*) and good life (*bios*). For Aristotle, *zoé* is that life that man as a living animal shares with other living animals, while *bios* signifies man's entry into the world of ratiocination, of the question of justice. *Bios* is therefore the sphere of language, the sphere that differentiates man from other animals. For millennia, this was the difference on which Western political thought was based. Agamben reverses the distinction to argue that the work of politics is precisely to monopolize the sphere of the living—merely living (*zoé*)—to reduce man to his bare existence, and more: to ceaselessly threaten with the prospect of annihilation: "Human life is politicized only through an unconditional power of death."[9] Therefore Agamben's focus is not on the life adorned with rights, but the life that fails to achieve humanity itself, "the remains as it were of our becoming moral, just and political. I say 'as it were' because political life's condition of possibility is the non-exclusion of bare life." And a little later: "There is politics because man is the living being who, in language, separates and opposes himself to his own bare life and, at the same time, maintains himself in relation to that bare life in an inclusive exclusion."[10] This erasural bond Agamben will call 'threshold': political life's relation with the non-relational. Politics must again and again enact its distinction with the bare life and thus again and again bring bare life within its scope as excluded.

Just as in the Foucauldian *dispositive* the pathological is mapped to indicate what normal is, for Agamben the sovereign too defines and creates the normal through the act of exception; exception is the distinctive feature of the sovereign, for only he has the right to decide on it. Early in modernity, Hobbes viewed the state of nature (or, premodern) not as a real epoch chronologically prior to the foundation of the City, but a principle internal to the City itself: *tanquam dissoluta*, 'as if it were dissolved.' It can emerge anytime and therefore proper vigil is essential. In continuity with Hobbes's formulation, the sovereign's precise function for Agamben lies in deciding what constitutes public order and security and whether the social order has been disturbed and conditions of chaos prevail. This decision is the immutable core of sovereignty.

Agamben endorses Schmitt's position that the exception is "that which cannot be subsumed; it defies general codification, but simultaneously reveals a specifically juristic element: the ability to decide in absolute purity. Therein resides the essence of the state's sovereignty, which must be juristically defined as the monopoly to decide."[11] Since for the legal order to operate there needs be an understanding of what constitutes the normal—and since this depends on the decision of the sovereign—the sovereign decision on the norm and the exception itself creates the basis for the law. Agamben calls sovereignty the 'border-line' concept of order and the exception. As he states, "what is at issue in the sovereign exception is not so much the control or neutralization of an excess as the creation and definition of the very space in which the juridico-political order can have validity."[12] People are given rights, there are norms and orders to follow. They can claim those rights if they wish and are supposed to follow those norms and order, knowing fully well that exception may erupt any moment.

Much like Hobbes' understanding of *tanquam dissoluta* in the City, therefore, in Agamben's scheme too there is the ever-present possibility of chaos in order and this possibility is determined by the sovereign's decision. Since the exception is the condition of law's operation, far from being outside to the realm of the law, it is cardinal to the law; it is what in a sense makes law possible. In other words, the law resides in its own suspension. Law can apply but it can also apply in not applying to a specific case. The exception is included within the scope of the law, points out Catherine Mills, precisely through its exclusion from it. "The effective consequence of this is that the exception confirms the rule by its being other than the normal reference of the rule."[13] This Agamben calls, 'inclusive exclusion'.[14] He concludes from this special grammar of the exception that "the rule applies to the exception in no longer applying, in withdrawing from it."[15]

To explain its relation with exception, Agamben locates the figure of the sovereign in a special topological arrangement, an architectonic that enables it to be at once inside and outside the juridical order. A sovereign is sovereign only in the act to exclude, while to exclude one has to be first included. To elaborate this position, Agamben quotes Carl Schmitt's key claim: "Sovereign is he who decides on the state of exception."[16] The essence of sovereignty, Schmitt continues, is not the monopoly of sanction or rule, but rather the monopoly of *decision*. Exception is the 'fundamental localization' (*Ortung*), inaugurating the topological complex of 'outside-inside'.[17]

Towards the end of his first Tanner Memorial Lecture, "Omnes et Singulatim: Towards a Criticism of Political Reason," Foucault observes: "Our societies proved to be really demonic since they happened to combine those two games—the city/citizen game and the shepherd/flock game—in what we call the modern states."[18] This is one of Foucault's typically cryptic, dense one-liners that he does not so much care to explain. Explaining the possible genealogy for this two-pronged modern power, Dotan Leshem argues that political sovereignty (as conceived by Schmitt and Agamben) and economic pastorship are distinct from one another in that the latter's primary relation is one of inclusion, while that of the former is exclusion. Consequently, the effects generated by the suspension of law are diametrically opposed: economic pastorship suspends the law in order to redeem both the individual and society as a whole by means of leniency and inclusion.[19] Agamben tropes the threshold state of inclusive exclusion as 'being-outside and yet belonging'. This is the point of convergence through the topology of exception between the homo sacer and the sovereign. For the homo sacer, it is the location of outside that is essence of of his being, which for being outside must first be included. For the sovereign, analogously but conversely, and much like Hobbes' Leviathan, he must remain outside the 'society' that he himself helps to constitute. Leshem: "Sovereignty operates in the mode of inclusive exclusion by banishing from the political body, while pastorship includes those who were excluded by validation of membership in the living body of Christ as a kind of exclusionary inclusion."[20] For Foucault, this transference between the political and the economic is the sign that within political sovereignty there emerges in modernity the civil society in the model of the economy which basically functioned as limiting the exercise of sovereign power by accommodating the rationality of the governed. For Agamben, on the contrary, it indicates that total capture of the outsider by making sure that they are included in the first place.

In his essay, "Desperate Vacuum," Peter Fitzpatrick tries to map 'that perilous but utterly necessary space' of liberal legality between the project of Enlightenment with its incurable energy in discovering the general (universal) in the particular (Europe) and 'the recalcitrant, intractable nature' outside the operative sway of this project. Reading in the light of Fitzpatrick, a certain pact between republican nations that Kant was talking of in "Perpetual Peace," then becomes the inside/Universal/Europe. Outside would be what lies outside it—namely, areas of Europe and other parts of the civilized world where this republican order will take time to come about (a temporal project), and the vastness that lies outside the civilized world, where it is held, tenuously, between the temporal and the anthropological and for which the outcomes would ever be uncertain. Historically speaking, the space that hinges between the historical and the anthropological is the space of exception, the colonial space. This is the original nomos, where nomos means not simply 'a "taking of land" (*Landesnahme*), the determination of a juridical (*Ordnung*) and a territorial (*Ortung*) order—but above all a "*presa del fuori*" (a "taking of the outside"), an exception'.[21]

Agamben points to the aporia of law and politics as they function in modern constitutions of nation-states: "If exceptional measures are the result of periods of political crisis and as such must be understood on political and not juridico-constitutional grounds, then they find themselves in the paradoxical position of being juridical measures that cannot be understood in legal terms, and the state of exception appears as the legal form of what cannot have legal forms."[22] The state of exception is not a special kind of law (like the law of war); rather, insofar as it involves suspension of the juridical order itself, it defines law's threshold or limit concept. For instance, on November 13, 2001, the president of the USA issued a decree which authorized the indefinite detention and trial by military commissions (not to be confused with the military tribunals provided by the law of war) of noncitizens suspected of involvement in terrorist activities. The USA Patriot Act issued by the US Senate on October 26, 2001, had already allowed the attorney general to 'take into custody' any alien suspected of activities that endangered the national security of the USA; however, as per the Act, within seven days the alien had to be either released or charged with the violation of immigration laws or some other criminal offence. What was new in President Bush's order is that it radically erased any legal status of the individual, thus producing a legally unnameable and unclassifiable being. Those captured as terrorists in Iraq did not enjoy the status of POWs as defined by the Geneva Convention, they did not even have the status of persons charged with a crime according to American laws. Neither prisoners nor persons accused, but simply 'detainees', they are the object of pure *de facto* rule. They are removed from the law by taking permission of the law itself. At Guantanamo Bay, bare life reaches its maximum indeterminacy.[23]

Here two things need to be kept in mind: one, exceptional measures are not a carry-over of the past absolutist state, but the creation of the democratic-revolutionary traditions that brought modern states into being. Second, even though exception is not codified in law, for exception to work, at least in the sense postulated by Agamben, it needs a legal, constitutional order in the first place. Here it may be interesting to compare Agamben's notion of the state of exception with the influential African political theorist, Achille Mbembe's notion of 'necropolitics'. In his 2004 essay, 'Necropolitics',[24] Mbembe maintains that the Foucauldian notion of biopower is insufficient to account for contemporary forms of subjugation of life to the power of death one experiences in certain sectors of international political life today. His examples come predominantly from the fringe states of postcolonial Africa that do not have monopoly of violence due to the eruption of many non-state players clustered around mineral extraction and export, activities that are linked to multinational conglomerates bent on taking full advantage of the unstable economies of those states. In such zones, Mbembe argues, death is arbitrary and commonplace as are those who constitute those roving marauding bands. In his bid to explain such emerging phenomena, Mbembe coins the term, necropolitics, borrowing, as he maintains, from Agamben's understanding of the modern cusp between biopolitics and sovereignty. But the examples Mbembe cites do not, strictly speaking, fall within the terms of Agamben's analysis because state of exception—as defined by Agamben—requires a constitution to be in place; the charge of the concept is precisely its juridicality. The extra-juridical, for Agamben, is not non-juridical and anarchy, but very much premised on the juridical.

As a matter of fact, Agamben is not so much interested in law as such, unless a specific article of the Constitution refers to the temporary seizure of legal procedures (like Article 48 of the Weimar Republic used eighteen times, as Agamben points out, during the republic's fourteen-year reign—i.e., 1919-1933). Otherwise, his interest by and large lies in decrees like the decree for the protection of the people and the state issued by Hitler as soon as he came to power. By virtue of such a decree Hitler could suspend certain basic rights and liberties. The concept of the state of emergency was never mentioned but the decree remained in force till the last day of Nazi rule, thus making impossible to distinguish between the rule and its exception.[25] Exception cannot be just a one time reality. It must first create its sphere of reference to 'normal' life, for which it must have a repetitive nature. It should be a style of ruling, a regular part of conducting affairs.[26] The logic of exception turns politics into a pure biopolitical agenda.

We conclude the discussion on *homo sacer* by pointing to two crucial analogues. First, the link-line between the sovereign, the *homo sacer* and the exception. It is exception, one ought to remember, that links sovereign and *homo sacer* together; exception is what constitutes both the sovereign and the *homo sacer*. Agamben defines exception in *State of Exception* much the same way he defines the *homo sacer* in his earlier book: "what cannot be included in the whole of which it is a member and cannot be a member of the whole in which it is always already included."[27] Second, the conceptual link between biopolitics and sovereignty which Agamben calls 'ban' (from Jean Luc Nancy's notion of 'abandon'). The originary moment of political relation is the 'ban': the establishment of a 'borderline' and the inauguration of a space that is deprived of the protection of the law. To ban the juridico-political community from the juridical and yet keep it within the scope of the latter is the primal act that defines the sovereign. As Agamben makes it clear, to be banned does not simply mean to be expelled; its basic political purpose is to expose and to threaten. "That which is excluded" Mills points out "is not simply set outside the law and made indifferent or irrelevant to it, but rather abandoned by it, where to be abandoned means to be subjected to the unremitting force of the law while the law simultaneously withdraws from its subject."[28] It is not so much the control or neutralization of an excess that the sovereign is concerned with as "the creation and definition of the very space in which the juridico-political order can have validity."[29]

The Musselman

Historically what manifests this state most acutely for Agamben is the epitomic figure of the *Musselman* of the Camp. Even though by 'Camp' Agamben means Auschwitz—i.e., the cruellest of them all—perhaps it is worthwhile to remember that the word is primarily used as a concept metaphor, one indicating the blurred threshold between juridical rule and bare life. In the state of exception, the law effectively coincides with life itself, such that fact and norm enter into indistinction, and the form of law can be understood as 'being in force without significance'. By this phrase Agamben indicates a situation in which "the law is valid precisely insofar as it commands nothing and has become unrealizable."[30] In 'being in force without significance', the law is emptied of all content or significance, and its suspension is precisely its mode of application. Mills observes: "It is not that the law no longer applies as in a state of lawlessness; rather, while applying, the law cannot do so in any concrete or immediate sense since it has lost any apparent meaning or intelligibility."[31] Agamben borrowed this phrase from the Judaic philosopher, Gershom Scholem. Benjamin, it may be pointed out, had reservations about Scholem's position on the law. For him, a radical conflation of life and law makes law unable to rule over life since it loses its claim to transcendence. Agamben, however, maintains that this conflation, this indistinction of life and law is real for both life under 'a law without significance' and life in sovereign exception. "In the state of exception, law without significance passes into life while life always subsists in relation to the law."[32] This indistinction Agamben finds maximized in the Nazi camp —at the same time, it remains an ever present possibility in the way modernity organizes political life.[33]

Agamben notes that apart from the decrees, the introduction of 'indeterminate clauses' into the law in the twentieth century —deciding in accord with 'good morals' or 'public security and order,' for example— rendered obsolete the illusion of a law that would *a priori* be able to regulate all cases and all situations and that judges would have to limit themselves simply to applying. This modality of blurring the distinction between fact and law reaches its climax in the Camp, the quintessential expression of the process of reducing the human to *homo sacer*. For Agamben, Auschwitz is the inevitable manifestation and ever renewed possibility of sovereign power and the production of bare life. Again, the paradigmatic figure of bare life in the Camp is the *Musselman*, a person rendered living dead due to treatment rendered in the camp, including sustained nutritional deprivation and psychological torture. Between those who survived the Camps and those who perished as soon as they arrived in Gas Chambers, were the clusters of walking dead: "an anonymous mass, continually renewed and always identical, of non-men who march and labour in silence, the divine spark dead within them, already too empty to really suffer. One hesitates to call them living: one hesitates to call their death death, in the face of which they have no fear, as they are too tired to understand."[34] Wolfgang Sofsky, in his book *The Order of Terror: The Concentration Camp*, describes the stepwise annihilation of human beings, what he calls the transmogrification of the *condito humana*: "Their skulls seemed elongated; their noses dripped constantly, mucus running down their chins. Their eyeballs had sunk deep into their sockets; their gaze was glazed. Their limbs moved slowly, hesitantly, almost mechanically ... Their increasing emaciation eradicated the dividing line between life and death."[35] Seeing the *Musselmäner* (the plural of *Musselman*) from afar, one had the impression of seeing Arabs in prayer. This image was held to be responsible—the original instigation—for being so named, a cluster of staggering, stooping corpses, a bundle of physical functions in its last convulsions.[36]

This is how Moses Schulstein, the Yiddish poet, writes about the Auschwitz in the poem, "I saw a mountain":

We are the shoes, we are the last witness.
We are shoes from grandchildren and grandfathers,
from Prague, Paris, and Amsterdam,

> *and because we are only made of fabric and leather*
> *and not of blood and flesh, each one of us avoided the hellfire.*

What interests Agamben primarily in Auschwitz is not the pile of shoes or other artefacts that shocked the sensibility of the poet or the countless dead bodies lying all around the place that numerous films and paintings would later depict, not the various surgical experiments performed on the living bodies of the inmates for 'the advancement of scientific knowledge' which the Holocaust museum so graphically illustrates but the figure of the *Musselman*, the moving threshold in which man passed into non-man, yet kept performing the bare rituals of living. In the vacuous, emaciated body of the *Musselman* was inscribed the law in its pure form, law that is 'all the more pervasive for its total lack of content' and has force precisely in this lack. It is in relation to witnessing that *Musselman* becomes important for Agamben.

Primo Levi has tried to show that the camps were beyond the understanding of good and evil, they were simply incomprehensible. But Agamben argues that simply to deny the *Musselman*'s humanity would be to accept the verdict of the SS and to create conditions for its recurrence. The *Musselman* is the site of an experiment in which morality and humanity are called into question, not extermination as such but the continuous production of material to be destroyed. Living becomes a performance of death. Commenting on Levi's *The Drowned and the Saved*, Berel Lang observed that the *Musselman* and its muteness signified not a loss of life, but of death itself.[37] Hurled to the precipice of life, life and death are blurred. So death loses its distinction, it becomes banal. As a mere physical presence without any remaining trace of humanity, the *Musselman*'s body becomes the signifier of the Nazi lexicon, the limit sovereign power cannot exceed: 'the invisible ark of biopower'[38] as Agamben puts it. Here we confront the primary problem of witnessing, or, to put it more emphatically, we confront the impossibility of testimony.[39] It is here that the ethical/legal project of Auschwitz lies, for Agamben.

For Primo Levi, the problem of the witness and the survivors comes from this very point of impossibility:

> I must repeat: we the survivors, are not true witnesses. ... We survivors are not only an exiguous (meager) but also an anomalous minority; we are those who by their prevarications or abilities or good luck did not touch the bottom. Those who did so, those who saw the Gordon, have not returned to tell about it or have returned mute, but they are the "Muslims," the submerged, the complete witnesses, the ones whose deposition would have a general significance. They are the rule, we are exception.[40]

For Agamben, however, the *Musselman* as the testimony of the survivor for and on behalf of the un-dead, offers an example of the embodiment of the ethical moment in the remainder (*le reste*), the trace and aporia of a relationship with the Other. It needs to be remembered here that Agamben does not exactly pose the problem of testimony as an ethical problem beyond suggesting that it is an aporia. Much of the holocaust literature does this, but it may be wrong to collapse Agamben's work in this sense with that of Friedlander or Lyotard.[41] In the preface to *Remnants of Auschwitz*, Agamben speaks about the inadequacy of available ethical categories. He says he would be content if in his study of the testimony he has "erected some signposts allowing future cartographers of the new ethical territory to orient themselves."[42] Agamben thus returns to a consideration of the intimate connections between language and death. To reconfigure the legal and ethical status of the only possible witnesses to Auschwitz, law, language and death must all be rethought, and thought together. The possibility of constructing a language of death which is neither a dead language nor a language of the dead: this is the ethical challenge that the mute impossible witness in the figure of the *Musselman* leaves for us.

We conclude with an attempt to link Agamben's deliberations on the questions of exception as worked out in the figures of *homo sacer* and *Musselman* with the wider question of the political. Alexander Garcia Duttmann begins his essay "Never before, always already: notes on Agamben and the category of relation" with this nuanced reflection: "To that which was never before we cannot relate, just as we cannot relate to that which has always already been."[43] The moment we relate to that which was never before, Duttmann explains, we have transformed it into something recognizable; similarly, the moment we relate to that which has always already been, we have made it into something new, something that never existed before. In other words, to relate is to accept that not all can be related, not all can be said, that there will be a remainder just as there will be a zone of the possible unexplored. So remainder does not make relation impossible, rather it is the very crux of relation, the silent folds within language itself and not an escape from language per se. For Agamben, this erasural identity of relation faces a void in a biopolitical context. He rules out therefore the notion of the political as the polycentric space of staking claims to denied citizenship, the terrain of the subversive or transversal of agonism. To come out of the ceaseless production of bare bodies in contemporary life, Agamben evokes the eschatological, messianic time when a new form-of-life would achieve a total overturning of the conditions of abandonment. This for him is the necessary condition of redemption from biopolitical capture. The only possible link to this messianic times with the present is perhaps the indestructibility of the human, or as he says, 'something always remains'.

NOTES

1. For a discussion of Agamben's subsequent books on political sovereignty like *Regno e la Gloria: per una genealogia teologica dell'economia e del governo* ('The Reign and the Glory: For a Theological Genealogy of Economy and Government'; as yet untranslated), *The Signature of All Things: On Method* (2009) and *The Sacrament of Language: Archaeology of the Oath* (2010), see Jeffrey Bussolini, "Critical Encounter Between Giorgio Agamben and Michel Foucault" and Anke Snoek, "Agamben's Foucault: An overview," *Foucault Studies*, No. 10, November 2010.
2. Foucault, *History of Sexuality*, Volume 1, p. 143. See also, Catherine Mills, *The Philosophy of Agamben*, pp. 58-59.
3. "The Foucauldian thesis will then have to be corrected or, at least, completed, in the sense that what characterizes modern politics is not so much the inclusion of *zoç* in the *polis*—which is, in itself, absolutely ancient—nor simply the fact that life as such becomes a principal object of the projections and calculations of State power. Instead the decisive fact is that, together with the process by which the exception everywhere becomes the rule, the realm of bare life—which is originally situated at the margins of the political order—gradually begins to coincide with the political realm, and exclusion and inclusion, outside and inside, *bios* and *zoç,* right and fact, enter into a zone of irreducible indistinction." (*Homo Sacer*, p. 9).
4. *Homo Sacer*, p. 6.
5. One example of such reciprocity is the Hobbesian social pact of taking away some rights from the subject-citizens and in exchange assuring them security and protection. Another example is Rousseau's general will.
6. Thomas Lemke, ""A Zone of Indistinction": A Critique of Giorgio Agamben's Concept of Biopolitics," Outlines—*Critical Social Studies* 7(1), 2005, p. 6 (http:/ /www.outlines.dk/contents/Outlines051/Lemke05.pdf).
7. Peter Fitzpatrick, "Bare Sovereignty: *Homo sacer* and the Insistence of Law," *Theory and Event* 5:2, 2001.
8. Ibid., p. 48.
9. Ibid., p. 56.
10. *Homo Sacer*, p. 8.
11. Schmitt, *Political Theology: Four Chapters on the Concept of Sovereignty*, p. 13.
12. *Homo Sacer*, p. 19.
13. Mills, Catherine, p. 63.
14. See *Homo Sacer,* pp. 19-20.
15. *Homo Sacer*, p. 28.
16. *Homo Sacer*, p. 11.
17. See Claudio Minca, "Giorgio Agamben and the new biopolitical nomos," *Geografiska Annaler*, Series B: Human Geography, December, 2006, pp. 389-90.
18. Foucault, Michel, "Omnes et Singulatim": toward a critique of political reason," Power, Ed. James D Faubion, The New Press, New York, 2000, p. 311.
19. Dotan Leshem, "Embedding Agamben's Critique of Foucault: The theological

and pastoral origins of governmentality," *Theory, Culture & Society,* Vol. 32(3), 2015. p. 109.

20. Ibid., p. 106.
21. See Minca cited above, p. 390.
22. "The State of Exception as a Paradigm of Government" in *State of Exception*, p. 1 To note, such understanding of exception matches well with the Emergency declared by Indira Gandhi in 1975.
23. For a discussion on this, Judith Butler: *Precarious lives: powers of mourning and violence.*
24. *Public Culture*, 15 (1): pp. 11-40.
25. See, *State of Exception*, pp. 25-6.
26. Agamben: (T)he juridical order does not originally present itself simply as sanctioning a transgressive fact but instead constitutes itself through the repetition of the same act without any sanction, that is, as an exceptional case. This is not a punishment of this first act, but rather represents its inclusion in the juridical order, violence as a primordial juridical fact (*permittit enim lexparem vindictam,* "for the law allows equitable vengeance" [Pompeius Festus, *De verborum significations* 496. 15]). In this sense, the exception is the originary form of law. (1998; p. 22).
27. *Homo Sacer,* p. 25.
28. Mills, p. 62.
29. *Homo sacer*, p. 19.
30. *Potentialites*, p. 172.
31. Mills, p. 63.
32. Mills, p. 64.
33. From Agamben's standpoint, therefore, the so-called 'relief camps'—say for riot or flood victims—would not qualify as camp in the first place.
34. Levi, Primo. 1987. *If This Is A Man—The Truce*, p. 96. Here it may be mentioned that those who were gassed were also best looked after, nutritionally and in terms of basic amenities—perhaps the harshest irony of the camp logic and the most effective way of making death banal.
35. p. 199.
36. The use of the term *Musselman* has caused considerable controversy, especially after 9/11 when clearly the Muslims are the new Jews of the western world. In any case, it has been pointed out that the word used by camp guards should not have been used without any qualifier.
37. See Lang: *Holocaust Representation: Art within the limits of History and Ethics.*
38. "(T)he absolutely unwitnessable, invisible ark of biopower," *Remnants of Auschwitz*, p. 156.
39. By inference, one could say that it is not simply the problem of putting the subaltern within the framework of history, of recorded history, but more profound: Can language capture what expired from language?
40. Levi, *The Drowned and the Saved*, pp. 83-4.
41. See Saul Friedlander edited, *Probing the Limits of Representation: Nazism and the 'Final Solution"*.

42. *Remnants of Auschwitz*, p. 13.
43. "Never Before, Always Already: Notes on Agamben and the Category of Relation," *ANGELAKI: Journal of Theoretical Humanities*, Vol. 6, No. 3, December 2001, p. 3.

REFERENCES

Agamben, Giorgio, *Homo Sacer*, Stanford University Press, Stanford, 1998.

Agamben, Giorgio, *Potentialites*, Stanford University Press, Stanford, 2000.

Agamben, Giorgio, *Remnants of Auschwitz: The Witness and the Archive*, Zone, New York, 2002.

Agamben, Giorgio, *State of Exception*, University of Chicago Press, Chicago, 2005.

Bussolini, Jeffrey, "Critical Encounter Between Giorgio Agamben and Michel Foucault," *Foucault Studies*, No. 10, November 2010.

Butler, Judith, *Precarious lives: powers of mourning and violence*, Verso, London, 2004.

Fitzpatrick, Peter, "Bare Sovereignty: *Homo sacer* and the Insistence of Law," *Theory and Event* 5:2, 2001.

Foucault, Michel, *History of Sexuality*, Vol. 1, Vintage, New York, 1990.

Friedlander, Saul (ed), *Probing the Limits of Representation: Nazism and the "Final Solution,"* Harvard University Press, Cambridge, 1992.

Lang, Berel, *Holocaust Representation: Art within the limits of History and Ethics*, Johns Hopkins University Press, Baltimore, 2003.

Lemke, Thomas, ' "A Zone of Indistinction": A Critique of Giorgio Agamben's Concept of Biopolitics,' Outlines – Critical Social Studies 7(1), 2005, p. 6 http://www.outlines.dk/contents/Outlines051/Lemke05.pdf).

Leshem, Dotan, "Embedding Agamben's Critique of Foucault: The Theological and Pastoral Origins of Governmentality," *Theory, Culture & Society*, 2015, Vol. 32(3) 93–113.

Levi, Primo, *If This Is A Man – The Truce*, Abacus, New York, 1988.

Levi, Primo, *The Drowned and the Saved*, Vintage, New York, 1989.

Mbembe, Achille, "Necropolitics," *Public Culture*, 15 (1), 2003.

Mills, Catherine, *The Philosophy of Agamben,* McGill-Queen's University Press, 2008.

Minca, Claudio, "Giorgio Agamben and the new biopolitical nomos," *Geografiska Annaler*, Series B: Human Geography, 2006.

Schmitt, Carl, *Political Theology: Four Chapters on the Concept of Sovereignty* University of Chicago Press, Chicago, 2006.

Snoek, Anke, "Agamben's Foucault: An overview," *Foucault Studies*, No. 10, 2010.

Sofsky, Wolfgang, *The Order of Terror: The Concentration Camp*, Princeton University Press, Princeton, 1999.

11

Aporias of Ethics: Looking at the 'Wholly Other'

Prasenjit Biswas

Derrida's idea that ethical undecidability about the correctness of an action follows from the law of the Other in me, a me surrounded by the wholly Other.[1] That consciousness of being oneself is never a being 'in itself' gives rise to divergent positions between a sense of responsibility and a sense of autonomy in an ethical agency. How does one speak about such an ethical agency in terms of an already formed subjectivity? Is such ethical agency formed on the basis of sociality of Subjects, or is it formed only as an Other to itself? The question can be answered by identifying complex phenomenology of human subjectivity as it developed from Hegel to Heidegger to Derrida and Agamben.

Hegel's 'Social' Subject

Hegel's reading of Kant's notion of Consciousness as noumenal being, a being that is in-itself and also a being of in-itself expounds the latter 'in-itself' only as a being-for-consciousness, which radically alters the very character of consciousness as a *being-toward in-itself of the Consciousness.*[2] Such a being is 'being' of conscious facts, as in psychology, while at the same time, it remains a being that possesses such conscious facts. Such a being cannot anymore be the being of 'in-itself' as in-itself is now altered into the 'being' of in-itself, which is Consciousness itself. Although Hegel considers this transformation of in-itself into consciousness, which is no longer a being-in-itself, which rather is a being-for-itself as *dialectical*, yet one has to probably make a distinction between *transcendental* dialectic and *immanent* dialectic. The transcendental dialectic concerns itself with the independence of being, while the immanent dialectic concerns itself with an interplay between being and consciousness in order to situate the outcome of this play. Kant can be credited with maintaining a distinction between analytic of Judgments and the function of pure reason, while he didn't venture into how such a distinction itself is possible because of the dialectical character of consciousness that overcomes the duality between transcendental and empirical/sensible. This combination of 'immanence' and 'overcoming' the diversity of phenomenological datum about consciousness assumes the role of a 'metaphysical substance' that belongs to a definite 'opening in the space.'[3]

For a post-Kantian Hegelianism of this sort, the overcoming of the duality between 'transcendental' and 'empirical' lies in being-in-the-situation, which is a collation of multiple possibilities that gives an ontological force to our will-to-know in order to count the multiple as one cardinal entity. Such an ontological force is explained by Heidegger, when he says, 'Metaphysics, insofar as it always represents only beings as beings [*das Seiende als das Seiende vorstelt*], does not recall Being itself [*das Sein selbst*].'[4] This *annulment* of Being in order to respond to the call of being, which is an ontological situation of naming Being as no-thing or void, which at the same time is the *difference* between beings and being-as-such. The description, 'being-in-the-situation' is the mark of this difference such that the *event* as present(ed) 'belongs to that-which-is-not-being-qua-being.'[5] But such a difference is the predominance of one signifying order over other, one can call it a 'presentation' of the presented as different from that which is present—an ontological duality that simultaneously denies the limits of presentation as well as transgression of the limit. In Heidegger's words,

> What is distinctive about man resides in the fact that, as the one whose essence it is to think, open toward Being, he is placed before the latter, remains related to Being and thus corresponds to it. Man properly is this *relation of correspondence*, and he is only this. 'Only': this does not mean a limitation, but an overabundance. In man, there prevails a belonging to Being, a belonging which listens to Being, because it is appropriated over to being.[6]

This foundational relationship of correspondence between 'human' and 'being' is a relationship between Beings's coming to presence and human's giving themselves to the presence, which is not necessarily a 'sacrifice', but a gesture of a giving of an 'it' that belongs to a prior Hegelian 'substance-subject'[7] that contains a differentiation between itself and its positioning itself as the being of a subject. A 'substance-subject' as a double movement toward being and conscious subjectivity, necessarily divided itself as a remainder to presence. This takes us to a plasticity of subjectivity that establishes the Heideggerian correspondence between being and consciousness, which later manifests itself in the form of a 'future' thought or subjectivity. Such a future thought is constituted by a temporal disjunction between prior determination of Being as a giving-to and a consequent affirmation of presence that leads one to a question, *how can the transition from the in-itself to the for-itself open a dialectic between being and consciousness*? The answer can be formulated in two different but inter-related ways:

1. Essenceless Subjects, called being-for-consciousness of the in-itself, which is 'pure being', which merely ascends without descending into the depths of subjectivity to become a Subject.[8] Such a being is a neuter, neither this nor that, it is rather 'to be in the middle of all that' and 'to be in the center'.[9] Such a positioning of being has too many *correspondences* so much so that there are as many idioms as there are things. The 'many' of things and entities correspond to 'many' idioms of Being, which is essenceless-by-play [*ein wesenloses beyherspielen*].
2. Essenceless subjects assume an architectonic, a 'totality of relations' within an episteme[10] that embodies the signifiers of correspondences between being and consciousness within a particular period or discursive context.

These two ways are inter-related as a binary relation between play and form, as Aristotle conceived it in terms of *aletheia* or disclosure. Such an idea is made further nuanced to include an idea of a ploylectic determination of Subject that lies at the *crossroads* of being and play. This determination remains polylectic on the ground that it not only involves the subjectivity of the singular self, but what accompanies the singular self is the disclosure of a plurality of beings that does not yield a place to a singular subjecthood.

Thrownness as Ethical Destiny in Dasein's Hold

This is explained further by Heidegger as Dasein's projection upon its own possibilities, which is explained by him as 'the possible impossibility of its own existence.[11] This possible impossibility is manifest in Dasein's anxiety that only manifests 'nothing' that produces a gap between Dasein's pre-ontological understanding of itself and the way the world appears to Dasein. The very being of the Dasein does not find its significance in the world. Heidegger expresses the state of anxiety as a double consciousness: (1) the presence of the being of entities in the world that makes it manifest as 'nothing of the world', which is an 'attunement' of being and (2) the being of 'nothing of the world' is disclosed only in anxiety and boredom, that is, an inner strife of 'being there.'[12] Both (1) and (2) taken together give us the existential reality of perpetual anxiety over the state of being, which is also the historical condition for Dasein's existence. This is stated by Heidegger as existence of Being-in-the-World in relation to Being-with-the-Other, which Heidegger called 'destiny' in a historical sense,

> The [destiny] is how we designate the historizing of the community, of a people. Destiny is not something that puts itself together out of individual fates, any

> more than being-with-one-another can be conceived as the occurring together of several subjects. Our fates have already been guided in advance, in our being with one another in the same world and in our resoluteness for definite possibilities.[13]

The notion of 'destiny' arises in Being-with that marks a common and shareable state of existence for Dasein. The fate of Dasein is guided in advance in so far as it shares a common destiny with other beings-in-the-world, which is the temporal-historical source of Dasein's fate. Such a fate is common, although it is not necessary that Daseins have a common identity. In a sense, Dasein simultaneously faces its being in concrete disclosure of historical moments as well as it transcends this facticity of being by way of overcoming its own no-thingness in the concrete role as an actor, with the possibility of being a victim or a victor. What is guided in advance as a common destiny appears in the form of the possibility that it has inherited, which is disclosed as a 'choice' for the Dasein, which Heidegger terms as a 'situation' in which the Dasein is thrown into. Such a 'thrownness', paradoxically, discloses one or other possibility for the Dasein as a projected fate that takes over its being there, which again at the same time, turns into 'attunement', which is a state of being 'anxious'. Anxiety is directed to the world without a specific object, while fear is directed to a specific object. In anxiety, the Dasein is indifferent towards entities, but the significance of entities is intact and it stands in purposive interrelations. Heidegger diagnoses that in anxiety, the world is turned insignificant and the Dasein collapses into itself. In anxiety nothing matters, there is no significance, no wholeness of relevance, so in a sense the world is not there. Heidegger speaks of 'the nothing of the world'. However, being affected by the insignificance of entities as a whole is quite different from experiencing no entities at all. Insignificance is not absence. "The nothing of the world ... does not mean that in anxiety we experience the absence of the innerworldly occurrent. It must be encountered, so that it can have no relevance at all and can show itself in an empty mercilessness." In their insignificance entities are very much there, they show themselves in their strangeness. Just as the indifference of deep boredom refers to Dasein's possibilities, anxiety, in its own way, comes with a kind of referring. It refers to entities as they are in themselves. As their significance recedes, they light up as entities in themselves, i.e. as entities that are independent of Dasein's possibilities. In pursuing a post-Kantian Hegelianism, one can characterize these entities as 'topological' that are encountered by Dasein in the crossroads of play between being and consciousness. Such entities in themselves acquire historicity by losing their essence as they annul the possibility of response.

This lack of response makes a reference to entities as a whole and not to any specific entity within the world. It does not refer Dasein to any possibilities, i.e. it does not refer Dasein's basic understanding of a way to be. This distinction that Heidegger draws between Dasein's possibilities and anxiety is reflected in the distinction between 'mere facticity' and 'historicity'. The former is termed as 'ontic' and the latter as 'ontological'. The 'ontic' is the non-objectifiable ground of experience that discloses the significance of the world in which the factical Dasein is said to 'live'. The 'ontological' is what is disclosed as 'possibility' in Dasein's Being-with, the modality of which lies in the encounter with the 'nothing of the world'. The encounter assumes the form of anxiety and/or 'not being-at-home' through which the world is disclosed to the Dasein as destiny.

Time Flying in Agamben

A very different notion of temporality arises here that even surpasses the Daein's destiny by way of the experience of limit as it arises in representation of reality and time in human subjectivity. Human subjectivity becomes the 'time *that* we ourselves are'. Following Paul's letter to the Romans, Agamben uses two different notions of time, resurrection and *Parousia*. Parousia is the second coming of Jesus at the end of time, while resurrection marks the 'end of time'. Similarly, Subject as spectator of time is a resurrected Subject at the end of experiential time of an event of 'time flying'. This resurrected subjectivity at the time of 'time flying' carries no-longer the sense of being a spectator but brings in the infinite possibility of being free of the temporal structure of consciousness and subjectivity. This is not the time of becoming Subject, as such a time has already lapsed in the spectatorial consciousness that the Subject has entered and it takes the Subject to the state of being uncaptivated beyond the 'open' to the not-yet.

The process of tracing an event is a process of undergoing the transformations that are a part of the series of heterogeneous differences that can only throw up an existential background for what is present, to itself and to the other. The particularity of what is present and the singularity of what is presented to the process of tracing is the impossibility of assuming the fullness of being in any fact or disclosure, but this impossibility brings into the field of consciousness the limits of Being's potentiality. An existentialist description of this limit takes the form of a distinction between 'potentiality-to-be' and the 'potentiality-not-to' as presented by Agamben in his reading of Existentialism.[14] Agamben's re-interpretation of Heidegger hinges on this notion of dialectic between 'potentiality-to-be' and 'potentiality-not-to' that coexist not as opposites, but as 'time-now' and 'time-that-remains.' The former brings facticity to a stop at a juncture of history with the disclosure of the potential, that is, potentiality-to-be as disclosed within the temporal horizons of a given structure of subjectivity. It is in this manner, potentiality-to-be is constitutive of history as time-now and as being-there. In contrast, time-that-remains is the time that remains after the constitution of subjectivity has reached a definite achievement in the sense of an end. In relation to this end, the historicized subject with its sense of the world arises beyond the 'horizon' of historical time that has thrown the being into a determined state of existence. As this determined state of existence is the potentiality-to-be, it does not address the *aporia* or *space of ambivalence* between the constituted subjectivity and the historicized subjectivity that emerges beyond determination. For example, in the event of Partition of Indian sub-continent in 1947, the aporia between the partitioned self/subjectivity as constituted by a chronological occurrences of events and the experiential and the lived subjectivity of being a refugee beyond the determination of history is an extremely rich resource of representation. This historicized Subject emerges in the 'operational time' that comes after the 'potential' that is realized as the "other side of Being" or "otherwise than being" (pace Levinas). In case of partition, such a potential is realized in the post-displacement search for home in an alien, if not hostile, country. This historicized subject becomes the 'logos' in the existential sense of disclosure that claims to 'realize an enunciation without any real reference' as a spectral/temporal entity. In Agamben's words,

> (...) our representation of chronological time, as the time *in which* we are, separates us from ourselves and transforms us into impotent spectators of ourselves—spectators who look at the time that flies without any time left, continually missing themselves—messianic time, an operational time in which we take hold of and achieve our representations of time, is the time *that* we ourselves are, and for this very reason, is the only real time, the only time we have.[15]

This is much more than *Dasein that* only encounters 'nothing of the world'. It is more in the sense that it distinguishes between state of existence as 'spectators of ourselves' that separates the being from the self/identity/subjectivity *and* the being that we are as represented in the temporalization of yet-to-come possibilities. The partitioned Dasein probably meets its destiny in the yet-to-come, without inheriting it from the already lived world, but in a sense by way of surpassing the lived and the realized in its non-coincidence with what their 'selves' are. Further, such an emergent subjectivity is also a contingent figure of representation, whose 'experience' can only be narrated as 'spectatorial'. As the partitioned self neither lies in the present nor in the past, its potential 'meets' what is yet-to-come in a spectatorial mode. This Agambenian twist to Dasein's possibilities sets aside the limits posed on consciousness by the ontology of no-thingness which for Heidegger is a counter-thesis of his notion of Dasein, as also it overcomes the gap between representation and reality by ascribing a different relationship with what we are. What is significant here is the space of the beyond that exists in the form of time that is yet-to-come, or the time-that-remains after the end is reached within a certain mode of being-in-the-world and/or being-for-itself. The space beyond is the messianic possibility of that which comes after the moment of historicization as an event that surpasses the potentiality-to-be by way of a surprise or an incalculable coming. How the incalculable can enter the realm of existence has been an untamable question within the notion of being qua being and being qua other. Agamben's distinction between chronological, operational and messianic time corresponds to these three Phronetic principles of Messianism. In Agamben's elucidation,

> We may now propose our first definition of messianic time: messianic time is *the time that time takes to come to an end*, or, more precisely, the time we take to bring to an end, to achieve our representation of time. This is not the line of chronological time (which was representable but unthinkable), nor the instant of its end (which was just as unthinkable); nor it is the segment cut from chronological time; rather, it is operational time pressing within the chronological time, working and transforming it from within; it is the time we need to make time end: *the time that is left us* (...).[16]

The ending of time is signified by a preparation for the future, which cannot be appropriated within the normal, as future, in Jewish Messianic thought comes with an absolute surprise. This is also a disruption of the present or the 'lived time' that is a synthesis of past, present and future. It is an 'other' time that is non-lived and extra-ordinary, a time not consistent with production and reproduction of 'real life'.

The question concerning Messianism has long occupied the place of a major thematic resource for developing an Existentialist perspective upon life, especially when it is damaged or it is in crisis. The experience of agony, holocaust, victimhood, trauma and other such states of being have been turned into a fundamental feature of the human condition, all of which either in their totality or in their partiality only disclose the limits of human existence. Such a picture only tells us that the subjects at the limit of their ability bear such dislocations simultaneously as victims as well as the 'imaging consciousness' of such victimhood. Victims of the life-situations have their being caught in a perpetual loss of a part of their own being, which they only pre-reflectively possess but do not know; while the experience of loss is already a part of being-in-the-world, i.e., already caught in a relation of intentionality. The experience of victimhood jibes with 'a pre-judicative comprehension of non-being' that acts as the ground of negative judgements and realities that inhabit the knowledge of one's own self and world. This nihilating relation of consciousness to the world is not just victim's self-knowledge, but it is made possible only because consciousness is of its very nature is a "no-thingness" that lies at the heart of being. This nihilating relation is Agamben's potentiality-not-to, without which, being-there cannot realize its own historicity, which interestingly, comes only after the realization of potentiality-to-be. Victimhood exhausts the potentiality-to-be to its nihilating end, where one is not what one is and therefore, the revival and redemption follows from such an end to emerge into that which is yet-to-come. This is the authentic experience of time from which the chronological time is derived in its identity with a given state of existence.

In its authentic mode, Consciousness appears to itself not as a thing, but as a non-being, as an 'other' with a non-self-identity. An existentialist like Sartre conceived such a non-being as being-for-other, whose being for-itself is only an act of presencing in relation to others. If being is being-for-other, then all its knowledge about itself and the world arises out of a relationship with the other. Therefore, the meaning of being lies in the nature of relationship with the other and knowing the being amounts to knowing the other. Existentialists contend that knowing oneself as an other *genetically* constitutes the otherness of one's own being. Being a victim of circumstances is being the other to one's own non-being, which the self or the subject can never own, as owning one's own being is an impossibility. This impossibility is simultaneously a relation to oneself and also it is a non-relation, as it is only a postponement or and undergoing of experiential time without 'any hold upon future'. Therefore, non-being or absence of being to itself does not allow one to be even a victim, rather the non-being appearing as a being-for-the-other provides a false essence to the state of victimhood. This false essence is experienced now as a relation to the other. In terms of Levinas, to be *being* is to be in a state of being *persecuted* by the other and for Heidegger, being-in-the-world never attains authenticity, as it can never attain its true essence. This ontological failure of being is taken to be the constituent of the very human condition that does not allow the being to attain its true nature, i.e., the desired freedom that eludes being.. This elusiveness is concomitant with experience of impossibility of the event of redemption or justice. Existentialist gave freedom a messianic image, which is always an 'yet to come', a forever waiting to make it happen. As it never comes, the agent or the subject of such messianic consciousness attempts to make this happen through their expectation and wait, i.e., they try to create another world in which it happens, an apocalypse that is conceptualized in terms of freedom and plenitude. Subjects surrounded by such existential incompleteness seek an escape route in events that are apocalyptic by their very occurrence, as if such ever-awaited moments of happening would transform the very human condition.

The human condition that allows perplexities of an ontological failure to comprehend Subject's relationship with its own modality of existence often contributes to the return of the desire of self-presence, a kind of proximity to oneself as well as to another. An idea of 'ontological sociality' marks a return to the desire of self-presencing that itself is an effect of being a subject of a participatory universalist planetary discourse. But this is a return definitely to a location different from the current space of self-affirmation, but well within the domain of proximity and alterity that never allows responsibility without equivocation and without contradiction. This characteristically distinguished domains of proximity and alterity as poles of ethical subjectivity creates a disjunction between an ethical imperative and the decision to follow it by the subject, as the subject faces an effacement of the decision to act.

For example, by way of representing the universal in the participatory agenda of global social movements of ethico-political multitudes, Levinas is posing a new challenge to a realist-foundationalist notion of Social Science as a science of alterity. What remains inarticulate in Rorty like anti-foundational critique of contextually specific social movements is a journey towards what Heidegger called 'homelessness', which possibly is a disclosure of plurality and alterity within the self-enclosed notion of self and its transcendental presuppositions of transformation. One needs to continue this therapeutic search for an alternative to the subversion of both the particular and the universal by way of a calling that annuls the call in order to respond to each other.

Justice without Law

An imagination of messianic justice carries forward this blurring of distinction between indication and expression in the process of repetition. Such a blurring produces an 'other context' that makes possible a projection of what is included/excluded, recognized/misrecognized not on the basis of real/ideal/imaginary kind of distinction, but on the basis of 'repetition'. Repetition is conceived as the 'threshold of indistinction' between an articulation of what is 'proper' to an identity or culture and what is 'other' to it. This indistinction creates a *messianic* structure around the event that is distinguished by Derrida from any determinate *messianism* of a biblical kind; one may always recognize there the arid soil in which grew, and passed away, the living figures of all the messiahs, whether they were announced, recognized, or still awaited.[17] This wait is it a limit that, as Derrida puts it in "Force of Law," "defines either an infinite progress or a waiting and awaiting"[18] because the political relationship to the "absolute future" also requires that one act, that one make political decisions. Derrida formulates this argument in relation to justice in "Force of Law":

> (...) justice, however unpresentable it remains, does not wait. It is that which must not wait. To be direct, simple and brief, let us say this: a just decision is always required *immediately*, right away, as quickly as possible. It cannot provide itself with the infinite information and the unlimited knowledge of conditions, rules or hypothetical imperatives that could justify it. And even if it did have all that at its disposal, even if it did give itself the time, all the time and all the necessary knowledge about the matter, well then, the moment of *decision as such*, what must be just, *must* [*il faut*] always remain a finite moment of urgency and precipitation; it must [*doit*] not be the consequence or the effect of this theoretical or historical knowledge, of this reflection or this deliberation, since the decision always marks the interruption of the juridico-, ethico- or politico-cognitive deliberation that precedes it, that must [*doit*] precede it.[19]

Agamben echoes this messianic structure associated with the promise. He says,

> Justice, like magic, is nameless. Happy, without a name, the creature knocks at the gates of the land of the magi, who speak in gestures alone.[20]

Justice comes with a subversion of the particular experience of forms of power and representation. As such it turns out to be a critique of the structure of identity and political mobilization, which is an attempt to rejuvenate an aesthetic of self-representation in the public space. The critique is possible by way of calling of a shared political space with the Other, which ironically repeats the experiences of xenophobia, racism and numerous other forms of colonization. In this context, it is necessary to recognize that every 'we' necessarily comes from the 'other' by way of a radical undecidability about who we are and this is the very possibility of sharing a common cultural space. This is also a profane sense of otherness, which is never identical to itself that ruptures the forms of misrecognition emanating from the immanent conditions of hegemonic difference. Derrida describes the situation in this manner:

> A certain experience of emancipatory promise; it is perhaps even the formality of a structural messainism, a messainism without religion, even a messianic without messianism, an idea of justice —which we distinguish from law or right or even human rights—and an idea of democracy—which we distinguish from its current concept and from its determined predicates today.[21]

Interpretation as an act of deciding the meaning of an event encounters this multiple possibilities of meaning not as an intended consequence but as an inevitable directedness to a referential frame, which cannot be determined by the interpretation of an event. Undecidability of the referential frame acts as a source of multiple interventions on the occurrence of an event, which provides support to the interpretation as well as re-orders it from a critical position of justice. This is how Derrida pronounces it, "I have only one language, but it is not mine." It indicates the possibility of search for the 'other' or/'and 'other of language'. The other, which is beyond language and which summons language is not a 'referent', but a 'dissemination' that is irreducible to language. For example, every claim of uniqueness of cultural and linguistic identity has the 'responsibility of testifying for universality'. But this universality is to be free from the violence of representing the universal in the particular—a hegemonic strategy that subverts the particular. It is rather an idea of universality that Deleuze articulated in this way,

> Neither particular nor general, neither finite nor infinite, it is the object of the Idea as a universal. This differential element is the play of difference as such, which can neither be mediated by representation nor subordinated to the identity of the concept.[22]

This notion of universality beyond the hegemony of the dominant discourse is the play between being and its condition of possibility that lies in a differentially structured universal that poses problems within the concept of 'universal'. The problem is to 'invent' a concept of difference that is without a concept sans an irreducible problem of being that exists. The 'problem' can be understood in the way one tries to make universal accommodative of a differential relation between one and many, the current problematic between pluralism and singularity as 'intrinsically defined' multiplicity that requires a repetitive internal plurality into many shades.[23] Methodologically we are a little liberated here from the constraints of holistic universality of cultural plurality as we need to operate within a fractured multiplicity of action and signification that calls for the possibility of extensive 'forms of self-ascription and self-determination' not just from the point of view of a fixed insider, but from the possibility of a free-moving and wandering entry and exit into multiple domains of culture. Such entry and exit provides new routes to universality that one needs to invent in pushing the cultural boundaries and the boundaries of culture. This should not necessarily mean a strong identification with the given norms of belonging, but leaving room for alternate belongings without necessarily subverting the closure of a particular culture. This can be articulated in a possible sense of learning from the other,

> I can learn the *wholeness* of the other(s) only through their narratives of self-identification. The norm of universal respect enjoins me to enter the conversation in so far as one is considered as a generalized other; but I can become aware of the Otherness of others, of those aspects of their identity that make them concrete other to me, only through their own narratives.[24]

This implies that the responsibility and moral obligation of understanding the other through their narrative claims cannot be mediated and altered by the predicaments of cultural and political dominance that sets up asymmetric terms for discounting the political legitimacy of cultural claims. The hybrid processes of boundary crossing between dominant and non-dominant cultures should open up processes of intercultural justice between culturally different identities.

The representational device of hybridity is not just loaded with concepts of cultural self and the unity between the self and the world, but concepts such as presence of the self and the world as the origin of representation are re-mark(s) that fold on itself and on thought. The fold acts as re-plica or re-application of quasi transcendental or quasi-ontological conditions within which the empirical or the ontical aspects of an identity/culture arises. This is putting the rigid cultural norms upside down: instead of knowledge or belief about a culture requiring the idea of objective practices and truths, the truth merely appears in practice and it presupposes the trace of language and a dissemination of language without return to cultural origin. This dissemination of culture is a device for an ontological re-interpretation of the "Other" as the proper Subject of the social. Derrida conceived this as 'what is proper to a culture is not be identical to itself'. In his words,

> (...) there is no self-relation, no relation to oneself, no identification with oneself, without culture, but the culture of one's self as a culture of the other, a culture of the double genitive and of the *difference to oneself*...signals that a culture never has a single origin.[25]

This brings us to a methodological acceptance of the 'other' as the source of one's own culture with the implication that it portrays the possibility of multiple meanings as a Nietzschean impossibility of having a language, which means a simultaneous *exscription* and *effacement* of meaning. None of us can be said to *possess* language, making it do our bidding, allowing us to subordinate it as a vehicle for the transportation of meaning. We are each possessed by the field of forces and powers with which language/culture/identity is always associated. The ironic gesture of the torturer, who would, through violence, demand his victim speak in the name of truth. But which speech is this? Not the speech of violence—unspeaking, false through and through, logically the only one it can hope to obtain—but a true speech, free and pure of all violence. So, for an idea of universal sociality, affirmation of is produced by negation, since negation maintains itself by positing being for an object. And it seems, in consequence, that affirmation, which is supposed to get past nihilism, ultimately fails to escape the contagion of the negation from which it came. This is to say that there is no outside of self-identity that did not itself authorize by inscribing itself within language. The meaning of such a conscious act of negation directs itself to the wholly other that involves a serial erasure of the trace of the self and the other,

It should be anticipated as the unforeseeable, the unanticipatable, the non-masterable, non-identifiable, in short, as that of which one does not yet have a memory.[26]

NOTES

1. Jacques Derrida, 'Abraham, the Other', trans. by Gil Anidjar, in *Judeities: Questions for Jacques Derrida*, eds. Bettina Bergo, Joseph Cohen and Raphael Zagury-Orly, Fordham University Press, New York, 2007, p. 17.
2. G.W.F. Hegel, *Phenomenology of Spirit*, tr. A.V. Miller, Oxford University Press, Oxford, 1977, pp. 55-6
3. Jacques Derrida, 'The Ends of Man' in *Margins of Philosophy*, tr. Alan Bass, University of Chicago Press, Chicago, 1982, p. 133.
4. Martin Heidegger, "The Way back into the Ground of Metaphysics" in Walter Kauffman, *Existentialism from Dostoevsky to Sartre*, Meridian Books, New York, 1975, pp. 275-6.
5. Alain Badiou, "Being's Prohibition of the Event" in *Being and Event*, tr. Oliver Feltham, Continuum, London, 2005, pp. 189-90.
6. Martin Heidegger, *Identity and Difference*, tr. J. Stambaugh, Harper and Row, New York, 1974, p. 31.
7. Catherine Malabou, *The Future of Hegel: Plasticity, Temporality and Dialectic*, tr. Lisabeth During, Routledge, 2005, p. 118
8. Hegel, *Phenomenology of Spirit*, p. 419
9. John Cage, *Pour les oiseaux*, interview with Daniel Charles, Paris, 1976.
10. Michel Foucault, *The Archeology of knowledge and the Discourse on Language*, tr. A.M.S. Smith, Pantheon Books, New York, 1972, p. 191.
11. Martin Heidegger, *What Is Philosophy?* New College & University Press, New York, 1956, pp. 11-12.
12. Heidegger, Martin. *Identity and Difference.* University of Chicago Press, Chicago, 2002, pp. 78-9.
13. Martin Heidegger, *Being and Time.* tr. John Macquarrie and Edward Robinson, Harper and Row, New York, 1962, p. 436.
14. Giorgio Agamben, *State of Exception* tr. Kevin Attel, Stanford University Press, Stanford, 2001, p. 40.
15. Giorgio Agamben, *The Time That Remains*, Stanford University Press, Stanford, 2006, p. 68.
16. Ibid., pp. 65-6.
17. Jacques Derrida, *Specters of Marx*, tr. Peggy Kamuf, Routledge, London, 1994, p. 168.
18. Jacques Derrida and Gil Anidjar, *Acts of Religion*, Routledge, London, 2002, p. 255.
19. Ibid., p. 255.
20. Giorgio Agamben, *Profanations*, p. 22.
21. Jacques Derrida, *Specters of Marx*, p. 59

22. Giles Deleuze, *Difference and Repetition*, tr. Paul Patton, Continuum, London, pp. 225-6.
23. Deleuze, Ibid., p. 231.
24. Seyla Benhabib, *The Claims of Culture*, Princeton Univ. Press, New Jersey, p. 331.
25. Jacques Derrida, *The Other Heading: Reflections on Today's Europe*, tr. P.A. Brault and M.B. Nass, Indiana University Press, Bloomington, 1992, p. 9f.
26. Derrida, ibid., p. 18.

12

Of Shame and Censure: Is An 'other' Politics Possible?

Debaditya Bhattacharya

I

The event of the 'scam' has become constitutive of a contemporary order of political 'commonsense'. As even the most cursory survey of popular discourse would testify, the primary mode of mobilizing public consciousness around the advent(ure) of the political is now in preparing the citizen-subject for knowledge in an act of revelation. To take the recent history of 'national politics' in India as an example, the overbearing predominance of Lalitgates and Coalgates, of 2Gs and Quattrocchis, or of Vyapams and Swiss banks[1] as an everyday frame of mass-communicative reference inflects our commonsense-perception of the 'political' with the thrilling theatrics of scams. The revelatory aesthetic inherent in the coming-to-knowledge of current-day (mal)practices of governance marks an interesting rupture in the technologies of knowing. It constantly promises the disclosure of a secret, but wraps it up in the unknowable sacrality of the 'miracle'. This idea of the *secular* miraculous—which lies at the heart of the 'scandal'—is merely a moment of the self-suspension of truth in a spectacular excess of the very taking-place of publicity. The 'scam' appears to pierce through the hymen that divides desire from consummation, the privatized 'secret' from the public 'spectacle'. It sensuously titillates a will to knowledge in the disaffected 'other' of the media-informed citizen, through an unforeseen excess of publicity masquerading as the self-present totality of meaning. In thus distributing itself along the aporias of reason impervious to all but the miraculous 'detections' of the secret sting-operation, the 'scam' constructs a new metaphysics of presence in the sheer making-visible of the possibility of publicity. It resembles an erotic desire for totalitarian knowledge, a scopophilic perversion of conquering 'openness' in the self-referentiality of a spectacle. What it offers by way of a 'gift' is not the 'secret' that it declares as an irreducible essence, but merely the remainder of a possible field of knowledge around its witholding.

Though the etymology of the word 'scam' is highly debated in that its use is largely found in very recent American legislative history, it is probable that its origins lay in the Germanic root 'skam' (Old High German '*scama*', Anglo-Saxon '*scamu*')— meaning 'an act of exposure or disgrace'. In its verb form, the root 'skam' has often been used to refer to the action of covering or hiding oneself. Interestingly, it is from this same etymological source that the word 'shame' takes its current form, in calling for a necessary concealment of the ashamed. However, this paper is an attempt to claim that despite their coincidence of lexical sources and an apparent history of identical articulations in popular discourse, the event of the 'scam' and the moment of 'shame' occupy distinctly different positions at the level of political practice. At the first instance, it is in their relationship with knowledge that their difference is marked. While the 'scam' has no referential relationship with knowledge but is merely a technology of unconcealment as an end-in-itself, the experience of shame—as I intend to show—is the only ethico-political precondition of 'knowing' as an act of marking difference by being *exposed in front of the Other*. It is in the event of this exposure that 'shame'—as the correlate of a knowledge threatened by non-coincidence with the hegemonic subject of self-presence— runs the risk of calling upon itself the objectifying violence of 'censure'. A third category in my analysis, the political violence of 'censure' issues out of a fear of the possible shamelessness of a difference-revealed-and-exposed before the Other. It forces an anthropologistic return to the subject-object binary, by which the potential effects of difference could be contained as objective empirical totalities ranged against the sovereign mastery of a transcendental humanist State. In this, the call to censure arrests the process of Becoming at the heart of the phenomenological project of Being— as always-already an effect of becoming-dangerous—and therefore necessitating subsumption within an empirical existentialism of the superior pre-dative/originary subjectivity of the State. Censuring is hence the predominant ideological operation of every fascist regime, thriving as it does on a public culture of shaming and criminalising difference. Every event of 'censure' is simply born of a desperation to control the potential infinity of shameless knowledge-prerogatives in the self by calling upon a legislative morality of 'guilt.' It attempts to outlaw 'shame' as the radical transgressive other to dominant orders of knowledge, and subsequently co-opts the experience within a moral-humanist economy of individual agency or culpability.

Such political terror of 'censure' mandates a containment of the disruptive experience of 'shame', by reading it within a causal pattern of action versus consequence. The phenomenological immediacy of 'shame' as characteristic of a reflexive self-consciousness is deliberately taken away from, by making it seem the logical outcome of a prior act of transgressive identification or determination. In this, 'shame' is politically constructed by the structures of power as *only* the 'negative' effect of a conspiratorial event of otherness and thus requiring a forced confession or conversion. Far from being an affirmative condition of *coming unto oneself in coming before the Other*, it has come to be viewed as the hidden conscience of being-other. Even while I write this paper, the nation reels under an organized culture of shaming-qua-censuring, as repressive agents of the state go about assaulting unmarried consenting couples on charges of hurting public morals and cultural sentiments, intelligence agencies witch-hunt rights activists fighting organised state-crimes as attacking the sovereignty of the nation, courts rake up selective memories of 'national shame' to justify the vengeful fictions of a 'collective conscience' and saffron-robed Cabinet ministers go out campaigning against minority-publics as 'anti-national' and 'illegitimately' begotten from a father other than the Hindu God Rama.

A sustained history of such state-sponsored censorship has by now naturalized the lexical complicity of 'shame' as but a 'call to censure'—whether it be in an erstwhile Law Minister's midnight-raid of a city neighbourhood to hunt down the shameful immoralities perpetrated by black immigrant-prostitutes or in the Hindu Right's crusade against a "woman hungry for sex" in Wendy Doniger or in Islamic fundamentalists taking up arms against the shame of granting asylum to an exile in Taslima Nasreen. Acclaimed writers and artists have in the same vein been charged with sedition and forced into exile or even threatened with banishment into Pakistan for having 'shamelessly' expressed as much as a disapproval of a Prime-Ministerial candidate. The recent annals of democratic reason have witnessed the Parliament debating the minimal social identity of a gangrape-victim as nothing more than a "living corpse," thereby almost legitimizing the 'shame' of survival in a patriarchal world. It is as part of a similarly censorious project of 'shame' that Dalit women have been stripped in public and made to live the ignominy proper to their caste-status or Kashmiri youth paraded naked by army personnel. The moralistic *a priori* of 'guilt' has conveniently erected a retributive equivalence between 'shame' and extreme acts of 'censure'. In the process, the experience of shame as an inescapable condition of the self has now translated into an other-directed technology for punishing forms and degrees of alterity. The phenomenological ground of the sentiment shifted from the self-conscious *feeling subject* to an *object-target* conceived as a thing-in-itself.

II

If, as I have maintained thus far, the true experience of shame as productive of knowledge is transcribable in neither the political theatrics of a 'scam' or of 'censure', then what indeed is shame? Inasmuch as the agenda of moral philosophy accounts for an intentionality behind every emotion and thus makes it part of a discourse on 'responsibility', what propels the birth of shame in the human psyche? To put it as a rhetorical conundrum, why is shame *shameful*—and what, in the history of human consciousness, imputes to it a will that can so easily be appropriated by commonsense perceptions of crime? If, in its coincidence with the auto-affective impulse, shame inhabits the space of a pre-moral sentiment, what makes it so vulnerable to assaults of the immoral?

Jean-Paul Sartre writes at length on the structure of shame in human consciousness with relation to the question of Being. In *Being and Nothingness* (1943), he explains:

> Consider for example shame.... [I]ts structure is intentional; it is a shameful apprehension of something and this something is me. I am ashamed of what I am. Shame therefore realizes an intimate relation of myself to myself. Through shame I have discovered an aspect of my being.... In fact no matter what results one can obtain in solitude by the religious practice of shame, it is in its primary structure shame before *somebody*.... [T]he Other is the indispensable mediator between myself and me. I am ashamed of myself as I appear to the Other.... Shame is by nature recognition. I recognize that I am as the Other sees me.... Thus the Other has not only revealed to me what I was; he has established me in a new type of being which can support new qualifications. This being was not in me potentially before the appearance of the Other.... Thus shame is shame of oneself before *the* Other; these two structures are inseparable. But at the same time I need the Other in order to realize fully all the structures of my being. The For-itself refers to the For-others. (pp. 221-222)

Shame, in the Sartrean imagining of the relation between being and becoming, is merely the experience of 'seeing oneself be seen by the other'. In this, it presupposes an event of unprecedented proximity with oneself—but only through the interposed presence of and difference from an other. It is the other which acts as the *remainder* of an ineffaceable distance between me and my apprehension of myself. And it is this distance within the very heart of being-for-itself that the sentiment of shame testifies to, through a constant menace of the vigilant but nonviolent other. The gaze of the other offers myself to my own consciousness, and prevents a coincidence with the being-in-itself despite absolute intimacy. This indeed is the founding moment of the self-conscious subject whose ownmost identity and identifications lie in a realisation of its *difference in the face of the other.*

Though the bulk of critical encounters has imagined Sartre as holding on to the idea of the Cartesian 'ego cogito' and subsequently reconfiguring the humanist project along existential lines, the text of *Being and Nothingness* would prove otherwise. It is true that Sartre later defends his existentialist project against a litany of such rash judgments by hastily and rather simplistically calling it an exercise in humanism – and one that vehemently denies the *a prioristic* assumptions of essence in favour of the actuality of *existentia.*

> What we mean to say is that man first *exists*; that is, that *man primarily exists* – that man is, *before all else*, something which projects itself into a future, and is conscious of doing so.
>
> (*Existentialism is a Humanism*, p. 23, italics mine)

Having thus ontologized the existence of man as prior to any conception of his essence, Sartre however does not exhaust his humanist imaginary in the rhetoric of self-presence. Instead, he hints at the existential *destiny* of the human as perpetually propelling itself "into a future" and thus out of sync with a self-contained metaphorics of presence. It is this effect of 'being-out-ahead-of-itself' that characterises the Heideggerian conception of Dasein in *Being and Time* (1927) and questions the metaphysical foundations of a self-identical subjectivity. Heidegger nonetheless, in his "Letter on Humanism" (1949), misrecognizes this Sartrean turn of existentialism and takes the French philosopher to task for what he deems a misplaced critique of metaphysics. He contends that though Sartre presumptuously claims to revolt against the originary ground of existence through an atheistic and non-essentialist anteriority of the human "before all else," he presupposes "an already established interpretation of nature, history, world, and the ground of the world, that is, of beings as a whole...without asking about the truth of being" (p. 245). In this, Sartre is accused of lapsing into a similar metaphysical essence of the 'humanitas' in *homo humanus* as opposed to *homo barbarus*. Heidegger's proposition for thinking about the truth of Being rejects the anthropologism discerned in empirical presence, and instead posits an ecstatic effect of '*ek*-sistence' as the true essence of Being. *Ek*-sistence, for him, is mere thrown-ness in the clearing of Being, as a movement towards its truth *not in coincidence but in distance*. It defines Being as nearness or proximity to itself, lacking forever a destiny in self-identity. It is this same effect of an intimacy forbidding identicality with the self that Sartre named as the intentional 'structure' of shame that lies at the root of Being. On closer analysis therefore, it seems that the imagination of subjectivity underlying both Heidegger and Sartre betrays the same suspicion of metaphysical humanism – and accompanies an ecstatic feeling of 'shame' that becomes the truest adjunct of a reflexive event of self-consciousness. For both, thinking the truth of Being involves a moment of ek-stasis —a movement outside of the self, a becoming-other in absolute nearness to the self—and this ecstasy of self-knowledge is fundamentally the experience of shame.

It was as early as in *The Transcendence of the Ego* (1936) that Sartre refutes the Husserlian paradigm of a transcendental ego as the originary site of subjective action, and instead imagines the latter as a synthetic construct external to the movements of consciousness. Thereafter, in *Being and Nothingness*, Sartre propounds a theory of the subject as one who is capable of a reflexive consciousness of itself. This instantaneous cogito, as the condition of possibility of a subjective Being, is but a demand for the self-presence of consciousness as capable of reflecting on itself. But the moment when consciousness reflects upon itself is the moment when it sees itself as *other*—or regards it as the other would see it; an object among others, self-divided in its ownness. The subject's capacity for self-identity is hence a "consciousness of consciousness" which is present to itself and yet never properly its own. It is an effect of self-presence perpetually fated to difference. This effect of nothingness that Being-as-subjectivity experiences at the heart of its own self-realisation is the ineluctable limit to its freedom as humanist transcendence. The experience of otherness is forever the condition of [im]possibility of pure self-knowledge, and takes on the structure of 'shame'. Interestingly, Sartre's positing of the nature of Being in his existentialist project not only seems sceptical of a humanist predicate of 'freedom', but also relegates the Heideggerian truth of Being (as essence) to the scourge of an eternal self-separation. Sartre clarifies it thus:

> I can be ashamed only as my freedom escapes me in order to become a given object... And this self which I am—this I am in a world which the Other has made alien to me, for the Other's look embraces my being and correlatively the walls, the door, the keyhole. All these instrumental things in the midst of which I am, now turn toward the Other a face which on principle escapes me. Thus I am my Ego for the Other in the midst of a world which flows toward the Other.... This being which I am preserves a certain indetermination, a certain unpredictability. And these new characteristics do not come only from the fact that I *cannot know* the Other; they stem also and especially from the fact that the Other is free.... Everything takes place as if I had a dimension of being from which I was separated by a radical nothingness; and this *nothingness is the Other's freedom*.... Thus each of my free conducts engages me in a new environment where *the very stuff of my being is the unpredictable freedom of another.* Yet by my very shame I claim as mine that freedom of another. I affirm a profound unity of consciousnesses, *not that harmony of monads which has sometimes been taken as a guarantee of objectivity* but a unity of being; for I accept and wish that others should confer upon me a being which I recognize.

> Shame is the apprehension of myself as... I grasp the Other's look at the very center of my act [of] solidification and alienation of my own possibilities.... The Other as a look is only that—my transcendence transcended. (pp. 261-63, italics mine)

What resonates in Sartre's discussion of "shudder" (p. 222) that is shame is precisely the fact that the coming to consciousness of the self must alternatively be a coming to terms with the *unalterable alterity of itself*. The event of a "transcendence transcended" that underlies the being-for-itself of the subject is a simultaneous effect of alienation from the Other as well as an affirmation of the profound "unity of being" with every potential other to come. The "unpredictability" and "unknowability" that conditions the 'radical nothingness' of coming-to-oneself in being-with-another (or, seeing-as-another) seems to be the very ethical premise on which "freedom" is realised as the internal limit to truth. The 'freedom' of the "Other as a look" is thus what must in essence be prepared for through the necessary correlate of shame. In other words, the default predicament of every consciousness' arrival unto itself is in a passage through its 'nothingness' before the radical potential Other. This political passage through 'difference' as the existential precondition for consciousness sounds unusually familiar to a poststructuralist ethics of the 'time of the Other'.

III

Though poststructuralist philosophers and scholars have remained insistently tight-lipped about their rather-tortuous relationship with Sartre, Derrida has—in a 1968 lecture in New York later published as "The Ends of Man" and in a couple of interviews thereafter—summarily disavowed of his philosophical debts to a Sartrean legacy. While in the former essay, Derrida accuses Sartre's work of a humanist metaphysics that borders on the anthropological, a 1989 interview with Catherine David for *Le Nouvel Observateur* sees him quickly judging the intellectual dominance of Sartre through an academic-and-publishing nexus as "nefarious and catastrophic" (p. 122). Derrida's primary point of contention against Sartre's theory of Being is in the latter's apparently Encyclopaedist presupposition of universals like "Man," "human-reality" and "freedom." He claims that his predecessor's challenge to metaphysics in the name of a "phenomenological ontology" is not only inadequate in that it presumes a "unity of human reality," but it also reduces the whole of existentialism to a humanist exercise that merely "reassembles the theological project of absolute knowledge" (1972, p. 115). Derrida goes as far as discerning a 'messianic' impulse in the Sartrean imagination, contrary to its insistent claims of secularity. Inasmuch as structuralism sought to question the logocentric cult of origins (at the heart of Western philosophical traditions) that imagined man as capable of self-[re]*presentation* in language, the subject was to soon become a mere *effect* of difference. For later deconstructive theorists, the humanist presumption of a possible self-presence as the condition of subjectification had only re-invoked the totalitarian paradox of theocentrism. Sartre's brand of atheism—in that it denied agency to the mythical construction of human essence as either instituted by an act of divine creation or governed by a Hegelian movement of the Spirit—seemed to Derrida to only substitute in its place an anthropological fact of existence. In thus granting the power of origin to the necessary antecedence of man, it apparently failed to interrogate the teleological 'end' of metaphysics or even herald the end of the totalising myth of man. Derrida vehemently critiques the Sartrean project of Being as self-contradictory in its secular pretensions that veered dangerously close to the terms of a "Christian personalism" (p. 115). Instead of forcing metaphysics towards a critique of substance, he finds it ironically replacing the transcendental urges of a Husserlian-Hegelian approach to history with a self-complete human consciousness as the singular 'responsible' force behind it.

Even if one does not wish to summarize Sartre's thought under the slogan "existentialism is a humanism," it must be recognized that in *Being and Nothingness*, *The Sketch of a Theory of the Emotions*, etc., the major concept, the theme of the last analysis, the irreducible horizon and origin is what was then called "human-reality"....

> [D]espite [the] alleged neutralization of metaphysical presuppositions, it must be recognized that the unity of man is never examined in and of itself. Not only is existentialism a humanism, but the ground and horizon of what Sartre then called his "phenomenological ontology" (the subtitle of *Being and Nothingness*) remains the unity of human-reality....
>
> ("The Ends of Man," in *Margins of Philosophy*, 1972, pp. 115-16)

It is evident here that Derrida's critique of existentialism takes off from the exact premise of Heidegger's argument in "Letter on Humanism," except insofar as the Heideggerian quest for the "truth of Being" is also finally subjected to that same critique. Derrida suspects Sartre of totalising the figure of the human under the guise of a popular anthropologism, and thereby representing a metaphysical analogy between Being and human-reality as unified in their very conceptual structures. This movement of thought, he claims, accords a *primacy of essence* to Being as self-referential in its unity and completeness—and thus may in turn replicate a horizon of infinity as the condition of possibility of the human. It does not question the conceptual universality of either 'man' or 'reality', and consequently falls prey to the same charges that Heidegger had eloquently levelled against the Sartrean analytic. Following this critical trajectory further through an interview for *Le Nouvel Observateur*, Derrida grants Sartre only as much as the authority of an anterior lineage serving for his own rites of initiation into the philosophy of Husserl, Heidegger, Blanchot, Bataille and others. But, soon afterwards, he detracts from this logic of ancestral affection by maintaining:

> But finally, Sartre was himself the 'unsurpassable horizon'!... One would have to devote several dozen books to this question: What must a society such as ours be if a man, who, in his own way, rejected or misunderstood so many theoretical and literary events of his time – let's say, to go quickly, psychoanalysis, Marxism, structuralism, Joyce, Artaud, Bataille, Blanchot – who accumulated and disseminated incredible misreadings of Heidegger, sometimes of Husserl, could come to dominate the scene to the point of becoming a great popular figure? ["Unsealing ('the old new language')," in *Points...: Interviews 1974-1994*, p. 122]

Derrida rests his evident disdain for the Sartrean mode of philosophical thinking as finally not belonging "to the age of those works that matter for me" (1995, p. 122). In my own deconstructive reading of the works that not only matter for Derrida but are also counter-signed by him and in his name, I do find—as would a few other scholars including Christina Howells, Hugh J. Silverman, Sebastian Gardner and Steve Martinot—some striking complicities of thought with the Sartrean oeuvre. Particularly with regard to the poststructuralist event of 'knowledge' conceived as an ethico-political 'promise' of the *other to come*, there indeed is much that cobbles more than an ancestral unity between Sartre and Derrida. At the risk of adopting what Martinot would call a structural 'homology' that looks beyond mere textual traces of congruence, I would insist that a re-evaluative rigour around poststructuralism definitely needs to confront the ghosts of an existential phenomenology only to measure their relative coincidences at the level of the ethical and the political.

Much like his predecessor Heidegger, Derrida seemingly performs an intentional oversight in his commentary on the existentialist question of Being. Instead of placing Sartre's thought within a larger and continuously evolving oeuvre of work (comprising philosophical-critical texts as well as novels, plays and stories) that spans from the 1936 essay on Husserl and *Nausea* (1938) to *The Family Idiot* (1972), Derrida selectively chooses sources fit for his critique. He deliberately skims through some representative sections of *Being and Nothingness*, and forces his deductions to rest squarely within the admittedly reductive formulisations permitted by Sartre's lecture to a lay-audience[2] in "Existentialism is a Humanism". Designed as a point-by-point rejoinder to his critics, Sartre went to the extent of publicly denouncing the text of this latter lecture for oversimplifying the breadth and philosophical density of his earlier work.[3] The sustained vehemence of Derrida's attack in "The Ends of Man" conveniently escapes the complexities underlying Sartre's positing of the question of the human, except by way of a few slender footnotes containing privileged references to *Nausea*. Consequently, the "unity of Being" in which Derrida discerns a metaphysical communion of the Being-in-itself and Being-for-itself loses sight of the constitutive self-division that characterises the Sartrean mode of reflexive subjectivity. In other words, the apparently 'apolitical' unity that Derrida identifies as the hubris of existentialism is in fact a declaredly self-divided being-of-consciousness that recognises its own potential for difference in the perpetual spectre of a vigilant Other. The necessary non-coincidence of consciousness with itself that I discussed earlier foils the metaphysical rhetoric of self-presence in every event of subjectification. Hence, Derrida's charge against Sartre's conceptualization of Being as "relating and appearing to itself" and thus re-presentable as the "totality of beings" is largely unsupported by an intimate encounter with the nuances enfolded in the latter's thought. It is true that a dialectical dualism seems to pervade much of Sartre's perception of 'freedom' as the difference between subjective acts and internalised conditions of objective existence, but that does not exempt his analysis from a rigorous phenomenological questioning of the nature of subjectivity. Sartre is acutely wary of the dangers of both a classical empiricism and a dialectical materialism (as developed through his later work in "Search for a Method" [1957] and *The Critique of Dialectical Reason* [1960]), and consequently addresses the immanent condition of otherness that enables and limits the freedom of consciousness. It is with sufficient reason that Steve Martinot, in *Forms in the Abyss: A Philosophical Bridge between Sartre and Derrida*, identifies a structural parallel between Derridean '*différance*' and Sartrean '*neantisation*' as simultaneously pointing towards the impossibility of presence at the heart of Being. He interestingly notes:

> Sartre's neologist term *néantisation* (nihilation) evinces a similar structure. Where différance is to be thought of as the exclusive ground of difference, nihilation is to be thought of as the exclusive ground of consciousness. That is, it makes nonreference to that essential and primordial "moment" of the upsurge of consciousness into the world, of which an awareness remains impossible.... Heidegger begins with the assertion that the question of Being had been forgotten by metaphysics; and Sartre argues analogously that we cannot forget the priority of negation, of what he calls *négatité,* even to the question of Being! To ask a question, to enter into inquiry as such, must leave open the possibility of a negative response, or the possibility that what is questioned is itself nothing. The possibility of the negative, that the answer is "no," is always immanent in the nature of questioning. (p. 33)

Néantisation or nothingness is the spectral parasitism of the Other at the moment of one's ownmost possession of the truth of Being[4]. Its characteristic passage through shame prepares the self for a being-for-itself by overcoming 'bad faith', and is decidedly a moment of nonviolent overtaking by the permanent possibility of *any* other. In necessarily traversing through the space of shame, knowledge is turned upon itself as an effect of incommensurable difference from the ever-present, ever-gazing and yet unknowable other. Isn't this accurately what constitutes the condition of possibility of a poststructuralist politics in itself?

IV

Derrida does turn once to a philosophical engagement with 'shame' with regard to the question of the limits of the human, in the first part of a ten-hour conference address in 1997 later published as "The Animal that Therefore I Am (More to Follow)." Here, he wonderfully interrogates the structure of self-affirmation in the humanities that assumes a necessary negation of the sovereign otherness of animality. Owing to the distinguishing singularity of the word, the Cartesian cogito assures itself of its being-human by signifying its difference from the animal. And yet, when faced with this absolute alterity of the animal's gaze—which is even logically excluded from the 'threat' of difference in being rendered incapable of 'response' —the human in Derrida feels bound by the affect of shame. This experience of shame, he explains through an anecdotal reference to his cat and in a peculiarly Sartrean analytical mode, is the most certainly ineffaceable 'trace' of one's being-human. The determinately marked 'other' of the animal in language ironically becomes the surest guarantor of the surpassing of man's linguistic sovereignty by returning him to a crisis of humanity in shame. And it is this moment of crisis that finally and completely returns man to a realisation of his ownness as distinct from the existential order of the bestial. Derrida elaborates this scene of a primal recoil before his cat, in a fashion that is particularly reminiscent of Sartre's analytic of shame in being-for-and-before-others:

> Since so long ago, can we say that the animal has been looking at us?
>
> What animal? The other.
>
> I often ask myself, just to see, who I am—and who I am (following) at the moment when, caught naked, in silence, by the gaze of an animal, for example the eyes of a cat, I have trouble, yes, a bad time overcoming my embarrassment....
>
> I have trouble repressing a reflex dictated by immodesty.... It is as if I were ashamed, therefore, naked in front of this cat, but also ashamed for being ashamed. A reflected shame, the mirror of a shame ashamed of itself, a shame that is at the same time specular, unjustifiable, and unable to be admitted to. At the optical

> center of this reflection would appear this thing [...] that is called nudity....
>
> Ashamed of what and before whom? Ashamed of being as naked as an animal. It is generally thought [...] that the property unique to animals and what in the final analysis distinguishes them from man, is their being naked without knowing it.... From that point on, naked without knowing it, animals would not, in truth, be naked.... In principle, with the exception of man, no animal has ever thought to dress itself. Clothing would be proper to man, one of the "properties" of man.... Man would be the only one to have invented a garment to cover his sex. He would only be a man to the extent that he was able to be naked, that is to say to be ashamed, to know himself to be ashamed because he is no longer naked. And knowing *himself* would mean knowing himself to be ashamed.... (pp. 372-74)

What is significant about Derrida's analysis of self-knowledge as "knowing [oneself] to be ashamed" before the radical other of the animal is the potential of shame to effect what Sartre—in the same vein—called a transformative *ekstasis*. Faced with a recognition of his own difference from the animal in shame, what man does is hide himself in clothing. This act of a transformation into apparent modesty in fact marks a further *difference* from the animal. Every release from the burden of the other's gaze (in shame) turns out to be ironically a radicalisation of one's otherness and thus a preparation for more shame. That is what Derrida calls the "shame of being ashamed," and therefore awaiting yet an other shame to come. Sartre argues along a strikingly similar line in *Being and Nothingness*, where he clarifies that every escape from the shame of being seen (as and against the other's difference) can merely be a retreat into 'bad faith'. The ashamed consciousness, in taking on a *persona* as the mark of an assumed *in*difference, re-lapses into 'bad faith' and heightens his difference. This in effect repeats the movement of the self-consciousness in a passage through successively greater difference each time and yet never coinciding with itself. The only possible response to the shame of a *different* knowledge, it seems, lies in the radical otherness of a shamelessness.

This ethical prerogative of knowledge to 'shamelessly' *return to itself in difference* is what finally brings about a 'strange alliance' between Derrida and Sartre as late as in 1996. Writing for the fiftieth anniversary edition of *Les Temps Modernes*—the journal Sartre started and which subsequently chronicled the turns of late-twentieth-century French philosophy—Derrida unequivocally affirms his "love" and "salutation" for his intellectual predecessor. Addressed in the form of a letter to Claude Lanzmann and titled "'Dead Man Running': Salut, Salut," Derrida discloses an unprecedented intimacy with the "*voice of Sartre*" (p. 262) and eventually wonders at its remarkable potential for '*différance*'. He invokes the time of the "anniversary" to announce the undying imminence of the "dead man" haunting our *relationship* with the present as "unstable, divided, split, antinomic" (p. 262). Commenting on *What is Literature? and Other Essays* in a series of preparatory notes appended to the letter, Derrida acknowledges a complicity with Sartre's imagination of 'literature' as replete with the *promise of an unveiling*, a giving without condition, a self-compromise. It begs the event of justice in the indignant shame of a *return* in an other['s] time—and, in the process, testifying to an undying potential for difference and deferral.

Taking off from this gesture of *solidarity* in an anniversarial return to an erstwhile adversary, the moment of *knowledge* translates into an ethico-political possibility for posthumous agreement[s] with the other.[5] An existential-poststructuralist analytic would regard this *shame of an intimate self-excess* as the *incrementally absolute other to authorised truths.*

V

It is because of its antagonistic relationship with power [of hegemonic knowledge-as-presence] that shame has, in a practical-moral history of emotions, been shown as *coincident with the event of sin*. This last section would briefly recount the ways in which sustained theological-theoretical interventions have served to convert what I call the 'existential-poststructuralist analytic' of shame into a negative moral affect meriting censure. Is a *return* to the shame of difference the only *possible* future of resistance, then?

To begin with, the scriptural paradigm has been repeatedly invoked to prove the natal synonymity of shame with the Original Sin that caused the Fall of Man from paradisal bliss. In *Genesis 3.7*, the effects of Adam's singular act of disobedience are described thus:

> At that moment their eyes were opened, and they suddenly felt *shame* at their nakedness. So they sewed fig leaves together to cover themselves.

What is significant here is the exact context of the production of "shame" and the consequences that follow. The fact that the effect of eating the fruit [of Knowledge] is described through an 'opening of their eyes' does not mean that Adam and Eve were blinded till "that [fateful] moment". On the contrary, it only signifies that the body of knowledge that exceeds the sanction of sovereign authority is relegated to an 'other' *ethic of seeing*. The very acquisition of self-knowledge is thus named as taboo in that it is supposed to be a moment of *shameful revelation to the other.*

The second function played by the image of 'eye-opening' as a logical outcome of the project of (self-)knowledge is that it confirms the visual technologies of *shaming*. That shame is a sentiment which requires apprehension of and by the other and concomitantly relates to a perceptual aesthetic of an *image of the self* are important effects mustered herein. Soon after, the need for a protective loincloth sewn of "fig leaves" further reconstructs shame as warranting avoidance in a *counter-aesthetic of optical opacity*. This signifies the call for concealment issued by an attempt at self-knowledge, and thus a tendency to *becoming-other as the only respite from a shameful intimacy of oneself to oneself*. The negativity inherent in our imaginaries of shame is reinforced through such desperate efforts at self-hiding.

Demonstrably, the relationship between *shame* and *bodily nakedness* takes us back to the etymology of the word in its Greek origins. The earliest literal equivalent of 'shame' in Greek is the term 'aidos'—which, coming from 'aidoia'—referred to the genitals. Across the whole body of classical literature and mythology, allusions to 'aidos' as rooted in the image of sexual or bodily disgrace abound.

The placing of shame within a moral consciousness is, as Bernard Williams contends in his work *Shame and Necessity*, a relatively recent tendency that often mistakes the former with a juridical (and thus punitive) idea of 'guilt'. He resolves this puzzle of "moral agency" later in the text by claiming that, in most cases of tragic import in Greek literature, the act that occasions shame is committed involuntarily and without any knowledge of its possible consequences. To take a paradigmatic example, the overbearing shame of Oedipus in committing both incest and patricide is constantly testified to as unwittingly completing a prophecy *without* any voluntary act of the will. But ironically this feeling of shame that, Oedipus claims, is exempted from the juridical compulsions of 'sin', had already turned moral by then. It is in the tragic protagonist's interiorization of the retributive function of justice—whereby, he aggressively performs violence on himself by plucking out his own eyes—that his shame gets appropriated within the *moral coordinate of judgment*. Interestingly, the act of self-chastisement in *blinding* serves as a crucial metaphor in transforming the nature of Oedipal shame into guilt. The symbolic deprivation of sight, while apparently being an instrumental representation of punishment, is also an attempt to relieve oneself of shame by taking away from the very visual nature of its apprehensions. *Shame is, as we have maintained, in seeing oneself be seen by the other*. Therefore, the loss of vision in either will automatically result in a loss of the condition for shaming. Oedipus accurately performs this function, and in the process confesses guilty by approximating to the technology of nemesis.

Williams maintained that within the normative regimes of governance via a positing of social heteronomy in Homeric 'shame culture', the natural legitimate reaction to 'aidos' was 'nemesis' (etymologically, Greek '*nemessetos*' meaning 'righteous indignation' or 'the act of giving one what is due'). Such shame culture, in foisting a distributive practice of 'giving one's due', interiorised the role of justice and thus *moralized itself from within* by unequivocally equating 'shame' with a reaction-deserving drive of 'guilt'.

However, on a different plane, each of the examples that we considered above presents us with pregnant possibilities of a *transformative* event of subject-(de/re)formation[6]. The sentiment of shame, in its most popular associations, relates to a "loss of face" in the *gaze* of potentially plural others. But, it is this same moment of a shameful facelessness that makes possible the event of taking on a different face—in Jungian terms, a *persona*. This persona is a mask that makes the most private—hence, shameful—nakedness opaque even in the very moment of its *closest proximity with the other*. What lies in excess of the mask is the self, but ironically what makes the self recognizable to an other is the mask. The persona thus is the perfect embodiment of a *non-coincidence of the subject with shame in the moment of their absolute mutual togetherness*. This is made possible by an affirmative gesture of *guarding the self as secret* in its being-as-other-than-itself. In responding to the demands of self-presentation *as such* by society, the shame-fearing "individual consciousness" conceals its own true nakedness in being *nakedly present as the other*. This is a paradoxical condition of *shamelessness*, produced by a transformative displacement of shame from being-before-the-other to being-as/with-the-other.

To conclude, it seems but all too apparent that the incarceration of 'shame' within a popular moral-punitive vocabulary of 'sin' qua 'guilt' is only an attempt to foreclose its *disruptive* potential for *différance*. Alternatively, the commonsense-perception of 'shame'—as a condition of powerless passivity in the self—always-already runs the risk of turning into a defiant politics of alterity in a '*differant*' shamelessness. In such an ethical manoeuvring of 'shamelessness' lies the most intimate challenge to fascist appropriations of a politics of shaming and censure—and thus a radical step toward that *wait* for a democracy to come, a democracy of infinite otherness.

NOTES

1. These refer to the popular media coinages around the most serious instances of political-financial misappropriations in recent Indian history. The continuous rhetorical juggling allowed by the media's *implosion of the event in the name* has in fact served the cause of a populist articulation of politics-as-corruption.
2. Anthony Richards Manser, in *Sartre: A Philosophic Study*, Westport and Connecticut: Greenwood Press, 1981, pp. 137-38, notes that this lecture was "comparatively superficial and often inconsistent with the views put forward in *Being and Nothingness,*" primarily because it was delivered at a "fashionable literary event rather than [as] a serious philosophic lecture". Further, Norman Nathaniel Greene, in *Jean-Paul Sartre: The Existentialist Ethic*, Westport and Connecticut: Greenwood Press, 1980, p. 13, sarcastically observes about the intellectual infirmity and decadent affectations of Sartre's upper-class audience

at this lecture: "An indication of the level of understanding to which Sartre was addressing himself is the reported fact that the opening reference to existentialism as a humanism provoked fainting among the audience." Gary Cox, in *Sartre: A Guide for the Perplexed*, Bloomsbury, 2006, p. 161, explains that the "distortion of [Sartre's] views" in this lecture was an obvious consequence of his popular appeal and his "desire to both entertain and shock" a rather uninitiated audience.

3. Joseph Fell, in a letter to Ann Fulton, dated 31 March 1980, laments: "It is unfortunate that the first and only work of Sartre's that most students and many professing philosophers in this country read was the 'Existentialism is a Humanism' lecture—a drastically oversimplified exposition that Sartre himself regrets having published" (as quoted in Abigail Cheever, *Real Phonies: Cultures of Authenticity in Post-World War II America*, Athens and London: The University of Georgia Press, 2010, p. 255). Significant for our understanding is Mary Warnock's introduction to Sartre's *Being and Nothingness*, where she refers to the lecture in question thus: "I mention this essay here only to dismiss it, as Sartre himself has dismissed it. He not only regretted its publication, but also actually denied some of its doctrines in later works." (p. xiv)
4. Sartre, in *Being and Nothingness*, pp. 23-24, elaborates: "[F]rom the very fact that we presume that an Existent can always be revealed as *nothing,* every question supposes that we realize a nihilating withdrawal in relation to the given, which becomes a simple presentation, fluctuating between being and NothingnessÉ. Thus in so far as the questioner must be able to effect in relation to the questioned a kind of nihilating withdrawal,Éhe detaches himself from Being. This means that by a double movement of nihilation [*néantisation*], he nihilates the thing questioned in relation to himself by placing it in a neutral state, between being and nonbeing - and that he, nihilates himself in relation to the thing questioned by wrenching himself from being in order to be able to bring out of himself the possibility of a non-being. This disengagement is then by definition a human process."
5. Derrida, passionately defending Sartre against the charges of "prophetism" leveled by Anna Boschetti in *Sartre et Les Temps Modernes*, Paris: Editions de Minuit, 1985, affirms by way of a question his 'fortuitous agreement.'
6. Giorgio Agamben, 1999, pp. 105-106.

REFERENCES

Agamben, Giorgio, *Remnants of Auschwitz: The Witness and the Archive*, tr. Daniel Heller-Roazen, New York: Zone Books, 1999.

Derrida, Jacques, "'Dead Man Running': Salut, Salut," *Negotiations: Interventions and Interviews 1971-2001*, tr. and ed. Elizabeth Rottenberg, Stanford: Stanford University Press, 2002, pp. 257-292.

— *Of Grammatology*, tr. Gayatri Chakravorty Spivak, Baltimore: John Hopkins University Press, 1967.

— *Speech and Phenomena, and Other Essays on Husserl's Theory of Signs*, tr. David B. Allison,

Evanston: Northwestern University Press, 1973.

— "The Animal That Therefore I Am (More to Follow)," tr. David Wills, in *Critical Inquiry*, Vol. 28, No. 2, (Winter, 2002), pp. 369-418 .

— "The Ends of Man," *Margins of Philosophy*, tr. Alan Bass, Sussex: The Harvester Press, 1982, pp. 109-136.

— "Unsealing ('the old new language')," *Points...: Interviews, 1974-1994*, tr. Peggy Kamuf et al., ed. Elisabeth Weber, Stanford: Stanford University Press, 1995, pp. 115-131.

Gardner, Sebastian, "Splitting the Subject," in *Auslegung* 13, No. 2, 1983, pp. 186-192.

Heidegger, Martin, *Being and Time*, tr. John Macquarrie and Edward Robinson, Oxford: Blackwell, 1962.

— *Hegel's Phenomenology of Spirit*, tr. Parvis Emad and Kenneth Maly, Bloomington: Indiana University Press, 1988.

— *Kant and the Problem of Metaphysics*, tr. Richard Taft, Bloomington: Indiana University Press, 1990.

— "Letter on 'Humanism'," *Pathmarks*, ed. William McNeill, Cambridge: Cambridge University Press, 1998, pp. 239-276.

Howells, Christina, "Conclusion: Sartre and the Deconstruction of the Subject," in Howells, ed. *The Cambridge Companion to Sartre*, Cambridge: Cambridge University Press, 2006.

— "Sartre and Negative Theology," in *Modern Language Review*, July 1981.

— "Sartre: Desiring the Impossible," in *Continental Philosophy VII: Philosophy and Desire*, ed. Hugh J. Silverman, New York: Routledge, 2000.

— *Sartre: The Necessity of Freedom*, Cambridge: Cambridge University Press, 1988.

Jacoby, Mario, *Shame and the Origins of Self-Esteem: A Jungian Approach*, tr. Douglas Whitcher, London: Routledge, 1996.

Martinot, Steve, *Forms in the Abyss: A Philosophical Bridge between Sartre and Derrida*, Philadelphia: Temple University Press, 2006.

— "Sartre's Being-for-Heidegger: Heidegger's Being-for-Sartre," in *Man and World* 24, 1991, pp. 63-74.

Rajan, Tilottama, *Deconstruction and the Remainders of Phenomenology: Sartre, Derrida, Foucault, Baudrillard*, Stanford: Stanford University Press, 2002.

Sartre, Jean-Paul, *Being and Nothingness: An Essay on Phenomenological Ontology*, tr. Hazel E. Barnes, New York: Philosophical Library, 1956.

— *Critique of Dialectical Reason*, tr. Alan Sheridan-Smith, London: New Left Books, 1976.

— *Existentialism is a Humanism*, tr. Carol Macomber, New Haven: Yale University Press, 2007.

— *Imagination: A Psychological Critique*, tr. Forrest Williams, Ann Arbor: University of Michigan Press, 1962.

— *Nausea, or The Diary of Antoine Roquentin*, tr. Robert Baldick, Middlesex: Penguin Books, 1965.

— *No Exit, and Three Other Plays*, tr. Stuart Gilbert and Lionel Abel, New York: Vintage Books, 1956.

— *Search for a Method*, tr. Hazel E. Barnes, New York: Knopf, 1963.
— *The Idiot of the Family*, Volumes I, II and III, tr. Carol Cosman, Chicago: University of Chicago Press, 1981, 1987, 1989.
— *The Transcendence of the Ego: An Existentialist Theory of Consciousness*, tr. Forrest Williams and Robert Kirkpatrick, New York: Noonday Press, 1962.
— "Writing for One's Age," *'What is Literature?' and Other Essays*, tr. Bernard Frechtman, Cambridge: Harvard University Press, 1988.
Silverman, Hugh J., *Inscriptions: Between Phenomenology and Structuralism*, New York: Routledge, 1987.
Williams, Bernard, *Shame and Necessity*, Berkeley: University of California Press, 1993.
Wood, Philip R., "Derrida Engagé and Poststructuralist Sartre: A Redefinition of Shifts in Recent French Philosophy," *Modern Language Notes*, Vol. 104, No. 4, 1989, pp. 861-79.

13

Body-Reparation-Invention: Cixous and Derrida on "Feminine Writing"

Sukalpa Bhattacharjee

> She must write her self, because this is the invention of a *new insurgent* writing which, when the moment of her liberation has come, will allow her to carry out the indispensable ruptures and transformations in her history.
>
> It is impossible to *define* a feminine practice of writing, and this is an impossibility that will remain, for this practice can never be theorized, enclosed, discourse that regulates the phallocentric system; it does and will take place in areas other than those subordinated to philosophico-theoretical domination.
>
> Hélène Cixous, *The Laugh of the Medusa*

Since the 1990s Cixous and Derrida had several dialogues on language and displacement, eventually constituting an archive of Jewish-Algerian-French thought and projecting through their work the inevitable link between writing, the body and dreaming. A major aspect of their dialogic exchange was on the notion of the 'feminine' and 'writing' which problematizes Cixous' notion of *écriture féminine*. Writing for Cixous is indissociable from reading, from living, and from her body. But Cixous refuses to present stable, mediated and phantasmic signifiers of body as evident in "The Laugh of Medusa," the most seminal of her texts on "Feminine Writing." Cixous displaces the debate of feminine and writing away from an inquiry of gendered subjectivity in the text, toward an analysis of the articulations of sexuality and desire produced through textuality. Cixous's position seems to constitute a powerful feminist appropriation of the Derridian approach of rejection of the logic of binary oppositions that characterizes the history of Western discourse. In 'Castration or Decapitation' as well as in *The Newly Born Woman*, she states that the dualistic structure must be rejected and in her theorization of feminine writing in 'The Laugh of the Medusa' she interrogates the Freudian and Lacanian models that see the phallus as the organizing point of sexual identity and desire. Cixous argues that "woman is body more than man is [...] more body, hence more writing." However, much of Derrida's idea of return to the secret of the symptom assumes what Cixous in her *Hyperdream* has called 'mourning for the mother' that never can reach the destination of death. But not reaching the destination, for Derrida, is haunting, or that 'what happens or arrives with phantasam'. So, in Derrida's view Hélène Cixous breaks the boundary between subjunctive and subjective, between moment and its escaping text. In *Hyperdream* as well as in a text like *A Silkworm of One's Own,* Hélène Cixous recollects how there is spinning of filiation within a shroud, which is a dream in reverse. Hélène Cixous noted that in such reverse memory, grief comes only as vertigo and not as determined grief and hence writing becomes "a hunger for flesh and for tears, our appetite for living, that, at the tip of forsaken fingers, makes a pencil grow." Writing goes to infinite giving and to dreaming, does not obey 'us' and becomes 'telephonic'. Such a shifting and yet a non-pronominal authorial "I" assumes the metafictional character of a semi-subject, that is never complete, but remains open to the door. Her writing always reconfigures intersubjectivity, with her "further-than-myself in myself" and "myself as the first other"; "the other in all his or her forms gives me I". Cixous, following Derrida, intends feminine writing as a decentring effect that expresses female fluidity, rebelling against masculine economy. In this sense writing through the body becomes reparation and inventive.

Body as Text

For Hélène Cixous the act of writing is about immense possibilities and yet it is about the impossible, as she says, "When I write, it's everything that we don't know we can be that is written out of me..." ("*Medusa*," 348) Cixous is also trying to write the other in the self when the other cannot be inscribed. The impossible possibilities of writing the other is reflected in Cixous's attempt to write everything that is not "me" and that which comes out of "me" in the act of writing. "Me" becomes other to "itself". But how does it become possible to write the other when the other cannot be inscribed? Cixous suggests that from mind to words, from body to paper, from signifier to signifier the possibilities of writing are made visible through various levels of translations.. Susan Sellers (Sellers, 1994: xxix) explains the two senses in which feminine writing can be understood. While this body of writing is the province of both the sexes, women are 'closer to feminine economy' than men and so women's writing has the potential to 'circumvent and reformulate' existing oppressive structures .Women are better equipped for feminine writing for which the body can be the most powerful site for inscription, because historically and sociologically the (female) body has been the space for articulating sexual differences and acute marginalization. Besides, the adult self is srill influenced by the pre-symbolic relationship with the mother and this is reflected in the adult's desire to inscribe the 'rhythms and articulations of the mother's body' in language and creative inscriptions. This necessitates the creation of an alter/native language which can articulate the textuality of the (female) body and the use of the body as a text in feminine writing. Secondly, feminine writing refuses to erase the other in order to inscribe the self and so it is more inclusive. Cixous asks "Who are I?" (Preface, 1994: xviii) because according to her "Pure I, identical to I-self, does not exist.I is always in difference." (Preface, 1994: xviii) So for Cixous it is the body which can be a a metaphor for woman's multiplicity, defying masculine language and interrogating restrictions on the female voice and body. Like the multi-directional serpents writhing on the medusa's head, woman can celebrate a creativity and sexuality that defies structure. A writer of feminine text is like a medusa, entering language through multiple locations of feminine desires—sexual, historical, or linguistic.

What this suggests is that women can be brought to writing through a reconnection to their bodies because a body is always already subjected to inscription. No writing can exist independently of the body and therefore 'this new insurgent writing' of the feminine should use the body as a text. For Cixous, the body is "already text" as a consequence of relations, in the interface, between the body and life. This brings Cixous to the point of boundary crossings between writing and life, one creating the context for the other. Life is both a bodily-text and a textual-body. Cixous seeks to collapse the mind/body binaries as reflected in masculine writings and embrace differences as, *tous les deux*. Masculine writing (re)produces binariess through hierarchy, linearity and logic whereas feminine writing is continuous with possibilities and potential of producing creative ways of thinking. The essence of feminine writing is in the celebration of differences and in upholding textuality of the (female) body. Hence, Luce Irigaray also points out the necessity of a women's specific language, which she calls '*le parler femme*', which operates through disruption of the phallocratic order by rejecting its unitary character that reduces everything else onto its logic of the Same. She argues that:

> [masculine] domination of the philosophical logos stems in large part from its power to reduce all others to the economy of the Same. [...] Whence the necessity of 'reopening' the figures of philosophical discourse—idea, substance, transcendental subjectivity, absolute knowledge—in order to pry out of them what they have borrowed that is feminine, from the feminine, to make them 'render up' and give back what they owe the feminine. (Irigaray, 1985: 74)

According to Cixous scholars like Banting (Banting, 225-46), Cixous is not inventing a new and exclusive women's language but creating new 'interlanguages' which is the linguistic interference from the source language

(SL). The text '*écriture féminine*' is located in-between patriarchal discourse and the new language that which is yet to be born., Therefore *écriture féminine* always anticipates the unknown, yet to be born language of articulation. The (female) body is not a site that represents a certain subjectivity, but the site in which interlanguages are played out to allow the construction of multiple bodies and subjectivities. This third body of writing which is born in-between is entwined and interwoven with voice/speech. However, this voice/speech is not "spoken" in that it opposes "written". When feminine speaks,

> ... she throws her trembling body forward; she lets go of herself... all of her passes into her voice, and it's with her body that she vitally supports the 'logic' of her speech... [and] she physically materializes what she's thinking; she signifies it with her body... she inscribes what she's saying, because she doesn't deny her drives the intractable and impassioned part they have in speaking. ("*Medusa*," 338).

But what is the 'elsewhere' of writing? Cixous writes,

> Writing ... does not happen out there ... [but] from the inside ... down below... a desirable hell ... deep in my body ... behind thought... [but it] does not mean that it does not think, but it thinks differently from our thinking and speech.

Cixous refuses to define the feminine mode of writing because it is impossible to define it. The flexibility and boundarylessness of feminine writing cannot be fixed within any definition.

> [it is] in the depths of my heart ... in my stomach, my womb, and if you have not got a womb – then it is somewhere 'else.' You must climb down in order to go in the direction of that place (*Three Steps,* 118).

This depth 'of my heart' is one's relationship to both pain and pleasure and this 'climb' downwards to the hell inside is the discovery of the 'other place' that will disturb the linearity and the rationale of a patriarchal social order. "It is here where desire makes fiction exist" (97). This is the space of alterity that makes feminine writing possible by 'stealing' or 'flying away' to an a-temporal space. But how does Cixous construct the feminine subject who would steal herself away to the inside of the heart/womb's hell? Cixous writes, "First she dies, then she loves" (*Coming to Writing,* 36). Death and love become synonymous for the feminine subject who should experience both simultaneously to escape the temporization of the a-temporal space of writing.

The Space of Writing

For Cixous, "Writing is not arriving... One must go... with the body... [and] leave the self....Walking through the self toward the dark" (*Three Steps,* 65). It is in the darkness of hell that one begins to write truthfully. Cixous writes,

> I move towards something that only exists in an elsewhere... writing is what deals with the no-deal, relates to what gives no return. That something else (what history forbids, what reality excludes or does not admit) can manifest itself there: some other. With the desire to keep this other alive – hence some living feminine—some difference—and some love... (*Sorties*, 97)

It is important to note that the Cixousian feminine economy does not operate through opposition to the masculine, because as mentioned earlier, women exist in a unique (non-) position as the excluded other of the masculine. Therefore Cixous's representation of difference and her notion of subjectivity appears more complex than that of Irigaray. While Irigaray bases her principle of difference mainly on the issue of biological sexes, Cixous points out the co-existence of multiplicity of differences within subjects even of the same sex. According to her,

> Pure I, identical to I-self, does not exist. [...] The difference is in us, in me, difference plays me. And it is numerous: since it plays with me in me between me and me or I and myself. A "myself" which is the most intimate first name of You. I will never say often enough that the difference is not one, that there is never one without the other. [...] I is never an individual. I is haunted. I is always, before knowing anything, an I-love-you" (Cixous, 1994: xviii).

Thus, Cixous's analysis for locating the space of feminine writing appears more complicated than that of Irigaray. Cixous appropriates the masculine lack as the necessary condition for feminine writing—"losing everything ... [and] this is not a thinkable 'condition'... if you want to [lose], then there is you and wanting, there is nonloss" (*Coming to Writing*, 38). Women's exclusion from language situates her beyond "the material that writing is formed of and extracted from" and thereby beyond language. The feminine is "the economy of positive lack..." (Cixous, *The Author in Truth*, 164). Being excluded from the masculine economy, she escapes the conventional representation and the grammar of language, which in turn gives her the liberty to play with language. For Cixous, "What is most true is poetic" (*Rootprints,* 3). Cixous cautions her readers about the hegemony of the signified on the signifier which would reduce the generative power of the feminine. Although it is necessary to have a theoretical framework for feminine writing Cixous privileges the poetic over the theoretical while recognizing the differences between the two.

Perhaps this is the basis of her recognition of *tous les deux* in which she seeks the reparation of the two, a separation-reparation. Derrida in his "Foreword" to *Helene Cixous Reader* (Sellers: 1994: vii-xi) begins with an example cited by Cixous in her *First days of the Year*, in a chapter entitled "Self-Portraits of a Blind Woman," a certain "Story of Contretemps." It begins on a bench. Derrida mentions that it is also a scene of reading of sexual difference: between separation and reparation, the in-between of the two. Separation and reparation are the impossible—difference in sameness—It is in the exchange that profits the other, the between that she is interested in. (Derrida, "Foreword," pp. xv-xxiii). That is why it is necessary "to shake them [words] all the time, like apple trees" (Cixous "Author", 150). Words therefore are born out of one's relationship with *jouissance*. *Écriture feminine* is grounded on the relationship with *jouissance*. Thus Cixous writes, "To write and thus forge the antilogos weapon" that will "submerge, cut through, get beyond the ultimate reserve-discourse" (*Medusa*, 337, 342). Writing has its source in the female—body from where multiple bodies emerge as Cixous mentions— "I am under the cosmic tent under the canvas of my body and I gaze out." (Coming to Writing, 53). More the writing more the body, more life, and more possibility. As Cixous puts it, "What enlarges a person's life are the impossible dreams, the unrealizable desires. The one that has not yet come true" (*Painting*, 129). Writing as the impossible makes this impossibility possible. Cixous calls it feminine writing because for her, "women will go right up to the impossible" (*Medusa*, 342). To construct the feminine space of writing is the impossible that must be embraced. "It is... that writing makes love other. It is itself this love. Other-Love is writing's first name." (Cixous, *Sorties*, 99). For Cixous,

> to love, to watch-think-seek the other in the other... is what nourishes life—a love that has no commerce with the apprehensive desire that provides against the lack and stultifies the strange..." (*Medusa*, 348).

To write is to love the other- as self-as-other, other-as-self.To write one must take a journey into the unknown (hell) and unfamiliar. Cixous says:

> Writing tries to undertake the journey toward strange sources of art that are foreign to us... The author writes as if he or she ...were a foreigner in his or her family. (*Three Steps*, 20)

Hélène Cixous's notion of the 'new insurgent' writing elaborated in her notion of 'écriture feminine', raises several other question-can the body be a source of self-knowledge? Does female sexuality exist prior to or in spite of social experience? Do women in fact experience their bodies purely or essentially, outside the damaging acculturation so sharply analyzed by women in France and elsewhere? What is the relationship between body and writing? How to define the 'feminine' and 'writing' without falling prey to the risks of essentialism? Can culture be rationally critiqued and then transformed? A review of available literatures on this themes inevitably draws our attention to the convergences and divergences—the between and beyond in the writings of Cixous and Derrida. The diagoues/monologues/differences and convergences between this two great thinkers of our times transgresses and transcends the boundaries of definitive categories like life and death, speech and silences, writing, speaking and hearing, theory, theatre and poetry, love, forgiveness, dream and reality. Many have termed these exchanges as a dialogue between philosophy and literature as well. Today it appears that it is impossible to read one without the other. It would be worthwhile to quote a few lines from Cixous's *Insister of Jacques Derrida* (2007):

> So we met each other in order to think in language, to speak language; between us it has always been a question of writing, of living in language, of hearing ourselves write, so as to write. We speak to one another so as to hear ourselves read, to know how to read, to write ourselves speaking, to give ourselves the writing that is in speech, sometimes so as to take words from each other's mouth.(13)
>
> Another thing, since I am on the side of the body: this text is full of bodily expressions, excretions, secretions, effusions. I think that Derrida is at once so well-read and so un-read, so loved and so aggressed because he is one of the rare 'men' or perhaps the only one, to risk his active body in the text. A body movement on the order of circling around inscribes and is inscribed in *Circumfession*. You yourself circle around this real and metaphorical penis, this blinded, wounded, healed, resuscitated, etc. penis, you circle around this sex, and at the same time your eye, our eye circles back on itself feeling faint. (*The Portable Cixous*, 2010: 54)

At the theoretical level thinkers like Spivak have questioned the very foundation of an oppositional theory (Spivak: 1987). But, Cixous's appropriation to oppositional theory has been through 'feminine writing', which transgresses, disrupts and destabilizes all binaries, particularly masculine/feminine. In the mid 70's when Cixous along with Irigaray, Kristeva and others developed a body of thought on the reading of women's experience in textual representations they followed Virginia Woolf's notion of a feminine writing that does not rely on the biological conception of the sexes—but on the mode of writing that characterizes feminine space and feminine writing. This perspective on feminine writing added to the climate of deconstruction and intellectual inquiry in post-May 1968 in France establishing the relationship between writing, politics and gender.

Another aspect to be noted is that Cixous writes by hand due to her belief that writing is a corporeal act, involving the memories and knowledge of the writer's body, and partly from her recognition of the fragile and intuitive nature of the writer's quest for truth. In the Introduction to *The Writing Notebooks* (2004) Susan Sellers quotes Cixous—

> I refuse... That this fabricated memory is for me contrary to the ripening of a text which wants to weave itself organically not by the accumulation of strata, but by erasings, siftings, virgin fresh starts I can advance ahead of me, without turning round, in the dark in discovery and far from the pollution of a churning out that would block my need to hear the unheard further off (x).

Writing therefore for Cixous is indissociable from reading, from living, and from her body. She wants to write on her own insides (womb/heart), not to know herself—although writing is writing oneself into existence. Perhaps what is significant is the instant moment/event without its event-ness Her passion for theatre lies in the fact that a staged play is always in the moment. She tries to write the present, which is an impossibility; yet in the trying, writing is transformed as the present plays truant and escapes inscription.

Jacques Derrida on the issue of feminine writing is known to resist a fixed technique or methodology in his practice of reading or writing, similar to Cixous's *écriture feminine.* Derrida's practice sets for itself an impossible task: "invention"— of "a novel world, another habitat, another person, another desire even" through multiple registers. Derrida attempts to suspend or deflect the very effect of universalization which for Kant and Hegel constitutes the heart of language. Again, Derrida allows for the *other* a place for the inscription of the other's difference. In *Psyche: Inventions of the Other* Derrida says—

> ...deconstruction loses nothing from admitting that it is impossible; ...The interest of deconstruction ... is a certain experience of the impossible:...the experience of the other as the invention of the impossible, in other words, as the only possible invention. (*PS*, 209).

Thus in the in-between of life and death, self and other, biography and autobiography like separation and reparation gets blurred. In *HC for Life* Derrida writes:

> Everything we write, she and I, remains strictly autobiographical, as they say. We only ever write ourselves, on ourselves. *Nous nous écrivons...* this indecision between two homonyms is not a game. It is so serious that it remains undecidable for me. An absolute difference which can come back to the same around here [*par ici*].... It is the truth: there are cases when, when two write, one no longer knows whether they write (to) each other or themselves [*s'ils écrivent ou s'ils écrivent*], and whether a lot covers all or part of the homonymy. (175)

Again, Feminine writing also promotes genre crossings by way of greater possibilities of articulating the other's position. Cixous's writing frequently incarnates and articulates the other in the form of characters. Whereas fiction writing for Cixous involves the staging of the self through language, theatre involves the creation of the other to be embodied in performance. Cixous like Derrida is anxious to embrace a sense of responsibility towards the other being. Once writing has shifted out of fixed parameters of logocentrism, *écriture feminine* flourishes, and the phallus disappears in Cixous' agenda for rewriting the female body.

Feminine writing thus, through its attempt at reaching out to the unknown other, invents the other. Masculine rhetorical economy rests on linguistic, historical, and sexual confinements and so women must evade the path of entering language through the masculine rhetorical space. Like Cixous, Spivak (1987) calls for the insurgent subaltern to act as an agent for change by destabilizing the patriarchal order. Cixous claims an insurgency through insurgent writing which becomes possible through a reclaiming of her own body. Following Virginia Woolf's (1966) position on the commodification of women through marriage as narrated in *Three Guineas,* Cixous assumes a critical stance against marginalizing women both as an economic and as a linguistic commodity. Therefore, Spivak, Woolf, and Cixous want woman to be empowered through language and reclaim her identity beyond and independent of the male symbolic order. Redeeming language from the phallic order has been one of the major struggles for women's writing. Elaine Showalter's (1977) concept of 'gynocriticism' has a lot in common with Cixous's *écriture feminine,* particularly in the sense that this form of women's writing resists the logic of linear, univocal narrative characteristic of masculine writing. However, as a resistant mode of writing the primary goal of 'gynocritics' is to appropriate, contest and subvert male strategies of writing as in *The Mad Woman in the Attic* (Gilbert and Gubar, 1979). Cixous's feminine writing however comes closer to Irigaray's views which link women's diffuse sexuality to women's language that awaits inscription on the body/text of women.

Taste of Dream

Cixous and Derrida return from a dream without a subject to touch back at self/itself, which is like 'dreaming the dream' and 'seeing oneself seeing.' Can such reflexive acts iterate and recreate the dream as an event that has a psychoanalytic depth of subversion of the dominant masculine? Is it an excess of anticipation, misguided or seduced reading? *HC for Life* or *JD, the Insister*? Can we name the unnameable in the language of dream? It is always a distinct possibility of repatriation through the acts of writing, dreaming and delivering. It is in this journey that one moves from Derrida to Benjamin via Adorno and one situates 'Benjamin's bed' and howls at the empty sky a name 'one knows lies hidden beyond the reach of human voice'. (*Hyperdream*, 131). Is dreaming then an act of phenomenological retention, or is it just writing about a dream that borders on the productive limits of politics of desire that arises before the subject and the object? Can this dream support mirror-effect that is needed to narrate it to *J.D. the Insister*? To whom does one recount?

> To a person who does not interrupt, does not crush the frail vapor, who tastes noiselessly, almost to no one. To oneself, near to oneself. To the ear. To the ear that keeps watch.
>
> (...) one redreams it to oneself once again.... And then adieu. (*Insister*, 133-4).

This cycle of dreaming-redreaming, Cixous contended, is the work of mourning, recounting and almost never-sleeping as insisted by Proustean aunty. If *J.D. the Insister* and if *H.C.*, the insister of J.D. are recounting to each other their dreams in the absent-presence of each other, the exercise is best captured in dreaming sleeplessly, a non-Faustean way to never know each oher's dreams, as it is embodied, deterritorialzed and without mirror-effects. This is what Cixous would term as 'greediness for tastetexts', which is part of an experience of never sleeping with fleeting, unrecountable and at the same time, housed-till-the-morning dreams and then comes the moments of writing: 'as soon as it is seized by writing, the concept is cooked.' (*Insister*, 137) This is erasure of the first intensity of the dream, a repression that one undergoes in writing, as Derrida would insist that such a contemplation or a fable must 'give itself' as a dream, as in a dream. (*Insister*, 144-5) But Cixous refers to the Proustean mirror-effect, when she said, 'Strange mirrors in which we contemplate ourselves in the other (in an) image.' (*Insister*, 144). The essential distinction here is between Freudian-Faustean mirror-effect versus Proustean sleepless dreaming of the dream in a strange mirror-image of dreaming, which is a Derridean giving to a supplement, to a process of larger semiotic creativity, where the search for the signifier, each of which is 'invited' in the other's dream. In Cixous's inimitable words, 'any move to lift the veil is a movement that submits to the law of the veil' (*Insister*, 144), as per Derrida. So, *H.C.* does not insist on submission to the law of the veil, which is the limits of imagining 'sexual differences.'

This invocation of dream, mirror and veil centres around writing differences, especially gender differences. The difference is unresolvable even in sharing dreams as such a sharing is only a desire, a 'greediness for tastetexts', or, lending an ear to see oneself see. Cixous calls it 'counter-genealogical movement of deconstruction', which pertains to the name Derrida, which is 'dissembled beginning with resemblances that are ephemeral.' (*Insister*, 155)

REFERENCES

Banting, Pamela. "The Body as Pictogram: Rethinking Hélène Cixous's écriture féminine." *Textual Practice* 6.2 (1992): 225-46. Cited in Sinclair Timothy Ang's "(Giving an Other) Reading (of) Hélène Cixous, écriture (and) feminine" *http://www.gradnet.de/papers/pomo98.papers/srang98.htm.*visited on 2.11.2015.

Cixous, Hélène. *The Laugh of the Medusa* (1975) in Elaine Marks, Isabelle de Courtivron (eds.) *New French Feminisms: An Anthology,* Minneapolis, University of Minnesota Press, 1984.

——, *The Newly Born Woman*, tr. Betsy Wing, Minneapolis: Minnesota University Press. 1986.

——, *Coming To Writing and Other Essays*, Ed. Deborah Jenson. tr. Sarah Cornell,

Deborah Jenson, Ann Liddle, Susan Sellers, Cambridge, MS, Harvard University Press, 1991.

——, *Three Steps on the Ladder of Writing*, New York: Columbia University Press, 1995.

——, "Sorties Out and Out Attacks/Ways Out/Forays," in Cixous, Hélène and Catherine Clément. *The Newly Born Woman*, tr. Betsy Wing, London: I.B. Tauris Publishers, 1996.

——, "The Author in Truth," in *Coming To Writing and Other Essays*, tr. Sarah Cornell, Deborah Jenson, Ann Liddle, Susan Sellers, Cambridge, MS: Harvard University Press, 1991.

——, *Rootprints: Memory and Life Writing*, New York: Routledge (1997).

——, *Insister of Jacques Derrida*, tr. by Peggy Kamuf, Edinburgh: Edinburgh University Press, 2007.

——, "Castration or Decapitation?" tr. Annette Kuhn, *Signs 7,* 1981.

——, *Hyperdream*, Cambridge, Polity, 2009.

——, *The Writing Notebooks,* tr. Susan Seller, New York: Bloomsbury, 2006.

——, 'Preface', in Susan Sellers *The Hélène Cixous Reader*, New York: Routledge, 1994.

Cixous, Hélène and Marta Segarra, *The Portable Cixous*, ed., tr. Susan Sellers, New York: Bloomsbury Publishing, 2004.

Derrida, Jacques. *Psyche: Inventions of the Other*, Vol. I, Peggy Kamuf and Elizabeth Rottenberg (eds.), Stanford: Stanford University Press, 2007.

——, *Margins of Philosophy,* tr. Alan Bass, Chicago: University of Chicago Press, 1982

——, *Positions*, (tr.) Alan Bass, Chicago: University of Chicago Press, 1982.

——, *H.C. for Life, that is to Say,* Stanford : Stanford University Press, 2006.

Gilbert, Sandra and Susan Gubar, *The Madwoman in the Attic: The Woman Writer and the Nineteenth-Century Literary Imagination,* New Haven, Connecticut: Yale University Press, 1979.

Irigaray, L., *This Sex Which is Not One*, (tr.) C. Porter and C. Burke, Ithaca: Cornell University Press, 1985.

Lacan, Jacques, *The Seminar of Jacques Lacan: On Feminine Sexuality, the Limits of Love and Knowledge*, W. W. Norton, 1999.

Moi, Toril. *Sexual/Textual Politics: Feminist Literary Theory*, London: Methuen, 1985.

Spivak, Gayatri Chakravorty. *In Other Worlds: Essays in Cultural Politics,* New York: Methuen, 1987.

Sellers, Susan. "Foreword by Jacques Derrida," *The Hélène Cixous Reader,* New York: Routledge. 1994.

Showalter, Elaine. *A Literature of Their Own: British Women Novelists from Brontë to Lessing*, Princeton, Princeton University Press, 1977.

Woolf, Virginia. *Three Guineas*, New York: Harvest, 1966.

14

Ecce Animot: Notes on the Animal Stigmatext

Sandhya Devesan Nambiar

I

The *Jungle*, Upton Sinclair's novel of 1906, dedicated to "the workingmen of America," portrays the lives of poor Lithuanian immigrants in America, their miserable working conditions, their crushing poverty, and the inevitable spectre of death all around. At one point, the novel describes in a somewhat hyperbolic fashion, the conditions in a meatpacking factory, where the workers who fall into the rendering tanks are sometimes rendered along with the meat into "Durham's Pure Leaf Lard". While this was extremely shocking to the readers of the time, Sinclair declared that what drew readers more than the account of the actually existing horrifying conditions of labour, was the aesthetic outrage against the idea of the meat being contaminated.

While Sinclair brought the human and the animal together in rather grisly conditions into a symbolic exchange, they have existed together, as well as not together, especially where the desiring productions of Capital have also led to massive factory production and spectrality of the animal as consumption.

As Novalis states,

> All enjoyment, all taking in and assimilation, is eating, or rather: eating is nothing other than assimilation. All spiritual pleasure can be expressed through eating. In friendship, one really eats of the friend, or feeds on him. It is a genuine trope to substitute the body for the spirit—and, at a commemorative dinner for a friend, to enjoy, with bold, supersensual imagination, his flesh in every bite, and his blood in every gulp.[1]

How do we then conceive of this messianic friend, and the power and force of her existence upon ours? Does not the human become radically altered by the sharing of space and time with all others that are not human, as Levinas was to finally concede? This carno-phallogocentrism as Matthew Calarco terms it, is one of the problems at stake in the human-animal relationship. At stake also is the animal *in* the human, which is sought to be repudiated in order for the 'purely' human to emerge into subjectivity.

Jonathan Swift's rant as letter to Alexander Pope in 1725, mobilizes an idea of a rational humanity which stands apart from what he calls the generally occurring *animal rationale*,

"But principally I hate and detest that animal called man, although I heartily love John, Peter, Thomas, and so forth... I have got materials toward a treatise, proving the falsity of that definition *animal rationale*, and to show it would be only *rationis capax*."

This Cartesian separation of categories, persists in contemporary phenomenological thinking, and remains a pressing problem of the subject, leading to questions also of pre- and post-subject formulations, where the animal constantly appears on the horizon, but vanishes into the body.

This paper then, shall attempt to explore the category of the 'animal', especially through readings of Derrida's own investigations in "The Animal that Therefore I Am," informed also by the observation in *The Beast and the Sovereign*, where he makes the rather Foucauldian claim that both are outlaws— "the beast ignorant of right and the sovereign having the right to suspend right, to place himself above the law that he is, that he makes, that he institutes, as to which he decides, sovereignly,"[2] continuing in his interview with Jean-Luc Nancy in 1989 titled "Eating well; or the Calculation of the Subject," which we shall return to.

These ideas shall be discussed along with the Heideggerean concept of the *Mitsein*, which finds a later resonance and unfolding in Deleuze's idea of *becoming-animal*, wherein that which we call the human can be explored in its being-with and becoming molecular.

The title, is partially borrowed from Hélène Cixous' recuperative *Stigmata: Escaping Texts,* where the idea of escape shall be looked at as a line of flight leading away from the Subject, and leading towards those who do not possess a face, except in engagement with the sovereign.

First delivered as part of a ten-hour lecture, in France in 1997, *The Animal that Therefore I Am* stands testimony to Derrida's continual engagement with the "question of the animal."

In the thirty years prior to this lecture, when he published his major works - *Writing and Difference*, *Speech and Phenomena*, and *Of Grammatology*, while he did insist, and repeatedly so on the animal, he did not publish his ideas comprehensively until *The Animal that Therefore I am* (henceforth AIA).

The chapter first appeared in English translation in *Critical Inquiry* in 2001 and has been the object of careful analysis by many scholars working in animal studies. We find that we enter Derrida's much-discussed nude encounter with a cat, a cat that he insists is a 'real cat'—and not the semblance of a cat that stands in for all cats. Opening with the Biblical account of the Genesis, Derrida explores the idea of human nudity in relation to the animal, where the human condition is territorialized on the eating of the fruit of the tree of knowledge, and the subsequent shame attached to the awareness of nudity, Derrida states,

> In principle, with the exception of man, no animal has ever thought to dress itself. [Thus] clothing would be proper to man, one of the 'properties' of man. 'Dressing oneself' would be inseparable from all the other figures of what is 'proper to man,' even if one talks about it less than speech or reason, the logos, history, laughing, mourning, burial, the gift, etc.[3]

These "properties of man" are the sites that Derrida attempts to bring into question. This encounter leads to a questioning of the very idea of human subjectivity when face-to-face with an animal, or when the gaze of the animal is upon oneself.

Derrida describes his encounter as being naked, and is ashamed of this nakedness in front of his little cat who follows him into the bathroom each morning and gazes inscrutably upon him. In Derrida's embarrassment before the cat, there is the act of 'Circumfession', where the limit separating the human from the animal also sets up the twin demands of sacrifice on the one hand, and apology or shame on the other. Talking about the self, he says, becomes an apologia of sorts—and he says that "another way one can confess (besides walking into the confessional) is by guiltily relating a story about oneself; a story, that is, which makes one look and feel guilty."

Throughout the essay, he contemplates the significance of his nudity before the animal, and the consequent shame that results from such as encounter. This leads to the question of the gaze of the animal upon us—it is a witness to the historicity of the human or it an Other who judges the sovereign in his distance?

Nakedness here becomes the paradoxical Event—which is both demanded, as well as unasked for apology. The animal as spectator therefore returns us to the question of the Subject—there is someone who has to meet the gaze of the animal and offer the apologetic though banal, supplicatory gesture as a kind of atonement for the Abrahamic exclusion for as Derrida mentions in *Eating Well*, his interview with Jean-Luc Nancy "...the 'Thou shalt not kill' is addressed to the other and presupposes him. It is destined to the very thing that it institutes, the other as man... The 'thou shalt not kill'—with all of its consequences,which are limitless—has never been understood within the Judeo-Christian tradition, nor apparently by Levinas, as a 'Thou shalt not put to death the living in general.' "[4]

Therefore while it could be argued that the body of the animal bears the stigmata of its sacrificial wound, the human subject is also a *stigmatext*, bearing the mark of responsibility of the animal death.

There is a temporal slippage between the shameful nudity of man and the parrhesiac shameless nudity of the animal, which is expressed in the ambiguous title of the essay, which could be translated as either 'The Animal that therefore I Am' (as if I were brought back to my own animality, for example, through the encounter with a cat), or 'The Animal that therefore I Follow' (as if I were following the animal on an evolutionary timeline, or following in obedience and submission, or following it in order to track it down like a hunter. (Derrida 2002, p. 380))

II

The doubleness of the signifier '*je suis*' in this context leads us to different modes of thinking the animal, and in terms of the response and responsibility attached to it. This slippery notion of both 'being' and 'following' points to the movement of the animal as Other in the interiority of being, as well its demands in the exterior—existing as evental difference to any possible totality of the self.

Derrida therefore deconstructs the Cartesian binary between the human and animal with what he calls *limitrophy*: where the dividing line between has turned into the abyss, which complicates the very notion of the dyad with the many, and the multiple. The line therefore turns blurry and abyssal, however maintaining the animal in its singularity.

> As with every bottomless gaze, as with the eyes of the other, the gaze called animal offers to my sight the abyssal limit of the human: the inhuman or the ahuman, the ends of man, that is to say the border crossing from which vantage man dares to announce himself to himself, thereby calling himself by the name that he believes he gives himself. And in these moments of nakedness, under the gaze of the animal, everything can happen to me, I am like a child ready for the apocalypse, *I am (following) the apocalypse itself,* that is to say the ultimate and first event of the end, the unveiling and the verdict. I am (following) it, the apocalypse, I identify with it by running behind it, after it, after its whole zoo-logy.[5]

There is a parallel question, not only to the one who follows the animal, but also to the one who follows the subject—who responds to the question of the Subject? On the one hand, there is the Other that is to be sacrificed in order for the Subject to appear; while the Other also demands an apology by its being-in-the-world where the Other's thrownness in the world also draws from us the care for the Other. There is the care of the self that demands the sacrifice of the other while there is also a certain care for the Other—that which is termed *Fürsorge*, in Heideggerean fashion—which is the being-with—the condition of *Mitsein*. Heidegger does not account for the Other as animal in his conception of the Care for the Other in *Being and Time*, as we know. As Derrida shows, Heidegger delineates an ontological separation: the living being (which is separated into the animality of the animal and the humanity of the human) and the nonliving being, and among all these distinctions, while "the stone is wordless, the animal is poor in the world," only man, he says, is 'world-forming'.

Derrida makes a mention of this qualified humanism in an interview:

> Only man has hands, says Heidegger, and, through the hand, he has access to a world of meaningful action. The ape, however, possesses only "Greifsorgane" (organs for grasping) and is therefore excluded from the realm of the human. This distinction between hand and organ for grasping is not something Heidegger arrived at by studying apes in the Black Forest, but rather has a purely stipulative character. Here, as always, humanism rests on the sacrifice of the animal, on the implicit swallowing up of the animal.[6]

This swallowing up of the animal renders Derrida's movement into a stasis, especially when he states in the interview as a reference to Novalis, "*To love without wanting to devour must surely be anorexic...*" This turn in Derrida himself towards what he repudiates in Heidegger, can also be read as a movement towards territorialization, the inscribing of oneself on the body of the friend. It is precisely this anorexic carnal dread that must be resisted, in order to be able to pose the question of who comes after the subject. Thus, *contra* Heidegger one could attempt a disarticulation of Heideggerian subjectivity from that discussed by Derrida and Nancy in "Eating Well," where one could bring *Fürsorge* to bear upon the profound responsibility that the Other in its multiplicitous difference draws from us.

In order to address this multiplicity, Derrida introduces the term "animot" in AIA, which he later replaces with the necrophagic desire resulting in the erasure of this difference in multiplicity. By replacing "animal" with "animot," Derrida hopes to remind us of the multiplicity of animal beings, and the question of the difference of the animal in relation to itself, as also from the human—

> Confined within this catch-all concept, within this vast encampment of the animal, in this general singular, within the strict enclosure of this definite article ('the Animal' and not 'animals'), as in a virgin forest, a zoo, a hunting or fishing ground, a paddock or an abattoir, a space of domestication, are all the living things that man does not recognize as his fellows, his neighbors, or his brothers. And that is so in spite of the infinite space that separates the lizard from the dog, the protozoon from the dolphin, the shark from the lamb, the parrot from the chimpanzee, the camel from the eagle, the squirrel from the tiger, the elephant from the cat, the ant from the silkworm, or the hedgehog from the echidna.[7]

Adding later, that "(t)he confusion of all nonhuman living things within the general and common category of the animal is not simply a sin against rigorous thinking, vigilance, lucidity, or empirical authority, it is also a crime."[8] Evidently, the very logic of deconstruction and difference has to be brought to bear upon that which complicates all subjective notions of self.

III

One could turn attention here to Gilles Deleuze and Felix Guattari who state in *A Thousand Plateaus* that natural history makes of the difference between animals in two ways—through thinking series and through thinking structure. Of the series, emerges also Jung's elaboration of the Archetype as collective unconscious—"it assigns the animal a particularly important role in dreams, myths, and human collectivities. The animal is inseparable from a series exhibiting the double aspect of progression-regression, in which each term plays the role of a possible transformer of the libido (metamorphosis). ... In contrast to natural history, man is now no longer the eminent term of the series; that term may be an animal for man, the lion, crab, bird of prey, or louse, in relation to a given act or function, in accordance with a given demand of the unconscious."[9]

Structural thinking however displaces completely this serial comparison, where "(i)t is no longer a question of graduating resemblances, ultimately arriving at an identification between Man and Animal at the heart of a mystical participation. It is a question of ordering differences to arrive at a correspondence of relations... When analyzing the institution of the totem, we do not say that this group of people identifies with that animal species...Structuralism represents a great revolution; the whole world becomes more rational."[10]

It is precisely this reason supposedly governing the human subject that Swift was protesting in the earlier-mentioned letter to Pope, and in contrast to a man as rational animal, he much preferred *rationis capax*, or man as possessing the ability to reason.

In contrast to these dilemmas of ratiocination, is the becoming-molecular or becoming-minoritarian, where one moves away from thinking through molar unities to thinking difference and the multiple. Deleuze's move towards becoming-animal here is a deterritorialization on this notion of the macro-political rational. He cites Faulkner who says that to avoid ending up a fascist there was no other choice but to become-black. "However," he says, "unlike history, becoming cannot be conceptualized in terms of past and future," and that "becoming-revolutionary remains indifferent to questions of a future and a past of the revolution; it passes between the two," that is to say, it is in *future anteriority* that one can locate the becoming-minor of the Subject. Deleuze and Guattari declare in *What is Philosophy?*, that the task of both philosophy and works of art is to strengthen the power of resistance, that is, "resistance to death, to servitude, to the intolerable, to shame, and to the present,"[11] where "to create is to resist," then the task is precisely to locate the unimagined or unimaginable in an already present actual.

It is of the order of the unimaginable, but it is a way of working a passage through the intolerable that exists, of thinking freedom within the cramped conditions of a necropolitical space, which can only lead to either death or sacrifice. Becoming-animal or with a slight shift—*becoming-animals*, as the case may be, since one replaces the animal with the Derridean multiple of the *animot*, becomes the event of deterritorializing the subject away from the *topoi* of a lonely being.

He invites us to look at a category of animals different from the domesticated or mythical—the demonic animal that exists in packs, in the wild, that form a shared multiplicity. These multiplicities with heterogeneous terms, co-functioning by contagion, enter certain assemblages; it is there that human beings effect their becomings-animal, or perform the who of the question "who comes after the Subject?," so that what is real is the becoming itself... *Becoming can and should be qualified as becoming-animal even in the absence of a term that would be the animal become*. The becoming-animal of the human being is real, even if the animal the human being becomes is not; and the *becoming-other* of the animal is real, even if that something other it becomes is not. This is the point to clarify: that a becoming lacks a subject distinct from itself; but also that it has no term, since its term in turn exists only as taken up in another becoming of which it is the subject, and which coexists, forms a block, with the first.

Deleuze also states that this becoming is not of the order of evolution, but instead an "involution"—for "(b)ecoming produces nothing by filiation; all filiation is imaginary. Becoming is always of a different order than filiation. *It concerns alliance*"[12]— where this alliance can only be of the nature of an infinite hospitality and virtual promise towards the Other, in the movement towards it, as *futur anterior,* where the real is not a molar classification, but is instead a molecular proliferation. He also issues a warning—"But we should not confuse these dark assemblages, which stir what is deepest within us, with organizations such as the institution of the family and the State apparatus."[13]

Returning to the story that we began with, Sinclair's *The Jungle,* it is instructive to also note, that ultimately what get ground together are the bodies of animals and men, but particular men—as labouring bodies, as the abjected subjects of the desiring production of Capital. While this may or may not be intentional, it points the way for the human-animal to be comprehended on the plane of immanence—not molar, but molecular and revolutionary subjectivities, resistant to fascist institutionality which when presented with the declaration of the becoming-minoritarian/becoming-black—"*I can't breathe*" —respond in the only way they know—with necropolitics and death. So while Deleuze responds to the eternal return, it "allows only the plebeian to return, the man without a name"— or the lumpen proletariat or new plebeians as Foucault terms them, or becoming-woman, as also becoming-animal.

These are perhaps some of the ways of responding to the call of who or what comes after the subject—where they create multiple lines of flight, and rhizomatic assemblages of unsettled nomadic animal meaning, which can perhaps lead us out of the loneliness of fixity and stratified time, into the fluidity of becoming as an infinite gesture of turning into, becoming, and taking within while also giving in.

I conclude here with Derrida's pithy yet profound declaration concerning the animal that we are—

"The animal looks at us, and we are naked before it. Thinking perhaps begins here."[14]

NOTES

1. *Novalis, Philosophical Writings,* ed. and tr. Margaret Mahony Stoljar. Albany: State University of New York Press, 1997, 102-103.
2. Jacques Derrida, *The Beast and the Sovereign.* Chicago: University of Chicago Press, 2012, p. 32.
3. Jacques Derrida, "The Animal that therefore I Am (More to Follow)," in *Critical Inquiry*, Vol. 28, No. 2 (Winter 2002), p. 373. < http://www.jstor.org/stable/ 1344276 > Accessed: 12/02/2011 17:22.
4. Jacques Derrida, " 'Eating Well', or the Calculation of the Subject: An Interview with Jacques Derrida," in *Who Comes After the Subject?*, Eduardo Cadava, Peter Connor, Jean-Luc Nancy (eds). New York: Routledge, p. 98.
5. Jacques Derrida, "The Animal that therefore I Am," Ibid., p. 381.
6. Daniel Birnbaum and Anders Olsson, "An Interview with Jacques Derrida on the Limits of Digestion," *E-FLUX*, Journal No. 2, 01/2009. <http://www.e-flux.com/journal/an-interview-with-jacques-derrida-on-the-limits-of-digestion/ > Accessed on 25 November 2014, 20:00.
7. Jacques Derrida, "The Animal that Therefore I Am," p. 402.
8. Ibid., p. 416.
9. Gilles Deleuze and Felix Guattari, *A Thousand Plateaus: Capitalism and Schizophrenia*, (tr.) B. Massumi. Minneapolis: University of Minnesota Press, 1987, p. 260.
10. Ibid.
11. G. Deleuze and F. Guattari, *What is Philosophy?*, (tr.) Hugh Tomlinson. New York: Verso, 1994, p. 110.
12. G. Deleuze and F. Guattari, *A Thousand Plateaus,* p. 263.
13. Ibid., p. 267.
14. Jacques Derrida, "The Animal that Therefore I Am," p. 397.

15

Learning to Live with Specters: Hauntology, Memory and Language in *Specters of Marx*

Vinod Kottayil Kalidasan

Introduction

Emerging as a book from a paper that Jacques Derrida presented in an international colloquium in 1991, *Specters of Marx* offers nuanced insights into the very question of the 'whither of Marxism'—an issue the colloquium in question was attempting to address. Derrida postulates that the scope and effect of Marxism, not only as a theoretical frame but also as a tool to understand history, can and must be studied in its 'hauntological' nature. In this sense, Marxism does not 'whither' nor does it require to be patronized. Rather, one must now be prepared to live with the numerous ghosts that Marxism has unleashed in the world. Marxism's 'spectral' entry (as a specter that haunts Europe), more like the entry of the ghost in *Hamlet*, forces us to look at history differently. I plan to probe here how memory plays a crucial role in the processes of haunting and mourning—themes often employed in literature from Shakespeare to Gabriel Garcia Marquez. All these haunting, ghostly apparitions and the exorcising of the haunting ghosts have been performed within the rubric of a 'spectral' language. For example, the claim of the ghost in *Hamlet* ('I am thy father's spirit') and the new narrative of history it offers Hamlet ('I could a tale unfold whose lightest word would harrow up thy soul') strikingly resembles the claim made in the *Communist Manifesto* ('A specter is haunting Europe—the specter of communism' along with its many 'prefaces') and the new narrative of history the text offers to its readers ('The history of all hitherto existing society is the history of class struggles'). I argue that the discursive forms of dialogue and argumentations available in the two aforementioned texts, their 'question-answer formats,' the presence of the 'questioning scholar' in both the texts (Horatio in *Hamlet* and the questions themselves in the *Manifesto*) and the ubiquitous ghosts open a window into the graveyard of history where the ghosts are at large. Derrida's text and its readers, more like the readers/audience of *Hamlet*, stand next to it watching not just the 'play' of the numerous ghosts 'out there' but the effect the play brings upon the living (play within the play) learning how to live/deal with the specters. The specter's multiple existence, as Ernest H. Kantorowicz (1981) points out, springs from a certain duality of its 'body'.[1]

Jacques Derrida's *Specters of Marx,* originally in the form of a lecture, engages with communism in a 'dialogical' mode and brings fresh insights into the theme especially when communism was at the centre of debates in a world very often argued to have been 'won' by liberal democracy and market capitalism. These arguments not only placed a capitalist mode of economy as the successor of communism but daringly proposed that, as a result of the 'triumph' of liberal democracy and market capitalism, human history itself has come to a standstill—the Francis Fukuyama moment of (no) history.[2] Derrida has not only argued against this 'end of history' debate, but proposed that the scope and effect of communism would be too numerous and far-reaching that its analysis would require a complex understanding of the ways it presents itself before us at various junctures of history. This must, thus, be seen in its entirety rather than as a system that merely governs/does not govern states. This is why we need to study the 'spectral' aspect of communism. In this paper, an attempt is made to study the concepts of Hauntology, memory and language as they are employed in *Specters of Marx*. I shall read Gabriel Garcia Marquez's *One Hundred Years of Solitude* in the light of Derrida's thinking as it is employed in his work, *Specters of Marx*.

Hauntology

In *Specters of Marx*, Derrida discusses in detail the promises of Marxism to the world. In a world beleaguered by authoritarian regimes, techno-economic and ecological disasters, communism promises a break with history, myth, religion and the nationalist mystique. Today in a country such as India where again communal and nationalistic regimes and forces are at large demonstrating how oppressive and dismissive they can be to and about their fellow men, their politico-religious alternatives and minorities, to the strong secular ethos the country stands for, a colloquium on post-structuralism such as this one, more like the colloquium in which Derrida spoke in 1991, makes us re-think the challenges of today.[3] This is why Derrida argues 'whether they wish it or know it or not, all men and women, all over the earth, are today to a certain extent the heirs of Marx and Marxism.' (*Specters,* p. 91) Being the intellectual heirs of Marxism also demands us to re-invent the world to change it. In Derrida, this re-invention begins from the very moment we encounter it; the very moment of its almost spectral arrival. This is the moment that *The Manifesto of the Communist Party* announced. The event of the haunting specter of Europe: 'A specter is haunting Europe—the specter of communism'. However, the specter's haunting is deeply linked to certain socio-political and historical events that have almost colonized our pasts secretly. For example, the European powers opposed to the idea of the specter of communism such as the Tsar, the religious entities and the German state have all stood for authoritarian regimes where not only freedom of expression was unpopular but also having a counter-view was a crime. This was the moment when they had all, despite differences, joined forces to 'hunt' and 'haunt' the specter of Marxism.

It appears that it is only when the graves are dug, that we recognize what we lost and how much we loved it as in the case of Hamlet. The grave is also the site of the ghost's origin. When Marx states that 'the history of all hitherto existing societies is the history of class struggles,' we are suddenly made aware of our pasts. However, Communism has this special thing about it: when it began, it hardly bagan. It was always already there. Communism is a philosophy that started to 'live' after its 'death'. As no specter could die, its death is impossible. The life after death of communism—its real life—assumes numerous shapes and hues. It gives us possibilities to free ourselves and to test its promises and revelations. The specter, in this sense, also exists in a multiple time-frame. In Derrida's own words, 'there are several times of the specter' (*Specters,* p. 99). Because of this 'proper characteristic' of the specter, if there is any, according to Derrida, it is impossible to tell whether 'its returning testifies to a living past or to a living future'. (99)

Communism, within the ambit of this argument, 'has always been and will remain spectral: it is always still to come.' (*Specters,* p. 99) All the powers of old Europe are afraid not of the arrival of a new system per se; rather they are afraid of the visitations of a ghost—a ghost that is going to torment them. The ghost they are worried about comes from the pasts of Europe and humanity—a past where monopolies of the old powers held sway. The ghost(s) of communism is exactly going to reveal the violence such monopolies had unleashed upon people and the ghost only speaks and it cannot be spoken to. It will 'deliver a series of blows to be deciphered'. (*Specters,* p. 99)

The fact that the ghost's presence itself is phantasmagoric, not always to be seen but capable of seeing, makes its 'presence' more powerful and awe-inspiring for the old powers of Europe and for its other enemies. What Marx does, in Derrida's opinion, is to announce the presence of communism—a promise to the future. It is a promise that was always there but still to come. The promise too, like the ghost, exists in its phantasmagoria. The hunt of the ghost gets spectral here too as Derrida calls it— 'exorcising' and 'conjuration'. The situation is such that 'no one speaks of anything anymore but this specter' (*Specters,* p. 99) and this specter is present and absent at the same time—presence in absence and absence in presence. Derrida takes the imagery of a 'television screen' to explain this ghostly phenomenon; it is more like 'all phantasms are projected onto a screen.'

Now the detractors of communism and the holy hunters of it conjure it and lure it into its doom by employing media as the medium. I think, the fascist propaganda against communism and the persecution of communists in Germany were examples.

Derrida's understanding of *The Manifesto*, emerged from a close reading of the same, locates it as a 'manifestation' of the elusive ghost—a self-manifestation of the manifesto that announced the birth of a ghost. A manifesto that manifests itself in the face of formidable powers that are up against it. A manifesto of the manifest—communism as a strong statement in favour of the communists of the world to openly publish 'their views, their aims, their tendencies, and meet this nursery tale of the specter of communism.' (*The Manifesto of the Communist Party*, abbreviated as 'CM' henceforth, p. 104)

The specter also evokes a sense of fear that it is present everywhere and it can appear from almost anywhere, anytime. The ghost evokes a sensation—'a make oneself fear' experience. The enemies of communism respond in panic—a reason why they are all in unison. I would like to take an instance from Gabriel Garcia Marquez's *One Hundered Years of Solitude* (abbreviated as OHYS henceforth).

Ursula Iguaran, in the novel, is afraid of getting married as she is scared of giving birth to babies with piggy tails—iguanas as they are called. But when she got married, she wears a chastity belt to thwart any possibility of her husband forcing himself upon her. Though the drama of the chastity belt wearing goes on for many months, her husband, Jose Arcadio Buendia neither forces himself upon her as she feared nor does he make a very strong point against his wife's taste for the bizarre fashion for metallic underpants until one day when he was ridiculed in the context of his wife's habit by Prudencio Aguilar during a cockfight (OHYS, p. 21). In a battle of spears that ensued, Jose Arcadio kills Aguilar and returns home to tell his wife to 'take off' the belt and announces:

> If you bear iguanas, we will raise iguanas... but there'll be no more killings in this town because of you. (OHYS, p. 22)

Marquez writes what happens next:

> It was a fine June night, cool and with a moon, and they were awake and frolicking in bed until dawn, indifferent to the breeze that passed through the bedroom, loaded with the weeping of Prudencio Aguilar's kin. (OHYS, p. 22)

Marquez mixes love with mourning—the memory of which would haunt Jose Arcadio Buendia throughout his life. It appears that when love was made and so was the ghost. It was like a love accompanied by mourning—all the more reason for Jose Arcadio Buendia to be haunted. As Derrida would observe 'Mourning always follows a trauma' (*Specters,* p. 97). The ghost of Prudencio Aguilar appears before Jose Arcadio Buendia in the dark, desperate nights with a spear stuck into its heart, still bleeding. Haunted by guilt and terror, Jose Arcadio Buendia decides to leave the town with Ursula Iguaran and many other young men and women to found a new village called 'Macondo' in a remote, hitherto unheard of valley. However, even in Macondo, Prudencio Aguilar's ghost chases him and it 'returns'.

When Macondo develops into a complex village, it leaves its own past behind. The war between the conservatives and the liberals leaves the city torn apart. The conservatives engage in electoral fraud and Jose Arcadio Buendia's son Colonel Auriliano Buendia leads the fight for the liberals. The 'liberals' in Marquez are closer to the 'communists' in Marx, who are urged to publish their views openly.

Macondo gets connected to the world outside and the fight between the liberals and the conservatives spreads into the world out there. Before the judge, the machineries of the state and a few other people entered Macondo, only two entities had ever visited the village. One is the ghost of Prudencio Aguilar and the other is the tribe of the gypsies under the mesmerizing leadership of their legendary hero Melquiades. The ghost appears before Jose Arcadio Buendia in different 'moods' and at different times. Once the ghost appeared to him 'sad, depressed and lonely.' Now this is something unexpected of a ghost. Probably the saddest thing on earth is death itself. Why must a ghost who is beyond the reaches of death be 'sad, depressed and lonely?' Though the wars and violence inside and outside of Macondo might give us a clue about the shifting moods of the ghost, the fact that what was so far seen as only 'spectral' now moves closer into the realm of the 'human' making their boundaries blur is noteworthy. This movement is very special because this is where we see the ghost as our own. The sadness, depression and the loneliness of Jose Arcadio Buendia are 'projected onto the screen' of the ghost as Derrida would have said. There are times when Jose Arcadio Buendia stops to be afraid of the ghost and allows it to come back. This is when one connects oneself to the ghost and that too to its plural. Derrida writes:

> ... let it be understood that we intend to understand spirits in the plural and in the sense of specters, of untimely specters that one must not chase away but sort out, critique, keep close by, and allow to come back. (*Specters*, p. 87)

Hauntology is also about the many times of the specter—its numerous returns. Derrida points out that the first noun 'specter' returns three times on the very same first page of *The Manifesto of the Communist Party.* Jose Arcadio Buendia's complex relationship with the ghost can be compared to Derrida's observation of the complex relationship that Karl Marx himself had with ghosts. Buendia despised the ghost of Aguilar but grows complacent with it in time even loving it in the end. He makes his tormentor his friend. Sometimes he even waits for its arrival. One night during the peak of the insomnia plague an old man enters Jose Arcadio's room. He fails to recognize him:

> ... when he finally identified him, startled that the dead also aged, Jose Arcadio Buendia felt himself shaken by nostalgia. "Prudencio," he exclaimed. "You've come from a long way off!" After many years of death the yearning for the living was so intense, the need for company so pressing, so terrifying the nearness of that other death which exists within death, that Prudencio Aguilar had ended up loving his worst enemy. (OHYS, p. 79)

The ghost in *One Hundred Years of Solitude* is almost human like the ghost in Hamlet. It can be emotional, it can also 'grow old'. The ghost's plurality is marked by its multiple appearances and the multiple feelings it brings in and its ageing. Derrida identifies this 'living connection' as an important idea in Marx's spectropolitics—a passionate attempt to connect to the world and change it The nostalgia that Jose Arcadio Buendia felt was also felt by Marx at the appearance of the spectral. What Derrida calls the 'spectral rumour' penetrates into all spaces. Derrida argues that the spirit of the sublime and the spirit of nostalgia cross all borders (*Specters,* p. 135) as one continuously engage with people. Here is Marx quoted by Derrida *(Specters,* p. 135):

> ... millions of spirits speak through the mouths of people.

Marx's spectropolitics aims to address this violence in the past more like the attempt by Prince Hamlet to address and correct the violence his father was subjected to. More like the deaths of Prudencio Aguilar and Hamlet's father, only one particular form of historical narrative ceased to exist. But it is not possible for history as such to come to any end. The ghosts of Aguilar and King Hamlet are going to haunt us, exactly like history, and we have to, as a necessary pre-condition, come to terms with them to learn to live with the specters.

Derrida also observes of Marx that 'like all obsessives, he harassed the obsession.' (*Specters,* p. 106) In his dissertation of 1841 Marx himself alludes to Ghosts in a letter to Ludwig Von Westphalen whom Marx addresses himself as 'son' and expresses filial love (*Specters*, p. 106) Derrida alludes this addressing to Hamlet ("Hamlet, I am thy father's spirit"). Derrida refers to Marx:

> *All the spirits of the world are called to appear ... and who never recoiled in fear from the shadows of retrograde ghosts. (Specters,* p. *106)*

Derrida points out that Marx loved the figure of ghosts and detested it at the same time. The specters of Marx are also his own projected on the screen. These specters stem from a deep awareness of the traumatic pasts. In the case of Marx, the ghosts come from the unjust, authoritarian, capitalist pasts and presents of humanity. That's why Derrida says the ghosts are in Marx's head. Marx develops his affinity to the ghosts. Derrida terms it 'spectropolitics' (*Specters,* p. 108). As Marx clearly indicates, man makes his own history not out of choice but under circumstances directly encountered, given and transmitted from the past—the tradition of all the dead generations (*Specters,* p. 108). The history of Hamlet too is not his own making but a result of his encounter with his 'spectrally' revealed past. When the *Manifesto of the Communist Party* states that '(t)he history of all hitherto existing societies is the history of class struggles,' it is doing the same thing—an almost spectral revelation of human history the ghosts of which are going to haunt us till the end of time. Instead and against an ontological and existential explanation of human misery and poverty, Marx puts forward a hauntological category that has a lot to do with both the past and the present conditions of human life. This is the moment of the arrival of the communist ghost and communism itself as a revolution and a radical break from history.

The Ghosts of Memory and Language

In this section, I would like to link memory and language within the ambit of spectropolitics. In Derrida, language is an inheritance of the spirits of the past. (*Specters,* p. 109) Derrida quotes Marx to state that revolutions of the past hardly disappear; they add on to the present ones as 'spirits of the past'. Marx goes on to say that the revolutions of the past that get assimilated into new ones are like mother-tongues. A beginner learning a new language always translates back into his mother-tongue but

> *... he has assimilated [appropriated : bat er sicb nur angeeignet] the spirit of the new language and can freely express himself in it [produce in it: in ibr probuzieren] only when he finds his way in it without recalling the old and forgets his native tongue in the use of the new.* (*Specters,* p. 110)

It is in this sense that Derrida states that the very assimilation of a new language is already an inheritance. (*Specters,* p. 110) Assimilation of a new language becomes a living appropriation of a spirit. The revolution here is the appropriation of another language. By memorizing the new, one attempts to 'forget' the old or its 'parody' in order to freely express oneself in the new tongue. This forgetting is also the forgetting of the specter of the old language—the spirit. The real problem here is that one does not forget things intentionally—that hardly becomes 'forgetting'. Furthermore, Derrida suggests that in Marx, when this forgetting corresponds to the 'living appropriation' of the new language that one is learning, the result will be bourgeois platitude—nothing but life. So, one must not 'forget' it. Rather, Derrida further argues, 'one must remember it while forgetting it enough'. In fact, one must keep the memory alive to absorb the new spirit one is appropriating at the moment without making its specter return. (*Specters,* p. 110)

Here, again, I would like to take an instance from *One Hundred Years of Solitude*. The insomnia plague that spreads across Macondo like wildfire brings into the village a continuous play of memory and forgetting. First of all, the plague seems to be transmitted by mouth. Now mouth (OHYS p. 47) represents language or speech since what they have effectively forgotten are the names and language itself. The passers-by are advised to ring bells so that the sick feels healthy. This happens because the sound of the bell does not confuse the people of Macondo as the toll of the bell gets registered differently. It creates an idiom both inside and outside of language. The bell reminds the people of Macondo something they still understand; a distinctly removed spirit of human attempt to communicate—something that the people of Macondo are yet to forget. Probably this will never be forgotten. What is bizarre about the insomnia plague is that it made people forget forgetting itself. When you forget to sleep, you forget an experience in which you can neither remember nor forget. In effect, you forget to forget. The real Marxian problem now can be seen at work here. In order to overcome the sickness of forgetting to forget, one has to remember to remember—repetitive acts of remembering and forgetting working at both ends.

The people of Macondo not only forget words; they also forget how to do things with words. They essentially go out of touch with the connections that they have unquestioningly made between words and things. The insomnia plague challenges this relationship and opens two parallel worlds. Firstly, a world of bare things; though they could still be meaningful. Secondly, a world of bare words sinking into an abyss of yet to be deciphered, remembered meanings. So they keep records of the things trying to connect the words with the things as they would do before the plague had invaded their land. A typical entry from the insomnia that invaded Macondo would look like this:

> This is the cow. She must be milked every morning so that she will produce milk, and the milk must be boiled in order to be mixed with coffee to make coffee and milk. (OHYS, p. 48)

Instead of learning a new language, the people of Macondo reinvent the same idioms differently. Since everyone has forgotten the quantum of knowledge acquired in a person's life-time, the re-invention of the same language is actually an invention itself for reinventing the wheel would almost always take a different route, a different heuristic experience so much so that it can only be invented now. It can never be the same ever again. Not strangely though, one of the first things the people of Macondo 're-invented' was nothing but a dictionary that Jose Arcadio Buendia calls a 'memory machine'. He feeds around fourteen thousand entries into it.

The new language invented, however, is also a borrowed one since it takes a lot from the 'other' Language—here a language the people have forgotten. In *The Eighteenth Brumaire,* Marx uses the tropes of language and spectrality to describe revolution. What I quote henceforth from Marx would explain to us what exactly Jose Arcadio Buendia in Marquez's text was doing:

> And just when they seem engaged in revolutionizing themselves and things, in creating something that has never existed [*nocb nicbt Dagewesenes Zuscbaffen*], precisely in such periods of revolutionary crisis they anxiously conjure up [*beschw oren sie angsticb*] the spirits of the past to their service *[die Geister der Vergangenbeitz...]* and borrow [*entlebnen*] from them *names*, battle-cries [*Cblacbtparole*] and costumes in order to present the new scene of world history in this time-honoured disguise and this *borrowed language [mit dieser erborgten Sprache] Specters* p. 108, *Eighteenth Brumaire.* (Italics in the original)

The insomnia plague can thus be seen as a revolutionary crisis that resulted in the attempts to make a dictionary, attempts to borrow language among other things. It is the conjuration that Marx discusses. The insomnia plague also brings up the idea of time being out of joint while the memory machine stands for a new vocabulary created. The dictionary emerges from the past meanings of words but it is composed for the world yet to come. The insomnia plague works as an event more like the event Marx describes in the arrival of a capitalist mode of production. In the *Manifesto of the Communist Party,* Marx clearly states how the poor and the working classes are different from the proletariat. While there have always been poor and working classes the proletariat emerged as a result of the introduction of the machines which have been invented since the middle of the last century and the arrival of capitalist systems in which men have to live exclusively by selling their labour. This lead to the aforementioned break and communism is presented itself as a specter revealing this historical condition from which it radically proposed a way out. The invention of a new language, a new sense of the world and a novel way of looking at oneself in the context of the specter would eventually go into the compilation of the dictionary in *One Hundred Years of Solitude* and the *Manifesto of the Communist Party*. Both ask us to articulate and to freely express our thoughts.

It turns out, in Derrida, that the death of communism, especially the collapse of Soviet Union, is not 'the death' since only a certain mode of communism has collapsed. The ghosts are to be understood strictly in their plurality and multiplicity.[4] It is time, Derrida, tells us,

> We'll treat him calmly, objectively, without bias: according to the academic rules, in the University, in the library, in colloquiua! We will do it systematically, by respecting the norms of hermeneutical, philological, philosophical exegesis. (*Specters*, p. 32)

Marxism's continued life re-invents the very language one has lost and it is done by continuously revisiting Marxism and to scrutinize the great promises it has extended to humanity. This also means that, for Derrida, an engagement with the specters of our own past and those of Marxism would be inevitable.

NOTES

1. Kantorowicz demonstrates the duality of the body of the king – 'the body politic' and 'the body natural'. The duality and, thus, the multiplicity of the 'body' is being investigated in his monumental work on medieval political theology. In his view, 'the body politic' appears to transcend the death of the 'body natural'—a kind of resurrection that Christ's own body had undergone. For an extended discussion, see Kantorowicz (1981).
2. Derrida trivializes Fukuyama's theory of the end of history. For Derrida the 'beginning' and thus,the 'end' are not as easily identifiable as they are for Fukuyama. In his view of history, predicting the 'end' of history is nothing short of a reductionist approach.
3. While a nationalist interpretation of present is seem as the 'authentic' version of Indian history by nationalists, this tendency is seen even amongst some Marxists according to G Aloysius. He writes: "In India where economic-and class-reductionism has collapsed, instead of developing more sensitive historical-materialist analysis, Marxists seem to be content with presenting variation of the nationalist historiography." (Aloysius, p. 22)
4. It has to be understood that not only Marxism is open to interpretation, but Marx himself amended some of his statements as in the case of Marx's own writings on India indicating a sense of plurality and evolution within the ambit of Marxist thought. For details see, Aloysius (1997) p. 34.

REFERENCES

Aloysuius, G. 1997. *Nationalism without a Nation in India*. New Delhi: Oxford.

Derrida, Jacques. 1994 [1993]. *Specters of Marx: The State of Debt, the Work of Mourning and the New International,* tr. Peggy Kamuf. New York: Routledge.

——, *Writing and Difference*, tr. Alan Bass. 1982. Chicago: University of Chicago Press.

——, 1998. *Of Grammatology*, tr. Gayatri Chakravorty Spivak. Baltimore: The Johns Hopkins University Press.

Kantorowicz, Ernst H. 1981. *The King's Two Bodies: A Study in Medieval Political Theology*.

New Jersey: Princeton University Press.

Marquez, Gabriel Garcia. 1996 [1967] *One Hundred Years of Solitude*, tr. Gregory Rabassa. New Delhi: Penguin.

Marx, Karl and Frederick Engels. 1969 [1848]. *Manifesto of the Communist party* in *Selected Works*, Vol. I, pp. 98-137. Moscow: Progress.

——, 1964 [1846]. *The German Ideology,* Moscow: Progress.

——, 1937 [1885]. *18th Brumaire of Louis Bonaparte,* Moscow: Progess.

——, 1975 [1885]. *Letters: Karl Marx and Fredrick Engels.* Moscow: Progress.

Nancy, Jean-Luc. 2008. *Corpus*, tr. Richard A. Rand. New York: Fordham University Press.

——, 2005. *The Ground of the Image*, tr. Jeff Fort. New York: Fordham University Press.

Ryan, Michael.1984. *Marxism and Deconstruction: A Critical Articulation,* Baltimore: The Johns Hopkins University Press.

Spivak, Gayatri Chakravorty. 2010 [1985]. *Discussion. Subaltern Studies: Deconstructing Historigraphy* in *Subaltern Studies IV: Writings on South Asian History and Society*, Ranajit Guha (ed.). Oxford: New Delhi.

Shakespeare, William. 1997 [1514]. *Hamlet: Prince of Denmark.* New Delhi: Cambridge University Press.

16

De-cision: Resisting the 'Tragic' and Surviving the Subject[1]

Sourav Kargupta

Introduction: The Argument

Ernesto Laclau and Chantal Mouffe carefully make possible a 'theory' of the 'subject of decision', even if that theory misses the temporal register which cuts decision internally, and stretches it as 'de-cision'. This paper goes beyond such a decisive predication through a reading of the 'spectral', not by staging the more familiar reading of the Marxian (exchange) value by Jacques Derrida, but the less discussed figuring of the spectral in Derrida's critique of the 'tragic' subject in Martin Heidegger.

Laclau and Mouffe test the impossibility of thinking society as a coherent structure in *Hegemony and Socialist Strategy*.[2] In their opinion, one has to abandon the model of society as a "sutured" and self-enclosed terrain since "every totality" is "necessarily" incomplete.[3] One may understand this incompleteness in the dual sense, of (1) the inside not being able to master its outside, and (2) not being constituted of fully present building blocks. Borrowing from Louis Althusser, they call the "field of identities which never manage to be fully fixed, [...] field of overdetermination."[4] The social space is a "discursive field," where the relations among its various elements have a "material character" (108). This argument resonates with the deconstructive notion of 'textuality', a weave neither fully closed off, nor totally open to the sign of the outside. I would, however, argue that the proposed 'material' character of the social field makes sense within a deconstructive fold only so far as 'materiality' is a lingering 'trace' in transaction with the 'non-material', and not a determining characteristic of the discursive, as Laclau and Mouffe seem to suggest.[5] I begin with a telegraphic figuring of the concept of the 'subject of decision' in Laclau and Mouffe, making way for a discussion of the problematic in certain texts of Jacques Derrida.[6]

For Laclau and Mouffe, 'hegemony' is the management-game through which certain discursive formations try to close off the dispersion of the social, in achieving a state farthest from instability, or "radical democracy" (189). Thus they re-inaugurate a theory of 'ideology', much ignored by recent scholarship. For Laclau and Mouffe, discourse has a material character which dismisses any concept of subjectivity modelled after unifying consciousness, proposing instead, "diverse subject positions" (109).[7] This immediately takes one away from the axis of the 'individual', who is not only an unified consciousness but also an indivisible body, individuated by and bound to the state-law as citizen, and therefore the foundational unit of that imaginary ('state'). For Laclau and Mouffe, the subject-position is not merely a node among many, rather it is a privileged node overdetermined by other nodes. They propose not one but two possible subject-positions, 'popular', which surfaces as the political is divided into "two antagonistic camps", and the 'democratic', which is also the subject of a "clearly delimited" politics (e.g. feminism), but which has not cut the society in half, and instead remains one among many such antagonistic positions. (131) They are more concerned with the distinction between these two subject positions, as they intend to track the marks of suture which knits a society as it unfolds in space. Notwithstanding the formal force of such an investigation, what if one inserts the problem of 'time' in this scheme? The question I would like to pose is this: can one think of this work of overdetermination in terms of a persistent process extended in both space and time? Without that, the subject-positions would still retain a similarity with the rational subject (present to itself and not overdetermined), in their very conception as points in space. Thought simply as spatial points it might also result in a theory of the subject as a stasis or 'embodiment of decision', again falling into the trap of the self-present subject. Laclau's self-confessed difference from deconstruction in settling for a "subject before subjectivation"[8] might be symptomatic of this ontologizing tendency.

I try to contest this position by posing 'decision' as furrowed-within and extended in time, and therefore, 'de-cision'. In de-cision, the 'hyphen' records the predication of the subject as 'graphematic', and not as pure intentionality.[9] I propose two ways of thinking the 'subject'—One through 'decision' in the axis of the 'event', and the other, through representation in the axis of 'survival'. However, these are not exclusive predications, not two contesting positions, but two related ways of thinking the same problematic, of conceptualising intentionality and responsibility through but beyond the category of the subject.

From Decision to De-cision

I want to move toward the figure of (the subject of) de-cision through a reading of Michel Foucault. The 'subject' never seems to be one of Foucault's preferred analytical categories, and one needs to be careful. Derrida recognizes that, "in his [Foucault's] last phase, there again, a return of morality and a certain ethical subject" (in Derrida 1994a, 256-257). I want to start with a short comment on Foucault's alleged unease with the category of the subject, which has marked similarities to Derrida's critique of it. I share Anirban Das's attention in reading the Foucauldian notion of 'anatomopolitcs' in its juxtaposition with ethicality, where power becomes "ontologically constitutive of the body" and therefore complicit with any investigation of being (Das 2010, xix). It is this imagination of a pre-ontological field which precedes the ontic nodes of the political subject that enables one to think ethics at the register of the pre-propriative. This is also the register of what Foucault has called the 'subindividual'. Gayatri Spivak is disapproving of Foucault for his "tenacious commitment to the sub-individual," (and, on the other hand, to "the great aggregative apparatuses") which seemingly prevents him from following the itinerary of the subject at the register of ideology (Spivak 1999, 252). And yet, this attention to the 'subindividual' cannot be given up either at a strictly theoretical level, if one wants to account for the lost steps taken before the thought of the subject congeals as individual (in her later works, Spivak herself has called this mid-way precipitation around a metonymic ground, 'agency'[10]). The individual as a subject of intentionality is implicated in a fabric of law and therefore cannot be the preferred category of studying the interstices of 'laws' and 'bodies' where they constitute each other. May be this, along with the 'critique of humanism', is the crux of Foucault's project when he endeavors to study "sex without the law" aiming to analyze "power which do not derive from the system of right and the form of law." (Foucault 1990, 90-91) Spivak recognizes this in studying ethicality through the precipitations of the subject in the "details of everyday," which also makes her revise her position on the Foucauldian 'subindividual'. She now sees in the move a close interaction between a deconstruction and the "ethical concerns of the final Foucault" (Spivak 1999, 38). The attention toward the 'sub-individual' can be placed in the ontico-ontological "force-field"[11] where one accounts for the presuppositions taken for granted in constituting the (ontic) subject of law. Consequently it might be a way to study the pre-propriative of the ethical. This project is sounded already in "Nietzsche, Genealogy, History" (1971) where Foucault sets up for a genealogical study, following Nietzsche, not the individual or the national, not "Greek" or "English," but "the subtle, singular, and subindividual marks that might possibly intersect in them to form a network that is difficult to unravel" (Foucault 1994, 173). Therefore, not merely the subindividual but "subindividual marks" which intersect to form a network. One cannot not ignore the distinction made between the subindividual as a thing, and the "singular" marks or traces of the subindividual. What the exact meaning of this singularity is not elaborated, but this might indicate Foucault's closeness to a deconstructive notion of the 'inscribed trace' as a mark of that violence which tries to name the singular, and the use of such a conception in thinking/undoing the subject of individuated body and consciousness. From a brief reading of this "final Foucault" and I go on to a moment in Laclau which I would show as running the risk of precisely that overt commitment to materiality which is evaded by Foucault's astute positioning of the subindividual.

I am reading here a late and important text called "The Subject and Power" (1982, in Foucault 2001). The first half of this article is written originally in English by Foucault himself and called "Why Study Power: The Question of the Subject." The crux of the 'subject' is approached here with a critical highlighting of the 'moment of intervention' which Foucault understands through the act of 'resistance':

> I would like to suggest another way to go further toward a new economy of power relations, a way which is more empirical, more directly related to our present situation, and which implies more relations between theory and practice. It consists of taking the forms of resistance against different forms of power as a starting point. (Foucault, 329)

Foucault is not merely talking about a middle ground between theory and practice but somehow trying to inscribe 'resistance' at a register where the two interact, a register which deals with the "relation between the two," where both operate but neither can dominate. He also indicates that resistance can be a "starting point" in understanding power. Let me elaborate on this reading. For example, if one thinks of a finite line with two extreme points indicating 'hot' and 'cold', is it possible to pin-point, exactly where, in-between these two points, 'hotness' gives up and 'coldness' takes over? To think of a thing, to measure a field, the thinking of a basic antagonism seems necessary. We have used the example of a scale of temperature, but Foucault himself uses a much trickier metaphor:

> To use [a] metaphor, it consists of using [...] resistance as a chemical catalyst so as to bring to light power relations, locate their positions, find out their points of application and the methods used. (329)

Thinking an antagonism, a break, is primarily a de-cision. This originary decision precedes and produces antagonisms. In this specific moment in the Foucauldian text, it is evident that an attention to the subindividual makes it possible to retain an opening toward a notion of ethicality before (both prior and subjected to) any decision. The attention to the sub-individual implicates the 'final Foucault' with an ethical thinking, and with a thinking of ideology, even if that part is never explicit in Foucault.

Foucault's argument stages the ethical along with the irreducible trace of 'reading', indicating a possible gloss on the idea of ideology. Ernesto Laclau, on the other hand, seems to reject the opening to the 'other' and therefore the 'pre-propriative' altogether in favour of a subject who traverses the gap between decision and undecidability. In a text intended to stage an encounter between his theory of hegemony and the Derridian deconstruction, Laclau notes that within a deconstructive frame, 'decision' "cannot be ultimately grounded in anything external to itself" (Laclau in Mouffe 1995, 52). This positioning of the decision beyond the calculable, Laclau contends, is deconstruction's central move. Quoting Søren Kierkegaard, Laclau writes that "the moment of decision is the moment of madness."(53) His next move is to take some "tentative steps" in "tackling this [...] problem" of decision as madness (53). For Laclau, one needs to leave the deconstructive aporia and approach the question of the subject in thinking the relationship between decision and undecidability. It is here that he introduces the subject, who, as if, comes to plug this aporia by *being* the decision. The subject is not predetermined by the structure and must "go through the experience of undecidability" (54). Laclau also adds that the subject requires a "jump" to traverse the distance between the undecidability of the structure and a "creative act" (54). This identification of a 'creative act' in the being-decision of the subject marks Laclau's departure from the slippery ground of madness. Laclau does suggest that no decision is totally free and yet, also stresses that the leap that makes it a decision cannot follow from any grammar or structure. But even after setting up such an aporia, Laclau tries to figure a definite ontology of the subject of decision. For him decision is that last instance, which always "swings free of all rational activity," and therefore remains at least pragmatically ungraspable, even if the pragmatist would be right in thinking decision (chiefly about 'meaning') non-foundational (70). Consequently, for Laclau, the connection between undecidability and decision is not to be grasped through any logical or ethical understanding. This rejection of the ethical in fact points to a crucial problem in Laclau's theory, for it tries to work with undecidability and difference without any detailed engagement with the problem of temporality, while I would argue that "the ethical relation to the other introduces time into the subject" and vice-versa.[12]

To recapitulate: the ignorance of difference in time (with the 'other', and with the 'self as other' at a different moment) makes Laclau's analysis too spatial and incapable of dealing with such a notion as the pre-propriative in terms of memory or the 'to come-ness'. For Laclau the "function" of decision ultimately embodies the impossible fullness of the subject (60). The sign 'I', as if lays itself down and embodies the bridge, resolving the aporia between structure and event. This position departs from deconstruction fundamentally in its effort to construe a 'theory' of decision. The insight of Spivak, that 'to come-ness' can be read also as a persistence, a living-on, might be helpful here. Commenting on Drucilla Cornell's idea a feminist ethics, Spivak writes, the mode of 'to come' is similar to being "always on the way," as "the nature of women's and subordinates' repetitive sustaining work," knowing that the "selvedge of that textile is always ahead."[13] Note the temporal extension of the decision as de-cision in this argument. For Laclau, however, the "otherness of the other" does not prompt the ethical, but it is the universal which appropriates the singular in its ethical injunction. The problem with this model consists in placing 'decision' in the position of the singular, and fusing the two (decision as 'jump', and as 'singularity') at the locus of the subject. For Laclau, the 'other' is merely the universal that "precedes and governs any decision" (55). Again, temporal distance is being missed, which could have interrupted this scene in thinking the locus of decision as extended in time. A notion like that would have recognized the production of decision not only shaped by the usurping authority of the universal, but also enchanted by the call of the undecidable, the undecidable which both opens and closes the law of decision-making. Instead, Laclau's model makes clear-cut divisions between contingency and predetermination, decision and the undecidable etc., forgetting their complicity as well as the 'restance'[14] of incomparability. This, I believe, comes from a desire to theorize, and to leave nothing un-theorized in a textual production.[15] Even after repeatedly stressing the importance of going through the 'experience of the undecidable', Laclau wants a narrative of that experience in theory:

> Hegemony requires deconstruction [...]. But deconstruction also requires hegemony, that is, a theory of the decision taken in an undecidable terrain: without a theory of the decision, that distance between structural undecidability and actuality would remain untheorized. (62)

For Laclau, even if the "trace of contingency" resides as "dislocation" within the structure, this trace seems too grounded and therefore easily claimed by the subject. To put it in deconstructive parlance, Laclau seems to prefer a notion of the trace-in-itself, or an ontologized trace. But in deconstruction, the trace cannot be a determined 'thing' or a being, but always a materiality haunted by spectrality. A claiming of this trace for a theory of decision becomes only too unquestioningly a way to theorize the subject. If materiality consists in not only thinking within the limits of the possible, but also in straining the limits of a certain un-thought through thought, then one needs to imagine a 'cut' even within the metaphor which apparently fixes or stops calculation, one needs to re-write decision as 'de-cision'.[16] 'De-cision' does not only interrupt the smooth deliberation of speculative reason and theory, it also interrupts itself through a 'cut' (*coup*, cision), both grounded and un-grounded. As Derrida replies to Laclau within the same debate, "if the decision is identification then the decision also destroys itself." (in Mouffe, 86) The problem for Laclau, then, consists in putting decision beyond any double-bind and yet within 'law' or that which can be theorized. The difference that for Laclau congeals between undecidability and decision can be said to exist within decision itself, never reaching the fullness of adequately answering to the call of the 'other', much like what Derrida calls, "messianic without messianism, a structural messianism."[17] Laclau is only too eager to choose between a true formalism and a pure materiality, even as the 'empirical' works in-between. This prompts a brief discussion of what Derrida calls 'hauntology', but I want to try here another path. A discussion of spectrality not following the Derridian reading of Marx, but of Heidegger.

Spectral de-cision: Resisting the 'Tragic' Subject

'Hauntology' in Derrida is usually understood through his engagement with the Marxian textuality of (exchange) value, even if there is another path through his reading of Heidegger. In *Specters of Marx*, Derrida renews one of his persistent questions: what is the difference between 'repetitions' and (a concept of) the "first time"? (Derrida 1994, 10). But this exercise is self-defeating since the moment one tries to figure any 'first time' into the conceptual weaves which depend on the generality of the repeatable instances, one reduces it. And yet, there still remains the very thought of a 'first time' which cannot be ignored. That lingering trace of a possible impossibility which both restricts and retains the trace of a 'first time' is also the coming of 'hauntology' in the Derridian scheme. Hauntology does not only make the thought of a 'first time' possible, it also signals its im-possibility as each first time is also the 'last time'. Singularity houses origin, and the death of it (Derrida, 10). What then, of the simulacrum, of representation, if each node is a singularity? This puts us face to face with the aporia, the one that stays between temporality of being, and its divisibility in fully present units of 'nows'. Derrida names this analytic of the spectral, positioned in the register of continuity or sur-vival: 'hauntology'. In the register of divisibility, it is named 'différance'.

Had Derrida only revealed that 'being' is "necessarily without heading and without assurance" (27) he would not have said anything new. In *Specters*, even before putting Marx through a slow cook, Derrida is interested in the Heideggerian textuality where the analytic of hauntology appears. He focuses particularly on Heidegger's reading of the pre-Socratic 'Anaximander

Fragment' (Heidegger 1975), where 'being' is seen as a 'jointure' applied to the necessary dis-junction of time. It is an echo of this basic move that Derrida reads in Hamlet[18] where the prince of Denmark wonders if it has come upon him to 'mend' the time that is 'out of joint'. "Jointure" (*die Fuge*) is Heidegger's preferred word for the Greek '*Dikę*' and not 'justice' as some other translations would have it, since he wants to stay clear of any "juridical-moral" notion. (see Derrida 1994, 27)[19] Therefore, the "lingering awhile" (*je-weilig*, 28) of 'Being' proposed by Heidegger activates a passage which remains persistent in joining the disjointed time. 'Being', in its 'lingering-awhile', tries to remain in the gap of disjuncture, and yet it cannot totally traverse this gap, since that would only fill it with presence. On the other hand, if it does not give itself to such a work, then time remains ever dis-jointed and impossible. What then gives 'Being' its purpose to make the journey? Reducing the conceptual model drastically, one can get the following image: a certain 'work' (of 'being') trying to bridge the gap between two points, points which, as if, stand as two extreme edges of a passage, like two pegs holding two ends of a curtain, never quite revealing the scene, both producing the passage and giving it a certain tension. Derrida proposes that in this scene (also used by Heidegger), the former point, one which stays in the past, is usually taken to be a mark of an originary violence or a 'crime', whereas the latter point, staying in the future, promises a 'justice' which nullifies the originary 'crime'. Derrida calls this structure, essentially 'tragic', which depends on the placing of the 'crime' in the anterior:

> There is tragedy, there is essence of the tragic only on the condition of this originarity, more precisely of this pre-originary and properly spectral anteriority of the crime—the crime of the other, a misdeed whose event and reality, whose truth can never present themselves in flesh and blood, but can only allow themselves to be presumed, reconstructed, fantasized. (24)

This anteriority of crime fantasized into precipitation calls for the other desire, that of justice, which is contingent on the crime and therefore works like a 'vengeance', Hamlet being the exemplary figure: "If right or law stems from vengeance, as Hamlet seems to complain that it does [...] can one not yearn for a justice that one day, a day belonging no longer to history, a quasi-messianic day, would finally be removed from the fatality of vengeance?" (25). Heidegger is implicated in this structure, for even if he tries to reject the word 'justice' and place the analytic of the lingering-awhile outside the ambit of law, he still imagines the passage perched between dis-jointure and jointure. Deconstruction, on the contrary, retains and yet questions the 'tragic' in at least two ways. Before anything it doubts the futurity of justice. Derrida writes, "is this day [of justice as vengeance] before us, to come, or more ancient than memory itself?" (25) This doubt radically interrupts the 'tragic' by putting on the table the possibility that justice might also belong to the realm of 'memory', or even be "more ancient" (25). Does this also not imply that the 'crime' on the other hand, can very well claim a placement in the future and therefore be rather a 'desire' than 'fantasy'? Deconstruction however would not resort to such a simple reversal and instead place both (crime and justice) in the non-place that is indicated by the expression 'more ancient than memory', where desire and fantasy coincide. If memory works like inscription or writing then 'justice', thought as 'more ancient' might prefigure memory itself as mark of an erasure which can also be named 'crime'. This considerably transforms the very concept of memory, making it undecidable if it is at all a chain of causal temporality which goes toward a future, where this future is an extension derivable from the present (and also existing before the present as a 'past'). The assurance of linearity is no longer possible, as there might very well be a 'futurity' which is more ancient than memory itself, producing memory through its own discontinuity. Moreover, and this is the second related departure of deconstruction from the 'tragic', undecidability stems from the fact that one can only think in the present, from within this present of (human) lingering which Derrida calls "today":

> If it is difficult, in truth impossible, today, to decide between these two hypotheses [of crime and justice], it is precisely because "The time is out of joint": such would be the originary corruption of the day of today, or such would be, as well, the malediction of the dispenser of justice [...]. Is it possible to find a rule of cohabitation under such a roof, it being understood that this house will always be haunted, rather than inhabited by the meaning of the original? (25)

The "house" is the closure of "today," and its placing is structured like a haunting of the memory that remains, a memory that is not certain of a distinction between past and future, crime and justice, as well as fantasy and desire. It is from this gap of the 'today' that one calculates, where the question set by deconstruction has farrowed 'time' and therefore inaugurated a différance which cannot measure its place or stance. Derrida is distinguishing between a disjuncture that presupposes the 'unjust' in the origin and 'justice' in the future (the register of the tragic) and one that "opens up the infinite asymmetry of the relation to the other" (the register of deconstruction, 26), which can also be named 'justice', but a deconstructive justice. This other 'justice', which does not depend on "the economy of vengeance or punishment" and therefore not "calculable and distributive justice" (26) is deconstruction's step away from the tragic. Heidegger's model does not let go of the time of the tragic, which reassures as if from above, giving the time of the 'today' some substance and measure and place, making it a fallen version of that meta-time. Heidegger, Derrida comments, adopts the Hegelian notion (which he himself calls a 'vulgar notion of time') where "history, which is essentially history of spirit [...] falls (*fällt*) *into time*" (Hegel quoted in Derrida 1991, 25). Deconstruction's separation from the Heideggerian argument is palpable. Forcing a translation between 'philosophy' and the 'fictional', Derrida makes Heidegger travel into Shakespeare and finds that literature has an excess, that of the returning revenant, which always already conditions the ontological question ('to be or not to be'). It is precisely this that produces Hamlet's precariousness before a certain limit which cannot be crossed merely by calculative steps. It is a "limit" that "prevents one in fact from understanding the very things which it wants to explain: tragedy, precisely [...] the hesitation to take revenge, the deliberation, the non-naturality or the non-automaticity of the calculation neurosis, if you like... ." (Derrida 1994, 30)

For Derrida, the lingering of the 'Being' does not 'join' (or jump to plug, to read contra Laclau) anything because it works only between two absences, "what is no longer and what is not yet," beyond which stays a time completely and wholly other, which can only be thought into existence as an anamnesis (30). The (non-)placement of 'today', therefore, cannot have a tension (like a tense cord held between two rooted ends), or any purpose until it names its 'former' and the 'latter' (and therefore places itself). The 'lingering' becomes tragic, if they are named 'crime' and 'justice' respectively, which, as is apparently the case with Hamlet, would be tied to the notion of a debt, a property handed over in a chain of patrimony. But Derrida proposes a different kind of debt, one that is not mastered by any property of the origin or injunction of the future, neither 'pre' nor 'post' but a logic of 'ex'-appropriation, which works through the prosthetic supplement of an anamnesis, 'imagined' as more ancient than memory where this imagination has a materiality as long as memory carries the trace of an intended 'image'. The trace returns and haunts, not as non-material, but as inscription. This move distinguishes hauntology from any onto-theological structure (named 'tragic' by Derrida), and takes one to the much mis-read argument about "messianic without messianism," beyond the limits of this discussion. One might also remember, as Spivak points out in her review of *Specters*, Derrida is only interested in the dilemma of the 'prince', (the hysteric figure of) Ophelia, who might have opened an-other analysis of patrimony, or Gertrude the mother have "no takers" (Spivak 1995, 66).[20] Derrida's challenge to Spivak, in turn, consists in the problem of mapping a feminist ethics remaining at the level of the sub-individual. This is an intricate confrontation to which we cannot turn.

I want to underline two gestures we have encountered, in initiating a discussion of spectrality upstream from the 'tragic'—(1) the precipitation of an anamnesis which is both memory and produces memory, and (2) the rejection of any 'calculable insurance' and therefore of any subject ensuring presence of things. How can the two go together? Is not the precipitation of a certain 'revenant' also an assurance that something is, that some thing moves and gives purpose to being and time? And if that is so, then can that thing not work as an ontological insurance? It can, but not within the limits of 'calculation', and hence it is a different kind of insurance one is tracking here. If calculable justice in the form of vengeance opens the way for a subject of calculable insurance, then the 'other' justice "as incalculability of the gift and singularity of the an-economic ex-position to others" (26) must think of a different insurance altogether. Derrida calls this a "doing" which persists as a work without having the arrogance of being the agent of vengeance or restitution, different from an "action" which just fixes, joins, and appropriates the other in a gesture of giving the other justice (32). Derrida's discomfort with 'action' or simply with a preponderance of the 'act' is manifest elsewhere too. For example in *Limited Inc* (Derrida 1988) Derrida likens 'action' to 'event' and remarks that the "value of the act (used so generally and analyzed so little in the theory of speech acts), like that of event, should be submitted to systematic questioning." (Derrida 1988, 58) He then widens the implication by pointing out that in the "entire philosophical tradition" there is a curious support given to the fullness of presence based on this notion of action and actuality of meaning, which he then proposes to "defer" through the notion of 'iterability' (Derrida, 58). The revenant is thus like the 'signature', the very signature that one inscribes as one's own, yet referring at the same time to a structure of repeatability which cannot be reduced to one signature only. In the logic of the signature therefore, implicated are both the 'event' and the 'repetition' ('becoming legend' of event), 'singular I' and 'universal I'. Together they stage the "paradoxology of the singular mark" (Derrida 1992, 58). The paradox consists in this: that one can only reply to the other by affirming the other (counter-signing), even if in doing so one tries to stage an unique event (signature), making an inimitable inscription proper to oneself. Derrida writes, "if I had to reply (responsibly, that's the point) to a different provocation or countersign a different singular work, signing but with a signature which countersigns and tries to respond in another way to the signature of the other..." (66). The work of the signature is the daily, empirical mark of the elusive de-cision to come, as it traverses the 'cut' of the mundane, unlike the Foucaulcian 'catalyst' (but like the work of it as metaphor), it leaves a mark, each time.

Is de-cision 'post-deconstructive'? In lieu of a conclusion

Here I want to emphatically insert a proposition, that there cannot be any 'post-deconstructive' subject, if one means by it a new 'theory' of subject predication that has taken deconstruction into consideration, only to go upstream. Deconstruction resists being read and sublated as one of many 'theories', instead trying humbly to be part of a project which it recognizes as unavoidable, calling it 'grammatology'.[21] This project is strictly fictitious, if by 'fiction' one means the recognition that every 'constative' is at its heart, 'performative'.[22] Another way of saying that the Derridian "Différance is one of the names for the necessity to obliterate the graphematic structure, and the necessity to misname it "graphematic," since there is no other way..."[23] This misnaming is a'performative' which one must account for, placing grammatology not outside the necessity of (human) subject predication. Even grammatology cannot be 'post-deconstructive', it remains a project which places the 'grapheme' not in the place of privilege that 'phoneme' enjoys, being the unit of presence, but as its double. Grapheme is that material moment without which phoneme cannot come to be, as a species term which inhabits both 'speech' and 'writing'. Only by means of a certain "mark-ability (graphematicity) in speech and writing" that analytic of both the structure and the subject (-to-come) is figured (Spivak 1996, 89). Derrida has repeatedly made this point that one is always already placed in the age (/edge) of this 'project', and any 'theory' is made only as a narrow instance of this general horizon. Each such 'theory'claiming to mark a new beginning remains, strictly, 'writing in the narrow sense', which works within a restricted economy. It would thus be enormously difficult to affirm deconstruction and yet, thinking of going upstream from the project of grammatology.

Derrida is also tempted to make a theory of decision, indeed the entire Derridian corpus can be read as an unfurling of this temptation which remains denied. As we see, it is denied since 'decision' is always already cut-within (therefore 'de-cision'). No decision is taken for the 'first time', every decision is taken based on previous experiences of decision-making. It does that by cutting itself off from its first occurrence, by re-presenting itself. This 'cut' is also the mark of the work of the other in self. This is the double-bind of decision. The newness and authenticity of a decision can only be recognized if it successfully cuts itself off from the unique eventness and sur-vives in a matrix of repeatability."Whenever I say "my decision" or "I decide," you can be sure that I'm mistaken," Derrida contends, for the decision "should always be the other's decision" (Derrida 2007, 455). Thus, de-cision. As if the little 'hyphen' inserts a certain 'machine' into the heart of the 'event' and makes it a 'work'. It also highlights the 'cision' or 'cut'[24] that it leaves at its wake like an open wound. The hyphen works not like a bridge, but like a hinge, resisting the full precipitation of the subject of decision. This hinge is much similar to the Marxian "pivot [*Springpunkt*]," a metaphor for the dual character of human labour-power congealed in the commodity, first as contract (to sell labour-power) and then as spectrality (of socially necessary labour power, and as 'value').[25] But that discussion is beyond the purview of the present essay.

NOTES

1. This article is an expanded and somewhat modified version of a chapter of my PhD dissertation, *Precarious Objectifications: Ethics of representation and the Figure of the Woman* (Kargupta 2014).
2. Originally published in 1985, Laclau and Mouffe 2001.
3. "Society is not a valid object of discourse," as they pithily put it. (111)
4. Laclau and Mouffe 2001, 111, emphasis in original.
5. However, the strength of their rigorous text consists in its multivocity. Indeed, 'materiality' is a term which figures in *Hegemony and Socialist Strategy* in many differing ways, and the following articulation not only fits the meaning I indicate here, but also anticipates partly the argument of the present essay: "the non-materiality of labour as a substance of value is expressed through the equivalence among materially diverse commodities" etc. (127)
6. Proceeding from Laclau and Mouffe is particularly helpful for our purpose here as Derrida himself has underlined. See "Remarks on Deconstruction and Pragmatism" by Jacques Derrida in Mouffe 1995.
7. One may ask: does the unifying logic of consciousness work like a hegemony, trying to unify the dispersed experiences and memory traces? And therefore, can one say that the 'subject' is structured like the social?
8. See Butler, Laclau, and Zizek 2000, 79.
9. This is consistent with the Derridian project of 'grammatology', see below.
10. See Spivak 2005.
11. Spivak's term in explaining a different Foucault attentive to the ontico-ontological difference, see Spivak 1996, 149-151.
12. Chanter 2001, 178. This has also inaugurated a debate on ethicality between Simon Critchley and Ernesto Laclau. See Critchley in Mouffe 1995 and Critchley 1993.
13. Spivak in Bilimoria and Al-Kassim 2014, 231.
14. For 'restance' see Derrida 1988, 51-57.
15. J. Hillis Miller, much in the line of our argument, has noted that a "salient difference" between Laclau from Derrida is contained in the latter's rejection of "spectral notions," which also means Laclau misses Derrida's point about the madness of decision being related to the trace of the "wholly other" (Hillis Miller in Critchley and Marchart 2012, 222).
16. In brief, as I have specifically explained, 'de-cision' can be seen as a deconstruction (deconstructive messianic understanding) of the commonsensical notion, decision. However, this specific way of writing the word has a complex theoretical history which we cannot discuss here (the major texts: Heidegger 1999, Nancy 1993). My use has intersecting lines with the magisterial trajectory of Heidegger which Nancy follows, but in my limited

use, it is also a notion meticulously argued in the first half of my thesis, through a reading of Louis Althusser and Jacques Derrida.

17. Derrida 1994, 59.
18. *The Tragedy of Hamlet, Prince of Denmark* (1599-1602) by William Shakespeare.
19. This has an uncanny similarity with Louis Althusser's rejection of the same word, 'justice' (see Kargupta 2014).
20. These require serious and separate considerations, the intricate weave of Spivak's comments on the Derridian readings of Marx have a force of their own. Even a quick glance would note the following trajectory: "Limits and Openings of Marx in Derrida" (1980/in Spivak 1993), "Scattered speculations on the Question of Value" (1985/see Spivak 1987), and "Ghostwriting." (Spivak 1995)
21. In an interviewwith Nancy, Derrida wishes that the work of subject predication would come out of its "pre-deconstructive" frame, i.e. recognize its graphemetic structure (Derrida 1994a, 266). This, however, is only a repetition of the declaration of the 'project' of grammatology, and not a call for a 'post' deconstructive subject, as Simon Critchely recognizes (even if he wonders, what if this was pursued by Derrida, in Critchley 1999, 72-73). 'Not pre-deconstructive' is clearly not post-deconstructive.
22. See Derrida 2002, 112.
23. Emphasis in original, in Spivak 1993, 147.
24. The figure of the 'cut' is discussed in detail in my unpublished thesis, see below.
25. As fleshed out meticulously by Spivak 1993, 119. The present article is indeed haunted by the Spivakian interruptions, most of which can be accessed with the password 'value', an abstraction to which (Spivak shows) Derrida is not fully attentive (he is attentive only as far as it concerns the necessary abstraction implicit in 'exchange', and not in Capital's transformation of surplus-value into its own body).

REFERENCES

Badiou, Alain, 2009. *Pocket Pantheon: Figures of Postwar Philosophy*, tr., David Macey. New York: Verso.

Bilimoria, Purushottama and Al-Kassim, Dina (eds.), 2014. *Postcolonial Reason and Its Critique: Deliberations on Gayatri Spivak's Thoughts*. New Delhi: Oxford University Press.

Butler, Judith, Laclau, Ernesto, and Zizek, Slavoj 2000. *Contingency, Hegemony, Universality: Contemporary Dialogues on the Left*. London: Verso.

Chanter, Tina, 2001. *Time, Death, and the Feminine: Levinas with Heidegger*. Stanford: Stanford University Press.

Critchley, Simon and O. Marchart (eds.), 2004. *Laclau: A Critical Reader*. New York: Routledge.

Critchley, Simon, 1998. "Metaphysics in the Dark: A Response to Richard Rorty and Ernesto Laclau" in *Political Theory* 26 (6): 803-817.

Critchley, Simon, 1999. *Ethics-Politics-Subjectivity: Essays on Derrida Levinas and Contemporary French Thought*. London: Verso.

Das, Anirban, 2010. *Toward a Politics of the (Im)Possible: The Body in Third World Feminisms.* London: Anthem Press.

Derrida, Jacques, 1988. *Limited Inc,* tr., Samuel Weber. Evanston: Northwestern University Press.

Derrida, Jacques, 1991. *Of Spirit: Heidegger and the Question,* tr., Geoffrey Bennington and Rachel Bowlby. Chicago: University of Chicago Press.

Derrida, Jacques, 1992. "Force of law" in *Deconstruction and the Possibility of Justice*, ed., Drucilla Cornell, Michel Rosenfeld and David Gray Carlson. London: Routledge, pp. 3-67.

Derrida, Jacques, 1994. *Specters of Marx: The State of the Debt, the Work of Mourning and the New International*, tr., Peggy Kamuf. New York and London: Routledge.

Derrida, Jacques, 1994a. *Points...: Interviews, 1974-1994,* tr., Peggy Kamuf. Stanford: Stanford University Press.

Derrida, Jacques, 2002. *Without Alibi,* tr., Peggy Kamuf. Stanford Stanford University Press.

Derrida, Jacques, 2007. *Psyche: Inventions of the Other*, Vol. 1, tr., Peggy Kamuf et al. Stanford: Stanford University Press.

Foucault, Michel, 1990. *The History of Sexuality*, Vol. 1: An Introduction, tr., Robert Hurley. New York: Vintage.

Foucault, Michel, 1994. *Aesthetics, Method, and Epistemology*, ed., James D. Faubion, tr., Robert Hurley et al. New York: New Press.

Foucault, Michel, 2001. *Power (The Essential Works of Foucault, 1954-1984,* Vol. 3), ed., James D. Faubion, tr., Robert Hurley et al. New York: The New Press.

Heidegger, Martin, 1975. *Early Greek Thinking*, tr., David Farrell Krell and Frank A. Capuzzi. New York: Harper and Row.

Heidegger, Martin, 1999. *Contributions to Philosophy* (From Enowning), trs. Parvis Emad and Kenneth Maly. Bloomington: Indiana University.

Kargupta, Sourav, 2014. *Precarious Objectifications: Ethics of Representations and the Figure of the Woman* (PhD dissertation). Unpublished.

Laclau, Ernesto and Mouffe, Chantal, 2001. *Hegemony and Socialist Strategy: Towards a Radical Democratic Politics.* New York: Verso.

Mouffe, Chantal (ed.), 1995. *Deconstruction and Pragmatism.* New York: Routledge.

Nancy, Jean-Luc, 1993. *The Birth to Presence*, tr., Brian Holmes et al. Stanford: Stanford University Press.

Spivak, Gayatri Chakravorty, 1987. *In Other Worlds: Essays in Cultural Politics.* London: Methuen.

Spivak, Gayatri Chakravorty, 1993. *Outside in the Teaching Machine.* New York and London: Routledge.

Spivak, Gayatri Chakravorty, 1995. "Ghostwriting" in *Diacritics* 25, 2, 65–84.

Spivak, Gayatri Chakravorty, 1996. *Spivak Reader*, eds., Donna Landry and Gerald MacLean. New York: Routledge.

Spivak, Gayatri Chakravorty, 1999. *A Critique of Postcolonial Reason: Toward a History of the Vanishing Present.* Cambridge: Harvard University Press.

Spivak, Gayatri Chakravorty, 2005. "Scattered speculations on the Subaltern and the Popular," in *Post Colonial Studies*, Vol. 8, No. 4, 475-486.

17

Wounding the Self—Writing the Other

Nimmi Nalika Menike and Sanjay Kaushal

The idea of violence has been approached and discussed by various thinkers from various disciplines. Rigorous researches on violence in academic sphere and its socio-cultural analysis in religious and juridical domains have endeavoured to develop a critique of violence in order to accentuate the necessity of preventing violence of all kinds. This necessity, on the other hand, in its yearning for a better world, seeks to spread love, friendship, forgiveness and care. Centuries of human history have been teaching, learning and commanding the condemnation and rejection of violence, while, on the other hand, innumerable experiences, stories and instances of hurt, pain, discrimination, and injustice as detrimental consequences of violence are highlighted. Despite this urge to get away from violence, the reason that we are still compelled to ask ourselves how successful our efforts have been to eradicate the violence is good enough to assess the failure and the complexities to appease the horrific consequences of violence. Acknowledging this failure at the outset to engage in a discussion on violence, we intend to address the idea of violence keeping Derridian philosophy as the backdrop of the analysis. In doing so, we do not intend to posit Derrida or his philosophy as a religion, tradition, discipline, method, or an answer that can be adopted or followed from now on; instead, taking his views, we seek to underscore the necessity of going beyond the given and popular idea of violence in order to think of a way that is not completely away from violence, but of a way that is violent yet ethical. Thus, we intend to think of a way in which both violence and ethics can be brought together in order to think of violent ethics and ethical violence.

The general idea or the meaning that the word 'violence' is concerned with, is on one hand, 1. a behavior involving physical force intended to hurt, damage, or kill, 2. on the other hand, a strength of emotion or of a destructive natural force. Accordingly, violence is destructive, harmful, and dangerous; also, if we refer to the first idea mentioned above, it is a power or force that is generated from or within one's body that damages, hurts, kills, and so on. This physical force is with everyone due to which everyone is violent; also, violence is with everyone. Therefore, everyone can be violent; everyone is a potential violence. On the other hand, this violence that everyone is capable of committing, can be directed towards one's self or another; also towards both self and another— another person or another being, also another thing— the other. Thus, violence can be done on both self and the other. However, it is true that there is also violence happening due to natural calamities— such as tsunami, hurricane, tornado, rain, and so on, yet that sort of violence cannot be rejected or aimed to be rejected since it is beyond human capabilities. Therefore, the idea of violence that we constantly refer to, is the one that is committed by humans, and it is that violence that is sought to be eliminated, condemned, and prevented in and through law, order, education, and religion. In that sense, eradication of violence from the world is an attempt that is taken up socially, religiously, legally, and politically; moreover, it is taken up both individually and collectively. Thus, every society, every culture, every religion, every system of law and order, operates against violence. In this regard, each of them makes a pledge that is kept against violence: *no more violence*. By today it has become a pledge, a step, a measure, a mechanism, a law, a practice that is taken up and undertaken nationally and also internationally, yet differently by different nations, communities, cultures, and religions. Hence, it is a national and international promise, also a decision—a decision to say *no* to violence, violence also in terms of discrimination, harassment, suppression, and so on. All are capable of making this decision because all are *capable of deciding*. It is this capability to decide which makes everyone powerful in their respective positions. Hence, everyone is capable, and everyone is able to be capable in making a decision-making a decision as *I*, wherein the particular decision becomes *my* decision. Here, the idea of decision needs to be considered in terms of ability, knowledge, and calculation.[1]

Every decision, including the decision to say *no* to violence, is a decision that affirms the possibility and capability to be oneself or the possibility to be *I*—the sovereign. The sovereignty of self is also the freedom of the self through which self appears as *the powerful*. Here, the idea of *the powerful* self suggests one's capability and possibility not only to act but also to be *able to be* conscious of one's own self and also of others— others in the sense of any being, world, also the future, as if others, the world and the future is at self's disposal.

Thus, it suggests a certain awareness, familiarity, and certainty that the self has about his own self, and also about others. It is through this awareness that one is able to distinguish one's own self from the others identifying himself as *I*, manifesting the identity of the self in terms of *I*. The ability to differentiate one's self from the others as *I* and *others* legitimates, affirms, and demands the necessity of a self-conscious and self-centered discourse. Thus, in the context of the self, the self-consciousness is a possibility, ability, necessity, and legitimacy. This idea of self-awareness in terms of self-consciousness that makes the self a "possibility," is extensively discussed by Martin Heidegger and Jean-Paul Sartre in *Being and Time*[2] and *Being and Nothingness*[3] respectively. They underscore not only the *possibility of the self*, but also the *necessity* of such a possibility of the self, keeping the self as the source of the truth and knowledge. In this attempt of self-affirmation, both the philosophers posit, yet differently, death as the limit, border, or the threshold of the self, where they bring the other into the discourse of the self.

According to Heidegger and Sartre, the possibility of the self is a *certainty*, that is to say, self becomes a certainty. But, this certainty is under constant threat—a threat coming from the other, for self is always in relation with the other. As Heidegger argues, this relation of the self with the other is due to "falling" of "*Dasein*" from its being,[4] owing to which the real self is covered or concealed in everyday life. In accordance with which, he infers two kinds of being within *Dasein*: "authentic being" and "inauthentic being."[5] Moreover, this inauthenticity, which is inseparable from *Dasein*, happens due to the other. Heidegger terms this other as "they-self,"[6] and the self is lost among they-selves in "idle talk" because of the "thrownness" and fallenness of being.[7] Consequently, one is not able to be one's own self in everyday world. Heidegger argues that, it is only at death one is able to be "Real" Self, for death is utterly *mine* as it is only *I* who die in *my* death. Hence, death is that which detaches the self from the other; the self is cut off from the other, due to which, other becomes an impossibility while making the self as a possibility. In contrast to Heidegger, Sartre views death as the impossibility of the self and the possibility of the other. The relationship between the self and the other cannot be eliminated even through death, for the existence of the other is irrefutable. Hence, in this undeniable relationship with the other, self is in a struggle to gain victory over the other who is trying to appropriate *me* with his interpretation. In this struggle, Sartre affirms the ability of the self to be powerful in defying the understanding and interpretation that the other has of *me*.[8] Victory of the self over the other is possible only when one is alive, because, according to Sartre, self loses this resistive power in the death. Therefore, it is only before death, one is able to be the Self despite the powerful other, due to which death is seen as the impossibility of the self and the possibility of the other.

However, considering Heideggerian and Sartrian views on the Self, it can be said that they attempt to resist the other in order to affirm the self, though they view death differently. Here, more importantly, the resistance is of two kinds: in Heidegger, it appears in terms of "care"[9], on the other hand, in Sartre, it is "choice" and "freedom."[10]

When these two ideas—care and choice or freedom—are compared with each other, the former does not seem to imply the idea of power[11], instead, it appears to refer to friendliness, lovingness, kindness, and so on. But, the terms "choice" and "freedom" bring images of power, strength, struggle etc. In this sense, Sartrian approach in demanding and affirming the self appears to be destructive in comparison to that of Heidegger's. Unlike Sartre, Heidegger does not seemingly give such sort of implication in his approach and the project of affirming the self. Rather, he tries to conceal it in his language. Yet, despite this strategy, it cannot withhold the traces of power in his idea of care. It is because of this idea of power emanating from the self, that the self becomes still the *powerful* or the one who is *able*. However in this affirmation of the necessity of resistance and care, both the philosophers have attempted to highlight the necessity of affirming and maintaining the Self in and through self-sameness. In doing so, they have necessitated the exclusion, subjugation, and separation of the other from the self. It is in this philosophical discourse of self-sameness where the other is subjugated and excluded by the power of the self. This power of the self has been coming up throughout the human history, and this discourse of the dominant self can be understood in relation to culture, community, nation, religion, gender, and so on, where every culture and community can be seen as closures which maintain *their own* space excluding the other through resistance.

Nonetheless, such self-affirming discourse becomes problematic, and also a discourse to be problematized when its position is seen in relation to ethics. As discussed above, self-dominant discourse is repressive and violent; its violence is directed toward the other, for other is *outside* the self, due to which the other is viewed as a potential threat to the sovereign space of the self. This threat can be understood with reference to the ideas such as, impurity, contamination, illegitimacy, inauthenticity, colonization, domination, enmity, and so on. In that sense, what is intended to be protected against the other is the sovereignty of the self; which is also purity, authenticity, legitimacy, superiority, and freedom of the self. In doing so, it creates a closure manifesting the self as a totality.

Under the power of such totalizing closure of the self, it is the other who has been discriminated and against whom injustice is done. Pain, misery, anger, despair, dissatisfaction, vulnerability, and so on demand the questioning of the self. It is in this context, the importance of Levinasian philosophy of the *other* along with "ethical responsibility" needs to be brought in, for the above kind of situation that unavoidably happens due to the domination of the self can effectively be addressed while affirming the inadequacy of questioning the dominant discourse. Inadequacy, not in terms of power, in which case it would again suggest retaliation, punishment, avenging, rejection, and so on, but in terms of ethics and responsibility which unfold beyond any politics or power *as such*. According to Emmanuel Levinas,[12] this ethical responsibility can only be approached by bringing the other into the domain of the self through questioning the spontaneity of the self. In this context of ethics and ethical responsibility towards the other, Levinas posits *self* in a condition of "no longer *able to be able*".[13]

Hence, it is important to focus our attention on this particular condition of the self as "no longer *able to be able*," that arises in the relationship of the self and the other, where other is unavoidable. This unavoidable other, as mentioned above, comes to the self from *outside*, and, as Levinas argues, this outside where the other comes from is also the zone where death comes from,[14] in which case death and the other are unknown to the self and knowledge of the self. Accordingly, since the other is outside the self and outside the knowledge and awareness of the self, self is not able to be aware of the other, in which case the other becomes a complete *stranger* to the self. Therefore, the other is not only unavoidable, but also undecidable and unpredictable, owing to which the *coming of the other* or the *arrival* of the other cannot be viewed in terms of *what*, *where*, *when*, *which*, or *how*. Here, the idea of the other needs to be understood not only in terms of another— another being or separate being, but also in terms of the other that *occurs* within the self. Thus, in the present discussion, while we present both—the former and the latter senses of the other, we specifically intend to highlight the *other* in the latter sense, i.e. the otherness that *happens* to the self despite the wish or will of the self. In other words, self is not aware of what happens to his *own* self; self is not able to control or resist this otherness happening to the itself; this frailty is precisely because of the inability to program, predict, or recognize the other.

Nonetheless, the other *arrives*. This *arrival,* as well as the *other* arriving in that arrival, is thus a *secret*. It is this secret, the other, therefore the *secret of the other*[15] that disrupts the sameness of the self. This disruption, which brings a *rupture* to the sameness of the self, makes a difference in the self, yet this difference cannot be recognized in terms of *what* or *who*, for it has no *figure as such*. Therefore, Derrida terms it as "*différance*" and "movement of différance."[16] This movement or the play of différance is something that self cannot hold back or control, due to which it becomes the condition of *not being able to be* the self that is discussed by Levinas, especially in his *Otherwise than Being or Beyond Essence*[17]. It is this philosophy of Levinas that is taken further ahead by Derrida in his discussion on violence, ethics, and responsibility.

Analysing the idea of violence and ethics with regard to the relationship of self and the other, Derrida puts forth his notion of *différance* highlighting the *unavoidable* and *necessary rupture* of the self. For him, this rupture is a "wound"[18] or chasm; and, this opening up of the self through the rupture, is violence. Thus, the rupture is violence, it is also violent. But, this rupture of the self is not intentional or programmed; therefore, it is not an action or re-action, it is also not a decision, rather it is de-cision —the cut. Despite this violence of the rupture, it is an ethical violence in the sense that it is opened up for the other, without knowing anything about *what* is going to come *from* the other, also *coming* as other. Therefore, as Derrida contends, the coming of the other is an "event,"[19] that is to say that the coming of the other is also the coming of the event. Explaining the idea of event in his *The Deconstruction of Actuality*, Derrida remarks that "coming of the event is what cannot and should not be prevented."[20] Hence, in opening up to the other, one, without having a prior knowledge of it, is going to welcome anything or anyone that is going to *come*. This impossibility of such awareness is due to the impossibility of the self to *determine* the other. Therefore, to open up for the other also means to welcome the other with utmost "hospitality". Explaining this idea of welcoming the other in terms of hospitality, Derrida writes:

> The one, *who*ever it is to whom "come" is said, cannot let him/herself be determined in advance. For absolute hospitality, he/she is the stranger, the one who arrives. I must not ask the absolute arrival [*arrivant*] to begin by declining an identity, by telling me who he/she is, under what conditions I am going to offer him/her hospitality, [...] If he/she/it is an absolute arrival, I must not propose a contract or impose any conditions. I must not: and furthermore, by definition, I cannot.[21]

This unavoidable *rupture* of the self that happens without any involvement of the self—without any intentionality, consciousness, awareness—is the very nature of being/self. However, it is not to suggest that the rupture is a *failure* or something *negative*. Certainly, this rupture does *dismantle* the possibility of *I* in the sense of totality; but on the other hand, it is this constant rupture which does not let any closure to be perpetual that would lead to the possibility of self. In this sense, the impossibility of the self is what makes the self possible; and this self is nothing but the *other*—self becoming the other. This way, what this constant rupture brings is not the infinite infinity of the self; instead, it is the *finitudeness* of the self that goes into *infinity*, or in other words, the *brevity* of the self. Consequently, there is no such possibility of identifying self *as such*, for there is no self *as such*—the totalized self or the complete self; instead, what appears as self, as mentioned above, is the *other*. Hence, it is the other who is being invented in the context of the self. Yet in Derridean view, "the other is indeed what is not inventible, and it is then the only invention in the world, the only invention of the world, our invention, the invention that invents *us*."[22]

In the task of inventing ourselves through the other, Derrida highlights the idea of literature through writing, where writing is viewed as the opening up of the given language—given language of the self to the other. Therefore, literature through writing is considered as the unfolding of the other, according to which literature is the space of the other. This space that is weaved in and through language has no particular border *as such*; it has no limit that can be crossed. In fact, it is the space where the distinction between *I* and the *other* becomes blurred, due to which one is *no more* self-identical; consequently, it becomes space of a third person—he/she/it—the other. Subsequently, as Blanchot writes referring to Kafka,[23] one is free; free from duties, responsibilities and law to which one is bound to surrender in everyday life; free from any order that demands identity; free from making decisions in terms of calculations and positions. This is the freedom that is experienced through language; through *opening up* of the *given* language. Language opens up through writing where language constantly breaks within.[24] In every moment of writing, language faces a risk— risk of losing what it *already is*, since in each act of writing, language undergoes a metamorphosis.

Thus, to write is to experience transformations or *différance*. Yet, this losing is not negative; because while it is losing what it *is already*, it is going to become something *other than*. As Derrida says, it is a game—where no one wins or loses; instead, "where whoever loses wins and where one wins and loses each time;"[25] it is a play of *différance*.

Nonetheless, to write means to break away from the *I subject*, which also means the death of the self or as Blanchot writes in *The Space of Literature*; to write is to "give[s] up saying "I"."[26] Hence, writing happens at the death of the self; but, not after or following the death; instead, writing "just following the death, *upon or on the occasion of the death*,"[27] owing to which, according to Derrida, it becomes mourning. One *mourns* over the death of another. In this context, it is important to look into the idea of death once again, but not in Heieggerian or Sartrian sense; instead, it has to be seen in Derridean view.

As in relation to Heidegger and Sartre, and also according to the general notion of death, death is considered as the end of life, also as the completion of life, due to which death becomes the last point. Accordingly, there is nothing beyond death; death is the border—border of life. However, in contrast to this general notion, following Levinasian idea of death, Derrida views death as "aporia",[28] where nothing can be seen as a joint or as a break, or else as *the* end or *the* limit, rather it is both joint and break in which case there is always something going to *remain*—going to remain *to come*. It is this remainder that he views in terms of "specters"[29] with which one is haunted over and over again, from which one is never able to be free. Thus, the *otherness* is that which is going to come even *beyond* death, and it is this otherness that one is haunted by, time and again; it is this otherness that is going to come beyond death over which one *mourns*. Thus, *coming* of the other is even *before* death—before the death of the self. As Derrida writes in his *Work of Mourning*,[30] this mourning is anticipated even before death. Hence mourning is the responsibility kept *in the name of the other* or *in the memory of the other*. In the introduction of *Work of Mourning*, editors Pascale-Anne Brault and Michael Naas remark that, "it is only through memory and mourning that we become ourselves, indebted even before we can owe anything to ourselves."[31] It is such an arrival that one is prepared to welcome. However, here, as Derrida explains, "one does not make the other come, one lets it come by preparing for its coming. The coming of the other or its coming back is the only possible arrival [*survenue*]."[32]

However, as previously mentioned, in literature through writing, one is able to break free from all the responsibilities. So doing, in a way, writing becomes a way of escaping. This escape is not only from responsibilities, but also and all the more from ethics: because to be responsible for *this* or *that* act or decision is also to be ethical in *given* terms, since the notion of responsibility in everyday life is determined by the binary classificatory system that is to do with good/bad, right/wrong, and so on. Thus, in living, to be ethical means to be responsible and vice versa. In that sense, the idea of writing appears to be mostly self-centred or selfish, therefore, more violent – violent than any other violence that happens at the level of taking actions, reactions, and decisions, as discussed above. It is here, at this point that the idea of ethics and responsibility needs to be viewed in an entirely different manner.

The idea of ethics and responsibility to be viewed in relation to writing is not determined by any ethics or responsibility *as such*. It is ethics *prior* to any ethics; responsibility taken up before being responsible, which means that, without knowing to whom one is being responsible or in what manner one is being responsible, and without knowing *what* it is to be ethical or *how* to be ethical. In that manner, there is no decided, programmed, calculated and defined responsibility or ethics as such. Here, the ethical responsibility is *undecidable* and *undefinable*. Thus, it is governed by urgency and immediacy—urgency and immediacy in an *emergency*. As Derrida says, it is a situation that arises with the question "What should I do?"[33] In such a situation, one is demanded to *decide*; yet, that decision should be a *responsible decision*. Moreover, this responsible decision, in Derridean terms, "must also and above all—and this is what I wanted to insist on—be made *with the utmost urgency*. And by *urgency* I mean the necessity of not waiting, or rather the *impossibility of waiting*."[34] Hence, ethical decision or responsible decision is far more difficult and risky; going to be risky since one is not aware of the outcome or the result— the "dangerous perhaps."[35] Therefore, such ethical responsibility is not for one's own benefit: instead, it *risks* one's own life. It is precisely due to this nature, that the ethical responsibility can be distinguished from political responsibility, also ethics from politics. Thus, as Derrida explains, it is the idea of *urgency* which asserts the necessity of interruption that can be seen as the most apparent difference between ethics and politics. Accordingly,

> [...] this ethical response can and should be immediate, in short, rather simple, it should make straight for the goal at once, straight to its end, without getting caught up in an analysis of hypothetical imperatives, in calculations, in evaluations of interests and powers. Because its urgency is infinite, immediately infinite, it is either absolute or null. It is no longer even an urgency insofar as a waiting time should not exist. Whereas, on the contrary, still according to the same appearance, political responsibility, because it takes into account a large number of relations, of relations of power, of actual laws, of possible causes and effects, of hypothetical imperatives, requires a time for analysis, requires a gamble, that is calculation that is never sure and that requires strategy. So many things that have no place, theoretically, in a pure ethical responsibility. There is neither gamble nor strategy in an ethics thus determined.[36]

Thus, it is in relation to such ethical responsibility, literature through writing needs to be viewed as "the nonethical opening up of ethics."[37]

NOTES

1. See Jacque Derrida's two essays "Deconstruction of Actuality" and "Ethics and Politics Today" in *Negotiations: Interventions and Interviews 1971-2001*, (2002).
2. Heidegger, M., 1962.
3. Sartre, J.-P., 1957.
4. Heidegger, M., 1962, pp. 210–214.
5. Ibid, p. 68.
6. Ibid, p. 167.
7. Ibid, pp. 211–221.
8. Sartre, J.-P., 1957, pp. 509–531.
9. Heidegger, M., 1962, pp. 370–380.
10. Sartre, J.-P., 1957, pp. 433–556.
11. For understanding the notion of care in relation to the self-centred discourse of power, see Friedrich Nietzsche in his *Thus Spoke Zarathustra* (1969) and Michel Foucault in his *Ethics–Subjectivity and Truth,* Vol. 1 (1994).
12. Levinas, E., 1969.
13. Levinas, E., 1989, p. 42.
14. Levinas, E., 1969, p. 233.

15. For a treatment of a philosophical understanding of the idea of secret, consult the following very useful text: Derrida, J. & Ferraris, M., (2001), *A Taste for the Secret* (tr. Giacomo Donis). Cambridge: Polity Press.
16. Derrida, J., 1973, pp. 129–160.
17. Levinas, E., 1981.
18. Derrida, J., 2007.
19. Idea of event has extensively been discussed by Jacques Derrida in many of his texts. *The Ear of The Other: Otobiography, Transference, Translation* (1985), *The Gift of Death* (1995), *The Politics of Friendship* (1997), *Negotiations: Interventions and Interviews 1971-2001* (2002), and *Psyche: Invention of the Other,* Vol. 1 (2007) can here be mentioned as some of those in which his idea of event unfolds in relation to various contexts.
20. See Jacques Derrida's two essays "Deconstruction of Actuality" and "Ethics and Politics Today" in *Negotiations: Interventions and Interviews 1971-2001*, (2002). p. 94.
21. Derrida, J., 2002, p. 95.
22. Derrida, J., 1992, p. 342.
23. Blanchot, M., 1982.
24. Jacques Derrida, in his "Roundtable on Translation" that appears in *Otobiographies: The Teaching of Nietzsche and the Politics of the Proper Name* (1985), discusses the idea of widening of language through breaking it within. Here He brings out metaphor of sea with its breaking waves to explain what happens to language in translation/writing. pp. 144-45.
25. Derrida, J., 1973, p. 151.
26. Blanchot, M., 1982, p. 26.
27. Derrida, J., 2001, p. 49.
28. Derrida, J., 1993.
29. Derrida, J., 1994.
30. Derrida, J., 2001.
31. Ibid p. 26.
32. Derrida, 1992, pp. 341-342.
33. Derrida, J., 2002, p. 296.
34. Ibid
35. Jacques Derrida, in his *The Politics of Friendship* (1997), discusses the idea of decision and event with regard to the *perhaps*, where he asserts that there is no event that is not preceded and followed by its own perhaps. "*Perhaps*," as Derrida argues, introduces the possibility of coming of something new or different other than what it is *already* or what it is *now*. But, the very nature of that which is to come is *unpredictable* and *undecidable*. Therefore, perhaps is *dangerous*, yet it is also the space of "chance".
36. Derrida, J., 2002, p. 301.
37. Derrida, J., 1994, p. 140.

REFERENCES

Blanchot, M., 1982. *The Space of Literature.* (tr.) Ann Smock. Lincoln: University of Nebraska Press.

Derrida, J., 1973. *Speech and Phenomena and Other Essays on Husserl's Theory of Signs.* (tr.) David B. Allison. Evanston: Northwestern University Press.

Derrida, J., 1976. *Of Grammatology.* (tr.) Gayatri Chakravorty Spivak. Baltimore: The Johns Hopkins University Press.

Derrida, J., 1985. *The Ear of the Other: Otobiography, Transference, Translation.* New York: Schocken Books.

Derrida, J., 1992. *Acts of Literature.* (ed.) Derek Attridge. New York: Routledge.

Derrida, J., 1993. *Aporias.* (tr.) Thomas Dutoit. Stanford: Stanford University Press.

Derrida, J., 1994. *Specters of Marx.* (tr.) Peggy Kamuf. New York: Routledge.

Derrida, J., 1995. *The Gift of Death.* (tr.) David Wills. Chicago: The University of Chicago Press.

Derrida, J., 1997. *The Politics of Friendship.* (tr.) George Collins. New York: Verso.

Derrida, J., 2001. *A Taste for the Secret.* (tr.) Giacomo Donis. Cambridge: Polity Press.

Derrida, J., 2001. *The Work of Mourning.* (eds.) Pascale-Anne Brault and M. Naas. Chicago: The University of Chicago Press.

Derrida, J., 2002. *Negotiations: Interventions and Interviews, 1971-2001.* (tr.) Elizabeth Rottenberg. Stanford: Stanford University Press.

Derrida, J., 2007. *Psyche: Invention of the Other,* Vol. 1. (ed.) Peggy Kamuf & E. Rottenberg. Stanford: Stanford University Press.

Foucault, M., 1997. *Ethics: Subjectivity and Truth,* Vol. 1. (tr.) Robert Hurley & Others. New York: The New Press.

Heidegger, M.,1962. *Being and Time.* (tr.) John Macquarrie & E. Robinson. Oxford: Basil Blackwell.

Levinas, E., 1969. *Totality and Infinity: An Essay on Exteriority.* (tr.) Alphonso Lingis. Pittsburgh: Duquesne University Press.

Levinas, E.,1989. *Levinas Reader.* (ed.) Sean Hand. Oxford: Basil Blackwell.

Levinas, E., 1991. *Otherwise than Being or Beyond Essence.* (tr.) Alphonso Lingis. Dordnecht: Kluwer Academic Publishers.

Nietzsche, F.,1961. *Thus Spoke Zarathustra.* (tr.) R.J. Hollingdale. London: Penguin Books.

Sartre, J. P., 1957. *Being and Nothingness: An Essay on Phenomenological Ontology.* (tr.) Hazel E. Barnes. London: Methuen & Co.

18

Remembering "The Purloined Letter": Letters from the Event Horizon[1]

Arup K. Chatterjee

Why do we remember the past, but not the future?[2]

Prologue

Edgar Allan Poe's "The Purloined Letter" (1845) proceeds on the following plot. The story is narrated by an unnamed character, who is a friend of the French detective, C. Auguste Dupin. The Prefect of Police in Paris comes to Dupin, for his help in a case of blackmail by the thief of a compromising letter. The letter is apparently addressed to the queen; the blackmailer being Minister D—. He had stolen the letter from the queen's possession and replaced it with a dummy scrap of paper. According to the Prefect, the contents of the letter have not been revealed, and the blackmailer has kept the letter very close to himself. Although the minister's apartment had been thoroughly searched by the police, the letter could not be retrieved. After a month, the Prefect returns to Dupin, frantic in his search for the purloined letter, having advertised for a reward of 50,000 francs if the letter were retrieved. Dupin produces the letter, and begins to explain to the narrator the manner in which he came to lay his hands on it.

Dupin explains that the Parisian police failed to recognize the thief's poetic and daring sensibility; that Minister D— had kept the letter very much in the open. When Dupin visited the Minister, in the disguise of a weak-sighted man, thus wearing sunglasses, he struck a conversation with him, and discovered a letter, chafed about its edge, on the Minister's table. Dupin left his snuffbox, so as to find an excuse to come back the next day. During his second visit, when the Minister was distracted by the fire of a gunshot, outside on the street, Dupin quickly stole the purloined letter, replacing it with a dummy, in his turn. As a consequence, one letter, whose contents are never revealed initiated the traffic (or sufferance) of two dummy letters; one in the possession of the queen, and another with her Minister. In this second letter,

Dupin had inscribed the following message to the blackmailer, who later critics have argued to have been Dupin's own brother: *Un dessein si funeste, S'il n'est digne d'Atrée, est digne de Thyeste* (If such a sinister design isn't worthy of Atreus, it is worthy of Thyestes).[3] It is supposed that the incriminating, twice-purloined, letter is safely handed back to the queen, by the Prefect.

Jacques Lacan and Jacques Derrida have both written their respective commentaries on Poe's story, besides numerous other critics. Lacan's "Seminar on the Purloined Letter" and Derrida's "The Purveyor of Truth" came at loggerheads to give rise to one of the formative debates of poststructuralism—that of language, meaning and interpretation of the floating signifier that the purloined letter transpires as. For Lacan, the fact that the letter is in sufferance (diverted or prolonged in its route) is the sign of the lack that the queen bears in her de-phallisized state; that the contents of the letter did not determine the meaning of the story (since both the king and the police were symbolically blind to its contents, as well as the sunglass-wearing Dupin) as much as the fact that the queen was dispossessed of the letter. Derrida responded by writing that the letter did not by itself lack meaning, but that Lacan had made the alleged *lack* appear to be the only meaning of the story: the symbolic lack of the contents of the purloined letter, and thus the lack of phallus in the queen. He further added that the more radical level of meaning was interred in the threat that in the hands of the queen, the letter was a potential castrating agent for the king, who would have fallen from his grace had the letter been made public. A third critic, Barbara Johnson, added to the debate in her essay, "The Frame of Reference: Poe, Lacan, Derrida," by suggesting that the letter is the property of the queen, all along, particularly as a surrogate phallus for the one she biologically or politically lacks.

The following series of fragments is an attempt to reconstruct the contents of the purloined letter. The basis of it, far from a hypothetical ranting, is to creatively reconfigure poststructuralist theory into the literary. Whether or not Poe wanted the reader to wonder about the contents of floating signifier (the letter); whether or not Lacan, Derrida or any of the later critics ever secretly considered giving the emptiness of the letter a subjective voice; and, whether or not the letter in a more popular course of interpretation can be simply forgotten as the MacGuffin[4] in the story; for all intents and purposes, the long tradition of criticism on Poe's ratiocination in "The Purloined Letter" are the real contents. Lacan and Derrida are literary in their own rights. Therefore, this thought experiment supposes their critiques to be the text of which the purloined letter is the footnote. And this sequence, when reversed, brings out the chronologically first love letter on top, annotated by the voices of Lacan and Derrida. Further, another voice that comes through in the letter is that of Stephen Hawking, a scientist and thinker, whose work is contemporaneous with the poststructuralist movement. To bring structural linguistics, deconstruction and positivist 20th century science (of black holes, event horizon and singular state) into the context of poststructuralism—a special context, that of travels of the purloined letter—provides an opening to imagine travel, in a positivist strain, as imbibing the strains from the movements of the universe and its language as observed during poststructuralism. The fragments of the hypothetical letter reproduced here, assume a new direction in, the language of travel, that of travelogy.[5] The reason why "The Purloined Letter" and black holes are brought together in this scheme is that like the latter, the author of the letter in question is nowhere—neither in the text nor in its analyses—questionable, or even brought into any light. The letter, and its bearers are convinced in moving towards orders of entropy, and the entropic flight of the letter is as convincing to us as objects getting lost in a depression—psychological, atmospheric or metaphysical.

Meaning/language/writing is totally pulverized inside these entropies, while the author remains invisible due to the failure of (linguistic) light to escape the boundaries of his black hole. He rests confident, however, in his hibernation that if anyone will fall from grace, it is the king, and if anyone will be incriminated, it is the queen. The question of whether the letter reaches its destination has been raised.[6] But why did one not even ask: who wrote the letter, or, is he alive? It/he, therefore, like a revenant, comes to us as a future, not simply in the future tense; but like the revenant, who according to Derrida comes in the ghost tense, or a future to come.[7] The letter is inseparable from the apparition that wrote it. Its visage and its contents are evanescent, and yet they come back to haunt like the spectre of Hamlet's dead father.

The first two letters are meant for the beloved (the queen). The next two, a little more scholastic and self-reflexive in their style and content, are letters written on the love letters, invoking the style in Derrida's *The Post Card* (1980), the section titled '*Envois*.' The writer of this letter belongs to a rather special habitus—the event horizon, or the boundary of a black hole He escapes the light of the universe, himself being infinitely concentrated with light. Thus, he is invisible to all detection and criticism on Poe's story. FIRST PERSON

I. UNDYING TO WRITE

The question is: did anyone ever know, or was anyone to ever know who I am? Who I *am*? Or, who I *was*? Which is the question? *Was* I before this letter was written, or *am* I still in the becoming of its reading? "You, my love, is it you I thereby name, is it to you that I address myself? I don't know if the question is well put, it frightens me. But I am sure that the answer, if it gets to me one day, will have come to me from you. You alone, my love, you alone will have known it."[8] This letter is written in the future; it goes back to you who must remember the future. For you to preserve this secret law of mine means to feign that *His*[9] law has not been thwarted. My law is the counterfeit of *His*. Whosoever knows this, *He* must not know.[10] You might like to expose this secret, keeping it out in the open, as though to flaunt your possession: of my sign, and my signature, which is addressed to you. That, in you, is the unpossessable.[11] But, even this possessiveness of the sign will be just a fiction.[12]

My writing to you about my travels may be based on the fiction that travelling is. However this fiction is based on the truth that I love you. What if this truth is only a fiction?[13] What if I have been made to travel only to play out the fiction that I love. That fiction suits not the truth but an autonomous design for this fictitious flight?[14]

Isn't it ironical? That the only apology for the redundancy or the violence of my language can be in this language alone? Is language thought, or is language knowledge? Do I know my language is violence due to language?[15]

This is not my letter, it is yours now. If it was found you would be incriminated in my love. But every letter should have a surplus, after the vows of love, the aesthetic of form, the incriminating evidence, and so much more of what is useful, has each been sifted out. What is the surplus then of *your* letter: the fact that it is also a letter apart from it being in writing? Or, the fact that it has a language that surpasses its use for you, in the time that you're reading it, which is a time of the past?[16]

This letter is like a return to our future.[17] In my descriptions, you will imagine the places I have travelled to, while I am only in the solitude of my confines now. There has been the passage of some time after I wrote it. Your reading of it was always in the time to come. And, now, I can only look back at the contents I wrote to you. Were there no language, we would only love... *now*. Nothing could be more absurd and meaningless than that loving, with nothing to throw us apart and make us owed to death.[18]

Being—*of* travel—you are twice bound. If you *are* because I travel, or if travel is my love, you simply cannot *be*. This is to say if your existence is served by your possession of this letter, it implies I have been travelling, that I am away from you, and you are not with me, who you love. If you *are* my love, I simply have not been travelling, but only drifting impurely from wherever you are. I must be distant from you so I may write, so I may *be*, if my existence is of the one who wrote this letter. If truly it was I that wrote it, I must have been away from you. If I was not, this would not have been a letter, it would have simply been a note. But letter as it is, its being and my trace are exiled again and again from you What you see now, this very *letter*, is not me as I am, but it is the *envois* of my unbecoming. If the letter eventually travels to you it will be in my catastrophe.[19]

This, my trait, is the way I write to you. When I write I am an immense concentrate of light. When it reaches you even the final spark is extinguished, and you think it is you who cannot comprehend.[20] It is the interceptionof the letter that has ravished its self-evident secret language,[21] or that merely the matter must have dissipated. The truth however is I have become a sage, so ascetic and so unfeeling that I cannot feel the pangs of being a hostage to my language. It is an absolute state of being bound one million times and more with my own being. I am of infinite density, in this singular state of language.[22]At the very origin of this womb my language was alienated from me, for it was another's too who named me, or left me be—as the writer of this letter will be—the unnameable. The only volition or role that I am left with, in this enigma, is of drifting away. For, if I choose to approach instead of drift, it would be out of a natural law, a design transcending myself. If I approach I would be giving in to *His* law, be apprehended and incarcerated. Like a black hole, I only drift. I advance, unknown to myself, towards that primitive singularity in an *envoyage* of ten thousand million years?[23]

This—my language to you—, being a letter...is in travel, or in sufferance.The cause of the letter is flight; for it to be in flight there can be no possession of it, and its meaning; one might merely hold it, and pass on.[24]

II. THE LETTER IS ABJECT

I wonder if *this* is writing too. I perhaps now know, as yourself, what writing is. However, I do not know that which it is not. *A writing is a writing because it is not...*(what is it not?) There should be some language which is not writing, for otherwise to *name* each of my experiences before you make me feel as though I am obliterating myself.[25] The freedom—or the shackles if you will—that bound me to a knowledge of that which was *not* writing is now shattered. Is this letter, a writing? Can writing be a letter?[26] What if in the course of this I keep struggling to find that quintessential name for that which is *not* writing, and succeed to fail in naming it? Will then have I explained some other language comes before writing, which makes me name, and write?

Why do I write a letter? Is it for me, or for you...to know? Or, is it merely for the simple fact that we cannot *know* together, that we have travelled apart? This letter is the sign of my obliteration, and I must cast it away. You, in the *promise* that you shall read this, defer my complete obliteration.[27] Since I must cast it away it is the abject, like a rejected artefact from which one does completely recede. My obliteration sets in when I've written the letter. You can only defer it when you find this, so you lag, as the deferral lags. Owing to this deferral, owing to this very fact that I must write this letter, is introduced the fear of my death, in me, as well as the fantasy of it in you. It is your lack that I must constantly conceal in the letter, and in this I fail. Hence I must disown the letter itself, and its contents. What I write here transcends the sign of the letter. The real letter is not in the fact that its contents are an indivisible whole. It is only in the fact that the letter is written, that it exists, and will so as the more abject, the more vandalised, the more ravaged it becomes. For, this will augment the obliteration of my being; this will justify the existence of the letter as a factory of mute speculations.[28]

The possessor of the letter is so feminine. I make you so by writing this to you, by making this *blissfully* enduring in its being possessed by you. Were I to possess something of a letter, which was also a secret, I would rather have burned it. If you had listened to me you would have burned everything and nothing would have arrived.[29] I alone would have possessed the sign, not the letter any more than me. But the letter in your case would have to be crumpled, dis-interred, ravaged, or rummaged for.[30] In that stripping of you would inhabit my death. This itinerary of my signature, this detour, this sufferance, this final preservation in the final act of pain you undergo...how true is it all? Is it not a fiction or just a performance to grant me a poetic and bearable passage to death?

Second Person

III

Abysmal Love

There would have been a certain pristine touch in the letter I wrote to my beloved from the hills, were I to have posted it to her. Instead of the immediacy of touch what would have touched her would be the distance, geographic and altitudinal. I was high up in the hills, and she, the plains. Just about then she was a plainer; she demanded a common language to understand my love. She and I both did not know, have never known, the letter is without the purity of love. It is a sign that we cannot love, *now*. The distance and the lack of touch enhance the seduction. She asked me for a postcard, as though to remind herself how far I was and to rue the displacement we have undergone—the image of the panoramic Doon Valley, or of London Eye—condoning her grief with the idea that I can look down on her; that I have retreated to a distant peak. Retreated, one asks? My beloved is a plainer and there is an abyss between her and my hills. She visualizes my fall into it, taking away my origin of the hills into this abysmal hollow. In my *retreat*[31] into the hills she wills my death, remarks in her memory her gift of death to the one she can only love more, more infinitely.[32]

Perhaps we imagine the lover-writer as fragile after the voyage. Not the voyage that has taken him far from me (from us), but the one whose embodiment the letter becomes. Perhaps the lover is always from the hills. He is plain and enduring in that postcard in which we *do not* see him, but which itself is an embodiment, not just of his existence, but of his mortality to come. He is mortal for he is to take the voyage of sending me the postcard. He is the envois of the *envoyage* to his death that we have granted him, owing to our absolute love. We are in perennial fear, even when we do not write the letter, of it being displaced. What if the letter did not reach my lover? What if it has poisoned someone else, who reads its contents now, or the one who cannot read any longer, for he is simply no longer alive, at the cost of my lover's death? Or is it so that if someone has to die it will only be *my lover*, and no one else? The displacement between him and me is the primeval fantasy for me to owe him to death. The suspension of death, the transference of poison, its perversions, its interceptions, its apprehensions, its loss, are all in a space where love has drifted. This deferral of love is due to the postal agency, where, to my love's imagination her lover is the courier. If he lives on she would think he has not loved her.

IV. PURLOINING MY DEATH

In purloining it I also prolong. This letter contains my sign. My will must be to make it lengthier than another's competing sign: between the legs of the woman?[33]

The beloved may be a commoner, while I am not. It is not as though one must pretend to come down to the *plain*, the land of what we refer to as the commoner. My language is so arbitrary that I cannot presume to speak the language of *another*, for *another*. Language cannot usurp, it cannot negotiate. Language is the event of the other, of the foreigner, of the inhospitable that commands our hospitality. Language is the deferral of travel. It is *desinterrance*:[34] The deferral of the message...the endless destiny of the *envois* to wander and to err. The very destiny of the secret is owed in the fact that it will not reach its destination.[35] The secret cannot inhabit. That we made love, not in love or in language. But that we made love in the secret, that I am still in the process of conceiving. The secret that is still to be written and the love that is yet to be made. This cipher of the secret, which belongs to *none other* than the lover: it is the purest home of the lover.[36]

Travelogy belongs in the realm of the letter's exile. The letter is meant to be exiled from the beloved. It does not breathe longer than it is revealed to the beloved. It is his own death that Socrates awaits at Cape Sounion. The cape is the passage to a *heim* he constructs as he waits for the boat to return from Delos. He practices inhabiting death for three days, since the time he foresees his death. Inhabiting is habituating. Is his waiting for death an attempt to exile it? Is travelogy in the beginning of the *desinterrance* of death? What is Socrates' travelogy if not the simple acquiescence to the fact that he must die, a simple owing himself to death? "Who is this, death? (Where is it to be found? as in the curious French expression *trouver la mort*, to find death, meaning, to die)."[37]

Is death the beloved I write to in the hope that my *writing* never reaches her?

NOTES

1. Event horizon is the boundary of a black hole. During the presentation of this paper the question was asked: is event horizon the event? To answer on the co-ordinates of the writer of the hypothetical purloined letter, it is important to remember that the letter itself is something that does not happen, or does not arrive. It is apprehended twice. Its contents are never revealed. According to Derrida the event is based on the possibility of its non-arrival, or 'disconvenience.' "An event cannot be reduced to the fact of something happening... it is what may always fail to come to pass." The letter is the event, therefore; not the exterior of the letter in its materiality, but the letter as a sign of something else that it conceals; of what may have come to pass, or will come to pass (when revealed) between the queen and the writer of the letter. It is that secret which is conceived by the writer (once again in this hypothetical letter written in the future or the ghost tense) from within the confines of the event horizon. Therefore, to answer the question here, the event horizon is not the event; rather, it is the horizon of the event, as it is of the black hole.
2. L.P. Hartley, in Stephen Hawking, *The Theory of Everything: The Origin and Fate of the Universe*. Mumbai: Jaico, 2006, p. 97.
3. In Crebillon's play *Atrée*, Atreus and Thyestes are brothers are brought to fatal opposition, owing to their innate capacity for malice and vengeance.
4. MacGuffin is a source or stimulant of a plot, wherein its main purpose is to get the plot/narrative rolling, without inherently mattering what it is, what it comprises, who it belongs to, and so on. See Slavoj Zizek, *The Sublime Object of Ideology,* New York: Verso, 1989, p. 163.
5. Travelogy is how much home (*heim*) the traveler or travelling artifact constructs in a space of the uncanny (*unheimlich*). It is the language of travel, in the space of writing; this is to say, any writing or speech addresses different components of social and personal life, along with addressing the notion or space of travel. This latter component is one of travelogy. See "What is Travelogy?" http://coldnoon.com/history-concept/ Accessed: 20/11/2015.
6. Slavoj Zizek, *Enjoy Your Symptom!: Jacques Lacan in Hollywood and Out,* New York:

Routledge, 1992, p. 11.

7. Derrida, *Specters of Marx: The State of the Debt, the Work of Mourning and the New International.* tr. Peggy Kamuf, London: Routledge, 1994, pp. 1-4.
8. Jacques Derrida, *The Post Card: From Socrates to Freud and Beyond.* tr. Alan Bass, University of Chicago Press, 1987, p. 8. In fact, Derrida in the *The Post Card* does refer to "The Purveyor of Truth," and himself engages in a mock-exercise of writing the unknown love letter, to which these fragments are dedicated.
9. The King's law and grace. The letter ordains the queen not to let the king fall from his grace. Royalty must be protected at all costs from the clandestine affair—romantic or political—whose nature can only be speculated, but never made public. While it is the secret law and will of the letter that reigns, the king must be made secure in the knowledge that it is the latter's law that is sovereign.
10. In the entire scheme of Poe's "The Purloined Letter" the common element in the course of the letter being in sufferance is the ignorance of the King. His symbolic blindness is seen as a metaphor both by Lacan and Derrida in their respective essays:"Seminar on 'The Purloined Letter,'" in Emmanuel Berman, ed. *Essential Papers on Literature and Psychoanalysis* (New York University Press, 1993); pp. 270-300; and "The Purveyor of Truth," tr. Willis Domingo, James Hulbert and Moshe Ron, in *Yale French Studies*, No. 52, *Graphesis: Perspectives in Literature and Philosophy* (1975) pp. 31-113. Although everyone else has necessary access to the contents of the letter, which in fact do not play any role except to create an entropy of sovereign knowledge, the king himself is shielded from this knowledge.
11. Lacan draws continual attention to the lack of the phallus in the queen. Since she does not possess a natural phallus, the letter or its sign acts as her surrogate phallus. Without this, she is dispossessed. Also, her phallus is unpossessable, by virtue of the simply lack.
12. Lacan also refers to repetition automatism; to how the letter is destined to be in sufferance by a repetition of changing hands. This signifying chain begins and ends with the queen. Being in possession of the letter once more, she is *rephallisized.* The question of *rephallisization*, in Lacan, is based on the presumption that the letter is phallic and whoever it touches it also feminizes it. However, the letter being vulnerable to a miscarriage, crumpling or stripping, is itself the wayward feminine *flâneuse.* Possessing it is in no way a *rephallisization*, except in a misogynist sense.
13. The truth at which both Derrida and Lacan try to arrive at, both the *truth of fiction* as well as the *truth of truth*, may be easily belied in the fact that there is probably an exterior design upon the sufferance of the letter. The sheer absence of sovereign knowledge about the letter may point towards progressive entropy of meaning and interpretation, despite the letter possibly reaching its original intended recipient (the queen). Lacan in asserting that the letter always will reach the receiver hints at a transcendental design only with the uneasy presumption of intersubjective and repetitive oedipal triangles. Derrida returns attention to the literary narrator of the story to disturb these triangles. But

even he is unable to fathom the entropic element of the letter's inherent travelogy (how much of an inhabitation does the traveller or the travelling artefact construct at every interval).

14. One can challenge with the surmise that the king, himself, or one of his allies, or a doppelganger (such as the effect brought about between Dupin and Minister D at the end) is behind the writing of the letter. This is to say in shielding the king from the unpleasant news the subject might be unknowingly carrying out the wishes of this autonomous schemer (the king or the ally) who himself is then the lawful patriarch. In that case the flight, or the free will of the letter, is an eyewash, as is the fact that the king should be protected from its dangerous flight. The shielded may well have willed his own shielding as part of his scheme.
15. Language is here used in the sense of writing, or an impression—the kind that names, creates nouns and nomenclatures. If writing is violence and this can only be explained in writing *this* should be the first contention for the irrationality of Lévi Strauss's patronizing representation (in *Tristes Tropiques*) of the Namibikwara's rather than Derrida's resorting to a more complex understanding of writing being the effacement of singularity in nomenclature (proper nouns). See "The Violence of the Letter: From Lévi-Strauss to Rousseau," in Gayatri Chakravarty Spivak (tr.) *Of Grammatology* (Johns Hopkins University Press, 1994), pp. 101-138.
16. The letter, if at all written by a lover or a secret ally of the queen, only comes to light in the future. That is, it *becomes* truly existential only when its contents are laid bare. Such a thing could only have happened much after the queen herself had read the contents, as she was the original recipient. The voice of the letter then—much like the voice of this hypothetical letter—is a voice from the future, a specter, come back to haunt the past. The voice is revealed only so much that there is always the promise of its coming back, such as in the revelation of the letter's contents, by and by. See Derrida's *hauntology* in *Specters of Marx*: "the specter is the future, it is always to come, it presents itself only as that which could come or come back..." (tr.) Peggy Kamuf (New York: Routledge, 1994), p. 48.
17. The letter becomes written in the future. Stephen Hawking asks why we do not remember the future. The answer he provides is the linearity of time in which we are bound. Time, however, is not necessarily linear; it has real and imaginary components which run perpendicular to each other. The imaginary component of time, or time running reverse, as in broken cups reacquiring shape in a film run backwards is generally not taken as real. This is so because of the second law of thermodynamics, which states that disorder or entropy increases with time. However, the laws of physics, according to Hawking, do not obey the laws of time, as in they do not distinguish between past and future. See Hawking, *The Theory of Everything*, pp. 97-99.
18. According to Derrida, Socrates while anticipating his death, in the anticipation of the boat's return from Delos to Cape Sounion, after having visualized his death in a dream, is "owed to death." One does not present/owe oneself or

another to death but is owed by a transcendental economy of debt, for the necessity of a (philosophical) continuation. See Jacques Derrida and Catherine Malabou's *Counterpath: Travelling with Jacques Derrida*, tr. David Willis, Stanford: Stanford University Press, 2004, pp. 201-02.

19. For Derrida, a catastrophe is a reversal, or a vacating of the origin, which he relates to the original absence of language outside of writing. See Derrida and Malabou, *Counterpath*, pp. 8-12. The reversal or the catastrophe of the writer of the purloined letter is in the fact that he is replaced by the destiny of the sovereign to who he writes. More than the author the recipient commands attention and custody.
20. A scientific understanding of black holes reveals that as a star contracts, the gravitational field at its surface intensifies, and light cones bend, until a point that the star has shrunk infinitely and light rays cannot escape it. Thus it appears black, but is rather only an immense concentrate of light, inside the boundary known as the event horizon. See Hawking, *The Theory of Everything*, pp. 37-41. Since light cannot escape from the event horizon, we, the spectators of the atoms lost within consider it to be a dark mass. Likewise, since the anamnesis of the lover-writer is so dense, that although lucid, his language is unclear to the beloved-addressee.
21. Derrida writes to his addressee that he would like to "write [to] you so simply, so simply, so simply," that the plainest language of candor itself became a self-evident secret, invented at every step, to pre-empt the gaze of the intercepter, like in a cipher, although out in the open. (*The Post Card*, p. 11) The cipher acts in the same way here as the letter kept in the open, both by the queen, and then by the Minister, so as to draw the least suspicion. And, yet, both the times it is purloined.
22. Before its expanding state, the universe was an infinitely dense concentrate of mass and light. This state is known as the singular state. This is also the state into which the universe contracts after the stage of expansion is over, at the end of the contracting phase. Language, which takes birth often in impressions and the activity of naming can also be said to expand and contract. The laws of the universe do not show positivist strains in the behavior of language. However, it such a scientific model is certainly helpful in understanding the processes of writing, which albeit a creative process, undergoes altering states of singularity (infinite density) and plurality (lightness or lucidity).
23. This according to Hawking is the time that it might take for the universe to begin contracting and return to its singularity.
24. The agency of the letter in "The Purloined Letter" comes not from the fact of its contents but of its potential to cause entropies in its transitional spaces. One may possess the meaning or the substance of the letter but without its own presence its text is inconsequential.
25. If naming of the proper noun for the purpose of summoning it is its obliteration, according to Derrida (in *Of Grammatology*), so should be the naming of an experience.
26. Although Derrida privileges the elements of the narrative and writing in his

analysis of "The Purloined Letter" he remains unconcerned about the relation of the sign that the letter contains—the writer's signature (not the sign the letter itself becomes)—and the sufferance it undergoes. Does this imply the letter's contents cannot be an example of writing as a case-study?

27. Zizek asks, why the letter need always reach its destination, for it can always go astray. He dwells however on the possibility that the letter, especially in the case when it lacks an addressee, may be addressed to none in particular, but a symbolic Other, who disburdens the sender of his responsibility for putting the letter into circulation. See *Enjoy Your Symptom*, pp. 11-12. For instance, a message in a bottle thrown in the sea by a shipwrecked passenger defers his complete obliteration in the promise or hope that it might reach someone.
28. Repetition Automatism: "The Purloined Letter" can never refer back to its author, but instead to an endless series of (possessors of) the signs the letter contains in what Lacan calls the "signifying chain." This implies intersubjective (triangular or otherwise) relations between the possessors or contenders of the sign in a space to which the author is extrinsic and thus forgotten, just as Derrida alleges Lacan of conveniently forgetting Marie Bonaparte's theses on "The Purloined Letter" and the rest of Poe's oeuvre.
29. Derrida writes of two lovers or correspondents being a miniscule residue, "left unclaimed." This is perhaps owing to the rift in time and space that both bounds and separates the correspondents. The correspondence, as a result, gets beyond the two writers: "which is why it should have been burned, all of it, including the cinders of the unconscious—and 'they' will never know anything about it. *The Post Card*, p. 7. Later, he tells his addressee, if s/he had listened to him, and burned the letter, then the possibility of its arriving back, coming back to haunt, would have been eliminated.
30. Just as the purloined letter is rummaged for by the police in the apartment of the Minister. When Dupin finds it, the letter is in a crumpled state, left so by the Minister to avoid suspicion of it being an artifact of any significance.
31. i.e. *retrait*
32. To be able to love more infinitely, it is necessary to make oneself more finite, incarcerate oneself more, in being able to love the *finite* other, or even the finitude of the other. To owe someone to death, or to sacrifice something implies infinite love for the sacrificed. What is not loved cannot be sacrificed. See Derrida, *The Gift of Death,* tr. David Willis, University of Chicago Press, 1995, pp. 50-62. Death is the ultimate finitude that the infinitely loving self can assign to the other.
33. Derrida, here, deals a double blow to Lacan by at once implying that it was he then who purloined Bonaparte's theses from "between" her legs, and dephallisized her therefore, as well as that Lacan is phallogocentric in his assumption of the letter's bearer being necessarily feminine, and already castrated by the fear and awareness of potential purloining. See Derrida, "The Purveyor of Truth," pp. 66-68.
34. Derrida and Malabou explain the neologism, in the context of modern day telecommunications, where opinions in favour of justice are made to wander,

and dissipate: "Destinerrance is in fact accentuated further by 'the new structure of spatiotemporal *différance* constructed by new techniques of telecommunication.' This 'new structure' is also one of 'deracination, delocalization, disincarnation, formalization,' rendering more undecidable still the frontier between here and elsewhere. See Derrida and Malabou, *Counterpath*, p. 18.

35. Derrida and Malabou, *Counterpath*, p. 18
36. *One never inhabits what one is in the habit of calling inhabiting. There is no possible habitat without the difference of this exile and this nostalgia.* Ibid. 47.
37. Ibid. 202.

19

Foucault: Optics and the Folding of Light

Abhilash Nath

I

> The bewilderments of the eyes are of two kinds, and arise from two causes, either from coming out of the light or from going into the light, which is true of the mind's eye, quite as much as of the bodily eye; and he who remembers this when he sees any one whose vision is perplexed and weak, will not be too ready to laugh; he will first ask whether that soul of man has come out of the brighter life, and is unable to see because unaccustomed to the dark, or having turned from darkness to the day is dazzled by excess of light.[1]

The cavemen and the Platonic allegory of the cave can be a point of departure to examine some of the central concerns of Foucault. The allegory of the cave explores questions central to the nature of reality, the condition of human being, and the ways to attain enlightenment. Intrinsic to it is also an exploration into the reality of light and a problematic of seeing, which are also central for Foucault. The present study, through its reading of Plato, locates Foucault in the general context of Western thought, particularly his leaning towards Stoic philosophy. The allegory of the cave is intrinsically linked to Plato's metaphysical and epistemological claims, especially, the dualism that he introduces in the realm of experience. According to Plato, the realms of experience are fundamentally of two kinds – the physical world and the world of forms. The physical world, that is, the world we perceive through our senses, is undoubtedly in a state of constant change. It is the realm of objects, images and shadows, and therefore, always an infinite puzzle. Here Plato clearly resembles the Heraclitean flux or even the Foucauldian economy of forces. On the other hand, the world of forms is stable and unchangeable. It is the world of pure *forms* and, therefore, it is more than one. Since it is stable, pure and ideal, the world of forms, in the allegory of the cave, constitutes the upper world, the outside of the cave—and for that matter, inaccessible to the ordinary life—and the world of senses, on the other hand, is the inside of the cave.

In the opening of the seventh book of the *Republic*, in a dialogue between Socrates and Glaucon, Plato introduces the allegory of the cave. It explicates the general condition of human beings, trapped in the depth of ignorance and unaware of the limitations of their own perspective. Socrates himself has suggested that the allegory of the cave is intended to illustrate the need for *education*. Socrates says, "Behold, a number of men living in an underground den that has a mouth opening toward the daylight. The cave is deep, and there, they have been in bonds since their childhood. Legs and necks fastened, they are unable to move and can only see before them. Imagine a fire blazing, at a distance, above and behind them and at an elevation, between this fire and the prisoners, there is a roadway. Then you will see, if you look, a low wall built along the way, like the screen with marionette players have in front of them, over which they show the puppets."[2] "I see," replies Glaucon. And along that low wall, men pass, carrying all sorts of vessels, statues and figures of animals made of wood, stone and various materials, which appear over the wall casting *shadows* on the wall in front of the prisoners by the light of the fire behind. Some of those men normally talk and others are silent, creating *echoes* in the cave. The simultaneous appearance of both shadows and echoes can only strengthen the prisoners' belief that the sounds belong to the shadows. Here the prisoners see shadows not as shadows, rather as unhidden. Anything unhidden is nothing but being and, therefore, the truth.[3]

Now imagine, what if one of those prisoners is released and compelled to stand up and immediately turn his neck around and he walks and looks towards the light. The glare of course is going to disturb him—suffering from sharp pains, the reality, at first, would not be accessible to him. Socrates asks, "will he not fancy that the shadows which he formerly saw are truer than the objects which are now shown to him?" "Far truer," replies Glaucon.[4] "Suppose he is reluctantly held fast until he is forced to see the sun itself, after dragging him up the steep and the rugged ascent of the cave. Would it be painful and irritating to him? It seems, very certain!" Socrates suggests here that it actually requires time and patience to get accustomed to the sight of the upper world. The prisoner who overcomes the limitations of the cave, through a long and painful intellectual journey, finally, discovers a higher realm and a true reality, through an awareness of goodness. Such a person, who could easily be mistaken by any of those folks, who hasn't left the cave yet, is the better equipped one, according to Plato, to govern the rest of the prisoners and, probably, rest of the society.

Before engaging ourselves in an agreeable analysis of the cave allegory, for the specific needs of the present study, it is helpful to identify, and differentiate ourselves from those few important concerns that Plato himself and Heidegger, in a later interpretation of the same allegory, have emphasised.

Plato's concern is that of education and the possible role of the educated in the society. Education is nothing but learning how to *hold* oneself in relation to objects, in the light of the ideas. Plato differentiates two distinct forms of experiences, and their respective spatial orders—the order of senses and that of ideas, the pure forms. The *inside* of the cave, for instance, is filled with fire-light and echoes, the lower forms, while the *outside* of the cave is shaped by the pure forms, sun-light and language, respectively. Plato through the allegory of the cave explicates an intellectual trajectory, one that is long and seriously painful, one that ultimately involves the movement of the soul from the world of senses to the world of forms. The allegory of the cave, from this standpoint, celebrates the primacy of the idea over any kind of practical knowledge.

Heidegger understands education in a purely Platonic sense. Educating oneself is precisely to comport oneself to the unhidden, the thing that which directly shows itself to us, without our effort. Heidegger, therefore, uses the allegory of the cave as a clue to understand the essence of unhiddenness—an enquiry into the being of the object. What is unhidden there? It is one question, according to Heidegger, that appears itself as the most simple and straightforward one. Yet, it is a question that demands the most dedicated attention. Heidegger's reading of the allegory of the cave progresses through tracking the more *truthful* and more *beingful* unhidden. Hence, the objects that appear along the lower wall behind the prisoners in the cave are more beingful than their shadows on the wall in front of them, and the sun, outside the cave, is more truthful than the fire in the cave. The process of comporting oneself to the unhidden then is inevitably a search for the degree of unhiddenness in objects. For that reason, Heidegger writes that what happens in the second stage of the cave allegory, when one of those prisoners is unshackled, is a failure, as "he who has been unshackled fails to encounter unhiddenness as such. He does not come to it."[5] Here the prisoner desires "to go back to the shackles, *away from the light*"—the light which is actually the true symbol of his liberation. It is towards the light that the "beings are to become more beingful, the unhidden more unhidden."[6] Heidegger's ontology is therefore directed towards a search for the essence of the unhidden, the beings, and the meaning of Being.

Thus one finds Heidegger focusing on the *unhidden*, the degree of unhiddenness, and the object in itself. But what has exactly revealed itself in light, before the prisoner, who had been unshackled. Is it the object itself? Plato suggests, and last of all, the most unhidden, the sun, reveals itself, and he continues, the unshackled prisoner then will "proceed to argue that this is he [the sun] who gives the season and the years, and is the guardian of all that is in the visible world, and in a way the cause of all things which he and his fellows [prisoners] have been accustomed to behold."[7] What is then exactly revealed to the prisoner is not the sun as the more true, unhiddenness—the object in itself—rather, it is the *a priori* condition of his own thought that is revealed to him. Once dragged out of the cave, into the sunlight, the prisoner suddenly becomes aware of the play of light (shadows) and language (echoes) in the cave that ultimately resulted in his false synthesis. The prisoners in the cave have believed that the echoes belong to the shadows and, therefore, they are one, and thought them as only one and, consequently, they tend to imagine shadows as true unhiddenness. The important point here is—and this is the reason why one needs to go through the Platonic allegory in a different light—the prisoner with such awareness of the ambiguity of the visible, rather than *comporting* himself to the unhidden, can only be careful to the visible. He will be reluctant to give himself up easily to the unhidden and a man such as himself ought to be one of the early Spinozians who walked on earth—a rare optician.[8]

The passing shadows on the wall, in front of the shackled prisoners, normally would have encouraged them to talk about shadows. Plato confirms that they have compared the shadows, judged them and this often developed competition amongst the prisoners on how to judge them better and come up with superior conclusion. Time, for the shackled prisoners, essentially is *succession*. Only the ongoing fleet of shadows on the wall, in front of them, can leave in them a sense of time. Time, therefore, is linked to space, to the objects and their movement, however, the prisoners shackled in the cave totally lack any knowledge of that space—the space that produces those shadows. For them the shadows are the only unhidden, therefore, they are nothing but objects themselves and any discourse of them is necessarily true. Since time is pure succession and non problematic, it is external to the shackled prisoners. Hence, at this stage of the allegory, the prisoners, essentially, lack the self; that is, the experience of I-myself or you-yourself. They, consequently, learn to believe whatever is perceived as truth. Even in the second stage, when one of the prisoners is released and the unshackled is provided with the necessary information related to the space that produced the shadows on the wall, he fails to grasp the truth and tends to go back to his former state of being—he prefers to be shackled. The glare from the fire in the cave, to him, is disturbing and painful to his eye. He struggles to look at the fire and pathetically fails in making any sense of it.

It is only in the third stage that a true struggle occurs in him between more than one concepts of truth. At this stage, the unshackled prisoner is forcibly dragged out of the cave and compelled to face the sun. The alterity of the outside, the upper world, compels him to rethink about the reality in the cave. Time consequently has become a problem to him; and it then moves into him, distinguishing the Ego from the I. Time here becomes internal to him. Relentlessly dividing him from within, splitting him from himself, the time finally becomes an unavoidable experience to the unshackled prisoner, and here *space* that has been defined as coexistence becomes a form of exteriority. The prisoner, who has been unshackled, finally, develops the self. It is his own self that he has constituted only through the folding of the forces, the forces of the exterior. Hence the unshackled prisoner, once liberated, would not be comforting himself to the objects, as Heidegger has suggested, rather would be interested in folding—the folding of the outside, in Foucauldian terms. Plato is himself convinced that, once liberated, the unshackled prisoner would not be interested any more in accepting the challenges of his fellow prisoners in judging the shadows on the wall in front of them.

The cave allegory—the way we have read it—has given us some important points. Time is eternal, yet it is internal to the subject. When time becomes temporal, it is no more a mere succession of moments, but rather time itself is an experience, constantly splitting the subject from within, differentiating the Ego from an always altering another—the I in "I think." Foucault writes: "to be modern is not to accept oneself as one is in the flux of the passing moments; it is to take oneself as object of a complex and difficult elaboration: what Baudelaire, in the vocabulary of his day, calls *dandysme*."[9] One can, therefore, notice that the concern here is not anymore of comporting oneself to the objects. Rather than posing the question, "what is there?" here one is inclined to ask "what am I?"

It is interesting, however, to note that, both these questions stem out of responses to Plato, his emphasis on the ideas—the forms—as the higher beings. The ideas belong to the upper world, and therefore, in a more general and abstract sense, they are the good. The temporal presence is always anchored in the atemporal, eternal presence—the presence of the Platonic forms. Hence the chair, in the context of everyday life, can only be a chair, if only there exists the very idea of a chair. Heidegger, in contrast, argues that Plato, by establishing the beyond-ordinary as the sole responsible for the ordinary, has in fact covered up *lichtung*, the clearing, an understanding of being. One's understanding of things is shaped in the background of those shared practices into which he is socialised. The craftsman is neither responding to the grain of the wood nor to the pure form, rather he is responding to the very need of the community itself. Since Plato, Heidegger claims, philosophy has overlooked the clearing that can both limit and open up beings—the clearing that decides the degree of unhiddenness of being. What, therefore, has concerned Heidegger the most is the question of being of things—how things become objects in modern world. On the other hand,

Foucault reworks Heidegger, and alters his focus. The things consequently have lost the podium, and the focus is shifted to the selves.[10] The essence of objects does not completely reveal itself in the presence of light. A phone or a knife for a kid is a toy. Hence the focus should be to understand the nature and state of the self and the spirit. Foucault writes: "Plato is said to have opposed essence to appearance, a higher world to this terrestrial world, the sun of truth to the shadows of the cave (and it becomes our duty to bring essences back into the world, to glorify the world, and to place the sun of truth within man)."[11]

II

Foucault's writing carries with it an extraordinarily sensual-visual. It is a world that hides as much as it reveals, constantly shaped by the tango of brightness and shadow; it is a world of depth and flows, where light floods in through invisible windows and inaccessible corridors. It is nearly a labyrinth. The flood of light that fills the space, spreading consistently across the surface of things and selves, illuminating them and presenting them as either transparent or opaque, is however the only common locus of representation. Hence one will confront a 'there is' of light, —just as there is a 'there is' of language— an irreducible being of light that illuminates and opens up the outside for sight. The panopticon of *Discipline and Punish*, the 'virtual visibility' of *The Birth of the Clinic*, the 'pastoral power' all are conditioned by such a 'there is' of light. Light is absolute, yet it is not ahistorical, the form and structure of sight are historically determined. Like language, it is the *a priori* of every possibility, the *a priori* that, in combination with the stimulus from other senses, positions the outside open to thought.[12]

The *Las Meninas*, the painting by Velasquez, for instance, is described, in one of the celebrated chapters of *The Order of Things*, as a system of light; a flood of light from an invisible window, at the right-hand side within the painting, opens up an entire space of classical representation. The light, here, by distributing both the objects and the models as either perceivable or non-perceivable, establishes among them a network of reflections and exchanges that consistently draw and redraw the line, which divides the outside of the painting from its inside. On the left-hand side within the painting, one finds Velasquez, the painter himself, working on a canvas. He is 'standing a little back from his canvas' and glancing at his models. The arm that holds the brush bent towards the palette, and Foucault describes, between the canvas and the palette his skilled hand, for an instant, is motionless. It is "suspended in mid-air, arrested in rapt attention on the painter's gaze; and the gaze, in return, waits upon the arrested gesture. Between the fine point of the brush and the steely gaze, the scene is about to yield up its volume."[13] Here the painter—as he is made visible in his own painting—is entirely illuminated by the same source of light, which has opened up an entire representation before him—the light from the window. The *first* proposition, therefore, is: since illuminated by the very brightness—the light—that grants him access to the outside, one can only sense brightness from its internal point of view. In other words, seeing, in itself, can never be an objective act. Since the subject is always internal to the very system of light that illuminates and thereby opens up the outside before him, it demands from his part a considerable intellectual and spiritual strength to overcome that very structure of his seeing and to find a vantage point from where he is able to examine the very conditions that grant him access to the outside.

Neither the painter's corporeal eye nor his models or even the spectator (of the painting *Las Meninas* itself) who is observing the painter at work, is the actual locus of brightness. Rather the whole possibility (that is the directedness of the painter's gaze, the possible exchanges that connect the spectator and the space that is represented within the painting, etc.) unfolds within the condition of light. The *second* proposition, therefore, is: light is neither anchored in the subject, who perceives, nor in the objects, which are perceived. It is rather the *a priori* condition of every possibility. For instance, in "Self-Writing," one finds Foucault reading Seneca and the culture of writing personal notebook (*hupomnemata*) and correspondences in the *light* of Greek practice of the care of the self. Seneca writes "I thank you for writing to me so often; for you are revealing yourself to me [*te mihi ostendis*] in the only way you can. I never receive a letter from you without being in your company forthwith. If the pictures of our absent friend are pleasing us...how much more pleasant is a letter, which brings us real traces, real evidence of an absent friend! For that which is sweetest when we meet face to face is afforded by the impress of a friend's hand upon his letter—recognition."[14] Writing, in the light of the care of the self, then is that possibility that can 'project oneself into view, to make one's own face appear' in the presence of the other.[15] Light is that through which one sees; it not only penetrates through, but also permits penetration. Light then is not just mere *visibility*, that is the opening and spreading out of the open, rather it is also that which lets through, and therefore, according to Heidegger, its essence is to be transparent.[16]

Matter can be neither transparent nor opaque in darkness. It is the very condition of light that gifts matter its character. By consistently spreading across its surface, light, at times, may only reveal the texture and colour of matter. Matter here folds light and creates within it an outside, which is actually inaccessible to light. It opens up capillaries of the *outside* within the *inside*, that is, within the system of light itself. The huge canvas on which Velasquez works in the painting, *Las Meninas*, is particularly of this kind. Since the canvas is placed precisely against the light and the standing spectator, it is inaccessible to his corporeal eye, and for that reason, it hides more than it reveals, initiating a succession of reflections and exchanges between the interior and the outside of the painting. However, at times, light may come from the depth of matter, revealing its very soul—such is the light that Foucault has identified in Seneca's correspondences.

Light here is deeply divided, and is divided into domains that are *not* at all related One will encounter, on the one hand, a sovereign white light that spreads and delivers the *being* of things; on the other hand, there is a different kind of light that is never from the depth of things. It "spreads over each thing in rapid bursts. ... in sharp surface bursts, in a fleeting plan, lightning falls on the surface of things, forming a sudden stroke, transitory, quickly darkened, etching an angle or a bulge, but leaving intact, obstinately in place, in their earlier presence, the things that it illuminates—without ever penetrating them. ..." Rare and slender illuminations run on the water ... on a boat at sea a man is leaning on a railing, his left hand holding the metal rail which runs along the deck; on the first knuckle of his third finger he wears a ring "which in its present position flashes lightning."[17] Contrary to the light that *spreads* and delivers the being of things, light here *contracts* and focuses on a particular point on the surface. It is, therefore, not a kind of light that lets through; rather a kind that only signals the existence of itself and the surface on which it focuses.

Light is divided into domains. Just the way attention (a concentration of intensities—which is essentially negation) and consciousness (a diffused intensity, or an *affirmation*) are difference of intensities of the spirit, these domains of light are differences in intensities, and therefore, it is inherently ambiguous and it inclines to hide more that it reveals. Only the wicked eye of the uninitiated will consider light as the element in which vision unfolds itself. The truth of light is concealed; and as a result, it has an esoteric structure. Here the eye however has a different function. From its normal position, it is forced to face the nocturnal. When the great iris turns itself to face the night, what the upturned eye reveals is clarity, its whiteness. In this state, the eye lacks the capacity of observing, and does not communicate. "A Preface to Transgression" locates the value of the eye as the figure of inner experience—the state of the spirit. From beneath the thickness of his narration, one may finally encounter in Foucault the surfacing of the oriental subtext. This should however be read against his reading of the Stoics, where he tries to undo the Platonic divide—the world of the senses and the world of the pure forms—and tries to see essence in what is mundane. When replying the question on the rising fashions of 'mind expansion,' the 'new sensibility' and oriental philosophy among the French youth following the May 1968 student revolt, Foucault in an interview scornfully rejected any link between Western individualism and Oriental spirituality. The mind expansion in Oriental spirituality, he has suggested, is directed particularly to *destroy the madness of normality and to regain true reality*, however; in Western individualism it is directed *to attain an individual madness beyond the rationality of the world.*[18]

III

Gustave Courbet's painting, *The Studio of the Painter: A Real Allegory*, appeared at a time when French art was seen internally divided into camps. The culture of high art that the idealists celebrated was facing challenge from a new force, realism. The realist, in the 19th century, explored the forces of the everyday sense and introduced direct painting from life. It was a period marked by a struggle between artists who lived in the realm of imagination and those who lived in the realm of vision. *A Real Allegory* is one such painting that appeared at a decisive stage in the history of modern art, a stage that is marked by the transition from the idealist-realist battle to an age influenced by Baudelaire and the arrival of the impressionists. Inspired by Velazquez's *Las Meninas*, this work has influenced some of the impressionist masterpieces. Edouard Manet, for instance, has drawn inspiration from it, while working on two of his early works: *The Old Musician* and *La Musique aux Tuileries*. It is a picture that is packed with forms and external life. It represents the condition of the modern artist.

A Real Allegory is a painting of Courbet himself, in the company of his friends, working at his Paris studio. It is painted with a lot of detail, yet the most brightly coloured objects are at the centre of the painting. The painting hardly authorizes any eye movement from one side to the other, leaving the centre of the painting as the only focal point. At the centre, behind the painter one finds a woman. She is exposed, yet seems relaxed and quite indifferent to her nakedness. She seems still and her head is slightly tilted towards the canvas on which the painter is working. She seems to be carefully reading the painting. In the painting, the naked woman represents the progression of time. At the centre of the painting, before the naked woman, the painter is making the last strokes on his work. He is not actually painting the naked woman; rather, he is painting the countryside. Next to his chain one finds his pet and a small boy. The boy, dressed in peasant dress, appears to be totally occupied by the painting. Possibly from the same countryside, which is painted on the canvas, he appears to be daydreaming. Behind the canvas on which the painter works, on the wall, one finds a mural of a naked man in a gesture of crucifixion.

Gustave Courbet, The Studio of the Painter: A Real Allegory

The whole seen unfolds around Courbet himself, who is at the centre of the painting. On the left hand side of the painting, the workers, and the men from the everyday life, share the space. There are priests, street-musicians, beggars, street vendors; they are people from the street and people, who have no place in 19th century Paris. Their actions and gestures in effect suggest the real condition of the working class. One finds them exhausted and tired by their work and poverty. On the right hand side of the painting, one finds the old Parisian bourgeoisie. There are friends and associates of Courbet; some are writers, some are novelists. At the far right of the painting, Baudelaire himself is portrayed; there he seems to be lost in one of his books. Contrasted to the working class, on the left hand side of the painting, the old bourgeoisie is marked by luxury and leisure. While the crowd that gathered at Courbet's studio represents a cross-section of the 19th century Parisian society, its inequality and class division, the figures at the centre of the painting suggest the real message of the painting. The image of a painter, as the creator of his creation, essentially invokes the function of the painter in the society. It is he, who organises the entire scene that unfolds in the painting. He is, therefore, elevated to the status of the creator of the painting.

The painting, on the other hand, also leaves traces of a much deeper thought. At the centre of the painting, the painter juxtaposes images; one finds Courbet painting a landscape that has absolutely nothing to do with the figures depicted in the painting. Here images overlap and cancel each other, opening a space of dreams. The little boy, who is seemed to have lost himself before the painting of the landscape, symbolises such an opening. He symbolises an ontological lack at the very heart of being, a yearning for a different time. That yearning for a different time is essentially rooted in the distrust of a continuum, the successive time. In dreams, the present is not strictly framed by the past and future. It is rather an individable present, that is, it neither has a beginning to connect with the past nor has an end to connect it with the future, and therefore, it neither has middle.[19] Hence this present, in a Foucauldian sense, is actually an *exit* or a way out. What Courbet achieved through the painting, *A Real Allegory*, is not a mere representation of a particular present; rather, he has succeeded in projecting the timeless themes in an immanent flux. The painting, through the juxtaposing of images, shows modern man's eternal *drive*—a drive that is rooted in an immanent lack—to change himself. It is a painting that celebrates the possibility of a painter; a painter, who is not a mere observer of the flux of time; rather he who takes himself as the 'object of a complex and difficult elaboration.'[20]

NOTES

1. Plato, *The Works of Plato, Vols. I & II (in 4 Volumes): Analysis of Plato & The Republic,* New York: Cosimo Classics, 2010, p. 270
2. Ibid, 2010, p. 265
3. Martin Heidegger, *The Essence of Truth: On Plato's Cave Allegory and Theaetetus*, London: Continuum, 2002, p. 19
4. Plato, 2010, p. 267
5. Heidegger, 2002, p. 28
6. Ibid, 2002, p. 29
7. Plato, 2010, p. 267
8. In Spinoza, philosophy does not revolve around the problem of the essence of unhiddenness. The unhidden is necessarily infinite and prior to its affections. The unhidden—the substance in itself —is characterized by its quality of affecting and being affected. The unhiddenness of a substance not necessarily directs straightaway to its essence, but only to any of its infinite attributes; to the predicate of one of the possible proposition. Each attribute, however, expresses 'a certain infinite and eternal essence.'
9. Michel Foucault, "What is Enlightenment?" *The Essential Foucault: Selections from the Essential Works of Foucault 1954-1984,* New York: The New Press, 1994, p. 50.
10. In one of his last interviews, Foucault, for instance, has confirmed that for him, "Heidegger has always been the essential philosopher."
11. Foucault, 1980, p. 167.
12. Gilles Deleuze, *Foucault*, London: The Athlone Press, 1988, pp. 57–60.
13. Michel Foucault, *The Order of Things: An Archaeology of Human Sciences*, New York: Vintage Books, 1994, p. 3.
14. Michel Foucault, *Ethics: Subjectivity and Truth*, London and New York: Allen Lane, The Penguin Press, 1997, p. 216.
15. Ibid, p. 216.
16. Heidegger, 2002, p. 41.

17. Michel Foucault, *Death and the Labyrinth: The World of Raymond Roussel*, New York: Doubleday & Company, Inc., 1986, pp. 108–109.
18. Paolo Caruso, *Conversazione con Levi-Strauss, Foucault, Lacan* (Milan: V Mursia and Co, 1969) cited in "Foucault's Oriental Subtext," Schaub, 1989, p. 308.
19. Jorge Luis Borges "A New Refutation of Time," *The Total Library: Non-Fiction 1922–1986*, London: Penguin Books, 1999, pp. 330–331.
20. Michel Foucault, "What is Enlightenment?" op. cit., p. 50.

20

This is (not) a Pipe: from Magritte to Bansky

Achia Anzi

Linguistics holds an exemplary position in de Saussure's semiology, but it is only one of the branches of the science of the sign."[W]hen semiology becomes organized as a science," de Saussure proposes, "the question will arise whether or not it properly includes modes of expressions based on natural signs, such as pantomime." (de Saussure, 68) If linguistics, according to de Saussure, operates through differences, pantomime allegedly communicates through identities or more precisely through mimesis. Saussure does not explore other branches of semiology apart from linguistics, but indicates how the so called "natural signs" might be incorporated into this newly established science. "Polite formulas" (such as bowing, handshake, *Pranamasana, mudras,* etc.) and symbols (such as the balance representing justice) are not wholly arbitrary as words. For instance, de Saussure explains, the symbol of balance cannot be replaced by a chariot. But since gestures and symbols are not free from conventions and regulations, they can also be explored, according to de Saussure, in a scientific manner. That is to say, the aim of the semiologist is to expose the general structure which rules and governs the operation of natural signs.

The question regarding the semiology of mimesis is left open in de Saussure's Course. The principle of convention cannot be applied so easily in the domain of imitation and resemblance. Michel Foucault approaches this question differently in his essay "This is not a Pipe". Instead of holding the lingual sign and the visual image, the arbitrary signifier and the natural mark, in distinct positions, he argues that the discourse guides our perception of images. Unknowingly language operates within the modes of our visual expressions. In a way, Foucault argument resonates inthe theory of the American theorist W. J. T. Mitchell: the image and the word cannot be separated and in fact operate many times in a similar manner. But while Mitchell proposes to read images as signs (in a new discipline of Iconology) and deconstructs the binary opposition between text and image, Foucault endeavors to free the image from the burden of language.

In the following I shall present a critical reading of Foucault's essay. Foucault interprets the famous painting of the Belgian artist René Magritte: "The Treachery of Images," and fastens the project of modern art to the project of semiology, by providing a (post)structuralist reading of artworks of modern artists such as Kandinsky, Klee and Magritte. According to Foucault, modern art challenges the basic norms of traditional western painting and liberates the image from the encumbrance of representation. Foucault distinguishes between resemblance and similitude: "Resemblance serves representation, which rules over it; similitude serves repetition, which ranges across it." (Foucault, 44) Thus he argues that Magritte undermines representation and introduces the art of the *simile.*

Foucault's criticism of the relation between images and words in western painting is crucial to the understanding of visual representation. Nevertheless, by adhering to the simile and highlighting the image's "filmy thingness," Foucault joins a long western tradition that celebrates the metaphysics of presence. I will conclude this presentation with the work of the British graffiti artist known by his pseudonym: Banksy, which addresses and challenges Magritte's pipe. Instead of a painting of a smoking pipe, Bansky installs a readymade water pipe, and instead of the sentence: "this is not a pipe," his work bears the title: "this is a pipe."

Let us return to Magritte's pipe or non-pipe. How should we understand the sentence: "this is not a pipe?" The painting's title: "The Treachery of Images" already reveals Magritte's intention:

> "The famous pipe. How people reproached me for it! And yet, could you stuff my pipe? No, it's just a representation, is it not? So if I had written on my picture "This is a pipe," I'd have been lying!" (Torczyner, 71)

At first glance Magritte's pipe is an exemplary expression of modern art's iconoclasm. The image is not only attributed with the impotency of representation (could you stuff it? Magritte asks), but is also charged with a moral misconduct: treachery, disloyalty and falsity. Foucault, however, does not accept this evident or simplistic interpretation. The image is obviously not the object which it represents. "Must we say," Foucault proclaims, "My God, how simpleminded!" But this statement is not as simple as it seems. An old lingual habit, argues Foucault, leads us to treat the image not as an arrow which points towards an object (in a manner similar to the way in which a word represents an object) but as the object itself. We don't say this is an image of a pipe but rather: this is a pipe. Hence, according to Foucault, Magritte's pipe (or non-pipe) does not announce the obvious but in fact reveals the unobvious: our confusion between the thing and its sign.

Two principles ruled Western painting from the fifteenth to the twentieth century. Contradictory as they were, Foucault argues, they rendered the apparatus of representational painting possible. "The first asserts the separation between plastic representation (which implies resemblance) and linguistic reference (which excludes it)." Image does not represent in the manner of a textual sign. The Image resembles while the text must speak across differences. While the first principle maintains an unbridgeable gap between text and the image, the second unknowingly reconciles between the two. Resemblance is at the same time affirmation. The painting does not simply simulate its model. At the heart of the silent exchange between the origin and the copy, the painting as representation must declare: "What you see is that." (Foucault, 34)

As opposed to these two principles Foucault posits the works of Paul Klee and Wassily Kandinsky. Klee juxtaposes textual signs along with visual figures on his canvas, creating "an uncertain, reversible, floating space" (Foucault, 33) that cannot obey a clear-cut separation between image and text. Kandinsky on the other hand challenges the theses of resemblance as affirmation. His paintings affirm only themselves and the shapes and colors appearing on the canvas. They do not refer to anything beyond themselves, beyond their pure materiality.

In comparison with the modernism of Klee and Kandinsky, Magritte's paintings along with the canvases of other Surrealist painters seem reactionary. "No one, apparently," writes Foucault, "is further from Klee and Kandinsky than Magritte. More than any other, his painting seems wedded to exact resemblances, to the point where they willfully multiply as if to assert themselves." But this is of course only on the surface. Despite the fact the Magritte's art seems "more committed than any other to the careful and cruel separation of graphic and plastic elements," it is committed to the project of Klee and Kandinsky, constituting "a figure at once opposed and complementary" to their works. (Foucault, 35)

Klee and Kandinsky invented new spaces in order to bypass the inner conflict of representational painting. Magritte on the other hand undermines the traditional apparatus of resemblance from within. Kandinsky created abstract images which allegedly affirm only themselves; Klee fused forms and signs on the same surface thus undermining their traditional separation; and Magritte creates a "non-relation—or in any case by the very complex and problematic relation—between the painting and its title." (Foucault, 36)

Klee and Kandinsky

Before considering Foucault's analysis of Magritte's work, let us examine how Klee and Kandinsky refute representation. The inner-contradiction of resemblance in traditional painting is clear: it appears to separate image from text thus retrieving the accuracy of the copy directly from the original (and not through difference as in language) but at the same time representational painting ignores the fact that the affirmation of the copy as a copy ("what you see is that") is based on a lingual procedure. The image as such does not affirm anything. It is beyond right and wrong. Only discourse can speak. Only text conforms with the categories of correctness and falsehood. The separation of text and image in traditional representation falls apart.

Were Klee and Kandinsky able to solve the paradox of representational paintings? Kandinsky in fact does not undermine traditional painting. He merely bypasses the problem of the image and paves a different way of treating the canvas. Moreover, in the clash between image and text, visual and discourse, he apparently chooses to advance the former. But despite his best efforts, his paintings preserve the same inconsistency of the traditional pictorial space.

Kandinsky's canvases, like traditional western paintings, supposedly communicate without words. His abstract paintings are mere things. But here we are again faced with the same contradiction of "realistic" paintings. In order for the painting to be a pure material presence it has to announce itself as such. Jacques Rancière writes about abstract painting in his essay "Painting in the Text": "The same surface must perform a dual task: it must only be itself and it must be a demonstration of the fact that it is only itself." (Rancière, 71) Abstract painting is not only a presence. In order to be a painting it has to announce itself as such. If traditional painting secretly proclaimed: "what you see is that," Kandinsky's canvas has to state: "what you see is a painting," "what you see is art". In a nutshell art cannot bypass the operation of language.

Klee on the other hand maintains a more complex pictorial space. Instead of separating image and text he conjures them together, thus creating an ambiguous space. But what is so ambiguous and uncertain about this space? *Villa R* does not look like naturalistic or realistic painting but this fact by itself does not undermine the apparatus of representation. One should not confuse painting as an image and an image appearing in the painting. For instance, by seeing the yellow orb in the upper right corner of *Villa R* as a moon, we confine the image to a certain discourse: "this is a moon". If we decide to leave the orb to its glorious materiality we are left with another discourse. In any case, there is no ambiguity here, but two ways of seeing the yellow orb By placing the letter R and the yellow orb on the same plan Klee does not change the way in which we perceive images.

Magritte

How does Magritte undermine the classical operation of representation? Apparently, as Foucault has noted, Magritte follows the same procedure of traditional paintings. And yet, the hyperrealism of his paintings conceals, according to Foucault, the strongest attack on realism. By using the tools of representation Magritte creates a collapse from within the classical tradition.

At the beginning of chapter five Foucault compares Magritte to Kandinsky. The latter, as mentioned earlier, challenges representation by separating resemblance from affirmation: the painting affirms only itself. Kandinsky liberates painting from resemblance and affirmation. On the other hand:

> Magritte proceeds by dissociating the two: disrupting theirbonds, establishing their inequality, bringing one intoplay without the other, maintaining that which stemsfrom painting, and excluding that which is closest todiscourse-pursuing as closely as possible theindefinite continuation of the similar, but excisingfrom it any affirmation that would attempt to saywhat is resembled. An art of the "Same," liberated from the "as if." (Foucault, 43)

Magritte dissociates resemblance from affirmation thus producing a new opposition: Same/As if. But this is not the precise relation of the "Same" and the "As if". The "as if" in fact consists of a mutual relationship between two elements: image and text. The "same," on the other hand, does not depend on a discourse. Similarity between two objects (the thing and the image) does not rest on a lingual apparatus. Presumably, same is same even without the finger that points toward the "original," the voice which authorizes this relation, and the text which affirms it. The mute exchange between two objects is interrupted by the unheard whisper of the discourse. The move from the image's sameness to the affirmation of the "as if via" discourse, produces a hybrid creature (as if = image+text) which assaults the purity of the modern aesthetic discourse. The same "stems from painting" while the affirmation or the as if "is closest to discourse". Accordingly, the text in the "treachery of images" does not indicate that the image is not the object it represents but dissociates the image from the text. By contradicting the lingual message of the image, Magritte liberates the image from the burden of the text.

But why should we disassociate the image from the discourse? If western philosophy, according to Derrida's critique, celebrates the presence of speech and denied the deferring apparatus of the text, we now witness in modern art and in Foucault's essay the opposite gesture which is nevertheless based on the same preference. While the text (or written image) is denied in favor of speech, in the domain of art the deferring power of the image is denied in favor of its material presence (Kandinsky) or its filmy presence or "filmy thingness" (Foucault, 41) as in Magritte's case.

Traditional western painting according to Foucault operates like a calligram. It conveys its messages in a dual operation: form and sign, image and text, visual and lingual. The image shows and announces or affirms itself at one and the same time. The problem according to Foucault is that these two operations cannot be performed at once. You can either see the painting or read it. If one tries to do both, one is already moving beyond the presence. The hybrid gesture of seeing and reading cannot be incorporated into the metaphysics of presence.

Returning to Magritte's non-pipe, we can now understand Foucault's interpretation and his own version of the metaphysics of presence. Magritte separates the operation of the image and from that of words. The image has no message to convey without the help of words. The image only simulates. By presenting an allegedly contradicting lingual message, the artist undermines the secret operation of words. Foucault reveals the semiology of resemblance and at the same time undermines its operation. But the liberation of the image as we have just seen is entangled with the violence of presence. Denying the secret bond between images and words is to favor presence over difference.

The semiology of the image and the image as a phenomenon

Until now we followed Foucault's understanding of the structure of the image and challenged his preference of the image's filmy presence. But does the message that Foucault deciphers in the image (this is that) is the only text to be read? Moreover does by analyzing the image in a structuralist fashion, by incorporating the image into the science of semiology and then liberating it from its burden, are we able to exhaust the operation of the image? Foucault liberates the image from semiology and presents it as a phenomenon; can we establish a different relationship between the phenomenology of the image and its operation as a sign?

As opposed to Magritte's art of similitude, Foucault posits the art of *trompe l'œil*, the most telling example of affirmative art according to Foucault. With regard to Magritte's art he writes: "We are farthest from *trompe l'œil*. The latter seeks to support the weightiest burden of affirmation by the ruse of a convincing resemblance: "What you see on the wall's surface is not an aggregate of lines and colors[,]" but depth, sky, clouds, that is the signified object. (Foucault, 43)

Foucault goes on to describe the experience of *trompe l'œil*: "a stairway that continues the steps you have begun to climb (already you start toward it, despite yourself)." But this description opens a new way of analyzing our perception of images. The image of the stairway does not speak. It forces itself upon the viewer. The viewer experiences the painting as a "real object" despite himself. At first encounter with the painting, the painting does not speak. If the painting signifies, the power of the illusion has already vanished. Analyzing the image in semiological terms does not exhaust the phenomenon of the image. The image entails a certain displacement. The *unheimlich* character of the image cannot be deducted to the operation of the sign. The image, to borrow from Nancy's terminology, is the *distinct*. Its abundance cannot be fully grasped when it is conceived as a sign.

But this does not mean that the image is mute. At the level of the deception the image must remain silent, but in order to become an image, the image has to reveal itself as an image. The image has to appear as an image. The *trompe l'œil* or any other image cannot become an image until and unless it refutes its deception. Semiologically, the image has to convey a dual message in order to become an image. If the image declares: "This is a pipe," it also has to announce: "This is not a pipe." "This is an image". The image should be explored at two different levels: 1) as a phenomenon (but not as a physical phenomenon because that would mean to ignore its true operation as an image), 2) semiologically, as expressing two contradictory messages: 'this is a pipe' and 'this is not a pipe.'

By now we can look at and read Bansky's pipe.[1] The informed viewer smiles at the sight of the pipe, an ironic smile. She already knows that the pipe she sees as a pipe is not a pipe. She might look for another essence beyond (or before) the visual trace: a materiality, a visual presence, or even a metaphor. But before (or after, or in parallel—it doesn't really matter) being able to do that, Banksy's text proclaims: "This is a pipe." The pipe that you see, readymade or drawn, real or fake, a presence or a trace, is a pipe. In the sphere of the image, it is a pipe. A pipe, it is.

NOTES

1. Bansky's pipe deserves a further exploration. In order to analyse Bansky's work, one has to consider other aesthetic and political issues: the tension between street art and institutional art, image and readymade, art and political resistance. I am grateful to Prof. Saugata Bhaduri (JNU) for his insightful comments.

REFERENCES

de Saussure, Ferdinand, *Course in General Linguistics* (tr.) Wade Baskin, New York: Philosophical Library, 1959.

Foucault, Michel, *This Is Not a Pipe*, tr. James Harkness, Berkeley: University of California Press, 1983.

Mitchell, W.J.T., *Iconology: Image, Text, Ideology*, Chicago: University of Chicago Press, 1986.

Nancy, Jean-Luc, *The Ground of the Image*, tr. Jeff Fort, New York: Fordham University Press, 2005.

Rancière, Jacques, *The Future of the Image*, tr. Gregory Elliot, London: Verso, 2007.

Torczyner, Harry and Bella Bessard, *Magritte, the True Art of Painting*, New York: Abradale Press/Abrams, 1985.

List of Contributors

Achia Anzi is an Israeli artist and scholar based in New Delhi. He obtained his Bachelor's and Master's degrees in Fine Arts from University of Rajasthan, Jaipur. He is an Assistant Professor at the School of Liberal Arts and Humanities at O.P. Jindal Global University, Sonepat, near Delhi. He has exhibited extensively in India, Israel and worldwide.

Gérard Bensussan is Professor of Philosophy at University of Strasbourg. Specialist of Modern German Philosophy, he has published several works notably and more recently *Les Âges du monde de Schelling. Une traduction de l'absolu*, Paris, Vrin, 2015.

Sukalpa Bhattacharjee teaches English at North-Eastern Hill University, Shillong. Her publications include *Society, Representations and Textuality: The Critical Interface* (ed.) 2012, *Postcolonial Literatures: Essays on Gender, Theory and Genres,* 2004, *Ethno Narratives: Identity and Experience in North East India,* 2006 and *Human Rights and Insurgency: The North-East India*, 2002.

Debaditya Bhattacharya teaches literature at Nivedita College, University of Calcutta. He works on continental philosophy and occasionally writes on issues of contemporary political interest. He is co-editor of *Sentiment, Politics, Censorship: The State of Hurt*, Sage, New Delhi, 2016.

Prasenjit Biswas is an Associate Professor of Philosophy at North Eastern Hill University, Shillong. His recent book is *Between Philosophy and Anthropology: Aporias of Language, Thought and Consciousness*, Notionpress, Chennai, 2017.

Arup K. Chatterjee was awarded Ph.D. at Jawaharlal Nehru University in 2015. He was a recipient of Charles Wallace fellowship to the UK, in 2014-15. He is founding editor of *Coldnoon: International Journal of Travel Writing & Travelling Cultures*. He is author of *The Purveyors of Destiny: A Cultural Biography of the Indian Railways*, Bloomsbury, 2017. He is Assistant Professor at the School of Law, O.P. Jindal Global University.

Marc Crépon is Director of Research and Chair of Department of Philosophy, École Normale Supérieure, Paris. He directs research at CNRS Husserl Archives. His publications address issues in moral and political philosophy, and focuses on the question of violence. Among his recent publications are: *Terreur et poésie*, Galilée, 2004; *Langues sans demeure,* Galilée, 2005; *Altérités de l'Europe*, Galilée, 2006 *La culture de la peur, identité, sécurité, démocratie*, Galilée, 2008; *Vivre avec, la pensée de la mort et la mémoire des guerres*, Hermann, 2008, (Eng. tr.) *The Thought of Death and the Memory of War*, University of Minnesota Press, 2013; *La guerre des civilisations*, Galilée, 2010, *Le consentement meurtrier*, éd. Cerf, 2012, *La vocation de l'écriture, la littérature et la philosophie à l'épreuve de la violence*, (éd.) Odile Jacob, 2014 & *L'épreuve de la haine, essais sur le refus de la violence*, (éd.) Odile Jacob, 2016.

François Cusset is Professor at the University of Western Paris and a committed intellectual historian, specializing in transatlantic exchange and the globalization of contemporary critical thinking. Cusset is the author of two novels and ten works of non-fiction, *French Theory,* Minnesota University Press, 2008, and *The Inverted Gaze*, Arsenal Pulp, 2011, among others.

Anup Dhar is a Ph.D. in Philosophy and Professor at Ambedkar University, Delhi. His recent works include *The Indian Economy in Transition: Globalization, Capitalism and Development,* Cambridge University Press, 2015 (co-authored), and *Breaking the Silo: Integrated Science Education in India*, Orient Blackswan, 2017 (co-edited), and *Psychoanalysis in the Indian Terroir* (co-edited, forthcoming)

Samir Gandesha is Associate Professor in the Department of Humanities and Director of the Institute for the Humanities at Simon Fraser University in Vancouver, Canada. He specializes in Modern European Thought and Culture and has co-edited with Lars Rensmann *Arendt and Adorno: Political and Philosophical Investigations*, Stanford, 2012, and *Spell of Capital: Reification and Spectacle*, Amsterdam, 2017, and *Aesthetic Marx*, Bloomsbury, 2017, both with Johan Hartle.

Siby K. George is Associate Professor of Philosophy at the Department of Humanities and Social Sciences, Indian Institute of Technology, Bombay. Specializing in contemporary continental philosophy, he writes from a phenomenological vantage point on such themes as development, technology, pain and dying, political ethics, and subjectivity, focusing specifically on Indian/nonwestern contexts. He is author of *Heidegger and Development in the Global South*, Springer, 2015, and coeditor of *Cultural Ontology of the Self in Pain*, Springer, 2016.

Vinod K. Kalidasan teaches English literature at St. Stephen's College, University of Delhi. His areas of interest include literary theory, questions of modernity and colonialism in Malabar. He has recently published: "The

Routes of Pepper: Colonial Discourses around the Spice-trade in Malabar," in *Kerala Modernity: Ideas Spaces and Practices in Transition*, 2015, and "A king lost and found: Revisiting the popular and the tribal myths of Mahabali from Kerala," *Studies in South Asian Film & Media,* 2016.

Sourav Kargupta is an independent scholar, formerly Erasmus Mundus Postdoctoral fellow at the Aarhus University, Denmark. He works on the intersections of deconstruction, Marxism and Feminism in the work of Gayatri Chakravorty Spivak, prose texts of Rabindranath Tagore, and theories of World Literature. He has published "Spectral Touring: Subject, Consumption, and the Wound of the Photograph," in: *Touring Consumption*, (eds.) Wee, D. and S. Sonnenburg, Springer, 2015.

Sanjay Kaushal is currently teaching at Amity University, NOIDA, near Delhi. He has worked on Maurice Blanchot in his doctoral thesis defended at Jawaharlal Nehru University in 2017. His research interests are centered on language, literature and philosophy.

Franson Manjali serves as Professor at Jawaharlal Nehru Universitty. He is engaged in a wide range of humanities areas, especially philosophy. Since his doctorate at JNU in 1986, he has researched in Paris and Strasbourg, and at IIAS, Shimla. His more recent publication is *Labyrinths of Language – Philosophical and Cultural Investigations,* Aakar, 2014. He has translated two scholarly books from French into English.

Nimmi Nalika Menike obtained her Ph.D. from Jawaharlal Nehru University. With a keen engagement in continental philosophy and literature, her thesis on *Religion, Nation and Gender: A Study of the Problematic of Representation and Violence in the Context of Sri Lankan Literature* (2016) focuses on Derridian deconstruction and its relevance in addressing the question of identity and violence.

Sandhya Devesan Nambiar teaches in the English Department, Jesus and Mary College, University of Delhi. Her Ph.D. thesis defended at Jawaharlal Nehru University, involved an exploration of conceptual structures in Continental Philosophy and of Deleuzean modes of philosophical thought in particular. She also works in the intersections of the philosophical and the political, especially on the question of the 'minor.'

Jean-Luc Nancy, born in1940, is Philosopher and Professor Emeritus at University of Strasbourg. He has published several works particularly on the community, deconstruction of Christianity, the political, and art. Long time friend of Jacques Derrida, he has remained very close to his thought.

Abhilash Nath has obtained a Ph.D. on Foucault's works at JNU, New Delhi. His research interests are centred on the philosophies of language, mind, and life, and the metaphysics of the nature of time and causation. His is currently engaged in a systematic study of the materialistic understanding of time.

Manas Ray is a Professor at the Centre for Studies in Social Sciences, Calcutta. He works at the interface of political theory and cultural studies. His recent publications are "Against Negation: Suicide, Self-consciousness and Jibanananda Das' poem, 'One Day Eight Years Ago,'" *Cambridge Journal of Postcolonial Literary Inquiry*, 2016, and "Goddess in the City: Durga Pujas of Contemporary Kolkata," *Modern Asian Studies*, 2017.

Jacob Rogozinski is Professor of Philosophy at Strasbourg University. His research focuses on phenomenological thinking of the ego and the body, and on the genealogy of exclusion and persecution. He has recently published *Le moi et la chair,* Cerf, 2006, (Eng. tr.) *The Ego and the Flesh,* Stanford University Press, 2010, *Guérir la vie – la Passion d'Antonin Artaud,* Cerf, 2011, *Cryptes de Derrida,* Lignes, 2014 (Eng. tr. forthcoming from Indiana University Press).

Rustam Singh Poet, philosopher and political scientist, he has been a fellow at Indian Institute of Advanced Study, Shimla, and, more recently, a Senior fellow, and Editor at Eklavya Foundation, Bhopal. He has published three books in English including *'Weeping' and Other Essays on Being and Writing* and *Violence* and *Marxism: Marx to Mao.* His four collections of poems in Hindi have also been published. His poems have been translated into several Indian and foreign languages.